REPUBLICANISM AND THE FRENCH REVOLUTION

Republicanism and the French Revolution

An Intellectual History of Jean-Baptiste Say's Political Economy

Richard Whatmore

OXFORD
UNIVERSITY PRESS

OXFORD
UNIVERSITY PRESS

Great Clarendon Street, Oxford OX2 6DP

Oxford University Press is a department of the University of Oxford.
It furthers the University's objective of excellence in research, scholarship,
and education by publishing worldwide in

Oxford New York

Athens Auckland Bangkok Bogotá Buenos Aires Calcutta
Cape Town Chennai Dar es Salaam Delhi Florence Hong Kong Istanbul
Karachi Kuala Lumpur Madrid Melbourne Mexico City Mumbai
Nairobi Paris São Paulo Shanghai Singapore Taipei Tokyo Toronto Warsaw

with associated companies in Berlin Ibadan

Oxford is a registered trade mark of Oxford University Press
in the UK and in certain other countries

Published in the United States
by Oxford University Press Inc., New York

First published 2000

British Library Cataloguing in Publication Data

Data available

Library of Congress Cataloging-in-Publication Data
Whatmore, Richard.
Republicanism and the French Revolution: an intellectual history of Jean-Baptiste
Say's political economy / Richard Whatmore.
p. cm.
Includes bibliographical references and index.
1. Say, Jean Baptiste, 1767–1832. 2. Economists—France—Biography.
3. Economics—France—History. 4. Republicanism—France—History. I. Title
HB105.S25 W47 2000   330.15′3′092—dc21   00–034009

ISBN 0–19–924115–5

1 3 5 7 9 10 8 6 4 2

Typeset in Dante by
Cambrian Typesetters, Frimley, Surrey
Printed in Great Britain
on acid-free paper by
T. J. International Ltd., Padstow, Cornwall

For
Ruth and Jess

'Nous serons toujours en accord dans l'amour de la vertu de la république et de ses amis.'

Abbé Grégoire, letter to Say, 1798

'Jean-Baptiste Say was a man of the later period of the French Revolution, a fine specimen of the best kind of French republican, one of those who had never bent the knee to Bonaparte though courted by him to do so; a truly upright, brave, and enlightened man.'

John Stuart Mill, *Autobiography*

Contents

Abbreviations   x

Preface   xi

Acknowledgements   xiv

Part I   Reinterpreting Say

1   The J.-B. Say problem   3
    1   *Say's Disputed Intellectual Legacy*   3
    2   *Smith's French Interpreters*   6
    3   *Say and the French Revolution*   10

2   Republicanism and Political Economy   17
    1   *Say's Ideology*   17
    2   *Political Economy in Eighteenth-Century France*   18
    3   *Eighteenth-Century Republicanism*   23
    4   *The Political Economy of Modern Republicanism*   28

Part II   The Intellectual Context of Say's Ideas

3   The Political Economy of French Decline   37
    1   *Dupont's Attack on the 'British' Say*   37
    2   *Explaining Britain's Strength*   39
    3   *Commerce and Constitutions*   41
    4   *Montesquieu's Critique of the British Example*   43
    5   *The Intellectual Legacy of the Seven Years War*   46
    6   *Physiocratic Strategy*   50
    7   *Reviving Reason-of-State Political Economy*   53

4   The Republican Turn in France, 1776–1789   61
    1   *Neo-Physiocracy*   61
    2   *Turgot and 'L'Organisation sociale'*   62
    3   *The Effects of the American Revolution*   66
    4   *Sieyès' 'L'Art social'*   68
    5   *Rœderer's Representative Democracy*   73
    6   *Clavière's Republicanism for Large States*   77

5   Revolution and the Political Economy of Terror   85
    1   *The Problem of Manners in the Revolution*   85
    2   *Clavière's* assignat *Solution*   86

3   *Regenerative War*   89
4   *The Terror Solution*   93
5   *Republicanism Transformed*   95
6   *A Science of* Mœurs   98

Part III   Republican Political Economy

6   Say's Republicanism, 1794–1798   111
    1   *Moral and Political Science at the* Institut National   111
    2   *Ginguené and* La Décade philosophique   114
    3   *Assessing the Revolution*   117
    4   *Secular Manners and the Problem of Religion*   120
    5   *Republican Political Economy*   125
    6   *The Reception of* Olbie   129

7   The Idea of a *Traité d'économie politique*   136
    1   *Say and the Consulate*   136
    2   Idéologue *Republicanism*   139
    3   *The 'General Fact' Approach to Political Economy*   141
    4   *Uniting Virtue with Self-Interest*   143
    5   *The Aims and Method of the First* Traité   145
    6   *Political Economy Ancient and Modern*   148
    7   *Say's Critique of Consular Republicanisms*   152

8   Defending Republican Manners   156
    1   *Say and Smith*   156
    2   *Industrious Manners and Egalitarian Ranks*   157
    3   *Frugality*   161
    4   *Moderate Wealth*   162
    5   *Moral Commerce*   165
    6   *Republicanism Revised*   167

9   Restoring French Glory   170
    1   *Britain's Weakness*   170
    2   *Perspectives on Smith in Consular Argument*   171
    3   *False Gods and Natural Liberty*   174
    4   *Natural Liberty in France*   177
    5   *The Fate of the First* Traité   183

Part IV   Republican Political Economy in Conditions of Monarchy

10 Rejecting the Post-War Settlement   189
    1   *The Return of the Bourbons and British Constitutionalism*   189
    2   *The Second* Traité   191

Contents ix

3 *Say's View of Britain*   194
4 *Say's View of France*   196
5 *Political Economy as Civic Education*   199

11 'Social Science in its Entirety'   205
1 *Ricardo, Malthus, Sismondi*   205
2 *The Influence of Bentham*   207
3 *The* Cours complet   210
4 *The Final Writings*   213

12 Conclusion   217

Bibliography   221
Index   233

Abbreviations

CdPp   J.-B. Say, *Cours complet d'économie politique pratique; ouvrage destiné à mettre sous les yeux des homes d'état, des propriétaires fonciers et des capitalistes, des savants, des agriculteurs, des manufacturiers, des négociants, et en général de tous les citoyens, l'économie des sociétés* (Paris, 1828–9), 6 vols.

ŒdC   M. J. A. N. Caritat de Condorcet, *Œuvres de Condorcet* (Paris, 1847–9), ed. A. Condorcet O'Connor, 12 vols.

ŒD   J.-B. Say, *Œuvres diverses de Jean-Baptiste Say* (Paris, 1848), ed. E. Daire.

LDP   *La Décade philosophique, littéraire et politique, par une société de Républicains* (after 1800 *par une société des gens de lettres*), eds. P.-L. Guinguené, J.-B. Say, F.-G.-J.-S. Andrieux, A. Pineux Duval, J. Le Breton (Paris, 1794–1807), 42 vols.

MdIN   *Mémoires de l'Institut National: Classe des Sciences Morales et Politiques* (Paris, 1796–1803), 5 vols.

TE   J.-B. Say, *Traité d'économie politique, ou simple exposition de la manière dont se forment, se distribuent et se consomment les richesses.* (Paris, 1803), 2 vols.

TT2   J.-B. Say, *Traité d'économie politique, ou simple exposition de la manière dont se forment, se distribuent et se consomment les richesses; Seconde Édition, entièrement refondue et augmentée d'un épitome des principes fondamentaux de l'économie politique* (Paris, 1814), 2 vols.

ŒdR   P.-L. Rœderer, *Œuvres du Comte de Rœderer*, (Paris, 1853–6), ed. A. M. Rœderer, 8 vols.

SVC   *Studies on Voltaire and the Eighteenth Century* (Oxford, 1955–).

Preface

Republicanism and the French Revolution has two central aims. The first is to provide a new understanding of the intellectual movements of one of the most turbulent periods of modern European history: France in the 1790s. In doing so it attempts to move beyond current historiographical fashion, something that requires justification. Emancipated from Marxist categories of analysis, much recent historiography—following Tocqueville in particular—has found the intellectual origins of the Revolution in certain political ideologies of the Old Regime.[1] Intellectual historians and devotees of 'the social history of ideas' have discovered continuities between the *philosophes'* desacralization of monarchy and church, and the *journées* of the early 1790s. All of the historians who have made these claims accept that the Revolution can be explained by reference to the gradual development of a 'public sphere', allowing 'public opinion' to become an independent, and unpredictable, actor in French political theatre. The assumption is that French political culture incrementally became more 'radical' in the late eighteenth century by contrast with that of other European monarchies. This process culminated in the events of 1789. Such ideologies as classical republicanism were able to take advantage of eighteenth-century social developments and become constituent elements of the revolutionary *mentalité*.[2] While such work has illuminated neglected areas of eighteenth-century life, problems arise when attempts are made to explain the intellectual movements of the Revolution itself. With regard to ideas about the public sphere and public opinion, the uniqueness of France in this respect is very difficult to discern, especially when compared with Britain, several Swiss cantons and certain Italian states. The move from a French subject acting in the public sphere of the Old Regime to a citizen of the revolutionary republic one and indivisible has not been sufficiently explained, except by a return to the old Marxist notion of *embourgeoisement*.[3]

The major difference between the intellectual movements of the French Enlightenment and those of the Revolution stems from the fact that few of the *philosophes* were republicans: the key term which enemies of the Revolution used to describe and deride the great upheaval from the transformation in June 1789 of the Estates General into a National Assembly founded on national sovereignty. In general, there was nothing more absurd to *philosophes* across Europe than the idea of making the vast, corrupt, hierarchical and commercial state of France into a republic. The distinction is compounded because most revolutionaries were republicans who rejected classical republicanism, the ideology that returned to public notice in the reign of Louis XV. Furthermore, notable writers in the classical republican camp, such as Mably or Rousseau, or those who were accused of it during their careers (such as Montesquieu and Voltaire) shared the view that whatever the merits of classical republicanism there was no state less suited to it than France. In their opinion, France was too large and commercial, with too established a social hierarchy and too divided a citizenry, to contemplate such revolutions of the constitutional architecture. There was, as a result, no straightforward development from *philosophe* to revolutionary, as the abbé Raynal made clear before the close of 1790.[4] He was dying in what appeared to him to be an alien intellectual world; one in which the political maxims of Old Regime France had ceased to function. Many historians have, as a consequence, been perplexed by the seeming paradox that the Revolution was an all-encompassing intellectual event that created the dominant political movements of the nineteenth century and yet was of an ideological nature that is difficult to pin down. Alphonse Aulard, writing in the 1880s, concluded that the French Revolution had no direct intellectual origins, because modern republicans writing before 1791 were impossible to find.[5] A tradition developed of seeing the Revolution as a unique event, one in which accident and circumstance played a greater role than ideas.

This book uses the writings of Jean-Baptiste Say, those of his mentors and their opponents, to tell a different story. Reassessing the categories that historians have used to interpret the Revolution, its argument develops by analysing ideas that would have been recognized by the historical actors we seek to understand. This is for the simple reason that the concepts they used are for the most part more precise and revealing than those which modern historians have tended to employ in explaining ideological change in late eighteenth-century France. It is shown, for example, that writers such as Say openly acknowledged that they were attempting to combine ideas in a manner which would have dismayed authors such as Rousseau, Montesquieu or Voltaire. Rather than pushing common enlightenment ideas in radical directions, Say was consciously contradicting them. The difficulty faced by revolutionaries such as Say was to move beyond enlightenment concern with small-state republicanism to justify the building of a regime unique in history. This was the modern republic, the centrepiece of revolutionary ideology. The revolutionaries recognized that they were doing something new. Developing commerce in a large republic revealed the extent to which they were moving beyond domestic traditions of political argument, and especially classical republicanism. In demanding a society without hierarchical ranks, where forms of commerce were compatible with republican virtue and where moderate wealth was the norm, they surpassed almost every *philosophe's* imagination. Theirs was a republic characterized by a political culture of industriousness, frugality, courage and moderation. The ideology of modern republicanism did, however, have origins in the French Enlightenment. The story of its birth in the 1770s and its development in the 1780s is told in the first two parts of the book. These outline a view of the revolution which Say and numerous leading revolutionaries shared, including Emmanuel Sieyès, Pierre-Louis Rœderer, Thomas Paine and Jacques-Pierre Brissot. All of these men played a part in convincing the Marquis de Condorcet to embrace the new ideology in 1791; he was the most important *philosophe* convert to modern republicanism of the revolutionary era.

The ideology of modern republicanism was articulated predominantly by adherents to the Girondin faction in the Convention. The third and subsequent part of the book explains why this ideology fractured with the Terror, leading to the development of diverse ideas about the best laws, constitution, and culture to make modern republics stable. Argument ranged from the necessity of civil religion to the functions of republican government and the virtues that underpinned it. Never resolved, these divisions were maintained into the nineteenth century, playing an important role in the development of post-revolutionary liberal and socialist ideologies. This story supplies the necessary background for the second aim of the book: to reinterpret Jean-Baptiste Say's political economy to reveal an unwavering commitment to the ideology of modern republicanism. His singular contribution to the debates about the future of the ideology is revealed, after the Terror shattered revolutionary optimism. In explaining Say's ideas by reference to modern republican movements, a stand is taken against the two orthodox interpretations of Say's ideas. The first stems from the view that Say was a liberal and that his ideas contributed to the formation of a liberal ideology founded on Adam Smith's *Wealth of Nations*. The second is that Say was a classical political economist, whose achievement was to popularize Smith's political economy in France and to have facilitated the progress of the science by discovering what has come to be known as 'Say's Law'. In fact, Say opposed the liberal creed when it was first popularized by Constant, Guizot and others in the early years of the Restoration. He was an unorthodox political economist, particularly in perceiving Smith's work to have been a precursor of his own republican ideology. Understanding the sense in which Say was Smith's disciple requires study of the peculiarities of, and different phases in, the French reception of Smith's books; a subject which, like the equivalent problem in Britain, has only recently begun to be understood. *Republicanism and the French Revolution* shows the variety of ideas about politics and political economy which Smith's work could be used to sustain. Say the classical political economist, who brought the ideas of the liberal Smith to France, is shown to be a historical myth. Say was rather a republican of a distinctive kind, having lived among the founders of the first modern republican ideology adapted to large European monarchies and having been directly involved in its subsequent successes and failures. Say's mature political economy attempted to create a new republicanism for a post-revolutionary world, something which numerous contemporaries recognized but which we appear to have forgotten.

NOTES TO PREFACE

1. R. Darnton, 'What was revolutionary about the French Revolution', *The New York Review of Books*, January 19, 1989; S. Maza, 'Politics, culture and the origins of the French Revolution', *Journal of Modern History*, 61 (1989), 703–23; K. M. Baker, *Inventing the Revolution: Essays on French Political Culture in the Eighteenth Century* (Cambridge, 1990), chs. 9, 11; R. Chartier, *The Cultural Origins of the French Revolution* (Durham, North Carolina, 1991), ch. 1; M. C. Jacob, *The Radical Enlightenment: Pantheists, Freemasons and Republicans* (London, 1981) and *Living the Enlightenment: Freemasonry and Politics in Eighteenth-Century Europe* (Oxford, 1991); D. Goodman, *The Republic of Letters: A Cultural History of the French Enlightenment* (Ithaca, N.Y., 1994); D. K. Van Kley, *The Religious Origins of the French Revolution* (New Haven, Connecticut, 1996), ch. 6.
2. J. Kent Wright, *A Classical Republican in Eighteenth-Century France: the Political Thought of Mably* (Stanford, California, 1997), pp. 198–211.
3. Colin Jones, 'Bourgeois Revolution Revivified: 1789 and Social Change' in C. Lucas, ed., *Rewriting the French Revolution. The Andrew Browning Lectures 1989* (Oxford, 1991).
4. *Tableau Philosophique de la Révolution en France en 1789* (Marseille, 1790), p. 6.
5. A. Aulard, *The French Revolution. A Political History, 1789–1804* (London, 1910), tr., B. Miall, 3rd edn., pp. 79–126.

Acknowledgements

It will be evident from reading this book that a debt is owed to the writings of numerous scholars. Special thanks are due to Istvan Hont, who first recognized the importance of Say's writings and set me to work in 1990. At Sussex, from 1993, Donald Winch proved an equally inspirational mentor and the final form of the book owes a great deal to both of them. Brian Young, Roberto Romani and Philippe Steiner kindly read versions of the entire manuscript at least twice and provided useful ideas for its improvement. The latter's work on Say remains the first port of call for any understanding of this author, and my gratitude for his help from the first requires particular emphasis. In 1995 Keith Tribe and Gareth Stedman-Jones scrutinized the thesis version of this book. In pointing out numerous weaknesses they supplied a plan of revision that I have attempted to follow. Since that time Keith Tribe has provided an endless stream of ideas intended to create a better book, for which I am extremely grateful. In addition, thanks to Michael Sonenscher for constructively criticizing several chapters and for providing a model for intellectual historians in his recent work on the French Revolution. James Livesey has been a help and inspiration since 1989. Thanks go not only for advice on the manuscript as a whole but through his own important work on the Revolution and beyond. I would also like to express thanks to Jason Pearce of Oxford University Press, Peter Starby, my colleagues, old and new, in Intellectual History at Sussex, John Burrow, Blair Worden and Martin van Gelderen, two anonymous referees of Oxford University Press, and librarians of Cambridge University Library, the University of Sussex Library, the London Library, British Library and Bibliothèque Nationale. The arguments of certain chapters were developed in the following journals and I would like to thank referees in each case: 'Commerce, Constitutions, and the Manners of a Nation: Etienne Clavière's Revolutionary Political Economy, 1788–1793', *Journal of the History of European Ideas*, 22 (1996), 351–68; 'Everybody's Business: Jean-Baptiste Say's General Fact Conception of Political Economy', *Journal of the History of Political Economy*, 30 (1998), 451–68; 'Jean-Baptiste Say's Republican Political Economy', *Journal of the History of Political Thought*, 19 (1998), 439–56; 'Good Books and Bad Morals': Jean-Baptiste Say's Assessment of the French Revolution, *Studies on Voltaire and the Eighteenth Century*, 378 (1999), 303–18. Without the practical help of Rosa Weeks this book would never have been completed. John Ramster and Kieran O'Halloran supplied aid with regard to style. John Pierre Alain and Aaron Callen provided advice in translating from French. The original thesis on which this book is loosely based was supported by a grant from the British Academy. Subsequent research was facilitated by grants from the Nuffield Foundation, for research in Paris, and the Arts and Humanities Research Board, for two terms of research leave. My greatest debt is to Ruth Woodfield, to whom the book is dedicated.

PART ONE

REINTERPRETING SAY

I

The J.-B. Say Problem

1   SAY'S DISPUTED INTELLECTUAL LEGACY

On his death in November 1832 Jean-Baptiste Say was lauded as a writer of singular importance. Fame as a political economist had been established across Europe and North America by the time of his appointment to the Chair of *Économie industrielle* at the *Conservatoire des Arts et Métiers* in 1819.[1] It had continued to grow throughout the 1820s, as the revolutionaries of 1830 acknowledged in granting him a Chair in *Économie politique* at the *Collège de France*. When Charles Dunoyer wrote in 1826, 'I am convinced with de Tracy that his is the best work that has been written in the science which is its subject', he was expressing a widely-held opinion.[2] Contemporaries recognized that Say's greatest concern had been the popularization of political economy, particularly among the middle and working classes of his native France. Political economy was to be a science within reach of the masses. It could, following the title of one of his most successful books republished several times from 1815, be taught as a catechism, allowing ordinary folk to live by its tenets. Clarity of expression was consequently of the utmost importance to him. It facilitated popularization but also fostered the unity of opinion Say believed to be every scientist's goal. Given such intentions, it is somewhat ironic that a controversy over the meaning of Say's political economy developed soon after his death. Its source was the perspective on Say's life articulated by his eldest son Horace. This served as the preface to editions of the *Traité d'économie politique* published between 1833 and 1848, at which time it also formed the introduction to the collection of Say's writings edited by Eugène Daire. Reflecting upon his father's views, Horace Say recalled that Jean-Baptiste Say had read the *Wealth of Nations* in 1789, when secretary to the Genevan financier Etienne Clavière, and was immediately converted to the conception of liberty which the book espoused:

perhaps the vocation of economist slumbered inside him at that time, for want of reading Adam Smith in the original. Clavière possessed a copy of the *Wealth of Nations*, but no translation was then known in France. On his [Clavière's] advice, Jean-Baptiste Say read the book: it was a complete revelation: he was henceforth an economist. A specimen copy was soon procured from London; he studied it, annotated it, and from this moment refused to be parted from it.[3]

According to his son, Say had drawn from Smith a 'calm and benevolent philosophy', supportive of the division of labour, free trade, and expanding commerce. This philosophy informed his writings throughout the 1790s until in the *Traité* of 1803 he condensed, clarified, and popularized the science Smith had created. The central aim of Say's work was described by means of a contrast with the intellectual movements of the French Revolution, which were condemned for having failed to distinguish political economy from morals or politics. According to Horace Say, his father's aim had been to challenge the Revolution in seeking 'to soundly establish the principal lines and fundamental principles of a subject of study which until then had been refused the name of science, on grounds of too frequent overlapping with politics and morals.' Both Say and Smith were described as 'liberals', exponents of the 'system of liberty', wary of government and opposed to state involvement in the economic lives of the people. A self-confident rhetoric was devised to describe the progress of the science since 1803, emphasizing the optimism felt by those positively inclined towards a Europe increasingly dominated by commerce and industry.

Horace Say was the first writer to link his father to the intellectual traditions of classical political economy and political liberalism, which were deemed to have developed from Smith and Turgot's economic writings. Jean-Baptiste Say became part of a canon that gave force to his son's perspective on the Revolutions of 1848 and the Second Empire.[4] Similar views were expressed by Say's successor at the *Conservatoire*, Jérôme-Adolphe Blanqui. In his popular *Histoire de l'économie politique*, first published in 1837, Blanqui agreed with Horace that Say was Smith's disciple and a critic of the political economy of the Revolution, having 'proved that his study was as valuable to monarchies as it was to republics'. He too distinguished Say from the revolutionaries in commenting that his writings lacked 'the social point of view' which had been fundamental to the intellectual movements of the 1790s. As a result, Blanqui did not consider Say to be a member of what he called 'the French school of political economy', defining the latter by the belief that 'the question is no longer, as in the time of Smith, exclusively that of accelerating production: the latter must be governed and restricted within wise limits.' Blanqui accepted that Say, however, through his theory of markets, had proved 'the general interest of men is to render mutual aid, instead of injuring each other as blind policy has too long compelled them to do.' Say's Law, from this perspective, distinguished Say's political economy from that of Smith in one important respect. Say had concretely defined the public good and demanded that legislators and citizens consciously pursue it, rather than relying on the hidden hand of private self-interest. Nevertheless, Blanqui agreed with Horace that Say should be classed as a political liberal alongside the British school of political economists headed by David Ricardo. Say's revolutionary 'political passions', the existence of which Blanqui acknowledged, were deemed to have left 'few traces in his writings.' Echoing Dupont de Nemours' opinion of 1814, Blanqui concluded that Say had from an early age been seduced by British intellectual traditions inimical to the unique interests of the French nation.[5]

Different conclusions were drawn by Say's son-in-law and former disciple Charles Comte, who, as secretary to the Moral and Political Science Class of Louis Philippe's *Institut Royal*, penned an appreciation which accompanied his editions of the *Mélanges et correspondance* (1833) and *Cours complet* (1837). Although he agreed that Say had devoted himself to 'the cause of liberty', he traced this to formative experiences during the Revolution.[6] In Say's writings of the 1790s Comte perceived the idea of 'bringing to the attention of all citizens the economy of societies . . . and making it accessible to every social class'. Rather than describe Say as a liberal, or Smith's disciple, Comte believed the key to Say's political economy lay in his attempt to influence the culture or what he termed the *mœurs* of nations, 'not by flattering the opinions of certain authorities or parties, and never by allowing a private interest to overcome the public interest.'[7] Comte was not uncritical of Say's conception of the public interest, but he wanted to praise the aims that he believed had inspired Say since 1789, and which marked him out from the majority of political economists in France and Britain in the 1820s and 1830s. It is noteworthy that several contemporaries shared Comte's interpretation. As early as 1819, having read Say's letter to Ternaux on the means of provisioning Paris, Alexandre de Lameth questioned Say's reputation as 'the French Smith'.[8] A similar view was put to Say by his younger brother Louis in a long-winded analysis of the new science.[9] Just after Say's death the first volume of Theodor Fix's *Revue mensuelle d'économie politique* contained an attack on Quesnay and Smith for having 'reduced this science to simple calculations of profit'. It was far better, Fix claimed, to return to what he termed 'the ancients' approach to political economy' based upon 'the domestic rules of a society', encompassing education, the virtues of labour, and the promotion of specific manners to underpin social structures. Otherwise, it was feared that commercial societies would collapse, as had Carthage, Athens, India, and Egypt. Although the British writers Ricardo, Malthus, and Buchanan, were taken to task for narrowing political economy, Say and Simonde de Sismondi were praised for creating a science of 'social economy'. Placing *économie morale* alongside *économie matérielle*, its central aim was to combat the moral evil done to 'the working classes', which Fix expected would ultimately foment revolution in Britain.[10] In his eyes, Say was not Smith's pupil. Rather, he remained the child of the Revolution, ever seeking the means by which all men and women could fulfill the moral potential of their natures in a society characterized by virtue, as opposed to one dependent upon the unintended benefits of egoism.

Although certain writers continued to view Say's work from Comte and Fix's perspective, Horace Say's interpretation proved victorious in the second half of the nineteenth century, not least because of the success of Say's grandson Léon in popularizing his father's account.[11] Marx certainly accepted it, and passed it on to his numerous disciples.[12] For the vast majority of mid to late nineteenth-century interpreters Say's ideas could be classified by reference to three related intellectual groupings: that of classical political economists, that of political liberals, and that of Smith's posthumous disciples. This interpretation has become still more dominant in the twentieth century, portraying Say as Smith's French heir, uncritically adopting economic liberalism and scepticism about excessive government interference in society alongside Constant, Guizot and other exponents of 'the liberty of the moderns'.[13] From a slightly different angle, several American historians have viewed Say as a theorist of 'modern industry', alongside *idéologues* such as Destutt de Tracy and Cabanis, who were inspired by Condorcet's defence of science and liberty in the last days of the Terror.[14] This portrait has proved equally appealing to historians of economic thought, although the story they relate has different emphases. Where Horace Say described his father and Smith as zealots of an enlightened 'liberal Revolution', from a modern economist's perspective the events of the 1790s are less important than the intellectual revolution presented by the science of political economy itself. Say's theoretical contributions as a classical political economist have been charted, however minor they may have been, to the 'history of economic analysis.'[15]

Consent has never been unanimous. Charles Comte's questioning whether Say divorced his revolutionary experiences from his political economy was addressed by Edgard Allix eighty years ago in articles which recognized an ambiguity in Say's response to the narrow science of wealth creation reputedly favoured by certain of his British contemporaries.[16] Allix's promised book on Say was unfortunately never published. French scholars have recently initiated more extensive investigations into Say's life and ideas and in the process have followed up many of Allix's leads.[17] Through such research, problems with Horace Say's interpretation have been clearly identified. Jean-Baptiste Say cannot be included in the camp of political liberals in the aftermath of the Napoleonic Wars because he opposed the model nation revered by all liberals at this time: the example of Britain's mixed constitution, system of ranks and commercial society. Against Constant, he held that Britain was a nation lacking liberty. In *De l'Angleterre* Say argued that the sovereign aristocratic oligarchy would sooner or later cause the collapse of the British economy and with it the state. It is equally misleading to straightforwardly unite Say with the British classical political economists, as Blanqui and later Marx did. Two notable contemporaries who were also Say's friends, Sismondi and Saint-Simon, believed that their own work had far more in common with Say's approach to political economy than that of Ricardo, Malthus or McCulloch.[18] Say's disputes with Malthus and Ricardo in particular underline a degree of mutual incomprehension and disagreement that can only make Say a classical political economist if the term is radically redefined. Say's association with Bentham's circle and his support for their views stemmed from a perception that alone among British writers they were developing French republican ideas first canvassed in the late 1780s. It is notable that the first translations of Bentham's writings into French were published in the *Courier de Provence* between 1789 and 1791, on which Say served as administrator at the time when he was also acting as Clavière's secretary. Say's view of Bentham can therefore be traced to the perspectives on utilitarianism that Brissot and Clavière developed at this time. That this was not Bentham's self-perception of his utilitarian science is obvious. It has to be borne in mind when claims are made that Say was a utilitarian who called Bentham, as well as Smith, his master.

2   SMITH'S FRENCH INTERPRETERS

The alternative strategy of calling Say a 'Smithian' is equally problematic because it is difficult to identify a 'liberal tradition' in French thought in which Smith's writings were prominent. This was the assumption from which Horace Say derived his interpretation. One means of doing so is by claiming that Smith owed his central ideas to Turgot. This has appealed to many French patriots eager to claim priority in the discovery of economic truths for their fellow-countryman.[19] When examined at first hand, however, Turgot's writings have proved as difficult to associate with liberal ideas as those of Smith. Although in favour of free trade in an ideal world, Turgot, like Smith, was a practical writer who limited his demands for reform to what he believed was possible in the second-best world of Old Regime France. He consequently never wavered in his support for absolute monarchy and was extremely critical of North-American republican experiments in politics. The added problem for contemporary interpreters of Turgot's work was his association with the physiocrats. Although Say, following Clavière, distinguished a 'republican' Turgot from the 'despotic' ideas of the physiocrats, he also made clear that the *Wealth of Nations* had played a far greater role in the formation of his own work. Recent historiographical trends with regard to both Smith and Turgot have largely mirrored each other. With regard to Smith, it is highly significant that historians of British political economy have revealed in recent years the limitations of labelling Smith a 'classical political economist' or 'liberal' without a great deal of qualification. What Smith meant by 'the system of natural liberty', and 'political economy' itself, has been shown to have been both controversial and innovative, notably in calling his work 'a branch of the science of the statesman or legislator.' Furthermore, the rediscovery of Smith's politics has raised questions for every aspect of his economic thought.[20] It has been recognized that the *Wealth of Nations* was interpreted in many different ways and used in very different kinds of argument from its first publication in 1776. Addressing this last problem has led historians of Smith's ideas to chart a great debate about the nature and meaning of his thought in Britain, and to underline its controversial reception.[21] It is obvious that progress in our knowledge of the reception of Smith's work raises a problem for interpreters of Say: was the 'liberal Smith' the creation of Say's disciples?

Given the interest in the nature of science in general, and economic science in particular, among the educated literary classes across the channel, and the interchange of ideas and persons between the nations, it is no surprise to discover that a debate about the meaning of Smith's ideas was conducted in the burgeoning journals, salons, clubs and correspondence of Parisian daily life. Although personally known to leading intellectuals such as Turgot and Quesnay from the 1750s, Smith's name became commonplace in more general writings on politics only in the 1780s. In 1784, for example, passages of the *Wealth of Nations* were used as the basis for articles on debt and credit in the *Encyclopédie Méthodique* volumes on *économie politique*.[22] Smith's ideas about public finance quickly became points of reference for writers involved in the debates which stemmed from Calonne's tampering with the value of gold in 1785 and the Anglo-French commercial treaty of the same year. Pierre-Louis Rœderer claimed that by 1788 Smith had become an important source of ideas for political reformers, although his works were more referred to than read.[23] Interest increased markedly during the Revolution. His work figured both in the debate on the manners concordant with national sovereignty and the continuing controversy over the relationship between property and citizenship.[24] Rœderer was perhaps the most important propagator of Smith's ideas in the 1790s, given his status and literary output, the range of his circle, and his ownership of several major journals.

Although the *Wealth of Nations* was probably more readily available, Rœderer later argued that when France became a republic it was the *Theory of Moral Sentiments* that was of greater import. It had been translated as early as 1770 by Briasson with the title *Métaphysique de l'âme*, but the translation was poor and those of Blavet in 1773 and 1774 were little better. A full and competent translation, by Sophie Grouchy-Condorcet, was published in Paris only in 1798. This did not prevent an informed perspective on Smith's moral science emerging in the early 1790s.[25] Rœderer called the *Theory of Moral Sentiments* 'the most excellent collection of observations through which the science of morals has been enriched' and enjoyed access to the work from 1789, having borrowed an English edition from Sieyès, who reportedly declared, 'It is an astonishingly good book'.[26] It was perceived to be an innovative and important work by Rœderer because it derived a theory of moral action from sources other than Hobbes or Helvétius. This became particularly important after the collapse of the constitution of 1791 increased interest in means of making individuals virtuous and fraternal.[27] Sophie Grouchy-Condorcet also came to prominence by using Smith to illuminate aspects of the Directorial controversy about national manners, from the reasons why crowds gathered at the guillotine to the moral consequences of regicide.[28] These uses lay behind the common perception of Smith's work as part of 'the system of social economy', embracing every aspect of the 'government of large empires'.[29] This was the dominant perspective upon Smith's work until the turn of the century, as Rœderer made clear in 1797:

Smith was a *philosophe*; he was one of the *lumières* of this century and perhaps the most useful . . . [because of the] *Wealth of Nations*, the most useful of book which has ever been written, and the *Theory of Moral Sentiments*, the first book to reconstruct the true foundations of morals, by analysing the phenomena of the heart in its entirety in order to discover the principles which direct it.

The *Wealth of Nations* was first translated in 1778, by the abbé Blavet, and published in four volumes in the Netherlands. Extracts from the work were popularized through the *Journal de l'agriculture, des arts et du commerce*, edited by d'Ameilhon, between January 1779 and December 1780. A second edition was produced at Yverdon in 1781, and a third at Paris in 1788. In 1790 'Roucher's' translation was begun in Paris by Buisson (Roucher could not understand English), and the first edition proved so popular that a second appeared in 1794. Rœderer argued that the debates in the Assembly of Notables over taxation first brought the work to public attention, something aided during the early years of the Revolution by Condorcet, although his promised critique of Smith never appeared.[30] Although often cited as a foil to the physiocratic approach to taxation and value, the work was nowhere portrayed as a systematic exposition of a new science called political economy but rather as a corpus of good ideas with disparate applications. Around 1800, however, a shift of interest occurred away from the *Theory of Moral Sentiments* and towards the *Wealth of Nations*. The movement away from a theoretically universal male franchise towards a property-based franchise was crucial for perceptions of Smith. The *Wealth of Nations* became one of the key texts that revealed to legislators the means to make good citizens, not by forcing them to be virtuous but by creating conditions in which citizens would enjoy a moderate income and thereby become independent. Support for mobile property and the critique of the physiocratic *impôt territorial* in the *Wealth of Nations* caused Smith to be portrayed as a supporter of the Consular constitution.[31] Smith was once again influential in an argument about the best form of republic, but was nowhere described as a liberal.

By 1803 St Aubin was claiming, 'It is no more possible to write political economy without detailed knowledge of Smith's book, than it is possible to write natural history while remaining a stranger to the works of Linnaeus.'[32] What is important is that Smith's work was sufficiently extensive and, in certain areas, vague enough, for him to become a source for writers of every political persuasion. Dupont de Nemours, and later Germain Garnier, used Smith's ideas to support physiocratic administrative reforms, arguing that Smith would have favoured the enfranchisement of the landed classes envisaged in the constitution of 1791, believing as they did that this mirrored the conception of the British constitution which Smith favoured.[33] Condorcet, by contrast, argued that the ideas of both Smith and Quesnay could be used to develop a new social science embracing politics, political economy and morals that would allow legislators to persuade citizens to act rationally without violating their liberty.[34] Sieyès was equally distinctive in using Smith's idea of the division of labour to demand a political order in accord with the social effects of this principle.[35] These are only a few examples of the uses to which Smith's ideas could be put. The idea of a 'liberal' Smith well known in the 1790s was clearly an invention of later commentators. As Simonde de Sismondi put it:

In vain the profound author of the inquiry into the wealth of nations has collected all the fundamental truths which ought to serve as rules to Legislators; his book, it is true, lacks method, is hardly understood by anyone, is cited rather than understood, perhaps without being read: the treasure of knowledge which it contains is lost to Governments.[36]

It should be clear from this evidence that when Say argued in 1803, '. . . there was no political economy before Smith', he was not making a common or uncontroversial statement.[37] Rather, he was contributing to a debate involving a number of his contemporaries who disputed Smith's legacy and relevance to the post-revolutionary generation. In this debate, a straightforwardly 'liberal' Smith can be found neither in Say's writings nor in those of any other political economist. If Smith was used to support a variety of political standpoints in the 1790s, how did Say come to form his opinion of Smith? This was the question which none of Say's family addressed, preferring to sketch an idealized growth of what was already deemed to be the most successful science of society.

By the 1830s liberalism in France was an established ideology with numerous eminent adherents. It became possible to project backwards into the eighteenth century a philosophic tradition that the liberals claimed to have inherited. The tradition included Smith but greater roles were played by Montesquieu, Voltaire and Turgot. The problem with this view was the decidedly illiberal Revolution, because it was unpardonable to claim that the French had betrayed their native liberal philosophy for twenty-five years between 1789 and 1815. Condorcet and Dupont de Nemours could be seen to have carried the liberal torch in the early years of the Revolution, beginning the long historiographical association of physiocracy and liberalism. Between the late 1790s and the end of the Empire, Destutt de Tracy and other *idéologues* were deemed to have defended liberalism in the midst of oppression. Say's particular role was to have maintained liberal political economy during the dark days of Bonaparte's censorship. From the perspective of the 1830s, Say could be criticized for having been too 'British': for having followed Smith too blindly when he ought to have been developing Turgot's ideas. One aim of this study is to show that Horace Say and his liberal associates misrepresented Say and as a consequence the history of political economy in eighteenth-century France. Comte's was a more accurate assessment of Say's ideas, giving prominence as it did to the 'social economy' that Say attempted to derive from Smith in the *Cours complet*. The question is what this meant to his contemporaries, and how it can be placed in the turbulent intellectual context of Revolution, Empire and after.

3   SAY AND THE FRENCH REVOLUTION

One fundamental aspect of Say's ideas, passed over by both Horace Say and Comte was imbibed at an early stage of his life from *philosophes* such as Voltaire and d'Holbach: hostility towards established religion of whatever form, but particularly Roman Catholicism. Of Genevan and Calvinist merchant stock, Say was born on 5 January 1767 at Lyon, where both branches of his family were prominent in commerce.[38] Despite his family's Calvinism, at the age of nine he attended a Catholic boarding-school at Écully. There he was taught by two Italian ex-Jesuits, named Giro and Gorati. In his *Mémoires* Say recalled that these men had instilled in their pupils knowledge and love of the deeds of the American revolutionaries, and provided an education in history, grammar, Italian, and Latin, in addition to physics. Above all they instructed him in the writings of the *philosophes*. This is signified by the fact that the school was, in Say's words, 'persecuted by the Archbishop of Lyon, who dreaded the pernicious effects of the century's philosophical spirit'. Opposition to Catholicism, which was to continue to his death, was first manifested at school, where Say recalled that the 'litanies to the Virgin and the Saints, which we were made to recite on our knees, were so long and so tedious that I became ill and fainted almost always before they were finished.'[39] The business problems of Say's father, Jean-Étienne, interrupted Say's education as the family moved to Paris in the early 1780s. Between 1784 and 1786, with his younger brother Horace, Say was apprenticed to a commercial firm in Croydon, reputedly against his wishes, as his preference was to become a *philosophe*.[40] Interest in the relationship between the arts and social well-being, made so central to French thought by Rousseau's first *Discours*, also fascinated Say, particularly in the early part of his life. It is noteworthy that he came to public notice not as a political economist but as a drama critic, imbued with Rousseauean concern for the effects of popular theatre, in the republican paper *La Décade philosophique*. On his return to Paris in 1787 Say was given employment by Clavière, then the administrative chief of a *Compagnie d'assurances à vie*. At some point before the Revolution Say became Clavière's secretary, a challenging task because of the latter's deafness. He remained in this position until he volunteered for the revolutionary army on 10 August 1792, in a company of *artistes et littérateurs* destined for Champagne.[41]

Serving Clavière was the defining moment in Say's early intellectual life. Seeds were sown which later formed the philosophy he was to defend in all of his works. Clavière, the most neglected figure within Say scholarship, is of an importance which it is difficult to overestimate because Say took so many of Clavière's ideas as his own.[42] Say's employment owed a great deal to their shared Genevan heritage, the maintenance of which in commercial and political circles has been charted across Europe by Herbert Lüthy's *La Banque protestante*. Clavière was born in the city of Geneva in 1735, like Say into a Huguenot family of merchants and financiers. Having purchased citizenship around the time of Clavière's birth, his family entered into the *bourgeois* class. Like many of his fellow citizens, Clavière was inspired by Rousseau's writings, and particularly the *Contrat social*, to oppose the corruption of the hereditary aristocracy of Genevan families who were then seeking to defend their political influence against the General Council of all citizens. The rebellion of the *natif* class excluded from citizenship in the spring of 1782 initiated the overthrow of the aristocratic Small Council by Clavière and *bourgeois* allies such as Du Roveray and François D'Ivernois; their intention was to create a constitution based on the *Contrat social* which would maintain a direct form of democracy in a society without social hierarchy and characterized by virtuous manners.[43] The Genevan revolution, however, proved short lived as Vergennes decided that it was not in the interests of France to have a popular republic on its borders. The subsequent invasion by French and Bernese troops led Clavière to flee the city. After adventures at Waterford in Ireland in 1783, where he intended to create a society based on the principles of the *Contrat social*, Clavière moved to Paris. In true Rousseau fashion, he originally believed France to be beyond the pale of political reform and Paris to be among the most corrupt of modern cities.[44] Life in Paris was, however, tolerated for at least three reasons. First, he accepted that the reform of Geneva would only be possible if it was accepted by the French court. Despite a bitter personal antagonism, Clavière had hopes that Necker's ascent in ministerial circles would end the French veto on constitutional innovation in their homeland. Second, Necker and later Calonne's defence and extension of the French national debt made speculation on the *Bourse* very attractive to financiers such as Clavière. He came to public notice in Paris as a leading player in the bull and bear games of the mid to late 1780s, attempting to manipulate the markets by employing hack writers such as Brissot and Gabriel-Honoré Riqueti, comte de Mirabeau to condemn by means of pamphlets the shares of certain companies, with the expectation of taking advantage of the resulting share collapse.[45] The third reason for Clavière's Paris residence was his gradual realization that Rousseau had in some ways been mistaken. He had always disagreed with his mentor that commerce was necessarily a force for political and moral corruption, preferring to follow British authors such as Richard Price or Adam Smith, whom he interpreted as defending forms of commerce fully compatible with justice and virtue. An equally significant disagreement with Rousseau centred on Clavière's conversion to the view that large states could be transformed into republics. His fascination with the rebellion of the North-American colonies played an important role in this process, which was shared with his great friend Brissot, a co-founder of the *Société Gallo-Américain*.[46] By 1787 Clavière had begun to argue that the salvation of France, and with it Geneva, lay in the establishment of a republican constitution, political culture and political economy. His political values and concerns remained largely those of Rousseau, but he believed that they had to be adapted to face the problems of modern states with the aid of Smith's and Price's insights. This was exactly Say's view of politics and political economy as he expressed it at the end of the 1790s and in the first *Traité*.

Clues to Say's intellectual relationship with Clavière can be found in the former's *Mémoires*, in which Say stated that 'since the time I was Clavière's secretary, before he was a minister, I studied political economy: he had a copy of Smith which he regularly studied.' It is certain that Say's hatred of hereditary aristocracy and emphasis on a virtuous political culture as the foundation of a free state can be traced to Clavière's influence. Before he was twenty-five Clavière gave Say access to one of the most radical intellectual coteries in Paris, which gathered at Clavière's and the banker Isaac Panchaud's residences in Paris, in the Kornman Mesmerist lodge, at the meetings of the *Société des Amis des Noirs,* and in the newly formed clubs of the capital.[47] Numerous figures who rose to prominence in the 1790s were well-known to Clavière. In addition to Mirabeau and Brissot he associated with Sieyès, Condorcet, Talleyrand-Périgord, and, after October 1789, Rœderer. These men determined the substance and form of Say's first writings, as is clear from the pamphlet *De la liberté de la presse* of 1789, in which Say imitated Mirabeau's welcoming of the Revolution. Every paragraph echoed arguments and discussion that he would have heard in Clavière's company. The most radical aspect of the Revolution was the transformation of a large state with an entrenched monarchy and aristocracy into a popular state founded on the sovereignty of the nation. While the aristocracy was abolished in 1789, Louis XVI initially remained as chief-magistrate with a suspensive veto over new laws. In September 1792 the revolutionaries removed this last vestige of the Old Regime and proclaimed the republic one and indivisible. Say's support for this act, and his republican perspective on the Revolution, was derived from his membership of Clavière's circle, many of whom were committed to justifying large-state republicanism. They defended it against the accusation, shared by such luminaries as Montesquieu, Voltaire, Smith and Turgot in addition to eminent contemporaries such as Mounier and Necker, that such forms of government were only possible in small states. Clavière's coterie was also intent on justifying a form of republicanism that was modern, in that it was fully compatible with the commercialization of French society. Through working on Mirabeau's letters to his Aix constituents, entitled *Courier de Provence*, Say came to share these points of view. After the Terror, Say was a founder member of the journal *La Décade philosophique*, which sought to promote modern republicanism in France. His writings of the period 1794–8 show an absolute devotion to the forms of republicanism first defended by Clavière's Girondin faction before the end of 1793.[48] Say was a rare figure among revolutionaries; he maintained his republican faith throughout the period of the Empire rather than allowing it to die with the Consulate. This is attested to by Say's close friend, the Genevan botanist A. P. de Candolle, who, in the 1830s, argued that he had been 'a committed republican and skilled economist' from the 1790s to his death.[49] Say's political sympathies were clear to everyone who was acquainted with him, as J.-A. Blanqui and the young John Stuart Mill, who stayed with Say's family in Paris in 1821, were fully aware. Rather than being a liberal, a term that was too fluid to serve as self-definition, Say considered himself to be a republican. The question is, of course, what was the relationship between his republicanism and his political economy? What did republican political economy mean in pre- and post-revolutionary France?

NOTES TO CHAPTER 1

1. T. N. Clark, *Prophets and Patrons: The French University and the Emergence of the Social Sciences* (Cambridge Mass., 1973), pp. 54, 133–7, 142; L. Levan-Lemesle, 'La Promotion de l'économie politique en France au XIXe siècle 1815–1881 , *Revue d'histoire moderne et contemporaine* (1980), 270–94; A. Alcouffe, 'The Institutionalization of Political Economy in French Universities 1819–1896', *History of Political Economy*, 21 (1989), 313–44; R. R. Palmer, *J.-B. Say: An Economist in Troubled Times* (Princeton, N.J., 1997), ch. 6.

2. Review of *Traité d'économie politique* (Paris, 1826), 5th edn., *Revue Encyclopédique*, 34 (1827), 63–90. See also C. Biddle, 'Introduction', *Treatise on Political Economy* (Philadelphia, 1832); M. Pickering, *Auguste Comte: An Intellectual Biography* (Cambridge, 1993), pp. 125, 313.

3. Horace Say, 'Notice sur la vie et les ouvrages de Jean-Baptiste Say', *Traité d'économie politique* (Paris, 1838), 6th edn., pp. iii–iv; Œ*D*), 'Introduction'. What cannot be doubted is that Say owed his interest in Smith to Clavière, which is confirmed by the draft *Mémoires* of 1818: Say papers BN Microfilm 6739, 151–212.

4. N. W. Senior, *Conversations with M. Thiery, M. Guizot and other Distinguished Persons*, ed. M. C. M. Simpson (London, 1878), 2 vols., ii, 144–6, 224–5.

5. *Histoire de l'économie politique en Europe depuis les anciens jusqu'a nos jours* (Paris, 1860), 4th edn., 2 vols., ii, 182; Dupont correspondence, Œ*D*, pp. 356–90.

6. 'Introduction', *Mélanges et correspondance de J.-B. Say* (Paris, 1833).

7. 'Notice historique sur la vie et les ouvrages de J.-B. Say', *Cours complet* (Paris, 1837), pp. v–xiii.

8. Review of Ternaux's *Sur les moyens d'assurer les subsistances de la ville de Paris, par l'établissement d'une compagnie de prévoyance*, *La Minerve*, (1819), pp. 164–71. Say himself made this point in a response to critics of the *Traité* of 1814: Say Papers, BN Mss. F 375.2, published in E. Schoorl, *J.-B. Say* (Amsterdam, 1986), p. 159.

9. Louis Say, *Considérations sur l'industrie et la législation* (Paris, 1822), pp. 324–40.

10. 'De l'économie politique: Quels en sont le but, les principes et les lois', *Revue mensuelle d'économie politique* (Paris, 1833–7), 4 vols., i, 1, 4–8, 12–14, 19.

11. Article 'J.-B. Say' by A. Clément, *Dictionnaire de l'économie politique* (Paris, 1852), 2 vols., ii, 591–5; 'J.-B. Say' in Léon Say and Joseph Chailley, eds., *Nouveaux dictionnaire d'économie politique* (Paris, 1891–2), 2 vols., ii, 783–90; Léon Say, *Turgot* (Paris, 1887), p. 40. On the tradition of Say economists see M. Luftalla, 'Jean-Baptiste Say et les siens: une famille d'économistes', *Revue d'économie politique*, 89 (1979), 389–407.

12. *Early Writings* (Harmondsworth, 1992), pp. 336, 361.

13. G. de Ruggiero, *The History of European Liberalism* (Oxford, 1927), pp. 171–2; Pierre-Louis Reynaud, ed., *J-B Say: Textes choisis* (Paris, 1953), pp. 48–58; Cheryl Welch, *Liberty and Utility* (New York, 1984), pp. 71–5; A. Jardin, *Histoire du libéralisme politique* (Paris, 1985), pp. 167, 187–8; B. Fontana, *Benjamin Constant and the Post-Revolutionary Mind* (Yale, 1991), pp. 24, 74.

14. M. James, 'Pierre-Louis Rœderer, Jean-Baptiste Say, and the Concept of *industrie*', *History of Political Economy*, 9 (1977), 455–75; T. E. Kaiser, 'Politics and Political Economy in the Thought of the Idéologues', *History of Political Economy*, 12 (1980), 141–61; *Minerva's Message. Stabilizing the French Revolution* (Montreal and Kingston, 1996).

15. Joseph Schumpeter, *A History of Economic Analysis* (Oxford, 1954), p. 491–2; Thomas Sowell, *Say's Law: An Historical Analysis* (Princeton, 1972), ch. 1 and *Classical Political Economy Reconsidered* (Princeton, 1974), esp. ch. 1; A. Tiran, *Jean-Baptiste Say. Manuscrits sur la monnaie, la banque, et la finance (1767–1832), Cahiers monnaie et financement* (1995), 1–229.

16. Edgard Allix, 'La méthode et la conception de l'économie politique dans l'œuvre de J.-B. Say', *Revue d'histoire économique et sociale*, 4 (1911), 321–60; 'J.-B. Say et les origines de l'industrialisme',

Revue d'économie politique, 24 (1911), 303–13, 341–63; 'La déformation de l'économie politique libérale après J.-B. Say: Charles Dunoyer', *Revue d'histoire des doctrines économiques et sociales*, 4 (1911), 114–47.

17. By far the best is Philippe Steiner. See especially, 'Politique et économie politique chez Jean-Baptiste Say', *Revue française d'histoire des idées politiques*, 5 (1997), 23–58; 'Comment stabiliser l'ordre social moderne: J-B Say, l'économie politique et la revolution', G. Faccarello and P. Steiner, eds., *La Pensée économique pendant la Révolution Française* (Grenoble, 1990), pp. 173–94; 'Intérêts, intérêts sinistres et intérêts éclairés: problèmes du libéralisme chez J-B Say', *Cahier d'économie politique* (1989), 21–41; 'J-B Say et l'enseignement de l'économie politique en France 1815–1832', *Œconomia* (1987), 63–95; *Sociologie de la connaissance économique: essai sur les rationalisations de la connaissance économique (1750–1850)* (Paris, 1998) esp. chs. 2–4; 'The Structure of Say's Economic Writings', *The European Journal of the History of Economic Thought*, 5 (1998), 227–49. In addition, the impressive work of the Dutch scholar Evert Schoorl, *J.-B. Say*: 'Bentham, Say and Continental Utilitarianism', *The Bentham Newsletter* 6 (1982), 8–18 and J. P. Frick, 'Philosophie et économie politique chez J-B Say: Remarques sur les rapports entre un texte oublié de J.-B. Say et son œuvre', *Histoire, Économie, Société* (1987), 57–66.

18. P. Roggi, 'Sette lettere di J.-B. Say a J. C. L. Sismondi', *Rivista di Politica Economica* (1972), 963–79; Saint-Simon, *L'industrie littéraire et scientifique liguée avec l'industrie commerciale et manufacturière* (Paris, 1817), in *Œuvres de Claude-Henri de Saint-Simon* (Paris, 1868–9), 6 vols., i, 185; ii, 155–6.; J. S. Mill noted that he once saw Saint-Simon at Say's residence in Paris (J. Stillinger ed., *The Early Draft of John Stuart Mill's Autobiography*, Urbana, 1961, p. 72).

19. Rœderer was among the first to have made this claim, stating that Turgot had sent copies of his *Réflexions sur la formation et la distribution des richesses* to Smith in 1766 (*ŒdR*, viii, 67). Another early defence of Turgot's priority is Dupont de Nemours' introduction to the *Œuvres de Turgot* (Paris, 1808–11), 8 vols., i, 118–9. For reviews of the controversy see P. D. Groenewegen, 'Turgot and Adam Smith', *Scottish Journal of Political Economy*, 16 (1969), 71–87 and D. Winch, 'Nationalism and Cosmopolitanism in the Early Histories of Political Economy', *Political Economy and National Realities*, eds., M. Albertone and A. Masoero, (Torino, 1994).

20. D. Winch, *Riches and Poverty: An Intellectual History of Political Economy in Britain, 1750–1834* (Cambridge, 1996); K. Haakonsen, *The Science of a Legislator* (Cambridge, 1981); I. Hont and M. Ignatieff, eds., *Wealth and Virtue: The Shaping of Political Economy in the Scottish Enlightenment* (Cambridge, 1983).

21. D. Winch, 'The Burke-Smith Problem and Late Eighteenth Century Political and Economic Thought', *The Historical Journal*, 28 (1985), 231–47 and 'Science and the Legislator: Adam Smith and After', *The Economic Journal*, 93 (1986), 501–20; R. F. Teichgraeber, 'Less Abused than I had Reason to Expect: the reception of the Wealth of Nations in Britain, 1776–90', *Historical Journal*, 30 (1991), 337–66; E. Rothschild, 'Adam Smith and Conservative Economics', *Economic History Review*, 35 (1992), 74–96.

22. *Encyclopédie Méthodique: économie politique et diplomatique* (Paris, 1784), 4 vols., ii, 147–55; T. Ando, 'The Introduction of Adam Smith's Moral Philosophy to French Thought' and D. Diatkine, 'A French Reading of the *Wealth of Nations* in 1790', *Adam Smith: International Perspectives* (London, 1993), eds., H. Mizuta and C. Singiyama; I. S. Ross, *The Life of Adam Smith* (Oxford, 1995), pp. 364–80.

23. Review of Prévost, ed., *Ouvrages posthumes d'Adam Smith*, *ŒdR* iv, 494–5, *Journal de Paris*, 20 Thermidor an V.

24. Saint-Just, *Discours sur les subsistances prononcé à la convention national dans la séance du 29 Novembre 1792*, *Œuvres complètes*, p. 383.

25. Rœderer, *Cours de l'organisation sociale*, 11 March 1793, *ŒdR*, viii, 188–200; review of Grouchy-Condorcet, *Lettres sur la sympathie*, *ŒdR*, iv, 499, *Journal de Paris*, 26 Messidor an VI.

26. Notes on *Théorie des sentiments moraux*, *ŒdR*, iv, 495–7.

27. *De la sympathie* (undated fragments), *ŒdR*, v, 417–18; '*Définitions diverses de la vertu*', *ŒdR*, v, 472.

28. Sophie Grouchy-Condorcet, *Lettres sur la sympathie* (Paris, 1798), third letter.

29. Le Breton, review of Roucher, tr., *Richesse des nations*, *LDP*, v, 401–9.

30. Condorcet, ed., *Bibliothèque de l'homme public* (Paris, 1790–2), 28 vols., i, 1.

31. Rœderer, *Mémoires sur quelques points d'économie publique, lus au Lycée, en 1800 et 1801*, *ŒdR*, viii, 41–97.

32. Review of Sismondi, *De la richesse commerciale*, *LDP*, xxxvii, 16.

33. Germain Garnier, *De la propriété dans ses rapports avec le droit politique* (Paris, 1792), p. 80. Dupont de Nemours, *Mémoires sur la vie et les ouvrages de M. Turgot* (Philadelphia, 1782), p. 110. In 1789 Dupont wrote to Smith: 'You have done much to speed this useful Revolution, the French *economistes* will not have harmed it.' E. C. Mossner and I. S. Ross, eds., *The correspondance of Adam Smith* (Oxford, 1977), p. 313. Dupont was to maintain this argument to his death; see *Observations sur les points dans lesquels Adam Smith est d'accord avec la théorie de M. Turgot, et sur ceux dans lesquels il s'en est écarté* (1809), *Oeuvres de Turgot*, i, 67–71.

34. Condorcet, Review of Roucher, tr., *Wealth of Nations*, *Bibliothèque de l'homme public*, i, ii–iii; 1790. Also, *Gazette national, ou Le Moniteur universel*, 24 August 1790.

35. M. Sonenscher, 'The Nation's Debt and the Birth of the Modern Republic: The French Fiscal Deficit and the Politics of the Revolution of 1789', *History of Political Thought*, 18 (1997), 64–103, 267–325.

36. Simonde de Sismondi, *De la richesse commerciale*, i, 12.

37. *TE*, i, xx–xxi.

38. Say's family history has been reconstructed by J. Valynseele, *Les Say et leurs alliances* (Paris, 1971). Say's *Mémoires* of his early life were partly published by Léon Say in *Journal des débats*, 8 July 1890. Regarding his grandfather Castenet, Say recalled that although he was eminent in the hierarchy of Lyon merchants he lacked an equivalent fortune because 'il était dépourvu de cette médiocrité d'esprit qui paraît nécessaire pour s'enrichir dans le commerce': an instance of Smithian disdain for self-interested merchants and financiers. See also Hitoshi Hashimoto, *Les lettres inédites de Jean-Baptiste Say*, *Treatises* 20 (1971), 74–99.

39. *Mémoires*, Say papers, BN Microfilm 6739, 152–60.

40. Say was responsible for one of the first maps of Croydon, which he sketched at this time. It can be seen in *Regional Survey Atlas of Croydon and District* (Croydon Natural History and Scientific Society, 1936). I owe this discovery to John Gurney.

41. Say described his experiences in a review of *La Campagne du duc de Brunswick décrite par un officier prussien*, *LDP*, 10 Prairial, an III (29 May, 1795), p. 412. In the Raoul-Duval family collection there is a revealing portrait of a red-bonnetted Say, based on Isabey's sketch of a healthy republican soldier, a photograph of which is printed in Joseph Valynseele, *Les Say et leurs alliances*.

42. For positive assessments of Clavière's ideas and their importance see J.-P. Brissot, *Mémoires, 1754–1793, publié avec étude critique et notes*, ed., Cl. Perroud (Paris, 1912) 2 vols., i, ix–xi; François D'Ivernois, *L'Histoire des révolutions de Genève dès la réformation* (Geneva, 1789), 2 vols., i, 115–16. On Clavière's life and financial activities see E. Chapuisat, *Figures et choses d'autrefois* (Geneva, 1920), pp. 1–119; J. Bouchary, *Les Maniers d'argent à Paris à la fin du XVIIIe siècle* (Paris, 1939), 3 vols., i, 11–101 (this work mentions a 'M. Say', probably Jean-Etienne, who was one of Clavière's financial agents in the insurance industry. It was probably Say's father who introduced his son to Clavière in the mid 1780s.

43. E. Chapuisat, *La Prise d'armes de 1782 à Genève* (Geneva, 1932); L. Kirk, 'Genevan Republicanism' in D. Wootton, ed., *Republicanism, Liberty, and Commercial Society, 1649–1776* (Stanford, California, 1994), pp. 270–309.

44. Brissot and Clavière, *Le Philadelphien à Genève, ou lettres d'un Américain sur la dernière révolution de Genève, sa constitution nouvelle, l'émigration en Irlande, etc, pouvant servir de tableau politique de Genève jusqu'en 1784* (Dublin, 1783), pp. 112, 152–5; As late as 1787 Dupont de Nemours was chiding Clavière for calling the French ignorant and corrupted: Hagley Library, w/2/a/2/292, letter of 16 June 1787: I owe this reference to Jim Livesey.

45. M. Marion, *Histoire financière de la France depuis 1715* (Paris, 1914), 3 vols., i, 348–85; Lüthy, *La Banque protestante en France* (Paris, 1959) 2 vols., ii, 420–5; M. Albertone, 'Political Economy and National Reality in France at the End of the Eighteenth Century: the Public Credit Issue', in *Political Economy and National Realities*, eds., pp. 127–46.

46. See Clavière and Brissot's revealing letters to Jefferson at this time: *The Papers of Thomas Jefferson* (Princeton, N.J., 1954), x, 261–4, 384–5, 514–15, 637.

47. J.-P. Brissot, *Correspondance et Papiers* (Paris, 1911), ed., Cl. Perroud, p. 108; R. Darnton, 'Trends in Radical Propaganda on the Eve of the French Revolution (1782–1788)', unpublished D.Phil. (Oxford, 1964), pp. 91–232.

48. 'Preface', *La Science du bonhomme Richard de Benjamin Franklin* (Paris, an II); 'Introduction', *Nouveau voyage en Suisse . . . par Hélène-Maria Williams* (Paris, 1798). Say's edition of Franklin's *Poor Richard* has been placed in context by A. O. Aldridge, *Franklin and his French Contemporaries* (New York, 1957), pp. 48–55.

49. *Mémoires et souvenirs de Augustin-Pyramus de Candolle* (Geneva, 1862), pp. 123–4.

2

Republicanism and Political Economy

1   SAY'S IDEOLOGY

Jean-Baptiste Say's intellectual career was divided by the Bourbon Restoration of 1814. Hitherto, Say had dedicated his life to the promotion of a form of republicanism that characterized one of the most important movements of the French Revolution: that of the Gironde faction as it developed between 1792 and 1793. Coming to prominence after the publication of the *Traité d'économie politique* in 1803, Say attempted in the book to describe a political economy supportive of the kind of republic he was committed to, adapted to the post-Terror circumstances of the Directory and the Consulate. If a republic was created in France, whose legislation embodied a republican creed adhered to by its citizens, he believed that the result would be the defeat of France's arch-rival Britain, and the beginning of an era of happiness and prosperity across the globe.

Napoleon Bonaparte's attempt to bribe Say into rewriting the *Traité* in praise of the First Empire is well known. Equally so is Say's refusal, the resulting censorship of the book and Say's period of internal exile in the Pas-de-Calais, which lasted until the collapse of the Empire. After his return to Paris Say was invited by members of the government of the restored monarchy to visit England, with a brief to discover the effects of a quarter-century of war on the British economy and more specifically the condition of British industry. This enabled him to renew an association with Bentham's circle, and in particular Bentham's editor and translator Etienne Dumont, which had first been established by Clavière and Brissot between the late 1780s and the outbreak of war in 1792. The journal for which Say had worked in the early years of the Revolution, the *Courier de Provence*, had been the first to praise, translate and publish Bentham's tracts on constitutional procedure and penal reform. The appearance in 1815 of the popular synopsis of Say's thoughts in the journey's aftermath, *De l'Angleterre et des Anglais*, marks the beginning of a rise to world-wide fame as a political economist. Eminence was affirmed by the praise received and sales achieved by the third edition of the *Traité* in 1817 and the widely-read summary of Say's views in the second edition of the *Catéchisme d'économie politique*. These works were pessimistic about the future prospects of the British state and evinced a scepticism about the chances of free government and civil liberty surviving. Such claims, far from making Say a liberal, underlined the similarities between his restated republicanism of the Gironde and the political ideas of Bentham and James Mill. At this time Smith's ideas were being claimed in France by writers as diverse as Saint-Simon and Constant, and in Britain by the disciples of both Burke and Paine. This makes the notion of a single 'Smithian' intellectual tradition, with Say as a leading member, meaningless. Rather, Say's writings continued to defend the central tenets of his republican creed in the conditions of the Vienna

Settlement. He perceived Smith's *Wealth of Nations* from this, historically inaccurate, perspective. In short, Say was attempting to promote his political faith by means of a specifically republican kind of political economy. Defining these terms, and explaining how their meaning determines the organization of this book, is the purpose of this chapter.

2   POLITICAL ECONOMY IN EIGHTEENTH-CENTURY FRANCE

The term political economy was coined in the seventeenth century to describe investigations into the management of nation states in conditions of international conflict. In particular, its exponents analysed the violent competition between two large empires, Spain and France. Political economy became popular at the peak of Bourbon–Habsburg rivalry, just as princes, legislators and philosophers were straining to discover new means of defeating their nation's rival. Significantly, it was at this time that, as Hume later said, commerce became 'a reason of state'. A good example of the genre is the tragedian Antoyne de Montchrétien's *Traicté de l'œconomie politique, dédié au Roy et à la Reyne Mère du Roy* in 1615. This patriotic book was written with the intention of extending the 'mirror for princes' literature by focusing upon the subject of comparative national prosperity. France was the *grand Estat* most blessed by God, being 'abundant in wealth, overflowing with people, powerful through healthy and strong towns, invincible in war and triumphant in glory.' Louis XIII was described as the heir to Rome, the King most able to defend the ancient maxim that 'the stability of the State comes from the conservation of its citizens; the safety of the people is the supreme law.' Montchrétien advised his prince to use all of his legal and cultural authority to foster the commerce of his subjects, with the aim of facilitating the stability and growth of the empire.[1] This sense of political economy dominated discussions well into the eighteenth century. Political economists perceived themselves to be writing to address problems in the context of antagonistic nation states. Political economy was broadly concerned with self defence and national glory. It was, as Smith famously wrote at the beginning of the fourth book of the *Wealth of Nations*, 'a branch of the science of a statesman or legislator'. The point of especial importance is that Smith's definition was as acceptable at the court of Louis XV as it was in the circles of the Scottish literati or the shifting political alliances of London party politics. One consequence of this was a mutual interest in the kinds of political economy being published on either side of the channel. Vincent de Gournay's direction and sponsorship of the translation of the works of a multitude of English and Scottish political economists from the late 1740s has been widely recognized. Although it was less necessary to make translations from the French at this time, English and Scottish political economists praised their French counterparts and acknowledged their influence. All were aware of the major writings printed at Paris, London or, more clandestinely, Amsterdam. Such close links were underlined by Smith's considering dedicating the *Wealth of Nations* to François Quesnay, had the latter lived until 1776.[2] Within national cultures, writers such as François Véron de Forbonnais or Quesnay himself may have disagreed about the legislation required to increase national wealth, but they acknowledged each other to be students of a common subject with a shared end in view.[3] The latter had altered somewhat since the days of Richlieu, Mazarin and Colbert. The object of French rivalry and the greatest threat to French power was no longer the Spanish empire. It was rather that of Britain. This fact was highly significant in the development of new ideas about political economy in eighteenth-century France. Britain's rise to prominence in Europe perplexed French, and indeed many British, writers. At the close of the seventeenth century the fear across Europe was that Louis XIV would succeed in achieving his long-cherished aim of universal monarchy.[4] Many Englishmen deemed him to be a worthy successor to the greatest of Roman emperors. In 1696, Gregory King acknowledged the dangers of 'a Potent Monarch, who alone has stood the shock of an Allyance & Confederacy of the Greatest part of Christendome.'[5] The logic of international power appeared to dictate French supremacy. France was the largest and most populous state in Europe, with the greatest natural endowment and the most advanced civilisation. Her only rival in terms of size, Spain, after Charles II died childless in 1702, appeared to be moving inexorably towards Bourbon dominion. Yet within a few decades such possibilities had become so inconceivable that they attained the status of national myths. Writers such as Montesquieu disputed whether anyone could have taken seriously a French attempt at world empire.[6] The central reason was not difficult to discern. Where Stuart monarchs had been pensioned by French kings, their successor dynasties were so militarily powerful that they were able to dictate the conditions of peace to their French rivals. Successive encounters proved that the victories of Blenheim, Ramillies, and Oudenarde were not merely the product of superior military strategy, but represented a shift in power away from Paris and towards London. The French attempted continuously to reverse a relative decline embodied by the treaties of Utrecht signed in 1713–14. Although the War of the Austrian Succession resulted in the stalemate of Aix-la-Chapelle in 1748, the peace of Paris, which ended the Seven Years War in 1763, set the seal on French inferiority. The result was that throughout the century French writers cast envious eyes over whatever they deemed to have made Britain distinctive and thereby more powerful.[7] Britain's constitution, commerce, religious establishment and system of public credit were at different times identified as necessary and sufficient reasons for her pre-eminence.

The effects of these perceptions on French political argument were manifold. French writers sought to explain British power and undertook comparative analyses of the attributes of and likely prospects for the two nations. For example, in the 1750s, when obsession with the British example was especially intense, French political economists disputed whether France should become a more commercial society and, in particular, whether the French nobility should imitate their British counterparts and embrace trade. Within this debate, attention was given to questioning the effects of the liberty of commerce, the extent of foreign trade, the importance of the agricultural sector, the relationship between commerce and national culture and, above all, the relationship between commerce and national defence.[8] The second major effect was a sense of crisis in French public life, and widespread fears of impending disaster. A man well-versed in French affairs, Lord Chesterfield, writing to his son in December 1753, noted that Parisian political culture was undergoing transformation. It was a genuine shock to see a French nation which 'reasons freely, which they never did before, upon matters of religion and government.' He added that 'all the symptoms which I have ever met with in history, previous to great changes and revolutions in Government, now exist, and daily increase in France.'[9] Such considerations gave particular potency to another of Louis XIV's legacies to his kingdom: the debate about the nature of the French state or, more specifically, the extent of monarchical sovereignty. Political economists in France were divided by their perspective on this issue. They shared the belief that the crisis of the French state was intimately concerned with the effects of different conceptions of sovereignty upon political economy. Failure to engage with this issue would have made their ideas as practical as Cyrano de Bergerac's lunar utopia.

Many political economists, such as Véron de Forbonnais, maintained the orthodox defence of sovereignty, namely that it resided in the person of the King. As Louis XV proclaimed at the *lit de justice* of 3 March 1766, directed against his critics in the *parlements*: 'Sovereign power resides in my person . . . Legislative power belongs to me alone, without dependence or division . . . The people exist as one only through me, and the rights and interests of the nation . . . are necessarily one with my own. They repose in my hands alone.'[10] As a consequence, public order was believed to emanate from the person of the prince. He was the representative of the nation in the sense that he alone determined what the public good was and what acts had to be undertaken for the safety of the people. No private person or corporation had any public existence or status except in accordance with the will of, and in deference to the authority of, the prince. The benefits associated with this perspective on sovereignty were evident in the history of *le grand siècle*. Kings from Henri IV had supplied the nation with unchallenged and enlightened leadership. They had the authority and the will to maintain the state. The greatest philosophers of the day had been their advisers. With the happiness of the people as their inspiration and glory their reward, absolute monarchy was for good reason perceived to be the most effective model of state organization for modern empires. Their efficiency, speed of action, and patronage of the sciences and fine arts affirmed this. Alone they had the power to prevent the recurrence of religious wars breaking out both domestically and internationally. The history of the previous five hundred years confirmed the limitations of alternative forms of state. The Renaissance republics were typical in being characterized by bellicosity, corruption, internal division, and permanent political crisis. Their replacement by the more efficient and less turbulent rule of all-powerful princes was unsurprising. Mixed monarchies in which powerful aristocracies enjoyed extensive political powers, such as those of Sweden or Poland, had rapidly declined, with the latter's political incapacity becoming a standing joke of every court in Europe. England's republican experiment had also given way to monarchy. Venice was a shadow of her former self. Successful alternatives to absolute monarchy that had risen in the seventeenth century, such as the Dutch Republic, had also experienced decline. The United Provinces were in practice divided by attitudes to the Stadholder, by religion, and by their relations with surrounding monarchs. The Swiss federation had become a satellite divided between the Holy Roman Empire and France. The majority of French political economists concluded that only the prince should be addressed in their writings. In considering the means to increase French power they refused to countenance any change to the perceived constitutional status quo. The problem which made the sense of French decline immediately alarming was the failure of Bourbon monarchs to raise the revenues which they believed to be necessary for the defence of the state. As a result, and particularly in the light of the debacle of John Law's experiments of 1716–20, a growing national debt became a source of fear and danger that had to be faced. In an original piece of research, Michael Sonenscher has shown how attitudes to resolving the problem of public credit can be used to distinguish between perspectives on sovereignty in France before 1789.[11] A general distinction can be made between those who believed the debt had to be abolished altogether, and those for whom public credit represented a source of national power that would allow France to extend her commerce and reap the political rewards consonant with her natural wealth and size.

The most prominent and influential political economists in late eighteenth-century France were the *économistes* or physiocrats. Led by Quesnay and the indefatigable Victor Riquetti, Marquis de Mirabeau, they promised to restore French glory by means of free trade, a single tax on the revenue of the net product of agriculture, the elimination of tax farms, and the re-establishment of provincial and municipal assemblies; the latter were intended to ease the burden of royal administration while increasing patriotism, by opening government to the true wealth-creating citizens of France, the landed proprietors.[12] Such a plan was attractive to the court because it did not entail any diminution of royal sovereignty. The King would be a legal despot, constrained only by the physiocratic laws interpreted by himself and his advisers. With the anticipated increase of agricultural productivity, and the self-sufficiency of France with regard to the satisfaction of basic needs, Quesnay argued that the administration of government would become cheap, and aggressive wars unnecessary. There would consequently be no need for public credit of any kind. With such attitudes to public credit and constitution-building, the physiocrats were the most opposed of all French political economists to the British model, holding that Britain was on the verge of economic and political collapse. Those who held that French power could be restored by utilizing public credit were themselves divided. On one side stood the anglophile advocates of mixed government. Inspired by Jean Delolme's *La Constitution de l'Angleterre* (1771), political economists, such as the Marquis de Chastellux, argued that the division of sovereignty would give the wealth-creating elements of the community greater opportunities to influence government policy, while increasing their willingness to underwrite the debts of the state. The British balancing act between different orders of the state was deemed to rest upon the most advanced constitution in the modern world. If it was adopted by France at the same time as French *philosophes* were able to make political administration a more certain science—something Chastellux was sure his works were on the verge of achieving—then governance would become straightforward; in the confident rhetoric of the day, it would become akin to geometry. France could face the future with the twin advantages of internal peace and renewed vigour. To such writers as the abbé Galiani, or his most influential disciple, Jacques Necker, Chastellux's ideas were impractical because they necessitated a constitutional revolution, the effects of which could not be predicted. The British constitution was singularly suited to the British Empire, being the product of a distinctive history and national character. By contrast, France had experienced absolute monarchical rule for almost two millennia and as a result it would be extremely foolish to challenge the existing conception of sovereignty. Where Galiani and Necker differed from the physiocrats was in their faith in public credit and commerce as forces compatible with contemporary politics. What was required was an able statesman, such as the admired Colbert, who would placate the critics of the crown's policy by granting them influence in provincial assemblies; these would gradually reduce government expenditure, and use credit to stimulate commerce and industry. Provincial assemblies, just as in the case of the institutions envisaged by the physiocrats, would provide administrative and advisory functions. They would never challenge the King's sovereignty. Each of these parties had advocates in the court, church and various *parlements*. Although Chastellux was the most radical, his ideas had a lineage dating from the early decades of the century; supporters included such luminaries as Voltaire and the abbé Coyer.

What united all parties was the view that France was, and would only ever be, a monarchy. Ideas about constitutional innovation would never change the fundamental nature of the state or challenge the hierarchical structure of French society. In short, all of these writers were 'moderns' when their ideas are seen against the background of the famous *querrelle* that had raged for over a century over the relative merits of ancient and modern civilization. Classical authorities had to be respected as sources of wisdom, but their ideas were to be interpreted within the context of an acceptance of the superiority of modern monarchy as a form of government and state. This meant that certain beliefs that had flourished in the ancient world were generally deemed irrelevant to contemporary political argument. Prominent among these was the claim that sovereignty was to be found in a body of equal citizens who enjoyed liberty by making their own laws, defending their own state, and creating their own wealth by farming the land. The associated contention that happiness could only be found in dedication to the public good, motivated by the love of the state, was equally disparaged. Neo-Harringtonian associations of citizenship with land ownership clearly influenced the physiocrats.[13] Other Roman republican ideas were held to be wholly anachronistic, including the beliefs—given a new life by Machiavelli's *Discoursi*—that political tumult between plebs and patricians was the fount of liberty, the view that the maintenance of a state or empire depended upon citizen armies, or that liberty was founded upon frugal and patriotic mores opposed to commerce and luxury. Still more ridicule was directed against the Spartan ideal of an egalitarian society characterized by agrarian and sumptuary laws.[14] Modern or civilized monarchies such as France were among the most stable and successful states in history. Supporters of modern monarchy believed that French subjects did not love virtue. They found happiness in forms of living far removed from ancient models. Many, led by Turgot, recognized that the division of labour had entrenched social hierarchy while commerce made the creation of alternatives to monarchy increasingly inconceivable. The greatest cliché of political argument by 1770, made famous by Montesquieu, Rousseau and Voltaire, was that republics were inconceivable outside of small states. The logical republic was Geneva, with its population of 25,000 citizens. When the term *république* was used in political debate, it was synonymous with the sovereignty of wisdom. This was, of course, an ancient tradition particularly associated with neo-Platonic philosophy and one which had revived from Bodin onwards. It was fully compatible with the sovereignty of an enlightened king. Indeed, it had been used in the seventeenth century to contrast the wisdom of French kings with the ignorance and excesses of the English republic.[15] Condorcet used the term in this sense when he called Turgot a republican in the influential *Vie de Turgot* of 1782. Yet what is peculiar about late eighteenth-century French thought is that the sense of national decline was so acute that very different republican demands for social reformation and political revolution were returned to, in the hope of restoring glory. Modern republican ideas were developed as an alternative to the British example of national flourishing.

3 EIGHTEENTH-CENTURY REPUBLICANISM

In France, as in Britain, it is strictly a mistake to talk about a revival of *classical* republicanism. Recreating ancient conditions was altogether inconceivable at the level of the large nation state. Andrew Fletcher put it very clearly at the beginning of the century and writers followed him in acknowledging that restoring ancient virtue would necessitate the reintroduction of slavery or 'domestic servitude' across Europe; otherwise the citizen would lack the time and peace of mind necessary for a life of dedication to the public good.[16] Few took seriously Rousseau's related demand that large civilized monarchies should renounce commerce and destroy themselves by becoming unions of small states, in order for virtue to survive.[17] A distinction must therefore be made between small and large state republicanism. The former flourished in the United Provinces and the Swiss cantons as well as being famously applied by Rousseau to such states as Poland and Corsica. Large state republicanism, rather than being a self-consciously advocated political option, appeared in a different form, at least before 1780. Prominent themes of ancient republicanism were revived in the guise of a literature of jeremiad, lamenting the loss of virtue and patriotism and attacking the spread of luxury. These are important because they contributed to an intellectual climate in which new theories about liberty in modern states were formulated. In France, these new theories developed in the wake of Turgot's fall from power as *contrôleur-général*, when many writers acknowledged that defence of the existing monarchical constitution, social structure, and national culture was no longer tenable if French decline was to be reversed.

It is significant that the writer most responsible for popularizing such a literature in France, the abbé Gabriel Bonnot de Mably, counted among his favourite authors the English cleric John Brown. Mably has attracted a great deal of attention in recent years because of his so-called 'script for a revolution', the *Des droits et des devoirs du citoyen*.[18] Although written in 1758 in response to the *parlements'* opposition to Louis XV, the pamphlet was not published until 1788, at which time it attracted notice as a call for a sovereign Estates General that would be the source of all future law.[19] When read alongside Mably's more famous *Entretiens de Phocion*, which saw numerous editions from 1765, some historians have concluded that Mably was that rare beast—a writer who advocated a French republic before the autumn of 1791. Few if any of Mably's contemporaries believed that he was in favour of such a transformation of the state. Mably certainly did believe that the philosophy and history of antiquity could teach kinds of morality which the moderns had forgotten to their cost. Works such as *Phocion* were damning indictments of contemporary manners and wholly opposed to public credit and commerce. They did not call for the creation of a republic in France. Rather, in *Phocion* Mably argued that a mixed government was superior to any other.[20] Another prominent work published during his lifetime, *De la législation ou principes des lois*, advocated 'tempered monarchy' for the dual reason that democracy risked creating political anarchy and that republican virtue could only subsist in small states.[21] The author of the 'Éloge historique de l'abbé Mably', the abbé Brizard, argued in 1787 that Mably opposed republicanism in large states. In this author's opinion Mably's intention had rather been to teach French kings to be more like their great forbears—Clovis and Charlemagne— and it is beyond dispute that reverence for these kings is a feature of all of Mably's writings.[22] Such an interpretation is also supported by scrutiny of the final work Mably saw published before his death, the *Observations sur le gouvernement et les lois des États-Unis d'Amérique*, which was notable for Mably's pessimism about the North-American republican experiment. He argued that where 'the liberty of the citizens has not been established and directed with the wisdom of the Spartans', the legislators 'must only establish democracy in a republic with extreme caution'. It was likely that North America's republics would soon be corrupted in the manner of the United Provinces. Mably discerned in the new world the replication of the manners that characterized, and in his view ruined, the old; as he put it. 'for a long time now the politics of Europe, founded as they are upon money and commerce, have caused all the classical virtues to disappear.'[23] Mably's book lamented the force of commerce and what he deemed to be its uncontrollable capacity to spread effeminacy, selfishness and sloth in the place of courage, patriotism and frugality. Although such works reminded their readers of the worth of political virtue, they described a world that had been well and truly lost. Mably acknowledged that it was too dangerous to risk its re-establishment in corrupt times. It is therefore unsurprising that *Des droits et des devoirs* accepted that when the state found itself in conditions of crisis its only recourse would be to a dictator with authority to take 'extraordinary measures, often contrary to the constitution of the state.'[24] Even at his most republican, he expressed little confidence in the rule of the people. Mably's preference was for an enlightened emperor dedicated to the public good. Given that he could see no possibility of such a ruler among the scions of the Bourbon family, he advocated making the landed nobility sovereign. It is probable that *Des devoirs* owed much to Harrington's *Oceana*. Mably strictly adhered to the neo-Harringtonian tradition of opposition to politically motivated transformations of the social order. Although more sceptical of commerce, his conception of the citizen was identical to that of the members of the other branch of the neo-Harringtonian brotherhood in France, the physiocrats. He would unquestionably have opposed the breadth of citizenship granted by the constitutions of 1791, 1793 and 1795. There was therefore little original in Mably's republicanism. Rather, his was the most cynical voice in the political choir. Republican themes which he revived were soon to strike a different chord in more innovative minds.

Those who shared Mably's contempt for French society and politics, such as the radical *philosophe* Helvétius, were as aware of the difficulties faced by republican conceptions of politics when applied to states such as France. Helvétius too has been labelled a revolutionary before his time; his bust was among the first to be erected in the vestibule of the National Assembly, and his works were counted among the most popular throughout the 1790s.[25] Republican themes can certainly be identified in his writings. He constantly attacked excessive inequalities of wealth as destructive of virtue. Machiavelli inspired his understanding of British power, tracing it as Helvétius did to 'the play of all the opposed passions'. Neo-Harringtonian concerns for the future of commercial societies were also expressed. In particular, he believed that British wealth would decline when domestic wages were undercut by the lower labour costs of poorer countries. In addition, an excessive love of luxury would corrupt ministers into abusing their powers, causing an already dangerously high public debt to increase further. As a result he described the collapse of Britain and its empire as inevitable. Moderating wealth and ensuring its distribution among as many hands as possible were the only solutions to the perennial problem of political corruption. As Helvétius put it, 'The more men in a state who are free, independent, and enjoy only a moderate income, the stronger that state will be.' He was sure, however, that the achievement of such egalitarian conditions was a pipe dream. The 'moral plant named empire' was certain to 'germinate, grow, mature, age and die.' One consequence of these opinions was that he had no faith whatsoever in changing the form of government of a state in order to solve its political problems. He warned Montesquieu, in a response to the latter's *L'Esprit des lois*, not to be over-impressed with Britain's form of government: the corruption embedded within it made her inferior to France.[26] The key to the reform of a state was a system of public education and good laws. His works were therefore dedicated to those who were in his view the greatest reformers of the age: Catherine II and Frederick the Great. As Diderot noted in his annotations to *De l'homme*, this man was as opposed to popular revolution as it was possible to be.[27] Helvétius' alternative to republican or monarchical conceptions of political practice derived from belief in the potential of reason to analyse human nature and determine the springs of human action. Armed with such knowledge, he believed legislators would be able to guide humanity. That the end result would be happy individuals living in peace-loving states was ensured by the identity of virtue and knowledge.[28] Legislators would, of course, have to deal with recalcitrant humanity by the provision of incentives to undertake virtuous actions and by punishing misdemeanours. This was the great challenge of contemporary moral science. Seeking to build the perfect constitution was a misplaced aim. It was also misguided because yearnings for political liberty usually resulted in the establishment of a state characterized by tyranny. Humanity had to have faith in the virtue of legislators and monarchs. Although there was no means of guaranteeing their ability, sovereigns would gradually recognize the benefits to themselves, their subjects, and their state, of creating a beneficent legal and educational system. In many respects, the most original aspect of Enlightenment political thought in France was the attempt to develop means of governing conduct.[29] The revolutionaries therefore turned to Helvétius not in the first days of the Revolution, when hopes were pinned on the erection of a new form of government. Rather, it occurred in the aftermath of the Terror, when committed revolutionaries realized that they would have to transform national culture before they could maintain a republican constitution.[30]

Helvétius' friend and fellow *philosophe*, Paul Thierry, the Baron d'Holbach, has also been numbered among those who inspired the republican movements of the 1790s.[31] D'Holbach's writings were closer to the former's ideas than they were to Mably's, aspiring as he did to govern by 'the Laws of Nature that always direct conduct towards virtue'. Yet he was as critical as Helvétius was of aspirations to republicanism in large states. As he put it, 'the people are ignorant and cannot govern themselves . . . democracy is only a modified anarchy.' Even republics that united the virtues of aristocracy and democracy would collapse through 'prejudice and faction, usurpation and tyranny'. Against Montesquieu, d'Holbach argued that the principle behind a republic was equality, and that equality could never be the basis of a stable state:

If Republics are founded and sustained by enthusiasm, greatness of soul, or virtue, these impetuous forces are always of short duration. The ease of oppression and unjust punishment encourage crime. The love of equality will in time destroy the edifice which virtue had raised and supported. Aristide fell victim to ostracism. After Phocion, who had the courage to be virtuous at Athens?[32]

Monarchies were superior to republics in being less fragile. D'Holbach did, however, predict that the most praised contemporary form, Britain's mixed monarchy, would enjoy only a short-lived fame. The end would come when the monarch either corrupted the House of Commons by patronage so as to have no need for it, or purchased a mercenary army willing to support a *coup d'état*. Britons, he believed, were too ignorant to defend their liberty. National greatness could only exist where the rulers and the people loved the public good. For this to be the case reason and good manners had to prevail. Teaching individuals to practice their social duties was therefore the key to political science. D'Holbach's application of these ideas was distinctive because of his argument that reason entailed condemning the traditional role played by religion in modern states. He believed Christianity in particular to be responsible for the failure of European societies to have established more rational and peaceful politics. True Christians were 'fanatics, enthusiasts and hermits'. A number of works issued from his pen seeking to prove that the reputedly sacred doctrines of every religion were in fact ancient dogmas dressed up in modern garb. Delight was taken in articles for the *Encyclopédie* that revealed similarities between ancient Inca liturgies and subsequent Christian practices. Religion was everywhere an escape from rational thought and a confession of ignorance. Organized churches had been invented 'only to save Sovereigns from aspiring to be just, from making good laws and from governing well.'[33] D'Holbach's hatred of the priesthood never became part of his proposals for the reform of France. Writers in the 1780s, such as Brissot and Nicolas Bergasse, used his ideas to demand the destruction of the first estate in existing large monarchies. This became one of the keystones of the republican programme in the 1790s, with which Say fully concurred.

What distinguished d'Holbach from Helvétius was the belief that enlightened legislators and princes could not be trusted to be wise. Citing the radical Whig Thomas Gordon, he contended that the problem with princes was that no one ever told them the truth.[34] Power had to be constrained by reason, or a state would be created where 'the people are all slaves, and the will of the master is the supreme law.' It was therefore necessary to reflect on the constitution most likely to promote the public good without increasing political authority to the extent of spreading ignorance and corruption. D'Holbach's solution is important because it was the first attempt to go beyond the British constitutional example and the orthodox defences of enlightened despotism, without rejecting commerce. It was first sketched in the article *Représentans* in volume fourteen of the *Encylopédie*, published in 1765, but was restated, in a more radical form, in subsequent works published before his death in 1789. The necessity of representation to a free polity is the key to d'Holbach's political thought. While he expressed a Hobbesian faith in the need for a sovereign who could exercise sufficient authority to compel the pursuit of *la volonté générale*, this was combined with the recognition that 'no man, however wise, is capable of governing a nation without support and counsel.' No rank within the state could know the needs of others. It was therefore essential that each rank be represented 'in assemblies which have the public good as their object.' D'Holbach combined this demand with a rejection of the neo-Harringtonian association of citizenship with land-ownership. Membership of his assemblies depended upon a more general property qualification because only such men had 'an interest and stake in the country . . . ownership of property makes a citizen.' His conception of wealth was sufficiently broad to include merchants, farmers, magistrates, clergymen and nobles in addition to the landed gentry. Each was an active citizen not because of their social status but because of their wealth. D'Holbach claimed that without such institutions the people's liberties would be unprotected. They would become ignorant and support the revolutions of 'dangerous and seditious men, such as Cromwells and Guises'. Moreover, without security there would be no commerce. D'Holbach's emphasis on commerce as a fundamental and necessary aspect of modern life distinguished him from Helvétius and Mably. Yet he combined this with opposition to the effects of excessive commerce, luxury and effeminacy, and also what he called 'commerce born of avidity'. The latter he associated with greed, war and exploitation, arguing that it was possible to develop forms of commerce that were compatible with virtue, the courage required for self-defence, and liberty.[35] Public credit remained unacceptable: 'an alchemical technique which dissolves the state.' Moral commerce was rather synonymous with moderate wealth, trade in necessities, and a national character which placed the love of liberty and virtue above that of financial gain.[36] This distinction was to prove of singular importance in the formation of modern republican conceptions of political economy, and of Say's in particular.

In *Représentans* D'Holbach was, understandably, unclear regarding the extent to which monarchical sovereignty in France might be challenged by the institutionalization of his assemblies. On the one hand, he implied that their powers would be advisory. This took him only one step beyond the physiocrats. On the other, he wrote of the monarch ensuring a balance between the representatives of different orders. The inference was that although the monarch had ultimate executive authority, the representatives would be responsible for the laws and administration of the state. Sovereignty would thereby be divided according to function, with the representatives exercising legislative power in accordance with the British model. D'Holbach was explicit at least in demanding a written constitution that would guarantee regular elections and the right of the people to call back their representatives. His later *Politique naturelle* was less equivocal, proclaiming that the plan for representative assemblies was 'not chimerical; the power of the Monarch is subordinate to those of the Representatives of the People, and the authority of the Representatives depends on the will of their Constituents.' In this work, d'Holbach combined the demand for unified sovereignty with acute criticism of mixed government and it is significant that it was written in the aftermath of studying Hobbes' works (his French translation of *De Corpore*, entitled *De la nature humaine*, appeared in 1772). D'Holbach believed, with many of his contemporaries, that 'liberty is man's strongest passion . . . It is founded on virtue and reason. All peoples have an innate right to it.' Identifying liberty with popular sovereignty and commercial society were more radical steps. Although he did not envisage transforming the social orders of France, accepting the necessity of a hierarchical society, d'Holbach had a republican conception of the monarch as chief-magistrate. He believed that without constitutional change legislation conforming to his conception of natural law would never be instituted. Proper education and governance was only possible within the confines of a constitution embodying the principles of what he called 'a true republic'. In his later works d'Holbach was opposed to mixed government and believed in rule by the people, by which he meant those who were citizens by virtue of their ownership of property and resulting interest in the public good. Alongside his virulent attacks on organized religion, his constitutional writings stand as indictments of contemporary France that were constructive as well as critical. There is no means of assessing the popularity of his many publications, all of which appeared anonymously and none of which received the approbation of the censors of the book-trade. Perhaps his most popular writings were his articles in the *Encyclopédie*, to which he was the third highest contributor, behind Diderot and de Jaucourt. It is certain, however, that he was a major influence upon *philosophe* thinking in general, not least because of the intellectual relationships he fostered and sustained through what Rousseau called *la coterie holbachique*. Dinners at his residence on the *rue Royale* every Thursday and Sunday united many of the leading *philosophes* of the day, including Diderot, Marmontel, Suard, Raynal, Chastellux, Helvétius, d'Alembert, Galiani, Grimm, Saint-Lambert, Morellet and, on occasion, Hume and Wilkes. During the first decade of their existence, from the late 1740s, Rousseau was a regular guest. After d'Holbach's death in January 1789 some of his disciples, such as Naigeon and Garat, played major roles in the formation of revolutionary republicanisms.[37] Garat was close to members of the editorial board of *La Décade philosophique*, which provides one link between d'Holbach and Say.

4   THE POLITICAL ECONOMY OF MODERN REPUBLICANISM

Despite his willingness to conceive of a state founded on popular sovereignty, d'Holbach's perspective remained within what might be termed 'Hobbesian' constraints. Like the English philosopher, his notion of popular sovereignty did not entail a right to resist. Rather, it was a warning to existing monarchs, and the Bourbon family in particular, to follow the public good and lead the people to virtue. As a consequence, there is no discussion in d'Holbach's works of the problems which might have arisen should a large state undergo a revolution and erect a popular government. As has been noted, he contributed to the political economy of modern republicanism through his distinction between moral and selfish commerce, but he made no attempt to link this to his reflections upon political transformation. The writer who did more than anyone to raise the issue of pushing large monarchies in a republican direction was Diderot. In many respects, the questions Say sought to resolve in his political economy begin here.

The expansiveness of Diderot's mind with respect to religion and morality are well known because of his atheism, materialism and vitalism. Opposition to Christianity was colourfully affirmed by less direct forms of ridicule than d'Holbach's, epitomized by the moral *conte* entitled *Supplément au voyage de Bougainville*. That Diderot was as original a thinker in politics is less widely recognized.[38] Early in his life, when he was closest to Rousseau, Diderot expressed reservations about the legitimacy of the French monarchy. An article in the first volume of the *Encyclopédie* (1751), *Autorité politique*, argued that the power of the prince was conditional, because his authority derived from being 'chosen by the people'. When their 'contract' was abrogated, 'the nation recovers complete freedom of action.' Although the radical nature of these ideas were masked by calls for a patriot king in the image of Henri IV, they caused a furore in the church and Paris *parlement*. 'Errata' published in the third volume included the assertion with regard to the article, that 'we never claimed that the authority of the prince did not come from God . . . The evidence of God's gift is the consent of the peoples, and such irrevocable consent bestowed by God to Hugh Capet and his descendents.' The article *Droit naturel* in volume five (1755), however, reaffirmed Diderot's rejection of the orthodox view of political obligation and claimed that adherence to the *volonté générale* was the only ground for obedience. The implication was that monarchs who violated the 'rights of humanity' ought to be opposed. If the *volonté générale* was synonymous with the public good, a question naturally arose concerning how it might be practically realized. The identity of Rousseau and Diderot's ideas ceases at this point as the former placed his faith in small state republicanism. For Diderot this was ultimately inadequate because it was inconceivable in large monarchies.

It was only in his final years that Diderot began to conceive of a genuine alternative to contemporary forms of monarchy. Like Rousseau he always rejected the British example. At different times different solutions were considered. In the early 1770s, for example, in his commentary on Helvétius' books, he placed his faith in men whom he called *honnêtes gens*; the ministers of France, such as Turgot, who were sufficiently enlightened that 'within ten years all our difficulties will be remedied.'[39] Diderot was conventional in considering republicanism to be a doctrine for small states alone at this time. Cynically, he stated that 'the sole form of government which grants happiness to humanity will always be precarious.' The event that changed his mind was the American Revolution, and d'Holbach was the indirect cause of Diderot's expression of a new-found optimism about political innovation. D'Holbach had asked La Grange to prepare an edition of Seneca's works. Diderot's *Essai sur la vie de Sénèque* was published as the seventh volume of the edition in 1778. It was then revised and republished in 1782 under the title *Essai sur les règnes de Claude et de Néron, et sur les mœurs et les écrits de Sénèque*. The second edition of the essay is notable for its defence of the right to resist tyranny, as Diderot asked 'who committed the crime of high treason? the Roman people or Nero himself?'.[40] Both editions, however, included an address *Aux insurgents de l'Amérique* that amounted to a synopsis of Diderot's political ideas. Diderot questioned the legitimacy of existing forms of government and claimed that America represented not only 'an asylum to Europeans against fanaticism and tyranny' but also a lesson 'to those who govern men, on the legitimate use of their authority.' In short, America had become a model for Europe. That Diderot was thinking about the French in praising republican America was revealed in additions he made to the third edition of the abbé Raynal's *Histoire philosophique des deux Indes*.[41] Here he stated that Frenchmen faced the choice of emigrating to North America or making a modern republic out of the ruins of their own monarchy:

We ourselves, oh my friends and fellow citizens, shall profit from your example. If our constitution is changed; if public wealth corrupts the court, and the court corrupts the nation; if our kings, to whom we have given so many terrible examples, finally forget them; if we, who were a distinguished nation, should be threatened with becoming the most abject and cowardly herd, by selling ourselves; then the spectacle of your virtues and laws could reanimate us. It could recall to our degraded hearts both the price and the greatness of liberty.[42]

Raynal's *Histoire* was one of the most widely read works of the time, with twenty official editions before 1789. It was here that Diderot made clear his belief that 'an empire cannot endure, any more than an individual family, without morals and virtue.' He claimed that Britain's greatness was traceable to the republican element in her constitution, the fact that 'man is in a word, a citizen, that is to say, an integral and constituent part of the state and the nation'. He also argued that Britain should not be seen as a model for other states because she was in rapid decline, with 'a government which you yourselves [the British] admit to be ignorant, corrupt, and reckless, [which] is arrogantly and with impunity hurtling you into the deepest abyss.' Genuine republics *could* be created in large states. It was necessary to combine political liberty with virtuous manners and, following d'Holbach, moderate wealth. Against Mably, Diderot argued that commerce was a necessity, but he pointed out that it could become a positive force in a republic if it was carefully nurtured and monitored by enlightened legislators. The alternative system of material equality was described as 'the most dangerous of all beliefs in a civilized society.' As in all of his works, Diderot's optimism was tempered. In addition to being an advocate of modern republicanism, he was also aware of the difficulties of transforming monarchies into their opposite form of state. Problems of the size of the state, disunity among the populace, and corruption in government had always been recognized, but Diderot believed that the North Americans had overcome them. Far more troubling, he believed, was the need to transform the national character of a people, the culture of the nation in its entirety, if a state was to remain republican.

As early as the annotations to Helvétius he had been aware of the issue: 'how can virtuous manners be restored among a corrupt populace?' The memorable and prescient answer was to 'adopt the means by which Medea restored youth to her father, by cutting him into pieces and boiling the whole.' This image recurred in the *Histoire*: 'A nation is only regenerated in a bath of blood. It is the image of old Aeson, whose youth was restored by Medea when she cut him up and boiled the pieces.' In the *Vie de Sénèque* he warned republicans that 'a State sustains itself neither by gold nor by the number of its people, but only by its manners'. In a commercial society, means had to be found by which the people avoided avarice and continued to love the public good. In addition to the classical ideal of being soldiers, farmers and law-makers they had to be merchants. These were exactly the problems which the republicans of the late 1780s and 1790s faced in justifying and putting their ideas into practice. Clearly, such constitutional and cultural transformations were difficult to conceive of and still harder to implement. Believing he could resolve such problems, Say followed Clavière and became a republican political economist.

Republican political economy demanded the establishment and maintenance of a moderate level of wealth for all citizens. Ranks had to be abolished to prevent aristocracy or inequality from recurring. The sovereignty of the people was to be coupled with the decentralization of political and administrative power to the citizens of a locality. Despite this, the republic was to remain a unified state. Its laws would embody the public good and its patriotic citizenry would be dedicated to defending and maintaining the state. The modern republic was a commercial society in the sense that wealth derived from trade and industry was to be encouraged as an antidote to the poverty of the state and the citizenry. Commercialization was to be welcomed as long as it remained compatible with republican morality and an egalitarian social structure. A republic was therefore not solely to be created by making laws that prevented domination and abolished monarchy, as many eighteenth-century British radicals supposed.[43] Far more important was the creation of a republican political culture based on a blend of commercial with traditionally conceived virtuous manners. Without cultural transformation any projected political innovations would be doomed to failure.

NOTES TO CHAPTER 2

1. *Traicté de l'œconomie politique* (Geneva, 1970), pp. 23, 121–2, 146–8.
2. Smith recounted this story to Dugald Stewart, as the latter reports in his 'Account of the Life and Writings of Adam Smith', Adam Smith, *Essays on Philosophical Subjects* (Oxford, 1980), p. 304.
3. *Quesnay et la physiocratie*, i, 260–71.
4. Charles Davenant, 'An Essay Upon Universal Monarchy', *The Political and Commercial Works* (London, 1770), 5 vols., iv, 23–30, 40–1. On France and Universal Monarchy, see I. Hont 'Free Trade and the Economic Limits to National Politics: Neo-Machiavellian Political Economy Reconsidered', J. Dunn, ed., *The Economic Limits to Modern Politics* (Cambridge, 1993), pp. 41–99; J. Robertson 'Universal Monarchy and the Liberties of Europe: David Hume's

Critique of an English Whig Doctrine', N. Phillipson and Q. Skinner, eds., *Political Discourse in Early-Modern Europe* (Cambridge, 1994), pp. 349–73.

5. *Natural and Political Observations* [1696], *Two Tracts by Gregory King* (Baltimore, 1936), p. 13.

6. *L'Esprit des lois*, 31 books, ix, chs. 7, 9; x, ch. 9.

7. E. Dziembowski, *Un nouveau patriotisme français, 1750–1770: La France face à la puissance anglaise à l'époque de la guerre de Sept Ans, SVC,* 365 (Oxford, 1998).

8. On these issues see G. Weulersse, *Le Movement physiocratique en France de 1756 à 1770* (Paris, 1910) 2 vols.; S. Kaplan, *Bread, Politics and Political Economy in the Reign of Louis XV* (The Hague, 1976), 2 vols.; J. Riley, *The Seven Years War and the Old Regime in France* (Princeton, 1986); C. Larère, *l'Invention de l'économie politique au XVIIIe siècle* (Paris, 1992); J.-Cl. Perrot, *Une histoire intellectuelle de l'économie politique* (Paris, 1992).

9. Philip Dormer Stanhope, fourth Earl of Chesterfield, *Letters to His Son*, ed. R. K. Root (London, 1929), p. 275.

10. Cited in Jacques Godechot, *Les Institutions de la France* (Paris, 1951), p. 4. On this view of sovereignty see A. Michel, *La Monarchie Absolue*, in K. M. Baker, ed. *The French Revolution and the Creation of Modern Political Culture: The Political Culture of the Old Regime* (Oxford, 1987); K. M. Baker, 'Representation Redefined', *Inventing the French Revolution*; F. Furet, *Revolutionary France*, tr. A. Nevill (Oxford, 1992), ch. 1.

11. M. Sonenscher, 'The Nation's Debt and the Birth of the Modern Republic'. The article should be read in conjunction with Istvan Hont's 'The Permanent Crisis of a Divided Mankind: The Contemporary Crisis of the Nation State in Historical Perspective', *Political Studies*, 42 (1994), 166–231.

12. On Quesnay's political economy see P. Steiner, *La Science nouvelle de l'économie politique* (Paris, 1998) and *Sociologie de la connaissance économique*, chs. 2–3.

13. K. M. Baker, *Inventing the French Revolution*, chs. 2, 4, 6, extending J. G. A. Pocock's *The Machiavellian Moment: Florentine Political Thought and the Atlantic Republican Tradition* (Princeton, 1975).

14. E. Rawson, *The Spartan Tradition in European Thought* (Oxford, 1969), ch. 17.

15. J.-M. Goulemot, *Le Mythe de Cromwell et l'obsession de la république chez les monarchistes Français de 1650 à 1700,* J. Viard, ed., *L'Esprit républicain* (Paris, 1970), pp. 107–10.

16. J. Robertson, ed., *Andrew Fletcher's Political Writings* (Cambridge, 1997), introduction.

17. *Œuvres complètes de Jean-Jacques Rousseau* (Paris, 1959–69), 3 vols., i, 935.

18. Baker, *Inventing the French Revolution*, ch. 4; Kent Wright, *A Classical Republican.*

19. *Des droits et des devoirs du citoyen*, ed. J.-L. Lecercle (Paris, 1972), letter vi.

20. *Entretiens de Phocion* (Amsterdam, 1765), conversation v.

21. *De la législation ou principes des lois* (Amsterdam, 1776), 2 vols., ii, 45.

22. *Éloge historique de l'abbé de Mably, discours qui a partagé le prix au jugement de l'Académie des inscriptions et belles lettres, Collection complète des œuvres de l'abbé de Mably,* ed. Arnoux (Paris, an III), 11 vols., i, 23–64.

23. *Observations, Collection complète des œuvres*, viii, 352–4, 461, 483.

24. *Des droits et devoirs*, pp. 219–20.

25. A. Guillois, *Le Salon de Madame Helvétius* (Paris, 1894); Mornet, *Les Origines intellectuelles de la Révolution française, 1715–1787* (Lyon, 1989), pp. 100–5; I. L. Horrowitz, *Claude Helvétius: Philosopher of Democracy and Enlightenment* (New York, 1954); D. W. Smith, *Helvétius: a Study in Persecution* (Oxford, 1965), esp. pp. 218–23.

26. *De l'homme, Œuvres complètes* (Paris, 1795), 12 vols., x, section 6, chs. 9–15; x, 121–2; x, 85–95, 114–15, xiii, 61–71.

27. *Réfutation de l'ouvrage de Helvétius intitulé De l'homme, Œuvres complètes de Diderot*, ed. J. Assézat (Paris, 1875), 15 vols., iii, 380–1.

28. *De l'esprit*, chs. 20–3 (Paris, 1852).

29. The phrase is James Tully's, although he does not apply his analysis to France. It is significant, however, that Helvétius saw himself following a Lockean tradition of philosophy. See 'Governing Conduct', *Locke in Context* (Cambridge, 1992).

30. M. Staum, *Minerva's Message*, chs. 8–12.

31. R. Hubert, *D'Holbach et ses amis* (Paris, 1928); W. H. Wickwar, *Baron d'Holbach: a Prelude to the French Revolution* (London, 1935).

32. *La Politique naturelle* (London, 1773), 2 vols., preface, i, 64–9.

33. *Le Christianisme dévoilé* (London, 1790, orig. 1756), p. 226.

34. *La Morale universelle* (Paris, 1820 [orig. 1776]), 3 vols., ii, 48.

35. *Représentans*, *Encyclopédie* (Berne and Lausanne, 1780), 36 vols., xvii, 367–8; *Politique naturelle*, vol. i, discours ii, sections 21–5, vol. ii, discours vii, sections 24–38.

36. *La Morale universelle*, ii, 14–20.

37. P. Kors, *D'Holbach's Coterie: an Enlightenment in Paris* (Princeton, 1975).

38. A. Strugnell, *Diderot's Politics: A Study of the Evolution of Diderot's Political Thought after the Encylopédie* (The Hague, 1973), chs. 4–5.

39. *Œuvres complètes*, iii, 275–6.

40. D. A. Bonneville, *Diderot's Vie de Sénèque* (Gainesville, Florida, 1966), chs. 3–4.

41. H. Dieckmann, 'Les Contributions de Diderot à la Correspondance littéraire et à l'histoire des deux Indes', *Revue d'histoire littéraire de la France* (1951), 417–40; M. Duchet, 'Diderot collaborateur de Raynal: à propos des fragments imprimés du fonds Vandeul', *Revue d'histoire littéraire de la France* (1960), 531–56.

42. *Histoire des deux Indes* (Amsterdam, 1780), 10 vols., viii, 292–3. Translations are from *Diderot. Political Writings*, J. Hope Mason and R. Wokler, eds. and trans. (Cambridge, 1992).

43. Quentin Skinner in *Liberty Before Liberalism* (Cambridge, 1998); Phillip Pettit in *Republicanism: A Theory of Freedom and Government* (Oxford, 1997).

PART TWO

THE INTELLECTUAL CONTEXT
OF SAY'S IDEAS

3

The Political Economy of French Decline

I DUPONT'S ATTACK ON THE 'BRITISH' SAY

Exiled from France after the Bourbon restoration, the aged arch-priest of physiocracy, Pierre-Samuel Dupont de Nemours, spent his journey across the Atlantic analysing the second edition of Jean-Baptiste Say's *Traité d'économie politique* (Paris, 1814). From the schooner *Fingal*, on 22 April 1815, he sent a detailed critique to Say in Paris. It is one of the most candid and revealing documents in the annals of French political economy. Dupont began by lamenting the dearth of disciples for what he dubbed Quesnay's science of political economy, and the vicious ridicule directed at the physiocratic movement, particularly by Say's 'satire' in the *Traité*. Nevertheless, Dupont retained the hope of converting Say to the old cause, and sought to combat despair by trying to force Say to recognize that he too was an *économiste*. Dupont explained that Smith, whom Say venerated above all others, was in fact a representative of one branch of Quesnay's broader subject, a claim that placed Say firmly in the physiocratic tradition of political economy:

I have just finished reading your excellent work . . . It interested me greatly and gave much conso-lation . . . You embrace almost all of our principles; excepting taxation, you draw exactly the same practical conclusions. The fancy you have of disowning us, which, my dear Say, you cannot quite conceal, does not prevent you from being, by Smith's line, a grandson of Quesnay and a nephew of the great Turgot.[1]

Dupont believed the gulf separating Say and Quesnay rested upon two disagreements that could both be resolved. Say did not accept that all taxes were ultimately paid by the landed proprietor who employed the primary producers, or that a single tax on the net product, the surplus revenue after the farmer's costs had been covered, would bring prosperity to agriculture in particular and commerce in general. Dupont remained convinced by these doctrines; but another disagreement was more divisive. Dupont accused Say of sketching only one branch of Quesnay's political economy—that concerned with the nature and distribution of wealth. According to Dupont, Say was abandoning the tradition of Quesnay and Turgot in neglecting the philosophical foun-dations of the science, emanating from the 'truths of natural law', and thereby the moral and political maxims which were an inseparable corollary of Quesnay's perspec-tive on the creation of wealth.

In Dupont's portrait, Quesnay was *the* philosopher of liberty. His genius had confined natural rights neither to the state of nature nor to social convention. Refuting Hobbes and Rousseau, he had erected a science which defined liberty *in society*, and which therefore did not entail the renunciation or dilution of natural rights by citizens entering the social state. Rather, Quesnay had given substance to the 'natural law' which stood above positive law, and which, when adhered to by legislators, would guarantee to every citizen the maximum liberty and security compatible with human nature. Each citizen who abided by the rules of enlightened justice Quesnay had discovered would receive a reward in accord with their contribution to the prosperity of society. In perhaps the most important passage in the letters, Dupont accused Say of discarding this heritage by '. . . cutting in two this beautiful science in order to separate concern with wealth':

You have narrowed the scope of political economy too much in treating it only as the *science of wealth*. It is the *science of natural right* applied, as it must be, to civilized societies. It is the *science of constitutions*, which teaches and will always teach not only what governments must do in accordance with their real interest, the interest of their nation, or their interest in *wealth*, but also what they are *forbidden to do before God*, under pain of the justified hatred and contempt of men, derision during their lives, and the bloody lash of history after their death.[2]

As a result of Say's error, political economy became redundant in the political sphere. Thus the *Traité* presented no challenge to the arguments popularly labeled 'reason-of-state' because they overrode existing legal codes and moral conventions and were associated with the intrigues of mercantile politics and the injustices of commercial empire. Dupont found the source of the problem in Say's undue regard for British ideas, which Dupont considered synonymous with reason-of-state arguments. Say was in real danger of unwittingly justifying an immoral perspective on society:

You believe that our broad manner of considering governments was *politics* and not *political economy*. In this case you have not spoken French, although you know it very well. Our language limits the meaning of the isolated word *politics* to diplomatic relations or relations of war between nations or other sovereigns. It is the science of Machiavelli, of Cardinal Richelieu, and of Bonaparte.

He therefore begged Say to 'leave the counting house' and return to the French language of liberty by repudiating the affected ideas and infected politics of the British:

do not imprison yourself in the ideas and language of the British, a sordid people who value a man only by the money he spends; they call public affairs the *commonwealth*, as if it did not include morals, justice, and the *droit des gens* (a term which has not even entered their language). They speak of their plants, their gardens, their rivers, their ports, their coasts, of their *country*: yet they have never acknowledged that they have a *patrie*.[3]

Dupont's letter might appear to be confused in praising Say for his work in a 'French tradition' of political economy while at the same time accusing him of over-fondness for British ideas. Such arguments are less important, however, than Dupont's recognition that political economists continued to be divided by the example of Britain. Differing attitudes to Britain provide an insight into the meaning of 'political economy' in Say's time. Indeed, the term 'the science of political economy' was coined as a means of attacking some of the perceptions of Britain prevailing in the 1760s.[4] On first examination these arguments could be perceived as being divorced from Say's work, but they were a powerful shaping influence upon his intellectual world. For the present, it is important to establish boundaries and distinguish different approaches and attitudes, in an attempt to define the kinds of political economy that Say would have recognized in the early years of his life.

2   EXPLAINING BRITAIN'S STRENGTH

Throughout his life Say was fascinated by Britain.[5] In every work of political economy published in his name there are constant references to British laws, policies, history, and national character.[6] As is well known, he and his brother Horace were given a commercial education in London in the mid-1780s. But Say's interest owed very little to his personal experiences. Long before his birth, the first concern of French writers was to explain the reasons for Britain's rise to prominence in Europe. Older problems, addressing the collapse of Spain, the effects of the influx of South American silver, and the possibility of establishing a universal monarchy, were perceived to be of secondary importance during the final years of Louis XIV.[7] National attention was rather directed towards Britain because an understanding of the vibrant health of this nation promised to illuminate the relative position of France and to provide an assessment of her future prospects. Say was therefore drawing on a tradition of reflection that was to be continued by the *Doctrinaires* of the 1820s and beyond.[8] The story is often presented as the victory of the 'laissez-faire' image of Britain over 'mercantilism', a development directly related to the transition of 'mercantile states' into 'consumer societies'.[9] Many historians now recognize the crudity of these general terms, not least because almost all writers claimed to be in favour of 'liberty' and 'commerce'.[10] Some have constructed more nuanced histories, for example based on the invention of sophisticated statistical and administrative techniques to analyse the economic world.[11] The present study takes a different path in allowing contemporary disputants to define their own positions, with the aim of recapturing their voices, as far as this is compatible with modern understanding of historically fluid terms.

The rise of Britain in the first half of the century had become a staple element of French discussion long before the Treaty of Paris was signed in 1763 at the summit of imperial rivalry.[12] Particular interest in the merits and demerits of the British polity can be traced to the 1690s, and to concern over the effects of the Glorious Revolution and the economic boom that accompanied it.[13] The outcome of the War of the Spanish Succession focused attention on the superiority of British public finances and sparked an interest in her political arithmeticians, especially the prescriptions for opulence of William Petty and Gregory King.[14] The war was also responsible for royal patronage of John Law's ultimately disastrous banking experiments.[15] By this time many writers were acknowledging the relative decline of France, making two questions of especial import; first, what were the causes of Britain's prosperity? Second, would it be possible for France to follow British practice? Early in the century, an influential view was formed in the merchant communities of Paris when John Law began to apply his schemes for Scottish regeneration to France.[16] In his view, the source of Britain's wealth could be traced to the extent of her foreign and domestic trade, and her national strength to public and private credit:

National Power and Wealth consists in numbers of People and Magazines of Home and Foreign Goods. These depend on Trade, and Trade depends on Money. So to be Powerful and Wealthy in proportion to other Nations, we should have Money in proportion with them; for the best Laws without Money cannot employ the People, Improve the Product, or advance Manufacture and Trade.[17]

In explaining Britain's wealth, particular emphasis was placed upon the institutions that facilitated trade by increasing the supply of money, specifically the national bank created in 1694, on the grounds that 'The use of Banks has been the best Method yet practis'd for the increase of Money.'[18] Law also commended 'Governments which Protect and Favour Trade' for having 'hinder[ed] the too great Consumption of Foreign Goods' by levying heavy duties upon foreign manufactures, ensuring the free export of British manufactures, and prohibiting the export of raw materials such as wool. Most important of all was the commitment of successive ministries to 'treasure by foreign trade', entailing the meticulous payment of public debts and support for merchant companies involved in trade across the globe. British governments were successful because they had recognized that, 'A Nation may gain where the Merchant loses, but wherever the Merchant gains, the Nation gains equal.' Law's additional proposal for stimulating trade was 'to make Money of Land' by the issue of paper bills, since 'Money is in the State what Blood is in the Human Body'.[19] By contrast, French governments were ambivalent about commerce, inconsistent in policy and fearful of national banks. Yet Law was convinced that the economic potential of France was greater than that of Britain; the 'mastery of the seas' was within the grasp of French ministers less constrained by the intrigues of parliamentary faction and less dependent upon public opinion. A Bourbon monarch could impose his own idea of order upon the economy by the implementation of Law's schemes, and harness national resources to create the self-sufficient commercial empire that had been Colbert's dream. In short, France could become what Law called 'a Commercial Kingdom', a 'Kingdom of Tradesmen, Traffickers, and Merchants.'[20]

Despite the failure of Law's attempt to regenerate France through speculation on shares in the Louisiana colony, he continued to have disciples dedicated to fostering commerce and credit in France. But in publications of the 1730s, Jean-François Melon and Dutot made clear the imperative of social change in France if Law's projects were to achieve success. As Dutot put it, if 'foreign commerce is the sole means to make a State rich and powerful' and 'to be the most powerful on land it is necessary to be the strongest at sea', then it was essential for the French nobility to renounce the 'shameful poverty' which accompanied obsession with the practice of arms; they were called on to return to 'the ancient practice' of mercantile commerce, which Caesar in his *Commentaries* had identified as the singular genius of northern Gallic culture. Dutot advised the establishment of new ports, ships, and companies to trade with the Indies and the Orient, able to take advantage of the low wages of these countries and undercut the commerce of Britain and Holland.[21] No constitutional impediments to France embracing commerce and credit were perceived, since, as Law had said, 'As far as authority is concerned, there is no state in which the Prince is not absolute'.[22] Noble prejudice apart, the social structures and cultures of the two nations were believed to be broadly similar. Later writers, such as Verron de Forbonnais, writing in the 1750s, were equally convinced of the potential flexibility of French policy and worked to *secourir la République* by similar means:

> Legislators have recognized a new source of glory and one which is far more secure, being founded on the happiness of humanity; it is a new kind of power, the acquisition of which is infinitely more useful, because without exhausting their treasuries and subjects, [legislators] have managed to increase their influence and importance in general affairs. The wealth of the People is of necessity the measure of that of the Prince; and *Finance*, or the art of issuing [money], of taxing, and of distributing the interest that office-holders gain from public ease, has always undergone the same revolutions as Commerce. These two branches of the internal administration of Empires today form the base of all political speculations, and their study is the principal occupation of true men of State.[23]

3   COMMERCE AND CONSTITUTIONS

A very different set of explanations for Britain's rise was given by writers inspired by Voltaire after the publication of his *Letters Concerning the English Nation* in 1733. Like Law, and following Defoe's *Plan of English Commerce* (1728), priority was given to commerce in explaining Britain's might: 'As Trade enrich'd the Citizens in *England*, so it contributed to their Freedom, and this Freedom on the other Side extended their Commerce, whence arose the Grandeur of the State.'[24] But the story of fostering commerce in a nation was, Voltaire suggested, entwined with the historical establishment of liberty. In the 1720s the writer perceived to have been responsible for the popularisation of this claim was Charles Davenant, and as such it became a major theme of discussion in Bolingbroke's circle during Voltaire's stay in Britain. Davenant had focused upon one of Machiavelli's most striking maxims: 'That no cities have augmented their revenues or enlarged their territories, but while they were free and at liberty.'[25] His conclusion was that commerce could only flourish in states where civil liberties were protected and in which all ranks were able to engage in trade. Britain's commercial success depended upon defence of the unique constitution of 1688, by which the interests of the king, the nobility, and the people had been balanced and, in theory, harnessed against misuse. Having accepted this view, Voltaire's message for Frenchmen jealous of Britain's strength was that power was intimately related to constitutional form:

> The *English* are the only people upon earth who have been able to prescribe limits to the power of Kings by resisting them; and who, by a series of struggles, have at last establish'd that wise Government, where the Prince is all powerful to do good, and at the same time is restrain'd from committing evil; where the Nobles are great without insolence, tho' there are no Vassals; and where the People share in the government without confusion.[26]

Different forms of government reflected diverse social structures and also what the British called manners (*mœurs*). The most important difference in these respects could be seen in the beliefs and practices of the nobilities of each nation. In Britain privileges were minimal: 'There is no such thing here as *haute, moyenne, & basse justice* . . . No one is exempted in this Country from paying certain Taxes, because he is a Nobleman or a

Priest.'[27] More revealing still, 'When the Lord Townshend was Minister of State, a Brother of his was content to be a City Merchant; and at the Time that the Earl of *Oxford* govern'd *Great-Britain*, his younger Brother was no more than a Factor in *Aleppo.*' The conclusion hardly needed stating. The British noble, in his capacity as a merchant, 'contributes to the Felicity of the World'; his French counterpart 'gives himself Airs of Grandeur and State, at the same Time that he is acting the Slave in the Ante-Chamber of a Prime Minister.' However useful national banks and navigation acts might be, their effects would be negligible without consideration of the constitutional and cultural forces that explained their origins and perseverance in Britain. Law's schemes had failed not because of their intrinsic malignity, but because they had been applied to a nation more hierarchical in structure and more feudal in aspiration than Britain; a state more absolutist than mixed, more monarchical than popular.[28] Voltaire upheld this view for the rest of his life. In the popular *Dictionnaire philosophique portatif* repeatedly published from 1764, he identified the Revolution of 1688 as the secret of prosperity because it had 'destroyed the fanaticism that shakes the most solid of states' and 'regulated the rights of the king, the nobility, and the people'. Such a mixed constitution he proclaimed, more glorious than that of Rome, 'will last as long as human affairs will last.'[29]

Voltaire's work was only one example, if the most widely read, of what became a leading theme of French debate in the late 1750s and particularly intense after abbé Gabriel Coyer published *La Noblesse commerçante* in 1756. Coyer was one of the most popular exponents of the depopulation thesis in France, but he believed it could be reversed by making French manners more like those of Britain. To this end he restated Voltaire's arguments, calling commerce 'the most efficacious means of [increasing] population', and inciting the nobility of France 'to serve the Nation by enriching them-selves through Commerce.'[30] Such demands were becoming so intrusive in public argu-ment that Louis-Charles Fougeret de Montbron coined the term *anglomanie* to describe the condition of national culture.[31] In the same year, Helvétius followed Voltaire in identifying Britain's 'mixed government', which had made men 'more Carthaginian than Roman', as being responsible for her commercial prowess. But he added a note of jeremiad to the general veneration of things British in prophesying decline through excessive reliance upon commercial manners:

the spirit of commerce, which necessarily leads to a taste for luxury and indolence, each day increases [in the eyes of the people] the price of gold and of labour, and each day diminishes their esteem for the art of war and even for courage: among a free people, this [last] virtue, sustains national honour; but in becoming weaker day by day, it will probably be the ultimate cause of the collapse or enslavement of this [British] nation.[32]

The long tradition of portraying luxury, inflation, effeminacy, and moral degeneration as the dangers inherent in commercial societies had revived in France by the late 1750s.[33] Luxury in particular was identified by all of Coyer's opponents as the 'most redoubtable of all the enemies of a State', the real cause of depopulation and a genuine challenge to the 'happy simplicity' of French life.[34] Another prominent thesis condemned commerce for the public credit it engendered, portraying it as a hostage to fortune and fool's gold, promising salvation and universal power but ultimately becoming the deadliest opiate. Statesmen and philosophers were wrestling with the question of how far the opulence that underpinned Britain's military success rested on her political system. If France was to flourish again was *constitutional* change essential?[35]

4 MONTESQUIEU'S CRITIQUE OF THE BRITISH EXAMPLE

The most distinctive voice of the 1750s to reflect upon these themes was that of Montesquieu, whose *L'Esprit des lois* contained a lucid and forthright assessment of France's relationship with Britain. In the famous eleventh book, 'On the Laws that Establish Political Liberty in its Relation to the Constitution', Montesquieu identified 'one nation in the world whose constitution has political liberty for its direct purpose', defining liberty as 'that tranquillity of spirit which comes from the opinion each has of their safety.' Since 'political liberty is found only in moderate governments' and 'present only when power is not abused' it was the essence of a constitution protective of liberty for 'power to check power by the arrangement of things'.[36] This was the abiding miracle of the British constitution, in which the legislative power was distinct from 'the executive power over questions decided by the rights of nations, and executive power over things decided by civil right', and in which checks were placed on the excessive use of any of the three powers. Nor was Montesquieu blind to Britain's commercial development, as he made clear in Book xx:

Other nations have made commercial interests give way to political interests. Britain has always made its political interests give way to the interests of its commerce. This is the people in the world who have best known how to take advantage of each of these three great things at the same time: religion, commerce, and liberty.[37]

Such praise led several contemporaries and subsequent historians to call Montesquieu an apologist for the British constitution, an advocate of French adoption of British practices.[38] This is an error. Montesquieu was as aware as Helvétius of the hazards facing Britain. The greatest of these he considered public credit, which threatened to destroy the delicate balance between the executive and legislative powers: 'If the legislative power determines the raising of public funds, not from year to year, but forever, it runs the risk of losing its liberty.'[39] Such fears caused him to conclude in a pessimistic rather than an adulatory tone, 'Since all human things have an end, the state of which we are speaking will lose its liberty; it will perish . . . This state will perish when legislative power is more corrupt than executive power.'

As to the possibility of France imitating Britain, Montesquieu argued against it at every juncture. Having praised the British constitution in Book xi he underlined his intention not 'to humble those who have a less extreme political liberty—I say that the excess even of reason is not always desirable and men accommodate themselves better to middles than extremes.'[40] He reiterated this point at the beginning of chapter seven when distinguishing between Britain and monarchies like France, while providing fulsome praise of the latter rather than the former: '[Monarchies] do not have liberty as their purpose but the glory of the citizens, state, and prince. But this glory results in a spirit of liberty that can produce equally great things and can perhaps contribute as much to happiness as liberty itself.' He sought to emphasize further the differences between the forms of government by showing their origins in the historical development of the social structures of the two nations. The political revolutions of the seventeenth century had ensured that 'the British nobility was buried with Charles I in the debris of the throne'. By contrast, in France 'the crown has always been sustained by that nobility which holds it an honour to obey a king but regards it as a sovereign infamy to share power with the people.'[41] This contrast runs throughout *L'Esprit*. In the second book, providing an early portrait of diverse forms of government, Montesquieu identified France as an archetype of monarchy and Britain as a popular state:

Intermediate, subordinate, and dependent powers constitute the nature of monarchical government, that is, of the government in which one person alone governs by fundamental laws. These fundamental laws necessarily assume channels through which power flows; for, if in the state there is only the momentary and capricious will of one alone, nothing can be fixed and consequently there is no fundamental law. The most natural intermediate and subordinate power is that of the nobility. In a sense, the nobility is the essence of monarchy, whose fundamental maxim is: *no monarchy no nobility: no nobility no monarchy*. Rather, one has a despot.[42]

As so often when discussing France, Montesquieu employed the device of direct contrast with Britain to add force to his argument. Montesquieu's well-known characterization of the British constitution as 'a republic hiding under the form of a monarchy' was as much a warning to France as a neutral description of its mixed form:

In a few European states, some people had imagined suppressing the jurisdiction of the nobility. They did not see that what they wanted to do the Parliament of Britain had already done. If you abolish the prerogatives of the lords, clergy, nobility, and towns in a monarchy, you will soon have a popular state or else a despotic state.[43]

In order to favour liberty 'the British have removed all the intermediary powers that formed their monarchy.' France was protected as a monarchy not only by the honour which characterized the nobility but by the 'depositories of laws' or *parlements* which 'bring the laws out of the dust in which they would be buried' and thereby guide the will of the prince away from tyrannical measures. In sum, 'Monarchical government assumes pre-eminences, ranks, and even a hereditary nobility. The nature of *honour* is to demand privileges and distinctions.' The most important conclusion to be drawn from these insights was that developing commerce in France would corrode ranks and initiate processes destructive of monarchy. In Montesquieu's eyes, 'the spirit of commerce brings with it the spirit of frugality, economy, moderation, work, wisdom, tranquillity, order, and rule.' In order for this spirit to be maintained it was essential for particular laws to be instituted that would support a commercial culture:

the principal citizens [must] engage in commerce themselves . . . all laws must favour it; these same laws, whose provisions divide fortunes as commerce increases them, must make each poor citizen comfortable enough to be able to work as the others do and must bring each rich citizen to a middle level such that he needs to work in order to preserve or to acquire a fortune.[44]

Commerce could clearly flourish only in certain kinds of societies, with specific types of constitutions and laws to protect and nourish it. For example, it suited small states with frugal and industrious manners, such as commercial republics or democracies, which enjoyed a minimum of inequality between ranks. Commerce would also flourish in popular states, such as Britain, whose nobility had embraced commerce and where wealth had gradually been distributed throughout the diverse social structure.

Another reason for Britain's commercial success can be adduced from Montesquieu's belief that 'the greatest enterprises are undertaken in those states which subsist by *economical* commerce.' Defining economical commerce as 'the practice of gaining little and even of gaining less than any other nation and of being compensated only by gaining continually', he employed it as the antithesis of commerce founded on luxury; the lesson was drawn that such commerce was 'scarcely possible . . . [in] a people among whom luxury is established who spend much and who value only objects of grandeur.'[45] Britain's commerce was economic while French commerce was characterized by luxury. Since, therefore, 'Commerce is related to the constitution', enormous changes would be necessary in French government in order to embrace the economical commerce which had made Britain great. Commerce contained a levelling principle tending towards equality, and it was this that Montesquieu feared most of all in France. Although commerce brought riches, luxury, and the arts, the social structure of France would be imperilled in choosing commercialization:

In a monarchical government, it is contrary to the spirit of commerce that any of the nobility should be merchants . . . Persons struck with the practice of some states imagine that in France they ought to make laws to engage the nobility to enter into commerce. But these laws would be the means of destroying the nobility, without being of any advantage to trade.[46]

Montesquieu was equally concerned to refute the other tenet of Law's policy, favouring national banks in France. Again distinguishing between economical and luxury-based commerce, he argued that banks were incompatible with monarchy on the grounds that 'in such a government there has never been anyone but the prince who has obtained or has been able to maintain a treasury, and wherever there is a treasury, as soon as it is excessive, it immediately becomes the prince's own.' Law was consequently 'one of the greatest promoters of despotism ever known in Europe.' The same problems would arise with the institution of trading companies, which would fall prey to the requisitions of princes whose orders could not be challenged. According to Montesquieu, however, there was no need for France to become commercial, being already rich in resources and almost self-sufficient. Commerce, he declared, had never been the bulwark of a truly great empire, being at best a Janus-faced force for prosperity. The crucial example of this was Rome, a state far more successful than Britain ever could be: 'Their genius, their glory, their military education, and the very form of their government estranged them from commerce . . . their political constitution was not more opposed to trade than their law of nations . . . the minds of the Romans were averse to commerce.'[47] For Montesquieu laws ought to vary with the form of government, the climate, size, opulence, ranks and manners of the state. There could be no universal science of legislation because the effects of policy were determined by circumstance; laws in favour of commerce were of benefit to Britain but unsuited to the stability of a large empire such as France. He was of course writing before France was ignominiously defeated in the Seven Years War, but his advice in the context of the 1760s was to await the commercial collapse of Britain. Agreeing with Voltaire that political change was a necessity if France was to pursue Britain's opulence, he nevertheless held that 'British' forms of wealth were inimical to his notion of a stable empire. Little succour could be given to statesmen opposed to constitutional change but in need of the immediate power which commerce supplied.

5 THE INTELLECTUAL LEGACY OF THE SEVEN YEARS WAR

Before the end of the Seven Years War, three perspectives upon the relative strengths of Britain and France can be identified. The first, including Law, Melon, and Dutot, advised the immediate encouragement of foreign commerce and public credit by ministerial means, and saw no impediments in the constitutions, ranks, and manners of the two nations. In the light of Law's débâcle, and the amount of public monies required to create trading companies capable of competing with the British, such standpoints were always treated with suspicion by ministers. The second perspective, that of Voltaire, Coyer, and Helvétius, expressed reservations about commerce and credit without first changing the form of French government and instituting measures to make national manners more like those of Britain. Although popular in times of crisis, no minister before the 1780s ever conceived of tampering with the existing form of monarchy in France before abandoning his career. Given the manifest loyalty towards existing monarchs, and the perception of greatness in a not-too-distant past, few members of the court or nobility favoured constitutional innovation. It was the least realistic response to military defeat and national humiliation. The third perspective articulated by Montesquieu was the most critical of policies imitating Britain, holding that government, manners, and ranks were so different in each nation that commerce and credit would operate in ways wholly detrimental to existing French life. His unparalleled study of national histories therefore associated precipitate constitutional, social, or economic innovation with disaster. Although Montesquieu's was the most sage approach, in the light of the recurrent political crises of the 1750s, such a response was inadequate. This was evident to François Quesnay as early as 1756, when he began to formulate a distinctive approach to French problems. It was soon to be entitled 'the Œconomic Science', 'the immortal base of our subsistence, of our manners, and, in a word, of all that can truly be called the fundamental Science of the Government of States'.[48] Quesnay's *Evidence* and *Fermiers* were published in volume six of the *Encyclopédie* in 1756, applying to society the physiological research of the *Essai physique sur l'économie animale* (published in 1736 and revised in 1747). In July 1757 he persuaded Victor Riqueti de Mirabeau to become his disciple.[49] In 1759 the first versions of the *Tableau economique* were published at Versailles, followed a year later by the *Théorie de l'impôt*, the controversy over which brought Mirabeau to Vincennes for criticism of the *Fermes générales*. When the Treaty of Paris was signed, the first textbook of physiocracy, *Philosophie rurale*, appeared, outlining a strategy for the reform of the kingdom. It influenced the Controller General Bertin and his successor L'Averdy, who, in edicts between May 1763 and July 1764, made the first legislative tests of Quesnay's philosophy by granting both internal and external freedom of the grain trade. It was also around this time that the young Dupont was ecstatically converted to physiocratic ideas, and produced his first written defence of the physiocratic cause.[50]

Quesnay was as critical as Montesquieu was of French advocates of British-style commercialization. Indeed, the origins of the policy maxims so prominent in physiocratic literature lay in a detailed critique of contemporary perceptions of Britain.[51] This was founded upon the distinction between 'an agricultural nation', or 'large agricultural state', and the 'commercial society' visible in Holland and epitomized by Britain. Whereas the prosperity of the former depended upon the quantity of primary investment (*avances primitives*) in agriculture, the wealth of commercial societies could only be maintained by pursuit of a precarious and unstable economic strategy. One of the most revealing early statements of this view can be found in the *Bref état des moyens pour la restauration de l'autorité du Roi et de ses finances*, composed by Mirabeau with annotated criticisms added by Quesnay some time between 1757 and 1758.[52] The economic vitality of commercial states was deemed to be contingent upon their ability to sell manufactured goods. In turn, this was determined by the low costs of such goods, the existence of markets, and the profits that merchants could draw from their various enterprises. The latter was particularly important because political institutions were erected on the revenue yielded by taxing such profits. To ensure these factors were realized it was important for commercial states to protect from external attack any smaller states with whom they traded. Maintenance of peace with agricultural states was also indispensable, ensuring access to large markets. Above all, means had to be found to keep profits buoyant. To this end, Quesnay noted that in order to maintain monopoly profits British colonies burned part of the tobacco harvest they so carefully nurtured, while Dutch merchants threw overboard a portion of the spices they carried. Against the conventional wisdom of the relative prosperity of the British poor, he drew the conclusion that commercial states had an interest in the absolute poverty of their citizenry because labour costs had to be kept to a minimum to preserve trade. A consequence of this was the meagre domestic market to be found in such states, because of the lack of purchasing power of the lower orders. Having exposed the economic logic underlying the prospects of commercial states, Quesnay went on to lay bare the dangerous social consequences of commercial economic strategies. The merchant on whom the state depended was not himself productive of wealth as he culled his profit from the cheap labour of fellow citizens or foreign subjects willing to exchange goods at disadvantageous rates. Owing allegiance to no man, the merchant was fickle, and a uniquely poor citizen with no stake in any particular nation. The point was reiterated with additional emphasis in the *Philosophie rurale*, Mirabeau's prolix compendium of what was being recommended as 'a new Economic science'.[53] Commercial societies were described as appendages to agricultural societies. They were the sickly dependents of agricultural nations, with weak constitutions prey to incurable afflictions. For example, the 'mercantile commerce' so essential to their existence was 'too exposed to competition and attack'; furthermore, the leading citizens of commercial states were more like bandits than luminaries, with equally unstable incomes:

All of their assets consist in dispersed and secret credits, in a few shops, and in long and short-term debts, whose Authors are in a sense unknown, since no one knows how much has been paid or how much is owing. All mobile and moneyed wealth is not available to the sovereign, and as a consequence yields nothing, a fact to repeat ceaselessly to the governments of Agricultural Nations who study with such care the means to become commercial; in other words, to plunder themselves. Large Shop-keepers, Merchants, Bankers etc., will always be members of Republics . . . In vain will authority try to force from them the duties of subjects.[54]

The decisive message was that France would 'plunder herself' in seeking after Britain's commercial wealth. Britain's recent strength, Quesnay made clear in the planned *Encyclopédie* article 'Grains', was due to her agricultural production. The politicians of the state, however, appeared to be abandoning agriculture to embrace the example of Holland, the 'warehouse state'. In making citizens of merchants Britain would destroy the class of landed proprietors so necessary to wealth creation in agricultural states. The form of government would ultimately follow the economy and sovereignty would become truly mixed, replacing the hereditary monarch at the apex of an ordered social pyramid with a disastrous division of social power.[55]

These lines of attack were carried further by Quesnay himself in the maxims and notes originally appended to successive versions of the *Tableau économique* and finally collated by Dupont in *Physiocratie* as a statement of *Maximes générales du gouvernement économique d'un royaume agricole*. Manufactured and industrial commodities, the eighth maxim declared, 'cannot yield any profit through sale abroad, except only in countries where manufacturing labour is cheap because of the low price of the produce'.[56] This was an inconceivable strategy in an agricultural state with a free and unobstructed external trade 'which keeps up the sales and the prices of raw produce, and which happily does away with the small profit which could be obtained from an external trade in manufactured commodities.' The inference was transparent. As far as Britain's wealth was based upon commerce it was weak rather than strong. France should never imitate such an example: 'A large state should not abandon the plough in order to become a carrier'. Her own history showed the dire consequences of commercial infatuation in the case of Colbert. Having been 'dazzled by the trade of the Dutch and the glitter of luxury manufactures', Colbert 'brought his country to such a state of frenzy that no one talked about anything but trade and money, and stopped considering the true employment of money or a country's true trade.'[57] That Quesnay considered Britain a prime example of a commercial society was made evident in an article for the *Journal de l'agriculture* of February 1766, which described Britain as an empire '. . . where not only the colonies but even the provinces of the metropolis are subjected to the laws of the carrying trade . . . where the interests of the soil and of the state are subordinated to the interests of merchants.' Mirabeau summed up the argument with a rare touch of eloquence: to seek commerce was 'to gather up the flowers of the economic tree and suppress its fruit.'[58] The mixed sovereignty that Quesnay associated with republican forms of government and commercial states also became an object of physiocratic hostility, and in 1767 several works were published which illustrated this opposition. The first, Quesnay's *Despotisme de la Chine*, condemned the disorder that accompanied any dilution of sovereign power: 'All the different ranks of the State can contribute in a mixed government to the ruin of the nation, through the discordance between private interests which divide and corrupt the tutelary authority, causing it to degenerate into political intrigues and abuses deadly to society.'[59] It was followed by equally vitriolic condemnations in the writings of P.-F.-J.-H. Mercier de la Rivière and Nicolas Baudeau, who attacked mixed sovereignty as a practical impossibility in France given the fact of material inequality between social orders and the size of the state.[60] Faction, confusion, and ignorance appeared whenever landed proprietors shared power with other classes. In such circumstances, destructive self-interest came to the fore, leading Badeau to conclude that in 'Aristocratic and Democratic Republics', legislation was arbitrary, property unprotected, and government tyrannical.[61] Only an independent absolute monarch had the authority to stand above the fray of private interests and impose the 'essential laws of the natural order'. The step identifying Britain as an exemplar of an insecure popular 'republic' had been taken by Mirabeau as early as *L'Ami des hommes*, in which he condemned 'a nation where the cries of the people too often prevail over reason.'[62] Turgot too was attracted to this line of argument in his *Éloge de Vincent de Gournay* of 1759, claiming Britain would suffer for failing to recognize 'there is no greater enemy of liberty than the people'.[63] Rather than have Britain or the 'arbitrary despotisms of antiquity' before his eyes, the wise monarch would imitate the Chinese, 'who reduce all Government to this sole law in conformity with the voice of Heaven', creating 'the State closest in the known world to a true *theocracy*, which I call *Economic monarchy*.'[64]

Quesnay's indictment of the economy and mixed sovereignty of commercial states did not preclude, as it did with Montesquieu, an attack upon the existing condition of France. Unlike Montesquieu he had a providential vision of the 'natural order' of economic life and the 'natural path' of economic development. Guaranteed by a benevolent deity, it was revealed to the reflective mind when the existential world was probed by reason.[65] Beyond human control, but open to human rejection, the natural order could be perceived in social structures and practices that had been organized by God as models of perfect justice for rational humans to embrace.[66] Natural laws unveiled the means to satisfy the first need of human beings, self-preservation, and described the more difficult further routes to the greater goal of social harmony:

Only the knowledge of these supreme laws can constantly ensure the tranquillity and prosperity of an empire . . . Together these laws form what is called the *natural law*. All men and all human authorities must submit themselves to these sovereign laws, instituted by the Supreme Being; they are immutable and irrefutable, and the best laws conceivable.[67]

This rationalistic providentialism was combined with a powerful conviction that France was the European state most likely to benefit from the natural order, having a greater economic potential than any other country. But Quesnay agreed with Coyer's pessimism that France was in the midst of 'a course of rapid decline'. Over a hundred-year period 'gambling, luxury, and wretchedness have taken their place among us'.[68] Mirabeau's assessment was more extreme: 'Gold and speculators have rendered the face of Europe abominable before God, just as the country of Canaan in ancient times.'[69] The problem did not lie with the constitution or the lack of moderation in governance.

Rather, successive ministers had favoured policies that departed from the natural order of economic development. Agriculture had decayed, with deleterious corresponding effects on wealth, politics, and social life. Quesnay condemned a country in which, '. . . the majority of the inhabitants lived in poverty, and their activities brought no profit to the state . . . taxes were almost all laid arbitrarily on farmers, workers, and commodities . . . The export of corn was forbidden . . . internal trade in corn was subjected to an arbitrary system of regulation.'[70] Following the agronomists he associated with, such as Duhamel de Monceau, Quesnay was certain that Britain's opulence was simply and solely due to superior investment in agriculture. In 1756 he contrasted the condition of agriculture in France and Britain, concluding that free trade ensured the stable prices so useful to trade and so lacking in the former state: 'Britain maintains its opulence by means of its real wealth . . . The Dutch and the British, whose corn trade is free, do not experience in their countries those huge variations in the price of corn to which we in France are always exposed because we have prohibited the foreign export and import of trade in corn.'[71] 'Exempting agriculture from all assessments' was the only aspect of British practice worthy of French emulation.

6   PHYSIOCRATIC STRATEGY

The critique and appreciation of Britain was the basis for a complex prescriptive doctrine with economic, cultural, and political consequences. Its foundation stone was Quesnay's conception of wealth. Central to his comparative analysis of the leading states of Europe was an association of the produce of land with what he termed 'real wealth'. This assertion was almost the defining motto of physiocratic commitment and could be found in every statement of physiocratic doctrine: 'Land is the universal blessing of humanity . . . an inexhaustible river of wealth . . . Land is the unique source of wealth, and it is agriculture which causes wealth to increase.'[72] The reasoning was initially straightforward. Cultivation of land ensured that the basic and most necessary needs of humanity were satisfied. Any sovereign authority that compromised national capacities to meet such needs was acting irrationally and, given the sanctity of the natural order, was almost blasphemous. The first duty of the physiocratic sovereign was therefore to protect the natural right to subsistence. The cardinal means to safeguard subsistence was guaranteeing an absolute right to property. Without this men would neither reap nor sow, associate or produce; they would remain in a barbaric condition of warring tribes, designated by Mirabeau as 'the errant society' of hunter-gatherers. As to the strategies to align France with the natural order, Quesnay divided his prescriptions into two categories. The first concerned the rules that sovereigns ought to adhere to in raising revenue, of particular import in France where most of the ills of the kingdom could be traced to taxes that destroyed wealth. Taxes had to be levied 'directly on the net product of agriculture, and not on men's wages, or on produce.' The net product, or wealth granted by land to its cultivators after subtracting the costs of subsequent cultivation, was conceived of as manna from heaven rather than a human creation with corresponding rights of ownership. If this view was accepted, it would be clear to owners of land that taxes on the net product were not in fact being levied on a tangible asset, but rather a 'portion of the property which [the landed proprietor] has not acquired, which does not belong to him, and which is paid to those to whom it is due.'[73] This was the most widely proclaimed tenet of the physiocratic creed, called by Quesnay the 'unique and direct tax', since, 'it must be exact and simple, and levied on the land which produces wealth.'

Once the taxation of the net product had been established and legally entrenched, ministers were not simply expected to enjoy revenues from bountiful agriculture. Absolute freedom of trade was of equal importance. Such liberty was not associated with the pursuit of unhindered self-interest, a view ascribed to Montesquieu, but rather signified a rational measure to increase national wealth by creating buoyant markets and efficient production.[74] It was expected to occasion other effects that distinguished the physiocrats from contemporary and later exponents of similar proposals. Quesnay believed that a thriving agriculture depended upon high profits for investors in land and consequently high prices for agricultural products. This was the most important consequence of free trade: investment in agriculture would be stimulated and competition to cultivate the land would drive up prices, making agriculture the most attractive of national industries. By contrast, low prices were not only the sign of an underdeveloped and therefore unattractive market but in international transactions manifested adverse terms of trade. For example, the low prices of agricultural products in France allowed commercial states such as Britain to levy a *de facto* tax upon the French nation, by exchanging manufactured goods for primary products which ought to have been valued more highly: 'If we buy from abroad a certain quantity of commodities for the value of one *setier* of corn priced at 20 livres, two *setiers* of it would be necessary to pay for the same quantity of this commodity if the government forced the price of corn down 10 livres.'[75] This belief explains Quesnay's view of the role of commerce and manufactures in an agricultural nation like France. Since free trade tilted the economic balance towards agriculture, commerce and manufactures would develop as the net product grew, and be stimulated by the agricultural surplus, thereby becoming symbols of national opulence rather than decrepitude. Once again, high primary goods prices was the mechanism by which this result would be achieved. Quesnay synthesized his view in a pithy set of epigrams: 'AS THE MARKET VALUE IS SO IS THE REVENUE: *Abundance plus valuelessness does not equal wealth. Scarcity plus dearness equals poverty. Abundance plus dearness equals opulence.*' High prices meant large revenues for the state and a thriving economy. Nor was Quesnay hesitant regarding the greatest test of such claims in the popular mind, premised on the association of high prices with impoverishment:

it should not be believed that cheapness of produce is profitable to the lower classes; for a low price of produce causes a fall in the wages of the lower orders of people, reduces their well-being, makes less work and remunerative occupations available for them, and destroys the nation's revenue. . . . A high price of corn, for example, provided that it is constant, is more advantageous to the lower classes in an agricultural kingdom than a low price. The daily wage of a labourer is fixed more or less naturally on the basis of the price of corn, and normally amounts to a twentieth of the price of one *setier.*[76]

Given the necessity of the consumption of agricultural products high prices would never discourage trade. Nor would they damage living standards, as the real wage of all labourers would be higher in the physiocratic system than in any other. Quesnay did not believe he was describing a utopia. The best state was one where justice reigned in the sense of allowing each person a reward matching their contribution to society, and particularly the cultivators and landed proprietors who had been neglected by commercial philosophers. Distributive justice of this kind could not be found in Britain, in ancient republics, or in other kinds of commercial state. He warned, 'Do not seek lessons in the history of nations or the aberrations of mankind, which represent only an abyss of disorders.'[77]

Mirabeau described the political structure consonant with Quesnay's economic strategy a 'theocracy', by which he meant a moral philosophy of certain and universal rules granted by a benevolent God for the guidance of all of humanity. In practice, however, pains were taken to identify *'le Roi pasteur'* with existing Bourbon monarchs, as the manuscript *De la monarchie* made clear. Mirabeau's *Lettres sur le commerce des grains* took an explicit stand in nominating France as the archetypal 'large agricultural State', necessarily governed by an hereditary monarch.[78] One of the maxims Dupont added to Quesnay's manifesto in 1767, placed before all others, called for 'a single sovereign authority, standing above all the individuals in the society and all the unjust undertakings of private interests'.[79] But in expressing allegiance to the existing political order Quesnay was not assenting to the *union des classes* defined by Bossuet, in which the whole state existed in the person of the prince, making his will the source of law.[80] The physiocratic 'legal despot' governed in accordance with rational rules of legislation, and was legally constrained to pursue them. Thus he did not *make* law because laws were already evident in the structure of the social world. His function was rather to use all necessary authority to enforce 'the natural and essential laws of the social order'.[81] For example, a physiocratic sovereign would subscribe to physiocratic taxation, expressed by the idea of the monarch as *co-propriétaire* with his subjects, by which he received a portion of the net product in return for protecting property. The monarch was equally constrained to recognize that 'the prosperity of humanity as a whole depends upon the greatest possible net product, in short, the best possible conditions for landed proprietors.' Quesnay hoped that the *parlements* then challenging the monarch's authority would see that their interests were best protected by such a powerful figure. The physiocrats also envisaged an independent magistracy able to compare 'Positive laws with the laws of Justice in its essence'. Rather than comprising a hereditary noble class they favoured enlightened individuals, the physiocrats themselves, who had undergone a rigorous training in 'the reciprocal duties of men united in society, and the physical laws of the reproduction and distribution of wealth.'[82] They planned to seduce the King and the aristocracy and persuade them to abandon war and the pursuit of military glory. In their place lay the glory of increasing the productivity of the soil and the management of large estates for the good of the individual, locality and state. Putting their ideas into practice entailed creating a more fluid aristocracy dedicated to the practice of agriculture. However, they had hopes that making enlightened proprietors out of the existing nobility would not entail a great change of personnel. The physiocratic regeneration of the kingdom necessitated the minimum of social upheaval. Theirs was a moral challenge to current philosophies of court and noble life.

The 'science of political economy' was evidently conceived as an antidote to the schemes of anglophile projectors and also to Montesquieu's claim that legislation for one state might be unsuitable to another. Such opposition symbolized the utility and originality of physiocracy in conceiving of national regeneration without constitutional change, and it was this idea that defined its place in contemporary minds until the Revolution.[83] Individuals were encouraged to embrace physiocratic practices in their everyday lives by renouncing luxury and investing in agriculture rather than the public finances.[84] An enlightened monarch could impose order on the world by abandoning public credit and foreign manufactures while relying upon the high domestic agricultural prices that sustained opulence in conditions of liberty. Thus the physiocrats were far more concerned with the popularization of their ideas than, for example, their Scottish counterparts, who were more sceptical of the power of reason and grandiose legislative projects.[85]

7   REVIVING REASON-OF-STATE POLITICAL ECONOMY

The physiocrats' influence on government lasted until the dismissal of Mayon d'Invau as Controller General in December 1769. His replacement by the abbé Terray and the *Arrêt du Conseil* of December 1770 suspended the export of grain. When Maupeou replaced Choiseul as Louis XV's favoured minister physiocratic access to the corridors of power was severely diminished. Several attacks upon them followed, centring on the advisability of internal and external freedom of the grain trade.[86] In the 1760s and 1770s, this was the test case of physiocratic doctrine, encompassing the question of legitimate government authority, the poverty of the lower orders, and the role of merchants in society. Most importantly, it led to a reopening of the dispute about the relevance of the example of Britain to French politics, commencing with a restatement of Montesquieu's condemnation of universal rules of national economy.

The most significant of Montesquieu's posthumous disciples was Galiani, whose brilliant assaults, entitled *Dialogues sur le commerce des bleds*, caused the physiocratic edifice to shudder. Having seen at first hand the diplomatic manœuvres of states between 1759 and 1769, as secretary to Naples' Paris ambassador, Galiani had become convinced that political economy was not a science of a perfect natural order with beneficent effects the world over, because all strategies were subject to varying political priorities in different kinds of states. Above all, they were affected by the power relations between states, leading him to conclude that political economy was in fact the science of 'reason-of-state'.[87] Different states with diverse forms of government and, most importantly to his mind, geographies, were unique, making 'Reason ill-used, experience misapplied, and examples drawn from dissimilar cases the causes of all our errors.' A prime example could be seen in those who ignored the fact that 'France today no more resembles the times of Colbert or Sully than present-day Britain and Italy.' So acute was this problem that even the great Montesquieu had too often succumbed to the 'generalizing spirit' that was the plague of the century.[88] For Galiani, by far the most grievous violators of common sense were the physiocrats, whose universal faith in uninhibited trade was so pernicious that it could initiate famine. Galiani claimed good grounds for apprehension, having seen the effects of the dearth in Tuscany, Naples, and Rome between 1764 and 1765. The physiocrats understated the malign properties of humanity that prevailed in all market transactions. They were blind to 'how the passions are made to play, the vices of men, their mistakes, their thoughtlessness and the disguised and false decorum of public affairs.'[89] In particular, the middle-men whom the physiocrats justified as necessary elements of a specialized grain market were in practice frequently the most avid of speculators, making governmental patrol of their activities essential.[90] Politics had to be analysed from this perspective, assuming the baseness of men rather than their aptitude for reason. Greed, delays, and the interminable clash of interests determined the operation of markets. In neglecting these commonsense truths, Galiani condemned physiocracy as a boon to the rich and a curse on the poor, an argument that persuaded Diderot to move against Quesnay.[91] The classic illustration was the grain trade, the *police* of which ought to vary with the nature of the state.[92]

A precise typology of prudent grain legislation was the aim of the *Dialogues*. In small states lacking cultivated land and threatened by large neighbours, free external trade would lead to dependence upon the grain supply of other states, leaving the small state open to economic blockade and defeat in war.[93] Since imported grain could only be paid for by domestic manufactured goods, low prices were essential, justifying the further *police* of markets in necessities. Galiani had Geneva foremost in his mind in concluding, 'reason-of-state, the first of all forces in the political order, obliges very small sovereignties to control commerce in grain, which is for them a weapon of war.' Such states had to be like convents, closing their doors to outsiders to ensure that their populations were static, and therefore supportable. By contrast, in moderately sized states such as Holland, where the lack of agricultural production had created a mercantile state dependent on the carrying trade, free trade was no danger, because a strong navy defended the state and gave access to international grain markets that were unlikely to collapse. Ironically, such states were more secure in food-stocks than agricultural states such as Sicily and Sardinia. The case of Britain was still more distinct, and Galiani confessed to bafflement in explaining her rise to prominence across the globe. This uniqueness made attempts to imitate its practices altogether futile:

In politics, Britain is the most complicated machine in Europe at present, and perhaps which has ever existed the world over. This country is concurrently agricultural, manufacturing, conquering, commercial . . . Its government is the most mixed, the most imaginatively composed that there has ever been. Finally, manners, character, products, political relationships, strength, weakness, resilience, are all particular to this country so distinct from the rest of the world and singular in form.[94]

Similar factors had to be considered with regard to France. France was an agricultural state but not exclusively so. Moreover, very different geographical conditions pertained in comparison with similar large states such as Spain. In the latter, free trade in grain was not to be feared because the grain basin of Castille was centrally located. Under these circumstances, a national market would ensure that grain circulated around the whole of the country. By contrast, the grain centres of France were to be found on the peripheries, such as Flanders, Normandy, and Picardy. Free trade would therefore have an opposite effect, and carry grain to markets abroad within easy reach. Furthermore, in pushing France towards agricultural production the physiocrats were again defying commonsense; manufactures and commerce were more valuable forms of wealth, as evinced by the opulence of Holland, Geneva, Genoa, and Frankfurt by contrast with Naples, Spain, or Poland. Far from being a state marked by equality, frugality, industriousness, and pure morals, Galiani argued that an agricultural kingdom was a gambler dependent on the fates, a state whose politics and wealth were tied to the vicissitudes of the harvest and grain market. Manufactures ensured work for the populace throughout the year, more stable prices, and wider markets. The only solution to French ills was to recognize these truths, and place all necessary authority in a wilful monarch who would stand above the antagonistic interests comprising the state and take prudent action for the safety of all.[95] Although the physiocratic response was typically vehement, with the abbé Antoine Morellet arguing that the rules of political economy were as universal as biological laws, Galiani was instrumental in undermining their reputation.[96] From the perspective of the *thèse royale* favoured by Galiani, the physiocrats were accused of undermining monarchical authority. As S.-H.-N. Linguet put it, placing the natural right to property above the need for the monarch to protect the poor from the rich violated the ancient Roman maxim, *Salus populi suprema lex esto*.[97] Having experienced the failure of free trade legislation after 1764 and the collapse of Maupeou's programme in 1771, this became a common reaction in the 1770s: demands for strong kings were united with calls for the pursuit of commerce and credit.[98] In this manner too, many of the themes of Law's writings were revived in the guise of reason-of-state claims. The most forceful of them came from Jacques Necker, writing in praise of the uniqueness of French culture and the resulting need for a prudential approach to problems such as grain scarcity, exercised by an unrestrained monarch.[99] In his writings, political economy as reason-of-state became an alternative to physiocracy, expressing allegiance to the 'moderation' of Montesquieu, but in practice following the schemes for commercial empire of Law, Melon, and Dutot. As Tocqueville famously noted, the French court in the 1770s and 80s was open to the most radical of reformist ideas, so long as these enhanced monarchical authority and respected the social structure of the Old Regime.[100]

It is instructive that Jean Delolme's paean to British liberty of 1771, *Constitution de l'Angleterre*, which noted that France had 'sunk under the most absolute monarchy', received little immediate comment.[101] The reason was that advocates of constitutional change towards Britain's mixed constitution were less conspicuous than they had been in the 1750s–60s. They could, however, be found, the most prominent being the Marquis de Chastellux, to whom the British constitution was the sole means of inculcating commerce, being a perfect balance of social forces.[102] But the successive editions of Chastellux's work served to underline fears about Britain's constitution rather than affirm the superiority of mixed government, making *De la félicité* the exception which proved the rule. In 1776 he appended an essay that expressed doubts about Britain's capacity to reduce the enormous burden of the national debt.[103] The abbé Coyer expressed similar fears in translating Wilkes' attack on governmental corruption occasioned by the war with the

North-American colonies.[104] The war was of course as much a source of apprehension and as divisive in France as it was elsewhere. For those who saw the economic realm as the domain of reason-of-state, it confirmed that Britain's greatness could be traced to state support for trade and empire. It also provided a salutary warning not to overextend a state's size or public credit.[105] Writers who had rather looked to Britain's constitution and culture as models for France concluded that they could serve as an ideal no longer. A decade after *De la félicité publique*, Chastellux was arguing that commerce undermined the spirit of patriotism essential to social harmony, and disturbed the system of orders which made France more stable than Britain.[106] He was a convert to the view of Montesquieu, Galiani, and Necker, that there was more to be said for the existing condition of France than had been supposed by anglophile advocates of innovation. Others judged differently. The United States of America was the first republic to be formed in a large state in existing memory. More radically still, it was a 'modern' republic because its government sought to extend both commerce and civilization. As was noted in chapter two, in his revisions to the abbé Raynal's *Histoire philosophique*, Diderot argued that the egalitarian social order of the new republic was worthy of imitation. The secret of American success was 'the equality of station' and 'universal ease' which 'has given rise in every breast to the mutual desire of pleasing'. America was the most stable and successful state in the world because it enjoyed the purest manners: 'Gallantry and gaming, the passions of indolent opulence, seldom interrupt that happy tranquillity . . . the female sex are still what they should be, gentle, modest, compassionate, and useful.' He advised the French to seek 'the restoration of primitive liberty' through 'the general assembly of a great nation.'[107]

Differing ideas about what constituted a nation divided political economists in the 1770s and 1780s. Physiocracy and British constitutionalism had declined. Traditional conceptions of monarchy, defended by Turgot and Necker in the midst of their reform projects, were challenged by writers who looked to America for inspiration. The American rebels made new kinds of constitutional innovation in the crisis-ridden debtor state of France more compelling.[108] More importantly, the 'transformation of the social order' became the watchword of a new generation of radical writers. Such ideas constituted the commencement of the republican turn in French political economy, which occurred when plans for reform which respected the political system had failed at the same time as rival states, pre-eminently Britain, had declined.

NOTES TO CHAPTER 3

1. Dupont correspondence, *ŒD*, p. 366.
2. *Ibid.*, pp. 367, 369.
3. *Ibid.*, p. 386.
4. A good example is Dupont's own 'Notice abrégée des différents écrits modernes qui ont concouru en France à former la science de l'économie politique', *Ephémérides du citoyen*, 63 vols., ix (1769), 12.
5. Letter on Britain, 14 October, 1814, published by Hitoshi Hashimoto, *Les lettres inédites de Jean-Baptiste Say*; Letter to David Ricardo, 1 May, 1822, *The Works and Correspondence of David*

Ricardo (Cambridge, 1952–73), 11 vols., ix, 188–90; review of Say's *England and the English People*, tr. John Richter, *The Quarterly Review*, 15 (1816), 544–5.

6. Contrast the entry 'Angleterre' with that of any other country in the index of editions of the *Traité* or *Cours complet*: e.g. *Traité* (Paris, 1841) 6th edn., p. 610 with pp. 619–20, 'France'. More specifically, for a statement of Britain's importance, *De l'Angleterre et des Anglais* (London, 1816), 3rd edn., p. 1–2.

7. On the rise and fall of these themes see A. Pagden, *Lords of all the World* (New Haven, 1995), esp. pp. 103–25; J. Israel, *Conflicts of Empires* (London, 1997).

8. See for example, François Guizot, *The History of Civilisation* (London, 1856), 3 vols., i, 3, 235, 246, 274–5; Ledru Rolin *The Decline of Britain* (London, 1850), Book 1, ch. 1; Nassau Senior, *Conversations with M. Thiers* (London, 1878), 2 vols., ii, 1, 79, 147, 178.

9. P. Harsin, *Les doctrines monétaires et financières en France* (Paris, 1928), p. 263, and the exhaustive bibliography, pp. xiv–xv; C.W. Cole, *French Mercantilism, 1683–1700* (New York, 1965), ch. 5.

10. As Claude Herbert said, 'All the world is convinced that liberty is the soul and the support of Commerce', *Essai sur la police générale des grains* (London, 1754), p. 16. The best reviews of modern literature are D. C. Coleman's 'Eli Hecksher and the Idea of Mercantilism', *Revisions in Mercantilism* (London, 1969), pp. 92–117, and 'Mercantilism revisited', *The Historical Journal*, 23 (1980), 773–91.

11. J.-Cl. Perrot, *Une histoire intellectuelle de l'économie politique*, pp. 7–59.

12. Contrast the confidence of Antoyne de Montchrétien's *Traicté de l'œconomie politique*, pp. 112–13, 147, with the fears of Pierre Le Pesant, sieur de Boisguillebert's *Factum de la France . . .* (1707), reprinted in E. Daire ed., *Économistes financiers du XVIIIe siècle* (Paris, 1843), pp. 266–9. It is noticeable, however, that Boisguillebert believed he had more to learn from the example of Holland than Britain; see *Le Détail de la France . . .* (1697), pp. 190–1, 207.

13. A revealing guide is J. Boislisle, *Correspondance des contrôleurs-généraux des finances avec les intendants des provinces, 1683–1715* (Paris, 1874–97), 3 vols., ii, 477.

14. On their ideas see Istvan Hont, 'Free Trade and the Economic Limits to National Politics: Neo-Machiavellian Political Economy Reconsidered', *The Economic Limits to Modern Politics*, ed., J. Dunn (Cambridge, 1994), pp. 41–119.

15. This is made clear in A. E. Murphy, *Richard Cantillon, Entrepreneur and Economist* (Oxford, 1986), pp. 65–87, 125–56.

16. A. E. Murphy, *John Law* (Oxford, 1997), chs. 9–11.

17. *Money and Trade Considered with A Proposal for Supplying the Nation with Money* (Edinburgh, 1705), p. 59. See also, *Premier mémoire sur les banques (1715–16)*, in Daire, pp. 549–53.

18. *Money and Trade*, p. 36.

19. *Ibid.*, p. 83; *Second mémoire sur les banques (1715–16)*, in Daire, p. 605; *Dixième lettre sur le nouveau système des finances (1720)*, Daire, p. 652.

20. *Essay d'un nouveau système sur les finances (1718)*, Harsin, ed., *Œuvres de Jean Law* (Paris, 1934), 3 vols., I, 301.

21. Dutot, *Réflexions politiques sur les finances et le commerce* (Paris, 1738), ch. 3, art. 7. Also J.-F. Melon, *Essai politique sur le commerce* (Paris, 1734), ch. 24.

22. *Œuvres de Jean Law*, iii, 189, cited in M. Sonenscher, 'Monarchical and Republican Reason of State: Public Credit and the Heritage of John Law in Eighteenth-Century France', *The Politics of Necessity and the Language of Reason of State*, unpublished conference papers, Cambridge University, 1992.

23. *Recherches et considérations sur les finances de France* (Basle, 1758) 2 vols., i, 2–3. Similar arguments could be found in Richard Cantillon, *Essai sur la nature du commerce en général* (Paris, 1952 [from the 1755 text]), pp. 48, 132–3, 171–2.

24. *Letters Concerning the English Nation* (London, 1733), Letter X. The *Letters* appeared in France as *Lettres écrites de Londres sur les Anlgois et autres sujets* ('Basle' [London], 1734) and *Lettres philosophiques* ('Amsterdam' [Rouen], 1734.)

25. Davenant, *An Essay upon the Probable Methods of Making a People Gainers in the Balance of Trade (1699)* in *The Political and Commercial Works* (London, 1771), 5 vols., ii, 336.

26. *Letters Concerning the English Nation*, Letter VIII.

27. *Ibid.*, Letter IX. Similar sentiments can be found in the 'Seconde épître dédicace' to *Zaire* (1736).

28. *Observations sur M. M. Jean Law, Melon et Dutot sur le commerce, le luxe, les monnaies, et les impôts* (1738), in *Œuvres complètes de Voltaire* (Paris, 1879), xxii, 359–60.

29. 'Gouvernement', *Dictionnaire philosophique portatif* (1771).

30. *La Noblesse commerçante* (London and Paris, 1756), frontispiece, p. 112. Also Coyer's *Développement et défense du système de la noblesse commerçante ou militaire* (Amsterdam and Paris, 1757), 2 vols., i, 10, ii, 82.

31. *Préservatif contre l'anglomanie* (Minorca, 1757). See Josephine Grieder, *Anglomania in France 1740–1789: Fact, Fiction and Political Discourse* (Geneva, 1985), ch. 1, ch. 4.

32. *De l'esprit* (Paris, 1757), 5 books, ii, ch. 22.

33. For numerous examples see F. Acomb, *Anglophobia in France 1763–1789* (Durham N.C., 1950), chs. 2–3.

34. P.-A. de Sainte-Foix, chevalier d'Arcq, *La Noblesse militaire ou le patriote françois* (Paris, 1756), p. 18. On the debate in general see E. Depitre, 'Le Système et la querelle de la noblesse commerçante (1756–1759)', *Revue d'histoire économique et sociale*, 6–7 (1913–14), 137–75.

35. F. Crouzet, *Britain Ascendant: Comparative Studies in Franco-British Economic History* (Cambridge, 1990), pp. 127–48.

36. *L'Esprit des lois*, XI, 4. Translations are based on the Nugent edition (New York, 1949) with emendations from the Cohler-Miller-Sone edition (Cambridge, 1989).

37. *Ibid.*, XX, 7.

38. Condorcet, *Essai sur la constitution et les fonctions des assemblées provinciales* (Paris, 1788), postscript; Phillipe-Antoine Grouvelle, *De l'autorité de Montesquieu dans la révolution présente* (n.p., 1789), pp. 92–8; J. Dedieu, *Montesquieu et la tradition politique anglaise en France* (Paris, 1909), ch. 12; Daniel Mornet, *Les origines intellectuelles*, pp. 95–9.

39. *L'Esprit des lois*, XI, 6.

40. *Ibid.*, XI, 6.

41. *Ibid.*, VIII, 9.

42. *Ibid.*, II, 4.

43. *Ibid.*, II, 4.

44. *Ibid.*, III, 5, V, 6.

45. *Ibid.*, XX, 4.

46. *Ibid.*, XX, 21–2.

47. *Ibid.*, XX, 10, II, 4, XXI, 14–15.

48. *Tableau œconomique avec ses explications par François Quesnay*, in V. R. de Mirabeau, *L'Ami des hommes, ou Traité de la population* (Avignon, 1756–60), part 6, p. 120.

49. Mirabeau's letter to Rousseau recalling his 'conversion' is in R. A. Leigh, ed., *Correspondance complète de J-J Rousseau* (Oxford, 1965–91), 50 vols., xvii, 171–2. A translation can be found in Ronald L. Meek, *The Economics of Physiocracy* (London, 1962), pp. 16–20. Translations are largely based on Meek's edition cited above and Meek & M. Kuczynski, *Quesnay's Tableau économique* (London, 1972).

50. *The Autobiography of Du Pont de Nemours*, tr. and ed., E. Fox-Genovese (Wilmington, Delaware, 1984).

51. See *Maximes de gouvernement économique* in *François Quesnay et la physiocratie*, ii, 496–510.

52. 'Bref état des moyens pour la restauration de l'autorité du Roi et de ses finances, Par le Marquis de Mirabeau avec des notes de François Quesnay', ed. G. Weulersse, *Revue d'histoire économique et sociale*, 6 (1913–14), 177–211.

53. The full title gives a good idea of Mirabeau's intentions: *Philosophie rurale, ou économie générale et politique de l'agriculture, reduite à l'ordre immuable des lois physiques & morales, qui assurent la prospérité des empires* (Amsterdam, 1764), 3 vols.

54. *Ibid.*, ii, 23.

55. *Ibid.*, ii, 24. Philippe Steiner has recently argued in his valuable study of physiocracy that Quesnay was in favour of large profits for the farmers rather than high prices for the consumers of agricultural products (*La 'science nouvelle' de l'économie politique*, ch. 3). While this is true, the opponents of the physiocrats, including Say, argued that their system necessitated high prices, because the productivity of agriculture could only be increased by expanding the commercial industries that they castigated.

56. *Physiocratie, ou constitution naturelle du gouvernement le plus avantageux au genre humain*, INED, ii, 962.

57. *Physiocratie.*, INED, ii, 963.

58. *Philosophie rurale*, iii, 317.

59. *Despotisme de la Chine*, INED, ii, 919.

60. Le Mercier de la Rivière, *L'Ordre naturel et essentiel des sociétés politiqus* (London, 1767) pp. 139–50; Nicolas Baudeau, *Première introduction à la philosophie économique ou analyse des états policés* (Paris, 1767), pp. 385–406.

61. Badeau, *Première introduction*, pp. 385–7, 420–1.

62. *L'Ami des hommes*, part one, p. 131.

63. Turgot, *Œuvres* (ed. Schelle), I, 601–2 and letter to Dupont, June 28 1780, *Œuvres*, V, 628–9. See also G.-F. Le Trosne, *De l'administration provinciale, et de la réforme de l'impôt* (Basel and Paris, 1788), 2 vols., i, 473. For Turgot's reservations about some elements of physiocratic doctrine see his letters to Dupont in *Œuvres*, iii, 398–9 (21 December, 1770), ii, 677 (23 December, 1770), ii, 507–9 (20 February, 1766).

64. Badeau, *Première introduction*, pp. 426–9.

65. *Evidence*, INED ii, 405.

66. *Despotisme de la Chine*, INED, ii, 921.

67. *Observations sur le droit naturel des hommes réunis en société, Journal d'agriculture*, September 1765. A revised edition appeared in brochure form in the same year: see INED, ii, 740.

68. *Questions interessantes sur la population, l'agriculture et le commerce, proposées aux académies & autres sociétés sçavantes des provinces, par François Quesnay, L'Ami des hommes*, part 4, p. 2.

69. *Philosophie rurale*, iii, 320.

70. *Physiocratie*, INED, ii, 960–1.

71. *Grains*, INED, ii, 501, *Hommes*, INED, ii, 531.

72. *Philosophie rurale*, iii, 317; Maxim, III.

73. *Physiocratie*, INED, ii, 956–7.

74. *De l'origine et progrès d'une science nouvelle* (London, 1768), pp. 25–30.

75. *Physiocratie*, INED, ii, 972.

76. *Ibid.*, INED, ii, 954, 973.

77. *Despotisme de la Chine*, INED, ii, 921.

78. *Lettres sur le commerce des grains* (Amsterdam, 1765), pp. 57, 107, 319. Also Dupont, p. 64–71.

79. *Physiocratie*, INED, ii, 949.

80. The most extreme critique can be found in Mirabeau's 'Notes sur Boisguillebert', ed. G. Weulersse, *'Revue d'histoire des doctrines économiques*, 3 (1910), 143.

81. Badeau, *Première introduction*, 425–6.

82. *Ibid.*, pp. 35–9; Mercier de la Rivière, pp. 80–6.

83. For example, Grivel's article *Droit naturel de l'homme, Encyclopédie méthodique: économie politique et diplomatique* (Paris, 1784), 4 vols., ii, 147–55.

84. This is made clear in Badeau's *Principes de la science morale et politique sur le luxe et les loix somptuaires, Ephémérides du citoyen*, 1767, 234.

85. See Mirabeau's revealingly entitled, *Entretiens d'un jeune prince avec son gouverneur* (London, 1785), 3 vols., i, xxix.

86. For example, abbé Mably, *Doutes proposés aux philosophes economists* (Paris, 1768); Friedrich-Melchior Grimm, *Sermon philosophique prononcé le jour de l'an 1770, Correspondance littéraire philosophique et critique* ed. Maurice Tourneaux (Paris, 1877–82), 16 vols., viii, 414–41.

87. *Dialogues sur le commerce des bleds* (London, 1770), p. 33.

88. *Ibid.*, p. 7, 15, 95.

89. LDP, xiv, 402–8, *Lettre de l'abbé Galiani à M Sartine*.

90. *Dialogues*, p. 168–70.

91. See Diderot, *Apologie de l'abbé Galiani, Œuvres complètes*, i, 118.

92. *Lettres de l'abbé Galiani à Mme. d'Épinay*, ed. E. Asse (Paris, 1882), 2 vols., i, 138.

93. *Dialogues*, p. 43.

94. *Ibid.*, pp. 49, 63–4.

95. *Ibid.*, pp. 24, 116, 215.

96. Morellet, *Refutation de l'ouvrage qui a pour titre dialogues sur le commerce des bleds* (London, 1770), pp. 30, 48–9.

97. *Lettre de M. Linguet, Journal de politique et de littérature*, 15 December, 1774, p. 232; *Lettres sur la 'Théorie des loix civiles'* (Amsterdam, 1770), p. 37; *Reponse aux docteurs modernes* (Paris, 1771), 2 vols., ii, 113.

98. For example, Condillac, *Le commerce et le gouvernement considérés relativement l'un à l'autre* (Amsterdam, 1776), pp. 354, 521, 533–5.

99. Necker *Eloge de Jean-Baptiste Colbert; discours qui a remporté le prix de l'Académie Françoise en 1773, Œuvres complètes*, xv, 5, 36, 85; also *Sur la législation et le commerce des grains* (Paris, 1775), 2 vols., ii, 169–72.

100. *L'Ancien Regime et la Révolution* (Paris, 1856), part three, ch. 1.

101. J. Delolme, *Constitution de l'Angleterre* (London, 1775), p. 18. Bachaumont noted that the book's attack on the French constitution led the ministry to restrict its circulation: *Mémoires secrets* (London, 1780), 9 November 1771, vol. vi, 29–31.

102. F. J. Marquis de Chastellux, *De la félicité publique,*, ii, 233, ii, 282–4.

103. *Ibid.*, *Sur la dette publique*, ii, 287–319.

104. *Nouvelles observations sur l'Angleterre, par un voyageur* (Paris, 1779), pp. 283–364.

105. Necker, *De l'Administration des finances* (Paris, 1784), *Œuvres complètes*, iv, 262.

106. *Du Progrès des arts et sciences en Amérique Septrionale*, appended to *Voyages dans l'Amérique Septrionale* (Paris, 1783).

107. Translations are from J. O. Justamond, *A Philosophical and Political History of the Settlements and Trade of the Europeans in the East and West Indies* (London, 1798), 6 vols., vi, 108–9; ii, 90.

108. J. O. Appleby, 'America as a Model for the Radical French Reformers of 1789', *William and Mary Quarterly*, 28 (1971), 267–86; P. Higonnet, *Sister Republics: The Origins of French and American Republicanism* (Cambridge Mass., 1988), chs. 4–6.

4

The Republican Turn in France, 1776–1789

In one of the letters Say received from Dupont de Nemours in 1815, physiocracy was described as the 'science of liberty'. The most wide-ranging inference drawn by Dupont from this grand claim was that all of the beneficial effects of the French Revolution could be ascribed to Quesnay's political economy. Dupont had been propagating this belief since the early 1790s. In 1794 a letter to the editors of the revolutionary journal *La Décade philosophique* stated that Quesnay had 'planted the tree of French liberty' which bore fruit in 1789.[1] Yet in the 1760s we have seen that physiocracy was popular with ministers and the court precisely because it opposed constitutional change, the very essence of the liberty attained in 1789. Physiocracy indicted the military nobility as idle parasites living off the labour of the wealth-producing classes. In the debate between the court and the *parlements*, they supplied the former with arguments supporting monarchical sovereignty by identifying *le Roi pasteur* with the enlightened physiocratic legislator. In all physiocratic writings the third estate were deemed too ignorant and were therefore in need of education if they were to participate in the formation of laws. Although many of Quesnay's ideas, most prominently the *impôt territorial*, were upheld by Dupont, physiocracy did in fact evolve between the 1760s and the 1790s. In Dupont's defence it could be said that the shift was one of emphasis rather than substance, towards an idea of 'legal despotism' compatible with 'national sovereignty, and owing a great deal to Quesnay and Mirabeau's criticisms of the *noblesse d'épée* in particular, and non-landed social structures (the 'sterile classes') in general. Nevertheless, physiocracy was a very different beast after Quesnay's death in 1774 because transforming the 'social organization of France' became the focus of physiocratic discussion. This was a response to the failure of Maupeou's institutional changes of 1770–1, perceptions of the continued decline of the French economy and, especially, the creation of a modern republic in America. Appeals to the French king and nobility to transform their political culture in accordance with physiocratic maxims had failed. Institutional changes were therefore demanded which would force the rational class of landed proprietors to enter political life and take responsibility for themselves and their *patrie*. In rejecting the British model of mixed government as excessively corrupt, biased towards commerce and prey to the passions of mobs and demagogues, the neo-physiocrats became sympathetic to republican ideas. They believed in a public good which could be practically realized by means of an aristocracy of land-owners contributing to the formation of physiocratic laws. Although he never abandoned his personal faith in absolute monarchical sovereignty, the neo-physiocrats were inspired by Anne-Robert-Jacques Turgot's later writings. He was among the first to argue in favour of remodelling French society by altering the political constitution of the state and this theme was taken up by Dupont and Condorcet, whose writings put physiocracy in the Patriots' camp in the late 1780s.[2] As in the 1760s, the physiocrats sparked a controversy which is important because it influenced the coterie surrounding Clavière and H.-G. de Mirabeau, and thus, in turn, Say. The aim of this and the following chapter is to explain how a controversy over the nature of a modern social order led to the development, in the hands of Say's associates, of arguments supportive of the transformation of French manners in order to create the kind of republic which no physiocrat could have conceived of, at least before Condorcet's conversion to Clavière and Brissot's republicanism in 1791.

2   TURGOT AND 'L'ORGANISATION SOCIALE'

Soon after the new king Louis XVI appointed Turgot *contrôleur-général* in August 1774 he received a letter sketching Turgot's ideas about public credit, the issue upon which he believed the future of France would turn. Promising 'the absolute devotion of my life', Turgot did not understate his fears for the future and requested that all of the ministers and administrators of the kingdom be warned of the impoverishment of the royal purse and the resulting need to work to reduce public expenditure. It was a simple fact that 'the prosperity of your Reign, the calm of the interior, the respect of our neighbours, the happiness of the Nation and yourself, all depend essentially upon economy.'[3] The policy advised to achieve this end had two strands. The first was encapsulated in the maxim, 'No bankruptcy, no more taxes, no more loans.' The second sought to increase revenue by putting an end to profits made by the *Fermes générales* when collecting taxes, and instituting measures to combat the costly privileges enjoyed by the first two orders of the state, the clergy and nobility. During the following year Turgot tried to realize these aims, culminating in the famous 'Six edicts', which included the abolition of the forced labour of the *corvée*, internal freedom of the grain trade, and inquiries intended to justify a land tax levied according to net income rather than social status or region. By the autumn of 1775, however, the extent of the opposition to these measures led Turgot to conclude that the link between the monarch and his subjects had been broken, resulting in social unrest and an increasingly parlous financial situation. As he put it, 'There is no public spirit because no common interest is recognized and visible.' Once more he addressed a *Mémoire* to the king, acknowledging the failure of previous attempts to redeem the debt and raise revenue, but recognizing too that the source of the difficulty lay in the fact that 'your Nation lacks a constitution: It is a Society composed of distinct and disunited Orders, and of a People with very few social ties . . . this results in a perpetual war of claims and ambitions that reason and common enlightenment have never regulated.'[4] The *Mémoire au Roi, sur les municipalités* used the word 'constitution' as an umbrella term for political devices with distinct functions, but which shared the ultimate aim of shaping a patriotic and egalitarian culture in France. The first device was 'a Council of national instruction directing the Academies, the Universities, the Colleges, and the Schools.' Turgot derived from Montesquieu, rather than Quesnay, the argument that 'the first bond of Nations comes from manners'. Since he believed that 'the foundation of manners is the education gained as children in all the duties of men in society', Turgot expressed surprise that 'There are methods and establishments for the creation of Mathematicians, Physicians, and Painters, yet there are none for the formation of Citizens.' The aim of the Council was therefore to establish a system of education 'to form in every class of Society men of virtue and utility, with souls of justice and pure hearts, thereby making zealous Citizens'. By means of a hierarchy of books and institutions, 'ranged in order of their usefulness to the Country', the 'duties of a citizen as a member of a family and a state' were to be revealed to all. Frenchmen would become aware of the interests they shared as members of a nation, and the duties they owed, in return for protection, to the first citizen, Louis XVI. Turgot was here rejecting the model of education favoured by Quesnay, founded as it was on learning a set of moral codes intended to make individuals more rational and productive. By contrast, Turgot wanted landed proprietors to become citizens, guardians of the public good in France: the political life of the nation in addition to the political economy. Once achieved, he anticipated a revival of patriotism sufficient to justify the prediction that 'in ten years your Nation will not be recognizable'. The transformation would regenerate France to become 'infinitely above any other People.'

The second element in Turgot's constitution sought in consequence to give a political voice to the interests which citizens shared as members of the nation. He envisaged institutions to distribute taxes between different classes, to recommend public works and foster better communications, to oversee the police and succour of the poor, to ensure peaceful relations with neighbouring areas, and to reveal the interests of each locality to higher authorities with powers to address common problems. By such means the *Fermes générales* and royal administrators, who had limited means and minimal local knowledge, were to be replaced by citizen administrators with an interest in efficiency and fairness in the distribution of taxes. Four levels of political assembly were to be instituted, beginning with the village and the town, with intermediate bodies for the *arrondissemens* or *élections*, and a provincial assembly for each region. At the apex a *grand municipalité, ou municipalité royale, ou municipalité générale du royaume* would advise the monarch and help him administer the kingdom by distributing taxes and carrying information forward regarding the condition of the realm. In defining citizenship, Turgot made clear that although a general interest uniting all individuals in a nation existed, only certain members of society could be expected to recognize and voluntarily abide by it. Furthermore, it was important to prevent assemblies from being over-large, to avoid tumult and to prevent the corruptible poor becoming members. No individual dependent upon another could be counted a citizen. Nor could those with movable wealth, because such riches 'are as fleeting as the talents'. Turgot confessed that he had been forced to the conclusion:

that only those who possess a part of the King's territory are the real people . . . those who possess no land have a Country only in their heart, by opinion, and through the happy accident of infancy . . . the possession of land puts a man in the class of contributors rather than the class of gamblers in Society; it is land that unites its possessor with the State, and constitutes the genuine Freedom of the City.[5]

Authority in a village assembly was to be proportioned to the amount of land owned by giving more votes to the larger proprietors. Small landowners were also encouraged to gain representation by pooling their resources to make up the 600 *livres* of net revenue that Turgot equated with 'a true interest, the freeholder, the right which the Romans called *pater familias*.' In towns, since 'house-owning is equivalent to barren land', only those with properties worth 15,000 *livres* were entitled to vote and to be elected to municipal assemblies, although once more Turgot favoured groups of *citoyens fractionnaires* to give representation to less wealthy landlords. Although Turgot confessed that he opposed venal offices, regional privileges, and tax-exemptions, his intention was not to reverse the traditional hierarchical system of orders, but rather to create an additional order of proprietors to ensure that 'property owners from the Third Estate have an equal voice to the members of the other two orders'. To this end Turgot conceived distinct modes of procedure for assemblies of different size and social order, in order to balance the interest of large and small landowners, and the interest of the existing nobility and the Third Estate. For example, a rule specified that if a very rich proprietor was in dispute with three-quarters of an assembly then the dispute would, after consultation with a higher assembly, be resolved by a majority vote by head. The over-arching goal of Turgot's constitution was to facilitate the reduction of the national debt by opening up some of the issues of local and national politics to the representatives of proprietor-citizens, thereby revealing the ties of need and interest that defined a modern nation state. He hoped that in return for political influence representatives of the different orders would agree to reform and accept a graduated tax on the landed assets of every individual. Ideally, having been given access to local politics, they would themselves recognize the imperative of increasing public revenue. Turgot was confident that through such measures the French populace would begin to love their country 'in the manner of the ancient nations' and yet be 'more wise, more consistent, and more attached to real happiness.' A 'new people' would emerge: 'In the place of the corruption, cowardice, intrigue, and avidity which has been found everywhere, virtue, disinterest, honour, and zeal will arise.' He also took pains to emphasize that his assemblies would acknowledge the king to be 'absolute Legislator':

They would present no challenge to your Authority; they would rather render you precious to Your People by increasing the People's happiness. They would make it evident to everyone that increased wealth and national well-being were due to your laws and your work.

Crucially, the assemblies 'would have no authority to oppose the indispensable and courageous operations which the reform of your Finances demand.'[6] Turgot saw no need for any dilution of royal power, but aimed to refine the exercise of such power by ensuring that the interests of the landed class were respected at court and in royal policies. His model attempted to unite the benefits of British parliamentary representation of national elites with the absolute sovereignty of French tradition.

Turgot's *Mémoire* was never sent to the king because he believed it to be in need of revision and wanted to select an opportune moment for its consideration, but it was widely circulated in manuscript by Dupont before its publication in 1787.[7] It became important as the first port of call for radicals in the late 1770s and early 1780s, who were beginning to demand more extensive constitutional innovations in order to reverse the decline of France. As is well known, Turgot was forced to resign in September 1776 after opposition from court factions centring upon the queen and Maurepas. Such experiences merely served to confirm his opinion of the necessity for constitutional change in France. This was evident in the letter he sent to Richard Price on 22 March 1778 commenting on the latter's *Observations on the Importance of the American Revolution*. Despite calling the new republic 'the hope of humanity', Turgot questioned Price's ecstatic tone by warning of the danger 'British prejudices' still presented to the nascent state. The North American constitutions, Turgot argued, 'rest upon the unsolid basis of the old and vulgar system of politics' because the 'spirit of party' and the 'system of monopoly' continued to divide the nation. North American statesmen had failed to:

attend to the great, and indeed the only natural distinction upon men, that between the proprietors and the non-proprietors of land, to their different rights with respect to legislation, the administration of justice and police, and their contribution towards public expenditure and the application of public money.[8]

National unity could only be the product of the representation of the interests of proprietors at the local level through assemblies with administrative powers, thereby confining a national legislature to 'general concerns'. This strict separation of powers, which developed the ideas of the *Mémoire*, was intended for America, but Turgot noted that if such ideas were applied to Europe, France was in a far better position than Britain. In Britain, he argued, 'all political writers, with the exception of Adam Smith and Josiah Tucker', were prejudiced by the false assumption of their superiority, a sure sign of the malaise of the nation. In the event of war, Turgot prophesied a social revolution in Britain in the wake of national bankruptcy, but continued stability in France. In Britain the landed interest was under-represented and monarchical authority was insufficient to face such challenges.

Turgot's achievement was to have revised physiocracy by showing that the identification of productive wealth with the 'natural product of agriculture' necessitated new institutions allowing landed proprietors to express their interests. Their wealth and aptitude signalled the transition from a 'feudal' to a 'modern' social order, with the military aristocracy being replaced by an elite of commercially-minded land owners. Turgot was also the first writer with physiocratic sympathies to focus on North America's potential to become an ideal physiocratic state, once 'British prejudices' had given way to 'French rationality'. One of the most important of his intellectual legacies was a conception of the American republic as being closer to the idealized 'civilized monarchy' of France than the moribund mixed government of Britain. His final writings contained the message that physiocracy had to be transformed from a moral to a political philosophy. He rejected Quesnay's conception of provincial assemblies in favour of assemblies of landed proprietors geared to generate a new political culture by playing a more active role in French political life; but he remained an orthodox physiocrat rather than a neo-physiocrat in refusing to endorse the notion of transforming French sovereignty.

3   THE EFFECTS OF THE AMERICAN REVOLUTION

Turgot made physiocracy into a politically innovative doctrine while upholding Quesnay's critique of Britain. The influence of his ideas can be seen in the writings of the leaders of the second generation of physiocrats after his death in 1781. To them, as to Turgot, it appeared self-evident that if political economy failed to concern itself with constitutional innovation, the French state would be imperilled by the 'arbitrary authority' found in tyrannies, popular republics, and mixed monarchies. Financial crisis demanded that the landed proprietors who provided the revenues of the state from the profits of agricultural investment were given a political voice at the very least. Le Trosne's *De l'administration provinciale et de la réforme de l'impôt* of 1779, one of the most conspicuous of the Turgot-inspired writings, made this abundantly clear.[9] But Turgot's most ardent disciples were Dupont and Condorcet. In each case dedication to Quesnay had precluded revisions to the form of French government from playing a role in their early political economy. Thus Condorcet's *Éloge de François Quesnay* of 1775 contained a defence of Quesnay as the ideal 'man of system', the founder of a 'perfect economic system', and the author of an economic science that would ultimately lead Quesnay to be venerated in the manner of Descartes.[10] Yet no reference was made to constitutions, constitutional change, or to the need for regeneration of the nation. Such themes were similarly absent from Dupont's *Abrégé des principes de l'économie politique* of 1772, which treated political economy as a moral code of physiocratic maxims independent of forms of government or national financial structures.[11] By the early 1780s, however, Turgot's insights into the problem of the national debt caused constitutional reform to become the leading theme of their writings, as a study of each reveals.

In Condorcet's case, signs of an altered perspective are clear from his *Vie de Turgot* of 1786, which argued that 'the right of contributing equally to the formation of laws is undoubtedly essential and belongs to all landed-proprietors.' The work also introduced the term 'republican', hitherto disparaged by all physiocrats, into discussion of political economy. Turgot himself, Condorcet asserted, had been 'in favour of a republican constitution above all others', defining a republic as a country where 'all the proprietors have an equal right to contribute to the formation of laws, to rule a constitution of assemblies which formulate and promulgate these laws, and to sanction them by their consent.'[12] While Britain was described as 'a more or less vicious aristocracy', France and America were considered examples of potentially successful republics, because laws existed 'not as the expression of the arbitrary will of the greatest number, but as truths deduced by reason from principles of natural right, and accepted as such by the majority.' The only difference was that in France 'consent to these truths is tacit in the constitution' while in America [assent] is public, and subject to legal and formal rules.' Condorcet followed Turgot in considering a 'republican' conception of the French monarchy to be superior even to the American form of government on the grounds that 'the monarch has not and cannot have any interest in making bad laws' and 'can act in accordance with the opinions of enlightened men without having to wait for the enthusiasm of general opinion.' A republic was not a warlike state characterized by the 'fanaticism of liberty', but rather a 'civilized monarchy' whose laws enshrined the natural rights to security of person and property. Condorcet defended these beliefs until the end of 1789. In his response to the abbé Raynal's prize competition sponsored by the Academy of Lyon, 'Has the discovery of America been harmful or useful to the human race?', he attacked 'zealous republicans', who considered the most fundamental right to be 'the making of laws', for failing to see that 'the virtuous citizen must know how to renounce [this right] in certain constitutions, for the sake of public tranquillity.'[13] The best constitution was rather one in which landed proprietors were given voice and influence, but did not present a challenge to monarchical wisdom. Condorcet's *Essai sur la constitution et les fonctions des assemblées provinciales*, completed in 1788 as his solution to the financial crisis of that year, was a hugely expanded version of Turgot's *Mémoire*. Condemning 'admiration for the British constitution that is more passionate than enlightened', Condorcet favoured the representation of landed proprietors. He expected their union to lead to the introduction of a uniform tax on land, in return for seeing the views of their assembly 'carried to the sovereign, as it would be consulted by him, and could be regarded with a fair degree of probability, as the general and reflected will of the nation'.[14] Seeing his plan being overtaken by the Estates General solution to financial crisis, which was forced on the King by the union of *parlements* and *notables* in 1787, Condorcet attacked such 'antiquated practices' as products of an aristocracy seeking to create a feudal republic in France 'which would make us permanently unequal'.[15] A declaration of rights became essential in such circumstances in order to hinder an Estates General or National Assembly dominated by aristocratic factions or ignorant ministers, which he believed had led to 'direct despotism' in Britain.[16] The plan of rights which Condorcet submitted to the constitutional committee of the National Assembly in the Autumn of 1789 was a concise statement of physiocratic doctrine after Turgot, making the class of landed proprietors the genuine 'freemen and citizens' of the nation, and enshrining the principle 'that no tax can be established which is not proportionate to the net product of agriculture.'[17]

Although Dupont's literary output diminished in the 1780s, as he continued in the service of the French government after Turgot's fall, by the end of the decade he too was acknowledging the necessity of constitutional change.[18] He canvassed this opinion after experience as secretary to the Assembly of Notables in 1787 made him fearful of the popularity of the English constitution as a model for French reformers. This was evident from the notes appended to his translation of Steven's *Examen du gouvernement d'Angleterre*. Dupont argued that in Britain neither civil nor religious liberty was genuinely protected because the powers of Parliament were ultimately arbitrary, being dominated by the pernicious influence of the executive.[19] Such corruption had generated a national debt that was propelling the state towards absolute monarchy and base manners, as Dupont claimed Hume had proved in his *History* and *Essays*. Instead of a mixed government balancing the interests of the nation, Dupont favoured a 'representative government' elected by the class of landed proprietors. As in Turgot's letter to Price, a strict separation of administrative functions replaced the balance of social orders or interests. It was for this reason that Dupont expressed reservations similar to Turgot's when reflecting upon the constitution, arguing that the unity of decision-making so necessary to good governance would be extremely rare. Dupont appeared to go beyond Condorcet's defence of monarchical sovereignty in arguing that 'The principle and source of sovereignty is evident in the Citizens'.[20] However, this was a rhetorical manoeuvre since, in making 'landed proprietor' and 'citizen' synonymous, the political economy each author expressed became identical. Dupont admitted this in the *Examen du gouvernement*, referring to Condorcet's work as the model for all constitution-builders.[21] Like Turgot, Dupont accepted that assemblies might initially be divided according to an individual's estate, and was dismissive of democracy. His only independent contribution was the idea of a second legislative chamber to balance the enthusiasms of a more popular assembly, composed of men of age and experience possessing scrutinizing and delaying powers.[22]

These writings placed neo-physiocracy in the vanguard of constitutional innovators at the beginning of 1789. In their advice to legislators 'not to exhaust themselves by seeking models in history, of which there is not one', and in their critique of feudal social structures, Condorcet and Dupont forged a powerful justification for social development towards a commercial society founded upon the exchange of agricultural products. They remained physiocrats, it is important to recognize, in their definition of citizenship as being founded on the exclusive productivity of agriculture and their continued acceptance of the view that all taxes fell on landed proprietors. This is what distinguished their ideas from Necker's schemes to alter French political architecture in the hope of generating a 'public spirit' that would ease the implementation of financial legislation. The provincial assemblies that he envisaged as means to such an end were not modelled on Britain or any idea of Turgot's. Necker simply did not believe in the necessity of consent to taxation or any dilution of monarchical sovereignty. His assemblies involved the nobility in the collection and distribution of taxes, and allowed them to advise, not influence, monarchical policy. Nobles would thereby, he believed, be won over to the cause of the crown against the *parlements*. Revenues would be increased, and more speedily raised, while the absolute sovereignty of the monarch remained intact. Economic health would then be assured, resting upon a union of the crown, enlightened ministers, and 'the rank and birth which favour distinction'. One of Necker's arguments in favour of luxury in a state derived from his claim that a contented nobility was all-important to a stable society. Thus he disagreed with Turgot that the social orders of France had altered in nature, and that such change ought to influence all future political decisions.[23] Turgot's model of the modern French nation was more realistic, accepting as it did that France had to change if it was to challenge Britain.

4   SIEYÈS' L'ART SOCIAL

To describe the forms of political economy developed in opposition to Turgot but not supportive of the constitutional status quo, it is necessary to go back to 10 February 1775, when Emmanuel-Joseph Sieyès' *Lettres aux économistes sur leur système de politique et de morale* was approved by the censor.[24] The work was written between 1770 and 1775, while Sieyès was secretary to the Bishop of Trégier, and is important because it served as a basis for the hugely influential political economy, called by Sieyès the 'social art', 'science of politics', 'social science' or 'science of the social order', of the *Vues sur les moyens d'exécution, Essai sur les privileges* and *Qu'est-ce que le Tiers État?*[25] Although his writings warned of the dangers of physiocracy, Sieyès is best understood as a thinker who considered physiocracy the greatest form of political economy yet conceived and as a necessary prelude to his 'political science', 'not of that which is, but of that which ought to be'. This becomes clear from an examination of some of the basic assumptions about the social world that they shared. The most revealing are Sieyès' definitions of society and citizenship. As in physiocratic writing, society was conceived as a means of better satisfying the subsistence needs shared by all of its members. 'All men', he wrote in the *Lettres*, 'wish to be happy'; since 'contentedness consumes goods', it was necessary to create 'a constantly acting force which produces new goods'. This force was labour, leading Sieyès to the conclusion, '. . . it is labour that creates wealth.' Society was consequently best defined as a 'living union of labour and its rewards':

An association is only a more perfect means [by contrast with isolated individuals] of procuring the wealth that everyone desires, in greater profusion and with greater security. Independently of the power of nature to produce goods, it is therefore essential for society to be a living union of labour and its rewards, and for the elements of this force, which society binds together, to produce far more than any individual acting in isolation.[26]

Once more following the physiocratic lead, Sieyès argued that citizenship was determined by an individual's contribution to the goals of society, measured above all by his ability to create wealth:

The sum of the labour of all the citizens forms the living union. If any citizen withdraws his share of labour he is thereby renouncing his rights, as no man should enjoy the fruits of another man's labour without reciprocity. Such labour is in this way the foundation of society, and the social order is no more than the best possible organization of this labour.

This illustration of the relationship between society and citizenship was physiocratic in inspiration. Disagreement stemmed from Sieyès' rejection of the exclusive productivity of agriculture and the resulting foundation of taxation in the net product. He considered it vital to give 'the name of wealth to all of the goods acquired by labour', deducing that 'there is no difference between landed wealth and the wealth of manufactures'. Although he agreed that the produce of the land best satisfied the most basic subsistence needs, 'this foundation does not complete the edifice of needs.'[27] But conflict over the nature of wealth foreshadowed Sieyès' main line of attack. The real problem was that the physiocrats' narrow view of wealth led them to a flawed idea of the social structure that most suited modern France. To Sieyès, France was not an exclusively 'agricultural kingdom' but a complex commercial society. Its social order made a mockery of the physiocratic division of society into productive agricultural and sterile commercial and manufacturing classes:

the arts and commerce have caused us to progress towards independence, they have liberated men from feudal servitude, and multiplied the classes which the aristocracy wants to reduce to three alone. Pastoral nations have only two [classes]: proprietors and their servants; feudal society has three, including a class of domestic servants because the proprietors are idle. Commerce establishes ten, twenty, or more.[28]

In Sieyès' eyes, the most important movement in modern history was 'the conversion of the largest part of the toiling class, who were forced to provide personal services, into free artisans who produce tangible wealth'. This had been responsible for 'the prosperity of modern nations' and was in opposition to 'all the different kinds of idleness' of pre-modern social forms. The physiocrats were therefore impeding the social structures generated in a commercial society by giving a privileged position to the class of landed proprietors. The problem was not only their idleness. Commerce depended on the free exchange of goods which embodied labour: 'If the labourer was free and his task was open to all, then the value of a good always expresses the quantity and quality of labour employed in its production'. Prices were fair if competition between producers ensured that costs were kept to a minimum; the division of labour had an important role to play in this process. Yet the class of landed proprietors could easily violate these requisites of commercial success by using their seigneurial privileges, most obviously the *corvé*, to shackle labour. Their market power in rural areas was at odds with free competition. Furthermore, excessive wealth made landed proprietors immune to the division of labour. Finally, the anti-commercial prejudices of the nobility were self-evident. Sieyès claimed that opposition to commerce explained the high prices to be found in French agriculture; as he put it, 'the lack of competition occasioned by the landed proprietors, or the exclusive privilege of land-holding, causes the rise of prices of primary goods beyond the value of the labour of the cultivator; it was the poor who paid the price'. In short, the physiocrats confused the social structure of modern society with the death-throes of a feudal aristocracy desperate to maintain its power. Sieyès thereby turned a physiocratic critique of military and feudal nobilities against the aristocracy as a whole by making the point that while their ideas for reform were to be welcomed, French decline would only be accelerated by giving political voice to the landed classes. To make citizens of the class least at ease with the transforming forces of commerce and industry was to Sieyès an error with other, equally lethal, effects. The physiocratic image of the landed citizen justified a tyranny as oppressive as absolute monarchy: 'Why admit as true citizens only landowners and consider all the rest as impostors who are obliged neither to contribute to the costs nor to the cares of the administration? This would be to sacrifice twelve million men to, at most, two million tyrants.' Sieyès claimed that proof of his concern about the politics of physiocracy could be found in Britain. By means of a brilliant rhetorical manoeuvre he claimed that Britain was an archetypal physiocratic state in spite of the physiocrats' abhorrence of the British constitution. In Britain the legislative power was dominated by a landed nobility. Like any privileged caste, they attacked any civil and political liberties that threatened their position at the apex of the social and political order. As a result, as commerce grew, a state of continual war developed between 'British manufacturers and merchants on one side and the owners of land on the other'. This explained Britain's relative decline during the previous decade, a perception that Sieyès shared with most French writers in the 1780s.

Sieyès' political economy did not end with a justification of a social order developed by commerce and industry, which ought to be made sovereign in the sense of having the power to define the public good for the nation. It further entailed rules for a wise legislator to follow to increase production, and the formation of a constitution within which a legislator was most able to exercise wisdom. Although more concerned with the latter, Sieyès made clear that the first role of the legislator was 'to enlighten men about their happiness'. This entailed fixing the meaning of the term 'industry', to make apparent the difference between productive industry and 'false riches, those of secondary importance, and especially wasteful, destructive, or ruinous wealth.'[29] Once these had been outlawed, it would be possible to create a more egalitarian society because commerce would tend towards greater material equality. With the progress of commerce and the division of labour, goods would become cheap enough to increase the real wages of the labouring classes. This argument, which had already been made by d'Holbach in France and Richard Price in Britain (Smith was also described as a source in certain French circles), was a central theme of all subsequent republican political economy, which tied together demands for certain kinds of commerce, national sovereignty and virtuous manners. To achieve it Sieyès followed Turgot and demanded a new constitution. But in sketching his idea of a constitution he claimed to have more in common with Adam Smith than any other political economist. After reading the *Wealth of Nations* and adding several notes to the *Lettres*, Sieyès claimed that he had 'gone beyond Smith' in 'recognizing the distribution of large professions or trades as the true principle of the progress of the social state.' What Sieyès meant by this was that the division of labour had altered the social structure of modern society and made imperative political change in accordance with these social movements. Smith, because of his British prejudices, had failed to acknowledge that modern constitutions had to ensure 'the representation of labour'.[30] If governed by wise legislators, commercial societies would avoid the extremes of feudal slavery as well as the 'general liberty' that characterized 'the unfortunate descent into commercial greed.' A 'moral civilization' would emerge, comprised of 'honest people'; citizens would be independent, but at the same time would be able to recognize their need for social ties and the duties that accompanied them. The ideal government instituted to sustain this social order was not a democracy. Sieyès believed it was unrealistic to advocate a popular constitution based on the political equality of all labourers. 'Equality' he argued, 'condemns the nation to a simplicity of industry and happiness which is sustained at the expense of the faculties of the imagination and the will.' Furthermore, if the social union was 'founded upon moral perfection', it was obvious that 'this morality can be found in only a section of the populace.' Therefore, since it was impossible to 'hold back humanity', experts had to be elected who recognized that the interest of society lay in extending commerce and the division of labour. The only means to ensure the involvement of such men was to give political rights to the wealthy and the educated within a framework of representative government. This was just, Sieyès argued, if everyone had access to instruction and opportunities to increase their property. The result was the division of the political nation into two classes of men:

A great nation necessarily comprises two kinds of men, citizens and auxiliaries; two peoples distinguished by education alone . . . Since this [social] union is founded upon the process of moral perfection, and such morals belong only to a fraction of the populace, the rest are admitted to society only as auxiliaries . . . I do not wish to divide men into Spartans and Helots, but into citizens and into companions in labour.[31]

In justifying what he was to later call the division between 'active and passive' citizens, Sieyès was describing a constitution barely more accessible to the general populace than Turgot's. Like Turgot and Dupont's later work, but in direct contrast to Quesnay, Sieyès favoured a rigid distinction between the sovereign legislative power and the executive or judicial branches. However, what he believed was most essential for France was the acknowledgement that the King was not and could not be part of the legislative power, because in any modern state the nation rather than the king was sovereign. In notes to the *Lettres* Sieyès argued:

If governments can act only by virtue of the law, it is evident that this law cannot be their will, but must be that of the governed. There is no difference between a king and a despot, if the king unites the two powers of the legislative and the executive. Despotism exists when one individual seizes the legislative power, anarchy when the people as legislator seizes the executive power. These are the extremes. Between them there are only distinct representative powers, the collective will and monarchical action, but distinguished in their branches as between so many monarchs.[32]

The *Lettres* and the notes added to them during the 1780s led Sieyès to demand the transformation of the French political order on the grounds that 'the corrupt manners of feudal society' had infested current politics and inaugurated a rapid national decline. The privileges of the first two estates were 'by the nature of things, unjust, odious, and a direct challenge to the supreme end of all political societies.' More dangerous still, they were destructive of 'all public economy'; the dire state of the national debt could be laid at their door. As Sieyès put it, ridiculing Montesquieu, 'If honour is, as has been said, the principle of Monarchy, we must at least agree that France has for a long time made terrible sacrifices in defence of this *principle.*'[33] The greatest threats to reform that appeared in 1788 were 'the multifarious agents of feudal society' because 'it is to the odious remnants of this barbaric system that we still owe the division of France, to her misfortune, into three mutually hostile orders.' To Sieyès, the plans for constitutional change that emanated from this camp included Turgot's provincial assemblies, which had been taken up by Calonne in 1787, and Mounier's support for a balance of social orders in the manner of the British constitution, which appeared in his *Nouvelles observations sur les états généraux de France* (Paris, 1789).[34] Rather than being a model, the British constitution was 'a gothic superstition' in which government had become 'an endless struggle between the administration and the aristocrats of the opposition', and where the nation and the king were 'virtually spectators'. The only solvent to the feudal ties in the French polity was a return to 'the fundamental principles of the social order' that would 'guarantee to the peoples their social and natural rights'.

The first branch of the 'social art' or 'social science' that Sieyès sought to articulate was 'the political constitution of society' founded on the sovereignty of the nation. As he put it, 'The nation is prior to everything. It is the source of everything. Its will is always legal; indeed, it is the law itself. Prior to and above the nation, there is only natural law.' In the commercial stage of society, national sovereignty could only be expressed by representatives who 'exercise those rights which are necessary for the preservation and good order of the community'. A 'National Assembly' of representatives from 'the forty thousand parishes which embrace the whole territory . . . and every element of the commonwealth' would be the new legislative power with authority to address the ills of the nation. It would be incorruptible, Sieyès claimed, with an argument reminiscent of Madison's tenth *Federalist*, because of its diversity. The second branch of the social art was called by Sieyès 'the constitution of taxation' because it contained proposals intended to resolve the national financial crisis. In the *Vues sur les moyens* he argued that the greatest threat to such a constitution was bankruptcy, then being favoured by all sides of the reform debate on the grounds that the debt had financed corrupt expenditures, that it had not been consented to by the nation, and was usurious. Sieyès sought to prove that bankruptcy was never an agent of liberty, but a tool of political authorities seeking despotic power. Bankruptcy, especially attractive to absolute monarchs during periods of uncertainty, would show that 'the abyss of despotism has swallowed everything'.[35] The creditors of the nation, a more numerous group than many realized, were 'co-proprietors' who had placed their trust in the government of France. The money they were owed had to be paid in full. Alternatives would only divide the nation or further imperil national finances. Rather than bankruptcy, existing taxes had to be levied and collected, not because they were just, but because the king, as the then sole representative of the nation, had consented to them. Once the National Assembly was established, the representatives of the nation would consent to new taxes and abolish all of those 'feudal revenues' incompatible with 'a free constitution in France.' But Sieyès was convinced that the problem could be solved without increasing charges upon the citizen. Bad administration had created the debt; as he said, 'to reestablish financial order it is not a question of taxing the peoples but of putting an end to abuses.' Thus national sovereignty was conceived as a means of addressing the financial and political crisis by giving power to the representatives of the social groups that defined the modern nation. These cogent solutions proved a manual for the Third Estate in the Estates General and continued to inspire the activities of many members of the National and Constituent Assemblies until the flight of the king to Varennes in 1791 destroyed the first French constitution. By 1789 Sieyès had provided a blueprint for a monarchical constitution compatible with increasing commerce, with a modern social order distinguished from Britain's. That he was a new kind of writer in French intellectual circles is beyond dispute. Alongside Diderot, yet far more optimistic, he envisaged the transformation of France by combining classical republican notions of virtue with certain forms of commerce. He was a modern republican in this and in his defence of national sovereignty, in which the king as chief-magistrate became the instrument of the public good.

5   RŒDERER'S REPRESENTATIVE DEMOCRACY

Sieyès was one of many writers who were inspired by physiocratic writing in general, and Turgot's work in particular, to formulate plans for a constitution which would at once address the debt problem and give political power to the new social orders of a commercial society. In the 1780s polemics and libels abounded with the intention of denigrating the outmoded practices of the court, the clergy, and the nobility. Clearly, in a work on J.-B. Say attention necessarily focusses upon the writers who influenced Say's subsequent political economy. Behind Clavière, the greatest influence on Say in the 1790s was Rœderer. A member of a noble family of Alsatian jurists, Rœderer was a counsellor in the *parlement* of Metz throughout the 1780s and an active contributor to the discussions of the Metz Academy concerning the future of France.[36] His earliest work in this forum, the *Idées sur un traité de finance* of August 1782 acknowledged that the only means of addressing the debt, which he considered essential for modern warfare, was a combination of commercial development and constitutional innovation. As such, it incorporated several themes which distinguished French political economy post-Turgot, and rigidly followed the latter's example in defining a 'constitution' as the assembled representatives of the three estates, whom Rœderer called 'sacred elements of the ancient republic', with responsibility for bringing the ideas of the nation to the foot of the throne. Five years later Rœderer's political economy was very different, and it explicitly rejected the traditional and feudal hierarchies that defined the Old Regime. Between 1783 and 1786, an intensive study of the economic circumstances of Alsace and Lorraine convinced Rœderer that Turgot was an inadequate saviour for France.[37] Although he supported physiocratic demands for the 'collapse of all barriers' that—in the form of tolls, prohibitions, and levies—impeded the trade of the provinces with the rest of France, Rœderer concluded that the creation of 'a new regime more friendly toward commerce and public liberty' required the destruction of all feudal orders and traditional estates. By 1788, he was using Turgot's view of the importance of capital investment against its author, with the argument that profits in commerce and manu-factures alone could generate the savings necessary to revitalize the French economy, making irrelevant physiocratic defences of agricultural production and political orders based on agriculture.[38] In Rœderer's view, 'commerce and manufactures command agriculture'; they had brought 'order and politeness' in the place of feudal strife. A typi-cal physiocratic state was Poland, whose grim predicament and feudal backwardness could be contrasted with the Swiss confederation, whose modern social order was worthy of emulation. In Switzerland, freedom of commerce and industry created a unity of interest between merchants and consumers signified by the term 'bon marché'.

The most important of Rœderer's works in the 1780s was completed just as Sieyès' *Vues sur les moyens* was being published, and shared the aim of directing the formation of an Estates General.[39] The works had a great deal in common. As Rœderer said in his later *Notice sur ma vie*, *De la députation aux états généraux* contained 'a theory of the well-ordered social state'. It gave reasons why the view of France as a system of corporations not only 'was not truly representative of the nation' but actually 'destroyed the unity essential to monarchical government' by making France 'so many small republics'. Turgot's idea of provincial assemblies was described as the worst example of the corpo-ratist perspective, because in giving political power to local institutions it would 'rein-troduce the ancient feudal anarchy' which was responsible for so many 'barbarous laws' and 'violations of the social contract'. This last point underlined Rœderer's debt to Locke and Rousseau, although his use of their ideas was distinctive. This argument was also effective against the physiocratic idea of citizenship, and Rœderer was as convinced as Sieyès that to give political power to the class of landed proprietors was to institute a vicious tyranny. As he put it, 'Men do not live from the land but from the fruits of the land', a proposition which led him to conclude that labour was the source of all wealth: 'Mobile property, from the fruits of the land, is alone essential to society, because the security of subsistence and of goods depends upon the existence of a certain right to consume these products'. Nor was the ownership of land essential to a healthy society, as the examples of Frankfurt, Augsburg, Geneva, Switzerland and Holland showed. To describe 'the industrious class' as 'salaried' by landed proprietors was to condemn them to 'the coarsest bread and the most common clothing and abode.'[40] There was therefore good reason to fear that the restriction of citizenship to landed proprietors would generate economic and political problems. Yet Rœderer agreed with Turgot that the only successful political economy in France was one which envisaged 'the remaking of society in accordance with the principles of justice and eternal order' by means of 'the preparation of a free constitution', on the grounds that 'only a regular constitution can establish and maintain order in a large society'. In formulating his idea of a 'free constitution' Rœderer turned away from Turgot and towards the writers he called *philosophes*, on the grounds that 'for forty years, a hundred thousand Frenchmen have been conversing with Locke, Rousseau, and Montesquieu; each day they received great lessons from them on the rights and duties of men in society.' The first part of *De la Députation* was almost a précis of Locke's *First Treatise on Government*, describing self-preservation as the fundamental natural law of the state of nature and the social state, combating patriarchal dominion as the source of political authority, and defining property rights as the product of mixing labour with nature's bounty. Rœderer was equally influenced by the *Second Treatise* and the first chapters of the *Contrat social*, as shown by his argument that political society was the product of 'a convention, a union of wills, with the object of giving each individual the equal certitude of exercising the rights natural to man', and by his statement that 'society cannot exist without the tacit consent of all those who compose it.' The simple conclusion was that 'it is essential for each member of the State to contribute to the formation of laws.' Any other form of government was illegitimate, being a species of despotism. The legislative power was the source of all authority in a state, but Rœderer moved away from Rousseau by acknowledging the need for large states in the modern world, and therefore government by representative rather than direct democracy. He was equally sceptical of the *mandat impératif*, which Rousseau defended in the *Gouvernement de Pologne*: the claim that national representatives should strictly enact the predetermined will of a primary assembly of all citizens. Rœderer held it to be a feudal vestige that entrenched social distinctions. Representatives were rather to be 'invested with all of the powers to be drawn from the social union' in assemblies where 'the will of the majority has the force of law.' Rœderer's acknowledged debt to Montesquieu is more difficult to establish, but he considered him 'the father of enlightenment and liberty in France, probably the greatest benefactor of the entire nation', because of his argument that if the feudal system of orders was abolished there would either be 'a popular state or a despotism'. In Rœderer's, mistaken, interpretation, Montesquieu was lending his support to the creation of a 'popular state' because he considered the 'system of orders' in France to be odious, and proof that a mixed government based on such a social structure would be disastrous. He concluded that Montesquieu was the inspiration behind a constitution based on what Rœderer called 'national sovereignty', meaning the sovereignty of the people as interpreted by a major-ity of representatives in a national assembly.

The difference between Rœderer and his juristic forbears, with whom Sieyès was at one on this point, was the breadth of civic participation considered compatible with national sovereignty. To Rœderer, liberty did not simply mean Locke's tacit consent or passive citizenship, but, following Rousseau, the *participation* of all citizens in the legislative power. Every independent male resident of the state was to be included as an elector and potential deputy, excluding only soldiers, prisoners, the infirm and domestic servants: 'the right to elect belongs to all men independent of domestic authority, born in the country or naturalized citizens, whatever their condition or fortune.' Rœderer was one of the few political economists of the 1780s to consider extending the freedom of the city to women, but he was optimistic enough about the exclusively male National Assembly to conclude that 'women should not fear slavery wherever men have been freely elected.' Assuming the dominant influence of fathers and husbands, and that 'women would be dumb before an assembly', Rœderer defined political society not as a contract between individuals, but as an agreement between 'heads of families, of men equally capable of labour and mutual aid.' He responded to fears expressed by Sieyès and Turgot concerning the potential for tumult, corruption, and ignorance in a popular assembly with the argument that 'the sole means of combating egoism' was 'to enlighten self-love' by 'calling for a discussion of their reciprocal ideas, and to submit these ideas to the will of the majority, after a fully public debate.'[41] Rœderer was more in tune with Sieyès, and also with Dupont and Condorcet, in accepting the need for an absolute separation of public functions, and the division of administrative labour between an executive monarch and an independent judiciary. He was also sure that the debt problem could be resolved through the institution of a constitution expressing national sovereignty. By such means the social groups with an interest in national preservation and commercial development would replace the feudal and physiocratic orders which posed a threat to good governance in France, Britain, and America.

Among Turgot's disciples, Rœderer's idea of a modern social order expressive of the national will was the most ambitious. It was also the most republican, adapting a consti-tution redolent of Rousseau's *Contrat social* to a large and corrupt state such as France. Unlike Rousseau, Rœderer considered that the political virtues for which the famous Genevan had argued were wholly compatible with commerce. Revising Rousseau from this perspective became a characteristic of political thought in the 1790s. As Rœderer's correspondence of 1788–9 shows, his schemes interested members of Necker's circle as well as the Old Regime's more voluble critics, such as Chamfort.[42] They also explained his election to the Estates General as a deputy for the third estate rather than the nobil-ity. Although a disputed election in Metz delayed his arrival in Paris until the autumn of 1789, this did not prevent Jacques-Louis David from giving him a prominent place in his portrayal of the Tennis Court Oath. In the National Assembly Rœderer sought to lead revolutionary politics by the principles outlined in *De la députation*. The links he forged with Sieyès caused him to be described as the latter's 'first lieutenant' by Sainte-Beuve. Nevertheless, the intellectual debts which Sieyès and Rœderer owed to different thinkers deserves attention, because this contributed to divisions of opinion about the politically active social order necessary to the resolution of the French financial crisis. Divisions of opinion between the two men regarding the course of the Revolution also made Rœderer rather than Sieyès the dominant influence upon Say after 1794.

6   CLAVIÈRE'S REPUBLICANISM FOR LARGE STATES

All of the writers who responded to Turgot's plan for constitutional and social change were convinced such innovations would solve the debt problem and make the finances of France stable enough to challenge Britain's ascendancy in Europe. They also shared an opposition to the classically-inspired republicanism then being defended most impressively by the abbé Mably. As we have seen, Condorcet had favourably used the term 'republican' as early as 1786. It was intended to refer to 'the general interest of society' or 'public good' rather than a defence of the right of the people to make the law. This was hardly surprising, as a succession of eminent thinkers had drawn an absolute distinction between ancient republicanism and modern civilization. To Montesquieu the fundamental problem was one of size. The virtue required of republican citizens required a homogeneous populace of fraternal patriots, something inconceivable outside a small state. Rousseau added that republican virtue and the kinds of culture generated by commerce were inimical to each other. The *Contrat social*, he made clear, was wholly inapplicable to a commercial society. Mably agreed, describing commerce and debt as social corrosives to be avoided by all true republicans. Similar arguments could be found in the work of every recognized *philosophe* as well as that of every physiocrat. As a consequence, writers impressed by the republicanism of the ancient world accepted that the sole means of making republican virtues compatible with commerce and civilization was by promoting a distinctly modern idea: representative government. Representation, as Sieyès and Rœderer made clear, would allow the natural right to self-governance to exist side-by-side with the necessarily coercive executive authorities characteristic of large modern states. While this required the transformation of French politics to accommodate the new social orders of commercial society the ultimate intention was neither to level ranks nor to obliterate political distinctions. For these writers, republicanism ended with national sovereignty, virtuous manners and moral forms of commerce. Those who supported Turgot's assessment of France's future prospects believed that the politics of commercial society were dependent on the activities of an elite whose interests were synonymous with the stability of the state and the protection of property. Even Rœderer, whose male heads of household represented the most numerous group of active citizens, made clear his opposition to 'mob' conceptions of democratic citizenship. Property-ownership and education were taken to be signs of potential public virtue and a capacity to act reasonably in the public arena. The optimism of the early revolutionaries was largely based on their belief that the old social order had capitulated to a new social order whose virtue had been fully proved in the *journées* of the summer of 1789; a notion epitomized in the restricted membership of the national guard by the *marc d'argent*. Sieyès, Condorcet, and Rœderer, all believed that the debt problems of the Old Regime would be resolved by the greater virtue of the newly enfranchised groups of industrious property-owners. The initial republican turn in French political economy entailed exactly this: a demand for increased political participation by the wealth-creating and civic-minded groups of French society. These groups would act on behalf of the sovereign nation and ensure that neither the chief-magistrate, Louis XVI, the ancient feudal nobility, nor the Catholic church, could abuse their powers. Republicans sought a new constitution and welcomed the social effects of the commercialization of society. Contrary to the views of such historians as Aulard, there was therefore a distinctive kind of republicanism before the Revolution, bitterly opposed to the British constitution and entailing the sovereignty of philosophers, merchants and farmers.

The majority of the National Assembly's supporters viewed the Revolution from this perspective; they were divided only by their conception of the constitution necessary to inaugurate the new era of harmony. The achievement of the Revolution was to be a set of political institutions protective of 'liberty' yet synonymous with a more fluid society of industrious citizens. The Genevan revolutionary and exile, Clavière, working with his friend Brissot, condemned such Turgot-inspired beliefs as incapable of supporting a modern social order in France. They were as committed as Turgot, Sieyès, or Rœderer, to transforming French society by means of constitutional change, and had been convinced by Richard Price that representative government was the only legitimate basis for a resolution of the debt problems of modern states. They were also convinced that economic development towards commerce and manufactures was imperative in France, and defended public credit as a necessity in any large modern state.[43] But Clavière and Brissot had a very different view of the forces that underpinned politics in general and constitutions in particular. This was undoubtedly due to Rousseau's influence, and most notably the latter's view of the importance of virtuous popular manners to a flourishing state. From 1785, Clavière, Brissot and other members of their circle made Rousseau's idea of manners the linchpin of proposals to transform France into a different kind of republic: one whose merits Say would quickly be persuaded to support.

Clavière had known Brissot since 1780, when, seeking the re-establishment of popular sovereignty in Geneva, he had travelled to Paris in the hope of gaining the support of Vergennes. Two years later, after the failure of constitutional revolution in Geneva, Clavière and Brissot were reunited in Neuchatel. They began their literary collaboration with a justification of popular sovereignty in small states.[44] It was from this time that Brissot began to consider Clavière his mentor and source of intellectual inspiration, particularly in political economy. Between 1782 and 1784 Clavière was engaged in creating a republican community of watchmakers in Ireland while Brissot sought to establish a *lycée* for independent *philosophes* in London. It was only when both men were living in Paris, after Clavière had rescued Brissot from bankruptcy and imprisonment in September 1784 that they began to collaborate in popularizing their ideas for the reform of France. Their proposals for constitutional change had a great deal in common with those of Sieyès and Rœderer because they favoured representative government and national sovereignty. Clavière and Brissot, however, had a far more popular conception of modern citizenship than either French writer, and a stronger republican faith in the need for the levelling of social ranks. This is evident from the *Observations d'un républicain*, completed early in 1787 and published at the end of the year. The book condemned the reformist strategies of both Necker and Turgot as inadequate responses to the ills of the kingdom.[45] Necker's *Administration des finances* was taken to task for defending the excessive powers of the monarch and his ministers. By contrast, Turgot was described as an enlightened genius who had perceived the real problem of France to be its lack of a constitution. Following Condorcet's *Vie de Turgot*, Clavière and Brissot argued that the great man 'belonged, by the liberty of his principles, to a Republic' but stated that Turgot had never been a 'true republican' because he had failed to recognize the need to combat directly the lack of virtue in the French populace. Turgot's educational schemes to instil patriotism were derided as monarchical fantasies because it was necessary to establish a republic where *all* of the people owned property and were protected in their use of it. Since Turgot supported the powers of the *intendants*, the epitome of a system of ranks, the people could never be free in his assemblies: 'Perhaps M. Turgot, in his economic system, had not tasted these republican ideas. He was persuaded, with the physiocrats, that Kings must govern according to evidence, that the people must submit themselves to it, that every counterweight was an obstacle and an abuse.' In fact, since all of the people contributed to the revenue of the government, everyone should be considered a citizen once they reached the 'age of reason'. France had to become a republic by means of 'a great upheaval' in which the people established themselves as sovereign, ranks were abolished, and manners were pure. The first step was universal male enfranchisement.[46] The second was to ensure that the legislators chosen by the people put into practice the political economy of Clavière and Brissot's second major publication of the period, *De la France et des États-Unis*, which had been completed at the same time as the *Observations*.[47] The serious nature of their intentions was signalled by the formation of the *Société Gallo-Américain*, which provided a forum for the discussion of events in France and America.[48] Meetings were held at Clavière's residence, at which Crèvecœur, Nicolas Bergasse, and Brissot were present, between January and April 1787. *De la France* appeared in the midst of the society's activities, and was read and discussed in the meetings. It promised a plan for the 'happiness of humanity', entailing the transformation of France by solving the debt problem and restoring what was described, undoubtedly by Brissot rather than by Clavière, as her 'ancient liberty'.

De la France succinctly stated the principles of Clavière's political economy. Security was the first concern of modern states. This required a capacity for self-defence that recent wars had proved to be determined by economic power. Although natural resources were the ultimate arbiter of economic strength, it was a peculiar fact that France was pre-eminent in this respect and yet had suffered successive defeats at the hands of inferior powers. The example of Britain's rise to prominence in the eighteenth century appeared to leave no doubt as to the dual sources of practical strength: trade and public credit. All of Clavière's previous writings made clear his absolute faith in expanding commerce and industry.[49] In *De la France* he added, 'credit has become ever more necessary to large nations, since borrowing is vital.'[50] Such claims were commonplace in post-1763 discussion. They explain the popularity in France of Hume's essay, *Of Public Credit*, in which Hume had underscored the importance of public credit to modern states while warning politicians of the deadly consequences of over-reliance or misuse. Clavière acknowledged Hume's warning in later writings; in 1787, he was all in favour of credit but in an analysis of the North American Revolution gave a distinctive twist to Hume's view of the origins of state power. For just as Britain's superior commerce and credit had proved too great for France, a similar logic ought to have ensured a far easier fight in North America. Clavière was certain that the outcome of this conflict had been influenced by American commerce and credit. But it had ultimately been governed by an even more fundamental factor: the public virtue of the American colonists. Their virtue was far greater than that of Britain's soldiers, and had consequently triumphed over superior wealth and arms. The liberation of America could therefore be traced to a trinity of forces identified by Price rather than by Hume; the Revolution 'underlined the importance of commerce to power, the necessity of public credit, and consequently the public virtues'.

Giving prominence to the synoptic phrase 'public virtues' underlined Clavière's commitment to his Genevan republican heritage, and above all to Rousseau. He was describing a republicanism that could be distinguished from that of Sieyès, Rœderer, and the neo-physiocrats. Where they held that an elite alone could be trusted to exercise the public virtues, Clavière argued that the masses must equally be persuaded to practice them. The first step was to abolish the aristocracy, the distinctive rhetoric that Clavière and Brissot's circle injected into pre-revolutionary political argument. Although Rousseau disdained commerce and condemned public credit, he had repeatedly argued that the health of a state was directly proportionate to its virtue. This meant the quality of the *mœurs*, or manners, of the citizenry, their willingness to sacrifice private interest to the public good, and their capacity to resist egoism. But where Rousseau held wealth and virtuous manners to be antithetical, Clavière followed Price, and also Thomas Paine, in forging a link between them.[51] Commerce depended upon mutual trust between individuals. If this trust was broken by dishonest practices or excessive inequality between social groups, then commerce would destroy virtue. 'Honest' forms of commerce, on the other hand, increased independence and fostered communication and movement between ranks. A similar view was taken of public credit. The decisive influence upon economic power then was public and private morality. As Clavière later said, 'prosperity will constantly follow principles conforming to the rights of humanity . . .'[52] In applying these assumptions to the case of France, Clavière concluded that French decline could be traced to an immoral culture, having 'exhausted everything . . . in futile sciences, frivolous arts, in fashions, in luxury, in the art of pleasing women, in the loosening of manners . . .'.[53] If one side of the immoral coin was ignorance, the other, also pure Rousseau, was luxury. The French economy, addicted to the provision of luxury goods, destroyed the industriousness of the lower orders of the population. Obsession with luxury goods was the product of the rigid system of French ranks, with an arrogant and overweening elite at the apex. Rejecting Montesquieu's claim that monarchy necessitated aristocracy, Clavière and Brissot argued that it was necessary to sacrifice the French nobility to commercial necessity:

This prejudice, which has falsely been held to be indestructible, because the nobility has wrongly been held to be one of the necessary elements of the monarchical constitution, this prejudice, I say, would alone be capable of preventing French commerce from having been active, energetic, and esteemed, if one did not have hope that wise philosophy destroys it and infallibly leads men to the great idea of only valuing individuals by their talents and not by their rank: an idea without which there are only aristocrats; that is to say, men incapable of welcoming the elevation of a city, and base men, unable to produce them.

The nobility were also held responsible for another powerful impediment to economic success, the anti-commercial culture. This manifested itself in the interests of French philosophers who, Clavière declared, remained embroiled in the hollow disputes of 'old political science', being, like Mably, 'too enthusiastic for the [ancient] Greek republics', too obsessed with the language of the 'vulgar politics of the balance of power', or too interested in 'futile sciences'. While the British nobility had realized that a commercial republican language sustained credit, the French nobility used an anti-commercial language to maintain its social position. For bizarre reasons, Clavière was fascinated by English. Here was a language to elevate citizens because 'a man accused of the greatest crimes, and of the most impoverished appearance, is called "Sir" when he is interrogated by his judges'. The French had forgotten the maxims of republican life to such an extent that they had committed the grave error of calling the American confederation an 'empire' rather than a 'free republic'. Without virtuous manners, any love of liberty would degenerate into 'a new tyranny', the great danger facing France, and the cause of the failure of English republican experiments in the seventeenth century. The latter's lack of virtue had been evident in the act of 'covering the vile Monk, with flowers', in the frivolity of English manners, and the national obsession with prostitution and gin.[54] To save the Revolution in France, tastes had to become simple because 'magnificent vases, tapestries, fine wines, mobs of servants, and a fine table' courted private deceit and public intrigue. Revolutionary legislators had to go beyond constitution building to foster an interest in the exercise of virtue by dividing property and encouraging savings banks, public instruction, and skilled labour. These lessons, neglected by Sieyès, Rœderer and the neo-physiocrats, and only hinted at by Turgot, had to become the fulcrum of the science. Clavière and Brissot agreed that France had to become a representative democracy, a fully commercial society. They added a demand for a social structure more akin to North America than contemporary Europe. Rousseau's writings were being reinterpreted to address the problems of a large commercial state. The result was more revolutionary than any other political economy available to the French reading public.

Their political message was popularized on Brissot's return to Paris from London in February 1788, after which he and Clavière founded the *Société Française des Amis des Noirs*. Seeking the universal abolition of slavery and, as an essential corollary, the development of free commerce and labour, it attracted prominent members, including Talleyrand and Lafayette.[55] It also led to the further exchange of revolutionary plans and the formation of party groupings before the opening of the Estates General.[56] Late in 1788, Clavière finally published in his own name, and began to campaign for a 'monetary constitution', embodying an economic strategy for the commercialization of the populace to underpin any political innovations.[57] This was conducted in partnership with a group of radical Genevans, including Etienne Dumont and Clavière's old ally

Pierre Du Roveray, who were largely responsible for Mirabeau's *Courier de Provence*. Through Mirabeau, Clavière became involved in the drafting of a declaration of rights for the National Assembly and characteristically included the statement, 'The conservation of manners is absolutely essential for the maintenance of the social contract, and all public financial activities must be scrutinized for their effect on manners.'[58] Brissot founded the *Patriote françois* in March 1789. Both men took advantage of the publishing opportunities subsequently presented by Nicholas Bonneville's *Cercle sociale* and journals such as the *Chronique du mois*. That Say's political economy was concerned with the improvement of private manners and the inculcation of public virtue in the mass of the populace was not surprising. He was following the script for a successful revolution outlined by Clavière and Brissot in the late 1780s.

NOTES TO CHAPTER 4

1. 'Lettre aux auteurs de la décade sur les économistes', *LDP*, iv, 70–83.
2. There has been much debate as to whether Turgot can legitimately be called a 'physiocrat', particularly as he declared himself independent of any sect. Although critical of *évidence* and *autorité tutelaire*, Turgot always defended the view that 'the landed proprietors paid all taxes', notably against Hume in 1767, and it is because of his development of this idea that he is here called a physiocrat: *Œuvres*, ii, 507–9, 658–67; iii, 398–9.
3. *Lettre de M. Turgot au Roi, Contenant ses idées générales sur le ministère des finances qui venait de lui être confie, Œuvres de Turgot*, vii, 6–7.
4. *Mémoire au Roi, sur les municipalités, Œuvres de Turgot*, vii, 390–1. Although Dupont had a hand in the work in his capacity as Turgot's secretary, he ascribed it in its entirety to his master.
5. *Ibid.*, vii, 404–8.
6. *Ibid.*, vii, 422, 478, 484.
7. Dupont gave his blessing to H.-G. de Mirabeau's publication of the *Mémoire* under the title *Œuvres posthumes de M. Turgot* (Lausanne, 1787). It was also published as part of Clavière and Brissot's *Observations d'un républicain* (1788).
8. 'A Letter from Monsieur Turgot to Doctor Price on the Constitutions of America', in Mirabeau's *Considerations on the order of the Cincinnatus . . .* (London, 1785), p. 161.
9. *De l'administration provinciale*, p. 329. On Turgot's general influence see P. Rosanvallon, *Le Sacre du citoyen: histoire du suffrage universel en France* (Paris, 1992), pp. 47–69.
10. *Éloge de Quesnay* (London, 1775), pp. 98–9. See also K. M. Baker, *Condorcet*, ch. 4.
11. *Abrégé des principes de l'économie politique, Ephémérides du citoyen*, 1772, i, 43–51.
12. Condorcet, *ŒdC*, v, 209–10.
13. *De l'influence de la révolution d'Amérique sur l'Europe* (Paris, 1786), introduction.
14. *Essai sur la constitution et les fonctions des assemblées provinciales* (Paris, 1788), *ŒdC*, viii, 126.
15. *Sentiments d'un républicain, sur les assemblées provinciales* (Paris, 1789), *ŒdC*, ix, 138.
16. *Idées sur le despotisme, ŒdC*, ix, 148–9.
17. *Déclaration des droits, ŒdC*, ix, 198–9, 206.
18. For an example see Dupont's *Rapports au comité d'administration de l'agriculture* (1785–6).
19. *Examen du gouvernement d'Angleterre, comparé aux constitutions des États-Unis* (London, 1789). Authorship of the American work, often attributed to Livingstone, has now been clearly established; see D. Lacorne's *L'Invention de la république. Le modèle américain* (Paris, 1991).
20. *De la périodicité des assemblées nationales* (Paris, 1789), p. 4.

21. *Examen du gouvernement*, p. 186.

22. *De la périodicité*, pp. 16–19.

23. *De l'administration des finances de la France* (Paris, 1784), *Œuvres complètes*, iv, 57–60; v, 50–64.

24. *Emmanuel-Joseph Sieyès: Écrits politiques*, ed. Roberto Zapperi (Paris, 1985).

25. On Sieyès' constitutional thought see P. Pasquino, *Sieyès et l'invention de la constitution en France* (Paris, 1998); Murray Forsyth, *Reason and Revolution: The Political Thought of the Abbé Sieyès* (Leicester, 1987); W. H. Sewell, *A Rhetoric of Bourgeois Revolution: The Abbé Sieyès and What is the Third Estate?* (Durham N.C., 1994), pp. 72–103; M. Sonenscher, 'The Nation's Debt and the Birth of the Modern Republic', *History of Political Thought*.

26. *Écrits politiques*, p. 32.

27. *Ibid.*, pp. 35–8.

28. *Ibid.*, p. 79.

29. *Ibid.*, p. 57.

30. *Ibid.*, p. 62.

31. *Ibid.*, p. 89.

32. *Ibid.*, p. 87.

33. *Essai sur les privilèges* (Paris, 1788), pp. 5, 21, 39, 48 f.

34. *Qu'est-ce que le tiers état?* (Geneva, 1970), pp. 153, 167.

35. *Vues sur les moyens*, p. 63.

36. On Rœderer's political thought see J. Roëls, *La notion de représentation chez Rœderer* (Heule, 1968), pp. 15–26; K. Margerison, *P. L. Rœderer: Political Thought and Practice during the French Revolution* (Transactions of the American Philosophical Society, 1983); M. Forsyth, *The Spirit of the Revolution of 1789: P. L. Rœderer* (Leicester, 1989).

37. *Observations sur les intérêts des Trois-Évêchés et de la Lorraine, relativement au reculement des barrières des Traites* (1787), ŒdR, vii, 437–523.

38. *En quoi consiste la prospérité d'un pays, et quelles sont en général les causes qui peuvent y contribuer le plus efficacement?*, ŒdR, vii, 600–4.

39. *De la députation aux états généraux*, (November, 1788), ŒdR, vii, 539–74.

40. *Ibid.*, vii, 540, 547, 550–1, 555–8, 564.

41. *Ibid.*, vii, 545, 552–4, 565–6, 570.

42. *Correspondance*, vii, 536–9.

43. *Point de banqueroute* (London, and Paris, 1787), pp. 5–7.

44. *Le Philadelphien à Genève, ou lettres d'un Américain sur la dernière révolution de Genève* (Dublin, 1783).

45. *Observations d'un républicain, Sur les diverses systêmes d'administrations provincials* (Lausanne, 1788), p. 113.

46. *Ibid.*, pp. 114 n., 155, 166–8.

47. *De la France et des États-Unis, ou de l'importance de la révolution de l'Amérique pour le bonheur de la France . . .* (Paris, 1788), p. 28. Although it appeared in Brissot's name, the introduction made clear the joint nature of the enterprise and its indebtedness to Clavière's 'commercial philosophy'. When a second edition appeared in 1791 in the hope of guiding revolutionary legislators, both authors were named.

48. Brissot, *Correspondance*, pp. 105–36.

49. *De la Caisse d'Escompte* (Paris, 1785), p. viii; *De la banque d'Espagne dite de Saint-Charles* (Paris, 1785), p. 108.

50. *De la France*, p. 20.

51. On Paine see Clavière's and Brissot's *Nouveau voyage dans les États-Unis de l'Amérique septrionale, fait en 1788* (Paris, 1791), 2 vols., i, xxviii.

52. *Lettre de la Société des Amis des Noirs, à M. Necker, avec la réponse de ce ministre* (July, 1789), p. 4.

53. *De la France*, p. 5; also pp. 8 f., 32.
54. *Nouveau voyage dans les États-Unis*, i, ix.
55. *Correspondance*, pp. 134–5, 166–75; *Mémoires*, ii, 71.
56. Clavière and Brissot united with Condorcet to direct the format of the Estates General in *Le Moniteur* (London, 1788).
57. *De la foi publique envers les créanciers de l'état* (London, 1788); *Opinions d'un créancier de l'état, sur quelques matières de finance* (Paris and London, 1789).
58. Draft declaration of rights, BN N. Aq. F. 9534. I owe this reference to Jim Livesey.

5

Revolution and the Political Economy of Terror

I   THE PROBLEM OF MANNERS IN THE REVOLUTION

In a letter to Etienne Dumont of 5 March 1829 Say modestly recalled his work on the *Courrier de Provence* by means of a contrast with what he considered to be the more meaningful labour of Bentham's famous translator: 'I remember that while you were advising Mirabeau all that I did was to receive subscriptions.'[1] Although we know little about Say's role in the production of the *Courier*, there is evidence to suggest that his subsequent recollection was disingenuous. Successive advertisements in the pages of the journal show that by 1790 Say was responsible for running the office in which it was produced. Furthermore, the founders of *La Décade philosophique* in 1794 made Say the editor-in-chief of that journal in part because of the breadth of his experience at the *Courier*. Most important of all, Say's aim was to make a contribution to the intellectual controversies of the Revolution. His first pamphlet, *De la liberté de la presse*, appeared in November 1789; in the early 1790s he was working on a translation of Helen-Maria William's *Letters on Switzerland* and a French edition of Benjamin Franklin's *The Way to Wealth, or Poor Richard Saunders*.

What unites this small body of work is a commitment to Clavière and Brissot's ideas regarding revolutionary culture, faith in 'reason', and making popular manners more virtuous. The latter issue became more important as the constitution building of the early years of the Revolution gave way to civil war and bankruptcy rather than peace and prosperity. Two phases of the Revolution can be discerned. The first sought the solution to France's ills in political architecture and was founded on faith in the united front that the public showed to the Old Regime. Such was the optimism of the early revolutionaries that Mirabeau's idea of the *don gratuit* or free gift of a quarter of each citizen's income to the treasury, was widely expected to succeed. The reality, after the Civil Constitution of the Clergy divided the nation, was civil war, empty public coffers and increasing animosity between France and other European states. To Clavière this was unsurprising. Legislators who erected constitutions but neglected strategies to reform manners courted disaster, and in his view the involvement of the populace in commercial activities was the only way to save France from moral and financial collapse. The second phase of the Revolution shared the concern of establishing a political culture that would at once resolve the financial crisis and restore public order. Other writers followed Clavière in focussing on the problem of manners but responded in different ways, not least because the spectacular failure of Clavière's policies after the Girondin ministries in which he served proved to be preludes to the radical Jacobin

Terror. From 1793, all of those who remained revolutionaries turned to the regeneration of manners in order to ensure the success of subsequent constitutions, sparking a great debate which raged until 1800, when Say's first work of political economy was published, the *Olbie, ou Essai sur les moyens d'améliorer les mœurs d'une nation*. This chapter explores some of the contributions to the manners controversy made by writers with whom Say came into contact in the 1790s, and particularly Rœderer, whose perspective on manners attracted Say in the aftermath of the Terror.

2   CLAVIÈRE'S *ASSIGNAT* SOLUTION

The political economy detailed in *De la France* and other pre-revolutionary work was directed against Calonne, whose policy Clavière sought to challenge and whose person he slandered. But Clavière was still more critical of Necker, in spite of the public confidence expressed in him at the beginning of his second ministry in late August 1789. Since 1781, Clavière had seen Necker as a traitor to his country of origin, Geneva, because he refused to condemn the growing power of the aristocracy. Necker's opposition to the popular Genevan revolution of 1782 provided further evidence of a commitment to inequality and social hierarchy. His antagonism towards free trade was consistent with Clavière's claim that his political economy rested upon a justification of oligarchy. In 1789 Clavière built on these accusations by mounting a vitriolic campaign, in league with Mirabeau, intended to show that Necker's political economy continued that of his despotic predecessors. As such, it would leave the corrupt manners of the French nation intact, and ensure the failure of any attempt to create a popular constitution or solve the debt problem. Necker's errors in public finance were ascribed to a misunderstanding of British experience. From Necker's perspective the issue was not whether the state was bankrupt but which political edifice could be relied upon to maintain credit. Although he had opposed the British model of constitutional form throughout his career, by 1789 he had become convinced that Britain's institutional example should be used to increase French credit. To this end he advised the creation of a mixed monarchy maintaining hierarchical ranks and the enactment of commercial laws in imitation of the mercantile system. To Clavière, Britain's successes were the product of the civil liberty, respect for industry and commerce, and the communication between ranks which had been a feature of British political culture since the 1690s. During the subsequent century, however, he was convinced, having read the third and fourth books of the *Wealth of Nations*, that British prosperity had been retarded by policies to control trade, a problem compounded by the excessive powers of the landed aristocracy in parliament and government. As a result, Necker was attributing Britain's commercial development to the shackles that in fact impaired progress. The leading example of this was his support for a national bank modelled on the Bank of England. To Clavière, the bank created in 1694 was the product of an aristocratic cabal in search of self-enrichment, 'a project of calculated speculation . . . of which some crafty individuals took advantage, at the same time as they took advantage of the consolidation of the revolution of 1688.'[2] Necker's faith in such an institution confirmed that he was a Janus-faced revolutionary. Rather than an institution based on hierarchical ranks, Clavière's republican perspective held that France was in need of greater equality. This could only be achieved by the commercialization of culture, involving the patrician classes and the third estate, with the aim of ultimately reducing the acute material inequalities between them. The first step was the creation of private savings banks with the power to underwrite private investment. These bastions of frugality would catalyse economic development, and direct it towards honest endeavours, fully compatible with Rousseau's idea of a good citizen.[3] His intention was to create a moralized political economy by making clear the public interest in economic and political virtue that every citizen could be persuaded or cajoled into embracing. Necker's revival of reason-of-state political economy could thereby be consigned to history.

Clavière's second proposal was conceived as an alternative to Necker's August loans, and subsequent support, in October 1789, for a *contribution patriotique*. To Clavière, such projects were misplaced because the root cause of the financial crisis was a lack of commerce. If commerce was stimulated and credit stabilized over a period of several years, debt and taxation would cease to be issues of public concern. Clavière's preferred first step focussed upon the perceived lack of coin in the realm. Paper money backed by national wealth (*biens nationaux*) was recommended as a solution to this problem. Clavière was tireless in his advocacy and leaned on the authority of the second book of the *Wealth of Nations* for the argument that 'commerce is secure in proportion to the amount of effective legal-tender.'[4] But he believed Smith had erred and tarnished his 'republican' credentials in arguing against a second means to stimulate commerce, the use of gold and silver plate to increase the coinage. Such a measure, Smith ought to have recognized, was worthwhile because it destroyed luxury and excessive wealth just as it affirmed patriotism and equality. This would be the basis for 'true credit', the key to 'a simple and gradual regeneration of the finances of the kingdom'. Tying private industry and public morality together created 'a great common interest', which was secure because it rested upon 'justice, the universal and fecund principle of all prosperity.'[5] Clavière's first project attracted the attention of the National Assembly, which had been issuing public bills carrying interest since September 1789. The nationalization of church property in early November, and the continued failure of Necker's schemes, led Clavière to lobby for large issues of *assignats* representing national wealth and operating as legal tender. His support for this measure, endorsed by the Assembly in April 1790, led him to claim paternity for the *assignats*.[6] He advised the National Assembly to 'unceasingly issue *assignats*, and make them in the largest quantity possible', on the grounds that 'their general use [as money] will reestablish affluence everywhere'.[7] Thus he expected the *assignat* to do far more than repair the hole in the nation's coffers. When an owner of *assignats* decided to redeem them, he would be rewarded with the ownership of tangible property. Commerce in *assignats*, and the national wealth they represented, would stimulate productive industry across the country. Although a slow process, the commercialization of the lower orders of the French nation would increase equality, extend independence, and encourage patriotism. These were the prerequisites of republican constitutionalism.

During the following five months, until Necker's fall from power in September 1790, Clavière continued his attack upon the chief minister and defended the *assignats* against the criticisms of several leading revolutionaries. Necker himself argued before the National Assembly on 27 August that the *assignats* were a paper money that would bankrupt France.[8] Talleyrand had also attacked them on the grounds that they risked the same fate as Law's schemes. Another critical deputy, Camus, stressed the inflationary lesson of American experience of paper money.[9] Condorcet and Dupont de Nemours argued that the *assignats* would drive out silver and other forms of coin, raise prices relative to paper, and thereby dangerously restrict commerce.[10] All of these writers preferred the issue of treasury bills at interest through the *Caisse d'escompte*, a revised tax-system, and increased loans. Clavière responded with the argument that by the summer of 1790 the *assignats* had averted imminent bankruptcy by establishing a working currency at a time of acute political uncertainty, and when taxes had become a symbol of servitude. As long as smaller *assignat* units of currency were issued so that the ordinary people of France gained a stake in the Revolution, political liberty would be safe from financial attack. Clavière again used Smith, without specific reference, to buttress his ideas, claiming that Smith would have given unqualified support to the issue of *assignats*.[11] Clavière emphasized that his faith in the *assignats* did not rest solely upon the wealth they represented. Rather it was their relationship with national sovereignty that made them so important to the Revolution. National sovereignty was a symbol of public unity, probity, and justice. It legitimized the issue of *assignats*, while they in turn promoted economic equality and popular interest in political liberty. He was convinced that the *assignats* were a product of the people's faith in liberty, and proof that they had abandoned the corruptions of the Old Regime. In short, popular manners were virtuous and patriotic enough to foster safe forms of commerce. The political economy of which they formed a part was wholly divorced from the financial practices of despotic states, as the history of France made clear. The association of the *assignats* with despotism, a claim made by all of their critics, was an error:

Have we transported ourselves to the time of Law? What was then the nation? A slave. What was then proposed? An operation founded only on the momentary enthusiasm of ignorant and excitable people, consisting of the issue of an enormous mass of bills, which at the end yielded NOTHING. What did individuals do? They were inflamed by the operation, agitated by extravagant greed, and ultimately ruined themselves and impoverished the nation. Return to the present. The nation is free. What do we propose? To acquit a part of the debt by selling an enormous mass of national wealth, shared-wealth, which is before our eyes and is to be spread everywhere.[12]

After Necker's fall from power Clavière sought to influence the National Assembly through his old ally Mirabeau, until the latter's death in April 1791. His writings justified what Mirabeau called 'the Monetary Constitution', an umbrella term for a political economy which sustained political liberty by securing public credit and creating affluence.[13] Its linchpin was currency reform. Necker had admitted to the National Assembly in October 1789, 'there is no more credit, and genuine currency has entirely disappeared'.[14] After November 1790 Clavière too recognized that the Revolution had failed to resolve the national financial crisis. He began to argue that circumstances required more than the establishment of the *assignat* as legal tender.

Before the end of 1790, Clavière's published writings had dealt with the reorganization of the national treasury, taxation, and freedom of trade both domestically and internationally.[15] He favoured a treasury with powers to borrow and lend at profit, independent of the executive, with permanent officials elected by taxpayers, and with inspection to be carried out by experts appointed by the legislature.[16] A *commissaire* appointed by the king would also monitor impropriety. Such an institution would distinguish French administration from the British, where 'the interest of a corrupting regime has prevailed.' The taxes considered most equitable were those levied on land and income. Although indirect taxes on consumption goods were held to be less fair, Clavière accepted their necessity and advised involving the 'entrepreneurial class' in their administration. When combined with free internal trade, and a commercial treaty with free states such as America, Clavière believed he had summarized 'the reforms linked with the system of liberty' stemming from the principle that 'morality is the sole sure guide in politics'.[17] These ideas made up what Clavière called the *principes libéraux* of a true citizen.[18]

3 REGENERATIVE WAR

As the divisions within the nation became more marked after the flight to Varennes and the massacre of the Champs de Mars, Clavière began to have doubts about his perception of national sovereignty. Voices in the new Constituent Assembly expressed greater concern about a perceived decline of trade. The *assignats* were rapidly being discredited, having fallen to 70% of their value in *livres* by the beginning of 1792. Clavière had always argued that creating liberty in France was far from easy and inevitably 'excited storms'.[19] But because of the fervour with which the nation had embraced liberty in 1789, he had failed to anticipate the civil war sparked by religious controversy and the flight of the emigrés. He was equally surprised by the continued financial collapse. The early acts of the National Assembly, and the support of the general populace, was evidence of an improvement in the quality of national manners. This was the premise of all of his reforms; the Revolution 'multiplies wise and honest men' and 'reconciles the passion for the public good with gentle sociability'.[20] Late in 1791 he accepted that he had exaggerated the qualities of national manners, and therefore the benefits to be reaped from national sovereignty. It became essential to formulate a political economy that more actively defended liberty, requiring measures far more extensive and intrusive than hitherto contemplated. Persuasion and incentives had failed to republicanize the populace. It became necessary to consider means of coercing and ultimately forcing people to be free.

Clavière's change in perspective can be traced to a pamphlet written for the *Societé des Amis des Noirs* in July 1791, the background to which was the question of what to do with France's colonial empire and more particularly the oligarchic and slave-based colonies of the West Indies.[21] A leading figure in the Constituent Assembly, Barnave, proposed on 15 May that France support the colonial sugar planters' refusal to allow non-whites to become citizens. He recommended that violent action be taken against the slave rebellions in St Dominique and Martinique. Clavière reiterated the popular arguments that such acts violated the right of all men to political representation, and the philosophical principle of human perfectibility, adding that abolition of slave traffic would increase French commerce. The claim of crucial importance, however, was that a class existed in the colonies that challenged both national sovereignty and liberty. The malign personal interest of the white planters impeded the exercise of political virtue. This could only be combated by asserting the powers of the metropolis to demolish the political power of the planters, and by establishing a free constitution, requiring 'national education [to] complete the revolution'. The relevance of this perspective to the upheavals of domestic politics needed no emphasis. Clavière believed that in the persons and ideas of Barnave and the Lameth brothers, a similar process could be perceived; self-interest was becoming a revolutionary solvent. Aristocracy had been formally abolished but a species of nobility had re-emerged in the midst of the Revolution. Furthermore, national education had clearly not prevented civil war in France. At this time, Clavière's unconvincing response was to restate his faith in peace through commercial development, 'which is more or less great, according to the extent of civilization and liberty'.[22]

Louis XVI's flight to Varennes, which marked the final crack in the foundation stones of 1789, led Clavière to address the problem more directly. The death of Mirabeau, so often Clavière's mouthpiece, was an additional source of the growing unease about national division. In August 1791 Clavière demanded an extension of the *assignats* through low value issues for the poor.[23] The arguments he now used were less confident, more sceptical about human nature's capacity for virtue and more immediately concerned with the future of the Revolution. The 'work of liberty' was described as being in jeopardy, necessitating national defence of the *assignats* not simply to avoid bankruptcy but to prevent manners being overwhelmed by poverty or profiteering. Such measures alone would 'sustain the Constitution' and combat egoism.[24] The crisis of late 1791 was described as a product of public and private immorality, pitting the forces of virtue against ignorance, idleness, and luxury. The work that most clearly sketched this new position appeared in November 1791; it maintained that public credit and commerce were favourable to virtue and had the power to resolve present difficulties.[25] Much of this rehearsed by-now-jaded arguments, using the statistics of Montesquiou to show the reduction of debt since 1789 and to prove that 'we have acquired, in becoming a nation, an inexhaustible source of wealth'. This countered the view that the *assignats* were unwitting enemies of the Revolution. Nicolas Bergasse had argued in *Le Moniteur* of April 1791 that the *assignats* were the antithesis of the ancient virtues France needed to sustain the Revolution; he supported an 'honest bankruptcy' to wipe out the debt and make it possible to abandon the *assignats*. To Clavière such a step would jeopardize the gains of 1789 by further dividing the nation, sowing mistrust where concord and sociability had steadily developed. Although Clavière's definition of bankruptcy changed when he accepted Delaunay's demand that the short-term interest payments on the debt be suspended, he continued to support payment for those who could prove that they were government creditors. Clavière developed this view against Condorcet's criticism that the fall in the value of the *assignats* would undermine all commerce, and thereby destroy the very industrious manners Clavière defended.[26] Before the Constituent Assembly Clavière announced that the value of the *assignats* would not fall so long as they were explicitly tied to tangible national wealth.[27]

However, he now declared that this would only be the case if speculators, employed by Pitt and the governments of Austria and Prussia, were prevented from conspiring against them. The speech revealed that Clavière was moving towards what was to be his final position on the *assignat* question, envisaging their defence through a general attack on the enemies of the Revolution. Republican political economy would not be complete without the destruction of the aristocratic ranks that continued to foster egoism, both in France and abroad.

Clavière's manifesto, intended to resolve the problems of the Revolution while bringing him to political office, was published by the *Cercle social* early in 1792 and serialized in the *Chronique du mois*.[28] The title of the work revealed the new element in his political economy. It identified a 'conspiracy against the finances' and contained 'measures to put an end to their effects'. As ever, he identified the *assignats* with 'French fidelity', the antithesis of 'intrigue and favour, corruption and wild prodigality.' But he acknowledged that the latter forces were now rampant: 'public spirit . . . is more uneasy than enlightened', and traced the problem to those classes which had put their own greed before the public good. First in line came the bankers, 'the most perfidious speculators . . . born for the misery of humanity' who 'enrich themselves on our ruins'.[29] They had attacked the *assignats* by speculating on their domestic collapse and by rejecting them as currency for international trade. More culpable still were 'the embezzler Calonne' and 'the aristocrat Pitt', representing the noble ranks who would stop at nothing to destroy the Revolution. From London they had unceasingly plotted to debase the currency and devastate trade, issuing counterfeit *assignats* in Paris, and organizing the governments and financiers of Europe to join a counter-revolutionary cabal. This had been successful because 'it costs far less to destroy the finances of a nation by the manoeuvres of a banker than by war.'[30] Extreme measures had to be taken to counter these machinations. The evils ranged against the *assignats* were so great that only a war against hierarchical ranks would save the Revolution: 'The people has suffered from aristocracy; now they [the aristocrats] will suffer from liberty'. The focus of Clavière's hatred was the coalition of states he held responsible for the collapse of the *assignat*: 'Therefore, our first financial operation will be a war against the coalition of princes.'[31] Clavière argued that this 'defensive war' would be successful only if it allied 'free and industrious nations' against absolutist states with hereditary aristocracies. He believed that this necessitated a British alliance to vanquish the central European powers threatening France. Given Pitt's place as Prime Minister such a demand may have appeared utopian, but Clavière, perhaps because of conversations with Paine, was convinced that if the French combined the 'constitutional renunciation of imperial conquest' with 'an appeal to public opinion in Britain' peace would speedily be established and Pitt thrown from office. After all, Britain was beginning to feel the effects of reduced trade with France, while the depreciation of the *assignat* had made French goods cheaper abroad. Furthermore, Clavière was certain that 'the national will' in Britain sought 'universal civilization', the 'great enterprise, sacred to all honest men, which ennobles commerce. . . .' Those who argued that Britain was a mercantile state, in natural alliance with Prussia and Russia, were mistaken, as the victories of the revolutionary armies revealed. Clavière's war was to be financed by the issue of interest-bearing treasury bills, a scheme similar to Necker and Condorcet's of 1789, and a general tax on inheritance, because it was the least damaging to 'industrious men'. Equally, the *assignats* were no longer to be associated with the debt but with national wealth in land, and gradually burned, as their owners took up the assets they represented. This radical plan for armed conflict against the immoral ranks of Europe would succeed, Clavière believed, because 'Our national resources have never been more active'. Patriotism and national morality would be strengthened in a civil war for the protection of republican virtue. Against those writers, such as Burke, for whom the war signified a return to traditional reason-of-state political economy, Clavière held the war to be a moral imperative.

In *De la conjuration* Clavière promised a general work on the principles of taxation for a new republic. His rise to power as Minister of Public Contributions in the first Girondin ministry, however, prevented him from publishing further theoretical works. His remaining writings were concerned with the promotion of the approach to political economy sketched in *De la conjuration*. Support for war was reiterated before the Jacobin club in April 1792.[32] During this month he responded to the critique of Montesquiou, previously an ally, who had attacked Clavière's proposed bank and suspension of immediate interest payments on the debt.[33] Their relationship was finally severed by Clavière's planned annexation of Geneva, which he believed would improve the finances of France, while bolstering republican manners.[34] Returning to power later in the year, from 10 August 1792 to 22 January 1793, Clavière's defence of republican manners and commerce was beginning to ring hollow. His October budget included schemes to raise revenue from landed and mobile wealth, from stamp and patent duties, and from state monopolies in the mint, the arms trade, and gambling. Although he remained fearful of the effect of lotteries on manners, Clavière acknowledged the dire need of the state for revenue.[35] Despite the proclamation of the first year of the French Republic, and Clavière's eminent place as its first minister of finance, his republican faith was on the wane. The rhetoric of his ministerial statements resounded to the 'victory of the cause of liberty', but could not hide the serious condition of the finances and the economy. He did, however, retain some confidence in the liberty of trade for the subsistence of the people.[36] These final ministerial statements were increasingly desperate. Having defended the *assignats* for four years, Clavière realized that his hopes had come to naught. The republic's finances remained in turmoil and the citizens prone to political violence; commerce was stagnating while the people were unable to throw off the yoke of monarchical manners. The *assignats*, an anonymous writer declared, were a force for despotism: 'The new regime of monetary administration, in making the presidents and counsellors disappear, has only created new abuses.'[37] By 1793 Clavière had lost all confidence in the perpetual peace between commercial nations that he had espoused in the 1780s. This was the republican crisis of political economy recognized by Saint-Just and many others; it was essential to use force to create virtuous manners in a country where monarchs had ruled for two millennia. Terror was becoming an extreme but oft-cited means to such an end.[38] Clavière did not live long enough to develop further solutions. With other ministers of the Gironde he was arrested in June 1793, having been vilified as a machiavellian English agent who had taken up French citizenship only to undermine the state.[39]

While imprisoned in Paris on 2 December 1793 Clavière killed himself by stabbing an ivory dagger into his own heart.

4   THE TERROR SOLUTION

Once Clavière's *assignats* had failed to provide a foundation for republican manners the compatibility of republican virtue with liberty and commerce came to be questioned. Yet on this issue the Girondins and the Jacobins were at one. In many respects the Jacobins who were dominating the Convention were developing the ideas of their enemies first outlined in 1791. For Saint-Just it was necessary to proclaim a state of martial law and in the name of virtue override the liberty that was hitherto perceived as the essence of the Revolution. Coming to public notice as a defender of the mixed constitution of 1791, which he believed combined the virtues of monarchy and democracy, Saint-Just had at first followed Clavière, expecting political liberty to stimulate commerce and thereby ensure a 'durable revolution'. He was, however, fearful of the 'misuse' of liberty and underlined the need for new manners to produce a stable polity. Clavière's perspective on the *assignats* was initially favoured for this reason.[40] When the constitution collapsed Saint-Just changed his mind. This was made clear in a speech to the Convention on 29 November 1792, responding to the demands for price-fixing by the commune of Paris and the committee of agriculture and commerce.[41] Saint-Just defended liberty of trade, but only in conditions where the people were 'uncorrupted'. He argued that Smith, Montesquieu, and the physiocrats, had been mistaken because of this last point. In corrupt conditions it was necessary to ask 'what are the limits of this liberty [of trade]?' This view accorded with Robespierre's rambling speech to the Convention on 8 Thermidor year 2 stating that 'The counter-revolution can be found in the administration of finances . . . It seeks to encourage speculation, to weaken public credit by dishonouring French patriotism, to favour rich financiers, and to push the impoverished poor to despair . . . The counter-revolution is in every branch of political economy.'[42] Political economists could not conceive of the variety of circumstances in which liberty might be exercised, and had therefore erected general laws of minimal applicability to France's condition. As Saint-Just put it, 'I dare to say that a good treatise of practical economy cannot exist.' The *assignats* had failed because popular manners did not accord with the economics of paper money. Liberty had made a war on morality, and the republic had therefore to be fashioned from base metal; the state was in the difficult position of making a republic from vices. The solution was to commence the reformation of manners in two stages. To reform manners in the economic sphere Saint-Just sought to reduce currency issues, cover the debt by grants of land, allow payment of taxes in kind, and rely on free internal trade and public granaries to combat famine. These measures would, he claimed, encourage the work ethic so crucial to republican manners and so alien to monarchy:

Under the monarchy the source of our corruption was the heart of all the kings: corruption is not natural to peoples . . . it is the fruit of idleness and power; the principle of manners is that everyone works for the benefit of the country, and that no one is enslaved or idle. Where there is work and activity in a State, the more this State is secure.[43]

The second step was to combat political corruption by pursuing the separation of powers to its logical conclusion. Saint-Just aimed to sever executive and legislative functions completely, strictly mandating representatives elected from the departments, and rigidly tying the hands of ministers. He thereby moved from the position of Rœderer before the Revolution to that of Rousseau's *Gouvernement de Pologne*.

The problem facing Saint-Just on attaining political power was that which had perplexed Clavière: bread, peace, and liberty remained elusive goals. Where Clavière had merely blamed the forces of counter-revolution, Saint-Just actively sought to destroy them. In doing this he moved beyond Clavière, by proclaiming that the reformation of manners necessitated the invocation of revolutionary government to stamp out the enemies of virtue. The tragedy was that he saw them everywhere—from being fellow representatives of the people the Girondins had become traitors[44]: 'the Republic will be founded only when the sovereign will restrains the monarchical minority, and reigns over it by right of conquest . . . It is necessary to govern by iron those who cannot be governed by justice: it is necessary to destroy the tyrants.'[45] Revolutionary government, controlling subsistence and justice, could put an end to the abuse of liberty that had so far tainted the Revolution. The result would be virtuous, republican, revolutionary men, able and willing to die for the state:

A revolutionary man is uncompromising, but he is judicious, he is frugal; he is simple without displaying luxury or false modesty; he is the irreconcilable enemy of every deceit, every indulgence, every affectation. As his aim is to see the triumph of the Revolution, he never censures it, but he condemns his enemies without allowing himself to be engulfed by them; he does not rage against them but he enlightens them . . . A revolutionary man is full of honour; he is policed without being weak, and willingly, because he is at peace with his heart . . . he is jealous for the glory of his country and for liberty, but does nothing hastily; he fights in battle, pursues the culpable and defends the innocent in the tribunals . . . for the Revolution to succeed he knows that he must be as good now as people were bad before; his probity is not the product of calculation, but a quality of the heart and something well-understood. Marat was gentle among his family and only terrified traitors. J.-J. Rousseau was a revolutionary, and never impertinent: I must conclude that a revolutionary man is a hero of good sense and probity.[46]

Policing the people did not merely necessitate revolutionary government and martial law. Saint-Just proclaimed: 'Create civilizing institutions . . . liberty cannot survive without them.' In the remaining days of his life Saint-Just repeated these injunctions.[47] After he fell victim to the guillotine a plan for a work on republican institutions was discovered among his papers, delivering his final verdict that institutions were vital to inculcate stoicism, the moral code which would protect commerce from tarnishing the Revolution:

Institutions are the guarantee of public liberty, they moralize the government and civil state, repress the jealousies which create factions, maintain the fragile distinction between truth and hypocrisy, innocence, and crime . . . Institutions are the guarantee of the government of a free people against the corruption of manners, and the guarantee of the people and of the citizen against the corruption of government . . . Stoicism, which is the virtue of the spirit and the soul, alone can prevent the corruption of a commercial republic which lacks manners. A republican government must have virtue for its principle; if not, there is only Terror. What governs those who wish neither virtue nor Terror?[48]

Like Clavière, Saint-Just did not perceive himself to be returning to reason-of-state justi-
fications of immoral policy. Rather, he shared with the Girondins the belief that without republican virtue, moral forms of commerce and a republican constitution,
modern citizens would never be free. Those who rejected these claims were deemed to
be so dangerous to France at this time that they had to be imprisoned, assassinated or
executed. In the battle to unify the republican manners of the government, differences
of opinion became exaggerated, resulting in the death of numerous innocents on the
false ground of treachery against the Republic. This extreme form of republican political economy did not end with the Terror. It was used by the Directory after the problematic elections of Prairial and Fructidor (1797), when the populace appeared to be
polarizing between Jacobins and Royalists. Although he opposed the Terror, Say was
fully aware of this form of republican political economy and justified it in his journalism for *La Décade*, once again showing the extent of Clavière's influence.

5   REPUBLICANISM TRANSFORMED

With the collapse of the constitution of 1791 and the failure of the *assignats* to restore
fiscal confidence, many revolutionaries perceived themselves to be in uncharted intellectual waters. Creating a republic in a large commercial state, where the citizens'
manners had been corrupted by monarchy, remained an unachieved project. Rœderer
captured the tenor of contemporary feeling in arguing that to establish a republic in
France it was necessary 'to expose the futility of historical reasoning on this subject.'[49]
Against Vandermonde, the first professor of political economy at the *École normale de
Paris*, who likened the ideal society to a hive of bees living without government,
Rœderer claimed that a republican constitution remained essential, but that the first
step towards such a goal was to resolve the problem of manners.[50] This issue was taken
up in 1792 and 1793 by numerous writers, including, significantly, Condorcet and Sieyès.
Condorcet, like Clavière, was unsurprised at the demise of the constitution of 1791. Its
'radical vice' had been to incorporate monarchical influence over law into a political
edifice erected on the principle of popular sovereignty. Condorcet's perception was that
its legacy would be the rise of a Cromwell figure who would ignore the demands of the
people and 'prevent the establishment of a republican constitution'.[51] He had become
convinced of the merits of 'the sovereignty of the people, equality among men, and the
unity of the republic' after the King's flight to Varennes, but he made clear in all of his
writings that the republican project was not synonymous with the abolition of monarchy but rather necessitated the reformation of manners.[52] This was a peculiarity of
French republicanism to be contrasted, for example, with that developed in North
America. Once more following in Clavière's footsteps, Condorcet had become fascinated by 'morals, or the art of good conduct'. This art was intended to stand beside 'the
social art', intended to establish political and constitutional rights, and 'the art of
administration', intended to resolve the problems of public finance. With Sieyès and
Duhamel, Condorcet founded the *Journal d'instruction sociale* in May 1793 as a means of
combating the 'prejudices which continue to enslave nations'; their avowed aim was to
'teach people to reason' in order not to be 'fooled by Caesars and Cromwells'.[53]

Condorcet believed it necessary to abandon *assignat* schemes and attempts to enforce models of republican behaviour, and focus on the civic education provided by 'a national programme of public instruction'.[54] His project entailed the creation of five levels of educational institutions, with *écoles primaires* for all boys and girls aged between six and eleven, five-hundred *écoles secondaires* providing a further three years of instruction, over a hundred specialist *instituts* intended to replace the *collèges* of the Old Regime, ten *lycées* in place of the twenty-two universities, and at the summit a *Société nationale des arts et sciences*. The first aim of these public structures was to provide a practical education in all that was deemed to be useful to the lives of republican citizens. For example, a premium was placed on the study of 'the moral and political sciences' and 'the application of science to the industrial arts'. The second aim was to provide state support for the men of genius whom Condorcet believed could best advise revolutionary legislators and thereby direct the course of the Revolution by the 'light of reason'. To this end the *Société nationale* was to bring together the most advanced minds in the mathematical and physical sciences, literature, and the fine arts, the best inventors, and the leaders of moral and political science, among whom Condorcet included exponents of 'social science, public law, political economy, and history'. But the key aim of public instruction provided the central argument of what was to become Condorcet's most influential work, the *Esquisse d'un tableau historique des progrès de l'esprit humain*: for a successful revolution every individual had to be taught to exercise their rational faculty. Written before Condorcet's death in prison in 1794, the *Esquisse* was a final attempt to combat the pessimism about the Revolution induced by the Terror, and to prove that the formation of a successful economic and moral republic was the ultimate destiny of France. It revealed what he termed the 'general facts' of modern societies, which were conceived as empirical foundations for the moral codes of republican life.[55] Proof of progress was factually evident in the works of the great philosophers through history. If such works were studied, universally certain truths could increasingly be seen to characterize the writings of philosophers and, more importantly, the laws of the societies in which they had lived. History became the leading human science: it was no longer a conjectural enterprise but the fount of certain information about the creation of the ideal republic. One of the most important examples of a general fact was the value of free trade. Condorcet argued that 'more liberal rules of commerce' were a force making for human perfectibility, regardless of the politics or conditions of particular societies.[56] Where the benefits of economic liberty were recognized, political liberty was promoted, and manners became more sociable and less corrupt. Equally, where political liberty reigned, economic liberty would inevitably follow. These species of liberty were mutually reinforcing, and had been beneficial in every kind of state. By developing legislative strategies based on general facts a republic would be created without privilege, the hierarchy of ranks, or dangerous forms of luxury.

In the *Journal d'instruction sociale* Sieyès too recognized that the constitutional innovations he had advocated in 1789 were doomed to failure without cultural regeneration. Sieyès shared with Condorcet the goal of equipping citizens with the moral and political information necessary to republican life, and proposed a scheme, to be sponsored by the state, for the propagation of elementary books in every branch of instruction: 'literary, intellectual, physical, moral, and industrial . . . to embrace every aspect of life.'[57] But Sieyès was less optimistic than Condorcet about the individual's capacity to reason independently, and thereby enlighten their own self-interest. He was acutely aware that human needs 'when the social state arrives, are not the work of nature.' Rather, habit, 'that second or third nature', determined the pursuit either of 'true happiness' or, more frequently, 'a mass of fictitious needs'. As a result, 'the most important object of morality and consequently instruction must be to recall men to simple and natural needs, to habits and passions lightly worn, but with a positive effect on happiness'.[58] To Sieyès, sobriety, economy, and industriousness were the cardinal virtues of republican society.[59] Their pursuit necessitated a republican constitution but also the creation of institutions to *direct* individual practices. Sieyès' plan, presented to the Convention's Committee of Public Instruction on June 26 1793, encompassed Condorcet's universal *écoles primaires* for the development of the mind and body. However, the centrepiece of his strategy was a system of local, district, provincial, and national fêtes, to commemorate 'the work of nature, of human society, and of the French Revolution'. For example, each locality, called by Sieyès a 'canton', would celebrate on fifteen distinct occasions the beginning of work in the countryside, enclosure and fencing, domestic animals, youth, marriage, maternity, old age, the perfection of language, the invention of writing, the origins of commerce and the arts, the art of navigation and fishing, the first political union, the sovereignty of the people, popular elections, and a selected subject of local pride. Each district would commemorate the return of spring, the harvest, the gathering in of grapes or some other local crop, ancestors, equality, liberty, justice, and benevolence. Each *departement* would celebrate the four seasons at the time of the equinox or solstice, the arts and sciences, printing, peace and just war, the destruction of social orders, the recognition of the unity of the people on 17 June 1789, and the abolition of particular privileges on 4 August 1789. The entire republic would come together to recall 'visible nature' on 1 May, fraternity on 1 January, the French Revolution on 14 July, the abolition of the monarchy on 10 August, and 'the republic one and indivisible' on the day the new constitution was to be accepted.[60] A system of prizes was intended to maximise competition among citizens and cantons in carrying out each fête. These institutions were to be seconded by national theatres with the identical aim of guiding popular manners away from violence and towards virtue, by means of constant practice and reward rather than reason.

Condorcet and Sieyès transformed their earlier faith in republican constitutionalism by accepting Clavière's focus on the centrality of popular culture, the *mœurs* of the people. Against Clavière and Saint-Just, however, they continued to oppose explicit coercion and they maintained faith in civic instruction. Condorcet, to the last, believed that men could be distinguished from animals by their capacity to reason and argued that once the sources of superstitition, aristocracies, churches and monarchs, were abolished, the people would be enabled to live rational and virtuous lives. As Sieyès had less faith in the people's potential rationality, he became convinced of the need to manipulate the passions and direct them towards republican virtue. An emphasis upon the primacy of the passions, redolent of Hume, distinguishes Sieyès's work from

Condorcet's, but they shared a belief in the possibility of the legislative shaping of modern political cultures. In Rœderer's hands the shift of the intellectual movement of the Revolution from constitution building to national manners was most pronounced and also developed as an alternative to Terror. His goal was a science of *mœurs*, the prospect of which fascinated Say as a journalist at *La Décade*.

6   A SCIENCE OF *MŒURS*

Rœderer's response to the collapse of the constitution of 1791, presented as a course of lectures delivered to the *Lycée* in the Spring of 1793, was more detailed and systematic, although it was indebted to both Condorcet's and Sieyès' perspectives on manners.[61] Rœderer was impressed by Condorcet's emphasis on teaching individuals—and especially children—to reason independently, and by the demand that the moral and political sciences be modelled on the natural sciences. However, he agreed with Sieyès that the force of habit was greater than that of reason, and consequently that institutions to instil the republican virtues by repetition and commemoration were at least as important as *écoles primaires*. What distinguished Rœderer's view was the argument that manners could be precisely defined for successful living and that the republican legislator, through exact physiological knowledge of the workings of human nature, could develop strategies to ensure the propagation and stability of such manners. As a result he believed he was 'doing something new' by 'observing for the first time the things which exist before the eyes of the world', and in the process developing a new form of republicanism for the modern world. The *Cours* that gave substance to these claims was written while the Convention debated the proper form of a republican constitution for France and as Robespierre was gradually tightening his grip on Paris and commencing the enforcement of his conception of republican manners by means of Terror. Rœderer confessed that his work was written 'from the tomb' with the aim of confronting 'the doctrine of demagogy' and defending property by revealing its just foundation and legitimate use in the service of humanity.[62] The lectures thus formulated an extensive critique of the republicanism derived from ancient sources, called by Rœderer l'*antiqu'archie*, which he believed to be intellectually responsible for the policy of 'the modern levellers' or Jacobins.[63] The books held responsible for reviving ancient republicanism were Rousseau's *Discours sur l'inégalité*, Mably's *Doutes aux économistes, Principes de législation*, and *Lettres sur les constitutions des États-Unis*, and finally a work which Rœderer ascribed to Diderot but which was in fact by Morelly, the *Code de la nature*. Such works had developed a critique of modern wealth and commerce, social structures, and culture, by contrast with the ethic of self-sacrifice for the public good, equality, and valour that were held to have characterized ancient Sparta, Athens, and republican Rome. Jacobins such as Robespierre and Marat had adopted these themes and applied them to France, perceiving the corruption of manners to be due to a failure to learn the lessons of the ancient republics, and mounting an attack on those who favoured the commercialization of French life.

Rœderer's attack on this position stemmed from his view that societies were successful not because of the form of government which they enjoyed, or the particular laws which had been instituted, but in proportion to the development of what he called 'the social organization', or the means of acquiring subsistence and securing self-preservation:

The social organization does not consist solely in the organization of government. Social science does not consist uniquely in public right . . . What then is the social organization proper? It is the arrangement of men and property which makes the human species reproduce and conserve themselves, so that the land produces subsistence for all men, and all the accumulated funds, or capitals, unite with all the forms of labour and the fruits of the land, as if they were the product of a property exploited in common.

All successful societies, he argued, have the same social organization, characterized by three forms of property and three forms of labour. Property had to exist in land, capital, and in the particular skills of individuals, and to have extended labour in agriculture, manufactures, and commerce. There was a natural historical progress of opulence from basic forms of agriculture to manufactures and foreign commerce, because 'there is a law of nature which carries men to experience new satisfactions' and 'to extend pleasures is to diversify them.' The division of labour led individuals to specialize and become interdependent, allowing the greater satisfaction of their own needs. Rœderer believed these claims were based on the facts of human nature and could be seen operating in the recent history of Europe, with the rise to prominence of states with specialized economies such as Holland and Switzerland, and those with mutually supporting agricultural and manufacturing sectors such as Britain. Those who favoured a return to ancient republicanism were confusing the old world with the new. By 'ancient states' Rœderer meant both ancient republics and early-modern monarchies, because he believed that feudal states were merely variations of an older social organization founded on slavery. The social organization of all these states was backward, because 'these peoples knew no property . . . and no commerce'. A small elite of citizens controlled the government and owned the slaves or forced the many to labour through the enforcement of feudal dues such as the *corvée*. Women and children were subjected to a patriarchal tyranny. Life was insecure and impoverished, foreign and civil wars frequent, and 'the happiness of the many was sacrificed to the happiness of the few'.[64] Above all, if such a model were adopted by a modern state in which the division of labour had created a more sophisticated social organization, the collapse of production would result, because it would entail 'giving land to the dissipator, the idle, and the impotent'. Rœderer countered the argument that ancient states were more powerful because of the valour of their devoted citizenry, claiming that the invention of gunpowder had reduced the need for individual valour, and that modern states were powerful in proportion to the size of their population and the extent of their commerce and manufactures. In any case, modern manners had 'softened', and could never be restored to their ancient state. What the modern world needed was 'equality with abundance and not with insufficiency', and 'a fecund liberty rather than one which impoverishes'. By condemning the forces of economic development, advocates of ancient modes of living were combating what Rœderer called 'the principle of conservation' with which he believed a benevolent Creator had endowed humanity, in order to ensure their progress.

The second mistake of the 'levellers' was to assume that creating republican laws and a republican constitution would remake French society in the image of the ancient Franks, Romans, and Spartans. In fact, Rœderer argued, the history of the Revolution itself revealed the limitations of republican constitutionalism and directed any independent spectator to 'a different guarantor of the social organization than the government, consisting of a perfect fusion of all the interests of society into one, in instruction or enlightenment, which creates public opinion, and also in the manners or habits which ensure that this opinion is respected.' Rœderer believed that 'manners are more powerful than laws, and that laws without manners have no empire'. His aim was to place manners 'next to enlightenment and public opinion, as means of reviving or replacing laws which are ancient or exhausted', developing institutions founded on 'the moral and physiological nature of man'. The springs of the social organization 'are the physical and moral faculties. Intellectual and moral qualities give this organization more or less force, according to their conformity with its power or disposition to weaken it . . . it follows that a greater number of political and moral elements [of man] are to be found under the scalpel of an anatomist than in all the recitals of the historian or the fables of the moralist or politician . . . It would clearly be worthwhile to reduce politics and morals to rules as certain and as evident as those of geometry.'[65]

Despite his attack on their ideas, Rœderer was no less of a revolutionary than the radical Jacobins. He was as critical as they were of physiocracy, 'the other known system of organizing society'. The social structures favoured by the physiocrats derived from a view of society 'as a great exercise in rural-exploitation', in which 'the farm is a vast workshop', dominated by a class of large proprietors 'who are by nature a corps of nobility on whom all the powers must be conferred.' At the apex of this social hierarchy stood the man who owned the most land, the 'sovereign–despotic king', whose power was limited only by 'the despotism of evidence' or physiocratic law-code, which demanded that cultivation be maximized. Rœderer condemned this perspective on society for combining the worst aspects of arbitrary monarchical power with a dangerously strong nobility. As a result, the lower orders of France had been oppressed by the physiocratic experiments of the 1760s and 1770s, and the movement had been 'unable to create twenty farms similar to those which have existed in their thousands for a hundred years in England', explaining the wealth of 'that beautiful country'. In Rœderer's eyes, physiocracy conceived of agricultural workers without land as slaves to be worked to death, and he damned the social organization erected on their principles as unstable.[66] A third way of organizing society, which avoided the pitfalls of levelling and physiocracy, was Rœderer's aim, a form of republicanism which combined the pursuit of wealth and the commercialization of society with the practice of traditional republican virtues. The most important of these was labour, but the virtues of moderation, frugality, reciprocal respect, and fraternity were added. All physiologists and anatomists knew that human beings were 'calculating machines' whose faculties responded to sensations by seeking to avoid pain and enjoy pleasure. Building on 'Bonnet, Locke, and Condillac's analysis of the senses', Rœderer wanted to imitate chemistry in seeking the moral *elements* of human behaviour, and thereby achieve epistemological certainty. Since the passions were the means of satisfying the desires produced by the working of the faculties on sensations, Rœderer commenced what he called 'a genealogy of the passions' in order to reveal their 'empire' and subject it to legislative control in the interests of humanity. All human beings, Rœderer argued, sought what he termed 'safety', the 'sentiment of security', and the certainty of self-preservation. This dominant need required the ownership and exercise of property, meaning 'the free use of all that is gained by labour, saving, or inheritance, and the use of the land for subsistence.' Equally important was liberty, 'the free use of the faculties which ensure that the ownership of property is translated into subsistence and enjoyment'. Human beings were created to seek safety by such means by their unique physiological organization, programmed to self-conservation by the union of the faculties and the experience of particular sensations. 'Sensibility' represented the union of these forces and determined the actions of the human will by creating fleeting or longer-term tastes and aversions, generically labelled 'affections'. Constant preferences or repugnances manifested themselves as passions which 'pressed on the will' by means of two levers, 'fear' and 'hope', directing the will to particular objects and experiences. Pleasures and pains could in turn be divided into physical and moral categories, and subdivided into resulting passions that sought to embrace or avoid them. While physical passions sought the biological needs of food, drink, physical love, rest after action, and activity after rest, the moral passions were composites of these needs in which the faculty of 'foresight' was exercised, and in consequence associated with the idea of future pleasures. Examples included wealth, power, glory, and moral love. Such passions were intellectual, and valued because they gave access to physical pleasures; and it was such moral passions which 'we see reign in the world'.[67]

What Rœderer called the 'direction' of the passions, making them virtues or vices when assessed by reference to public interest, was in his view determined by 'the spirit that enlightens us', the rational or calculating faculty that sought the safety and interest of the self. This could be reinforced or overruled by a still more powerful force, the 'moral habits or manners learned in infancy'. Rœderer acknowledged that this force was of little importance in contemporary France, where the goal of all republicans was to extinguish the monarchical manners and deferential habits of the Old Regime. The intensity of the passions was affected by a 'temperament' that could be 'bilious, sanguine or phlegmatic', and in consequence 'act with more or less effect on the fibres and fluids of the body' and 'give more or less energy to the will'. Temperament did not govern the passions but reinforced the effect of the spirit, making men courageous or cowardly, virtuous or examples of *honnêtes gens*, who, if they did not commit crimes, turned a blind eye towards infractions of the public good. The combined force of spirit and temperament created an individual's 'character', which influenced the duration of each passion and 'the habitual state of a man'. Rœderer's grand conclusion to this dissection of the psyche, in the stating of which he acknowledged a debt to Helvétius, was that 'social institutions can act upon men, and make them fulfil their common duties . . . the legislator can ensure that the only actions open to the will are useful and virtuous.' The practices associated with the empassioned pursuit of wealth, glory, love, or power, could be directed towards virtuous or vicious deeds. For example, 'To make a Leonidas, Horatius Cocles, Curtius, or Decius, it is only necessary to place [individuals]

in a similar country and circumstances to these great men.' Similarly, 'in a country
where the force of government makes it impossible to attach glory to the public good,
pride becomes vanity'. Rœderer's example was once more derived from Rome, 'where
tyranny bred evil heroes' such as 'Marius, Sulla, and Octavian'. An identical analysis
could be undertaken for each passion. He claimed that 'the love of women can produce
the most sublime virtues or abase and degrade women themselves.' Under a despotic or
monarchical government, where women were a species of property, their actions 'extin-
guished civic passions'. By contrast, in free states, 'where government has allowed profit
to be attached to the need for love, and where institutions and manners ensure the
possession of women as prizes for valour and service', Rœderer claimed that 'heroes
and men of virtue' were commonplace. France should follow the Spartan example of
allowing young women to crown publicly heroes and censor criminals and cowards.
The result would be what he described as 'a super-magistracy . . . the surest guarantee
of social order.' Allowing women to abandon public functions through 'alienating their
liberty in a conjugal union' was a most short-sighted policy. But Rœderer's overriding
concern was to prove that the love of wealth could serve the public good. In a corrupt
state it would be 'the source of intrigue, baseness, and fraud', yet if the legislator associated wealth with public esteem and a virtuous character it would then stimulate 'industry, economy, modesty, and frugality'. Rœderer drew on modern history for
illustrations of these claims, and praised Dutch and Swiss manners as models for the
French in matters of wealth.[68]

At the root of Rœderer's analysis was a belief that virtuous actions and egalitarian
social structures would best secure the 'safety' that all humans sought by protecting property and giving the greatest scope to liberty. He believed that humans were motivated by
self-interest towards this end in all of their actions, and claimed that he was writing in the
tradition of 'Pufendorf, Hobbes, Mandeville, La Rochefoucauld, and Helvétius', in
grounding sociability in self-interest and need, by denying the existence of a spontaneous
moral sense or 'universal benevolence'.[69] Against Hume and Smith, the latter being for
Rœderer the more perceptive and profound thinker, he argued that the faculty of sympa-
thizing or identifying with the pain of others was one more example of 'rational benevolence' or 'the enlightened and perfected reason which determines the happiness of men.'
The danger of the idea of sympathy in Smith was its use in an attack upon the possibility
of social equality. Smith had argued that the poor accepted their position in society
because of their sympathy with the successes of the ambitious, the powerful and the
wealthy. Rœderer claimed that this justification of the social hierarchies of the Old
Regime was dangerous but based on a misunderstanding of the love of acquisitiveness.
He explained that deference was a product of the corrupted manners of an inegalitarian
society rather than a universal social fact; given the prevalence of virtuous manners,
acquisitiveness could be positive in its effects. Smith's view was a vain illusion; the artisans
would never be satisfied with low wages because of sympathy with their masters.[70] Some
self-interested practices, such as commercial transactions, would result in the increase of
wealth by the very exercise of the moral passion of acquisitiveness. Others had to be scrutinized by the legislator to direct men by hope and fear towards a socially beneficial result.
An excellent example of the failure to direct individuals was perceived by Rœderer in

gender relations. Although women were deemed to be masters of 'domestic society', and therefore denied access to the 'civil society' of men (the function of which was to protect women and children) Rœderer believed that women were unjustly prevented from enjoying the fruits of liberty and property by tyrannical laws governing inheritance, divorce, and adultery. Men's lust for power had subjected women to life with 'a bastille in every house', establishing an ethic of chivalry which corrupted manners by enjoining women to be superficial and asinine. Rœderer called on French legislators to counteract 'antiquated piety' in declaring that 'men are not kings in their houses, women are not property, and marriage must be based on heartfelt love'. They should follow the novels 'which are the true declaration of the rights of heartfelt love' by 'allowing our men and women to love freely'. The problem was clearly that too many individuals succumbed to extreme passions or were mislead by ignorant self-interest. Since enlightened self-interest was a rare commodity in the 1790s, Rœderer believed that the control of manners by wise legislators was the only hope for the first generation of French republicans by making virtuous actions unreasoned and habitual.

The manners of white Europeans were most susceptible to legislative guidance, Rœderer believed, because the 'transparency of the skin' facilitated the communication of sensibility and the imitation of positive feelings. By contrast, the subjection of dark-skinned people could be explained by their 'lack of transparency', which caused 'the suffering of the negro to interest us less than those of a white'. Rœderer claimed that this explained why non-white races 'have difficulty forming true societies'.[71] It also explained why 'the pains . . . of a brown-haired woman affect us less than a blond'. The mobility of the body was another physiological tool by which humans communicated feelings of sensibility; he held that part of the attraction of children was their constant movement combined with the ease with which their skin coloured in response to external stimuli. When a society had developed codes of behaviour which were associated with particular physical signs, its manners could easily be directed. Rœderer believed civil laws to be the most important influence upon manners because of the system of punishments, rewards and laws they instituted. For virtuous manners he demanded equal inheritance laws among children, the legal defence of civil liberties through a bill of rights, and open divorce laws. Above all he requested laws to favour labour, for example, by forcing men to obtain a trade before they were able to marry. Only by such means would labour become 'the natural force which perfects men and leads them to meet their needs, and knits the interests of all men together.'[72] Second in importance were the institutions and practices which legislators could promote to guide popular culture. Examples ranged from public instruction for children in 'useful arts', to public prizes, allegorical spectacles, monuments, festivals and dances. An industrious culture could be fostered by such means to underpin French prosperity, but Rœderer maintained that similar techniques could be used in times of crisis. Statues could be veiled, or mysteriously shaken by means of secret levers in order to underline a particular threat to public tranquillity. Rœderer favoured laws to regulate modes of dress under different circumstances to transmit similar messages to the public, and also popular manoeuvres in times of war to warn enemies of the strength of national arms.[73] These strategies echoed in several respects those of Sieyès and Condorcet. In particular, Rœderer

followed them in maintaining that once measures to reform manners had been initiated, a republican form of government could successfully be created, and the final
lectures of the *Cours* detailed the political architecture he favoured. But Rœderer was
more precise and encompassing than any previous author who had examined the problem of manners in the 1790s. His grand claim was to have created a *science* of manners
by means of which a particular republican culture could be introduced into the monarchical soil of contemporary France. Only specific manners were compatible with a
flourishing social organization, and only particular means could be used to foster them.
These distinctions are captured in Rœderer's analysis of 'political or national music',
which he believed could become a force 'more powerful than language' in shaping
French culture. Drawing on Plutarch and Polybius, Rameau and Rousseau, he cited in
support of the influence of sound the examples of Timothy of Athens 'who subdued a
violent Alexander with his music', and Stradella, a Neapolitan violinist, who in 1762 had
not only 'seduced a young lady with his playing' but also 'calmed a jealous rival with his
serenades'.[74] Where modern music served the potentially violent passions of volup-
tuousness, Rœderer sought to develop 'music for morality', and distinguished between
'memorative music', such as chanting, which inspired specific virtues, and 'imitative
music' of a particular tone or melody, which governed the intensity of feeling and
'could inspire great actions.' He praised Gossec as one of the few composers who
understood that republican music could be made for the inculcation of manners, and
demanded public money for the support of such work, as well as the less powerful influences of sculpture and painting. By such means a republican art of conducting wills, 'of
making the pleasures taken in actions conform to the general interest', could 'create a
true public opinion which is enlightened, virtuous, united, and, in a word, moralized'.[75]

The major intellectual movement of the early 1790s concerned the creation of citizens by extra-constitutional means. This was why there was a renewal of interest in
such books as Rousseau's *Contrat social* and it explains the mass publication of the works
of ancient and modern philosophers who had explored issues of national character and
moral culture. The problem was how to achieve the goal of a committed republican
citizenry without using Terror or exacerbating the civil war. Say too addressed this
question, which Clavière had so clearly defined, and he followed Rœderer in developing
new answers to it.

NOTES TO CHAPTER 5

1. *ŒD*, p. 556.
2. *Opinions d'un créancier de l'État, sur quelques matières de finance importantes dans le moment actuel*
   (Paris, 1789), p. 45. A separate section entitled *Motifs de réunion pour les créanciers* was
   appended.
3. *Opinions d'un créancier*, p. 30.
4. *Motifs de réunion*, p. 119. Clavière said he was using the chapter 'Of Money considered as a
   particular Branch of the general Stock of the Society . . .', Book II, ch. 2 of the 4th London
   edition of the *Wealth of Nations*.
5. *Courier de Provence*, 17–18 August, no. 27, pp. 12–13, 17.

6. *De la France* (1791), 2nd edn., p. viii.
7. *Courier de Provence*, 20 March 1790, no. 120, *Suite des observations nécessaires sur le mémoire de M. Necker*, p. 81.
8. *Contre l'émission de dix-neuf cents millions d'assignats*, Œuvres complètes, vii, 430–47.
9. *De l'opinion de M. Camus* (Paris, 1789).
10. Condorcet, *Sur la proposition d'acquitter la dette exigible en assignats* (Paris, 1790), *ŒdC*, xi, 485–516; Dupont, *Opinion de M. Du Pont . . . sur le projet de créer pour 1,900 millions d'assignats monnaie* (Paris, 1790).
11. *Réponse au mémoire du M. Necker, concernant les assignats, et à d'autres objections contre une création qui les porte à deux milliards* (Paris, 1790), pp. 13, 86, 125, 155, citing *Wealth of Nations*, Book II, ch. 2, p. 293.
12. *Réponse au mémoire du M. Necker, concernant les assignats, et à d'autres objections contre une création qui les porte à deux milliards* (Paris, 1790), p. 200. See further Clavière, *Coupons d'assignats. Pétition proposée aux quarante-huit sections de Paris* (Paris, 1790).
13. *De la constitution monétaire* (Paris, 1790), p. ix.
14. *Œuvres complètes*, vi, 122.
15. *Réflexions addressées à l'assemblée national, sur les moyens de concilier l'impôt du tabac avec la liberté du commerce, et les rapports que la France doit entretenir avec les Américains libre* (Paris, 1790).
16. *Lettre de M. Clavière à M. Beaumez, Sur l'organisation du trésor public* (Paris, 1790).
17. *Réflexions sur les formes et les principes auxquels une nation libre doit assujétir l'administration des finances*, pp. 48, 174, 159.
18. *Observations sommaires sur le projet d'une refonte générale des monnoies* (Paris, 1790), pp. 6, 24, 41.
19. *Courier de Provence*, 6–8 April 1790, no. 128, p. 313.
20. *Réflexions sur les formes*, p. 151.
21. *Adresse de la Société des Amis des Noirs à l'assemblée national, à toutes les villes de commerce*, ed., E. Clavière, (Paris, 1791).
22. *Ibid.*, pp. 103–6, 122–55.
23. *Lettres écrites à M. Cerutti, par M. Clavière, Sur les prochains arrangemens de finance* (Paris, 1791), pp. 5–6.
24. *Pétition faite à l'assemblée national par E. Clavière, député suppléant de Paris. Sur le remboursement des créances publiques non vérifiées* (Paris, 1791), p. 3.
25. *L'État actuel de nos finances* (Paris, 1791). In December it also appeared in *La Chronique du mois*.
26. Condorcet, *Sur la distribution des assignats et sur l'établissement de paiements par registre*, published in *La Chronique du mois*, January 1792, pp. 64–75.
27. *Etienne Clavière à l'assemblée national, sur les finances* (Paris, 1791), p. 1.
28. *De la conjuration contre les finances et des mesures à prendre pour en arrêter les effets* (Paris, 1792).
29. *Chronique du mois*, January 1792, pp. 104–6.
30. *Ibid.*, February 1792, pp. 87–92.
31. *Ibid.*, January 1792, pp. 132–3.
32. *Discours de M. Clavière, ministre des contributions publiques, À la Société des Amis de la Constitution, séance aux Jacobins Saint Honoré, le 4 April 1792*, p. 4. See also *Mémoire envoyé par le ministre des contributions publiques à l'assemblée national, le 9 Mai 1792*, pp. 4–6.
33. *Réponse de M. Clavière à la lettre de M. Montesquiou* (Paris, 1792), p. 9. Clavière had advocated measures to control industries of interest to national security; see, *Sur l'état actuel des manufactres des poudres et salpêtres du royaume* (Paris, 1792), p. 9.
34. *Correspondance du Ministre Clavière et du Général Montesquiou* (Paris, 1792).
35. *Mémoire par le citoyen Clavière, ministre des contributions publiques, à la convention national* (Paris, 1792), pp. 30–38, 49, 62.
36. *Proclamation du conseil-exécutif provisoire, relative aux subsistances* (Paris, 1792), p. 17.

37. *Coup d'œil sur les monnoies; Sur leur administration, et sur le ministre des contributions publiques* (Paris, 1793), pp. 3, 23.

38. *Fragments d'institutions républicaines, Œuvres complètes*, ed. Michèle Duval (Paris, 1984), pp. 977.

39. Joseph Marie Belgodere, *Supplément aux éclaircissements, pour servir de base à l'opinion qu'on doit avoir sur le citoyen LAMARCHE, directeur de la consection des assignats, & sur ls ministres Clavière qui en à la surveillance* (Paris, 1793). Clavière defended himself with *Clavière, ex-ministre des contributions publiques, à la convention national. Réponse à A.G.J. Ducher des deux hémisphères* (Paris, 1793).

40. *Esprit de la révolution et de la constitution de France, Œuvres complètes*, pp. 277, 301, 305.

41. *Discours sur les subsistances prononcé à la convention national dans la séance du 29 Novembre 1792, Œuvres complètes*, p. 382.

42. *Œuvres*, eds., Marc Bouloiseau and Albert Soboul (Paris, 1967), 10 vols., x, 570–1.

43. *Discours sur la constitution de la France, prononcé à la convention national dans la séance du 24 avril 1793, Œuvres complètes*, pp. 318, 320, 418.

44. *Rapport fait au nom du comité de salut public sur les trente-deux membres de la convention détenus en vertu du décret du 2 juin, présenté à la convention national edans la séance du 8 juillet 1793, Œuvres complètes*, pp. 457–8.

45. *Rapport fait au nom du comité de salut public sur la nécessité de déclarer le gouvernement révolutionnaire jusqu'à la paix, présenté à la convention national dans la séance du 19 du 1er mois de l'an II, Œuvres complètes*, pp. 520–1.

46. *Rapport au nom du comité de salut public et du comité de sureté générale sur la police générale, sur la justice, le commerce, la législation et les crimes des factions, présenté à la convention national dans la séance du 26 germinal an II, Œuvres complètes*, pp. 809–10.

47. *Discours du 9 thermidor an II, Œuvres complètes*, p. 912.

48. *Fragments d'institutions républicaines, Œuvres Complètes*, pp. 966–7, 977.

49. *Entretien de plusieurs philosophes célèbres, sur les gouvernments républicain et monarchique, ŒdR*, vii, 61–71. See also the article *Querelle de Montesquieu et de Voltaire sur les deux principes du gouvernement monarchique et du gouvernement républicain, ŒdR*, vii, 55–60.

50. *Est-il possible d'unir si parfaitement les hommes en société qu'ils n'aient pas besoin de chefs, et de lois coactives pour vivre ensemble en bonne intelligence?, ŒdR*, v, 153; also, *Du néologisme de Sieyès, ŒdR*, iv, 204–7.

51. *Sur la nécessité d'établir en France une constitution nouvelle, Chronique du mois*, March, 1793, *ŒdC* xii, 531–42.

52. *Fragment de justification*, (July, 1793), *ŒdC* v, 575–605.

53. 'Prospectus', *Journal d'instruction sociale* (May, 1793), *ŒdC* xii, 605–13.

54. *Sur l'instruction publique*, in J. Guillaume, *Procès-verbaux du comité d'instruction publique de la convention nationale*, 6 vols. (Paris, 1891–1907).

55. *Esquisse d'un tableau historique des progrès de l'esprit humain*. ed., O. Prior (Paris, 1970), pp. 117–18.

56. *Ibid.*, pp. 51, 58, 132.

57. *Du nouvel etablissement de l'instruction publique en France, Journal d'instruction sociale*, 3 June 1793, pp. 82–3.

58. *Des intérêts de la liberté dans l'état social et dans le système représentatif, Journal d'instruction sociale*, 8 June 1793, pp. 44–5.

59. Additional support can be found in Sieyès' autobiographical *Notice sur la vie de Sieyès, membre de la première assemblée nationale et de la convention* (Paris, 1795).

60. *Projet de décret pour l'etablissement de l'instruction nationale présenté par le comité d'instruction publique, Journal d'instruction sociale*, 29 June 1793, pp. 99–104.

61. *Cours d'organisation social fait au Lycée en 1793, ŒdR*, viii, 129–305. It is possible that Say

attended the lectures at the *Lycée* as he had returned from the army by this time. Georges
Gusdorf has claimed that Say attended the lectures of Vandermonde, his brother's tutor, in
1794 at the *École normale* in *La Conscience révolutionnaire: Les Idéologues* (Paris, 1978), p. 532.

62. *Notice sur ma vie pour mes enfants*, ŒdR, iii, 287.
63. *Cours d'organisation sociale*, ŒdR, viii, 134, 179.
64. Ibid., viii, 131, 136, 145–9, 155.
65. Ibid., viii, 131, 182.
66. Ibid., viii, 150–8.
67. Ibid., viii, 183–4.
68. Ibid., viii, 186.
69. Ibid., viii, 187–191.
70. ŒdR, viii, 200. See also the review of Madame de Stäel, *De l'influence des passions sur le bonheur et les nations*, ŒdR, iv, 473–94.
71. Ibid., viii, 193.
72. Ibid., viii, 265–6.
73. Ibid., viii, 205–6, 267–8.
74. Ibid., viii, 208–14.
75. Ibid., viii, 227–8.

PART THREE

REPUBLICAN POLITICAL ECONOMY

6

Say's Republicanism, 1794–1798

In the aftermath of the Terror increasing numbers of *émigrés*, ex-revolutionaries, and foreign polemicists were portraying the Revolution as a moribund project. French manners were perceived to be antithetical to republicanism, and endemic bloodshed the unavoidable consequence of their conflation.[1] Once a supporter of the liberty gained in 1789, Antoine de Rivarol had become a leading sceptic after his experience of the events of 1793–4. His *De la philosophie moderne* of 1796 blamed modern philosophy, and Condillac in particular, for the excesses of the Revolution, arguing that the Terror tarnished both the *philosophe* enquiry into the nature of virtue and its practical political application. The only means of preventing philosophy from decomposing property, Rivarol claimed, was strict enforcement of Catholicism through institutions such as the Index. Although less enamoured of Catholicism, the Protestant Jacques Necker had for many years been issuing similar warnings, founded on the belief that religion was the only secure foundation for manners, and that without the strict enforcement of religious practices anarchy would result. To Necker, the traditional manners of French society had to be rescued from the attacks of republican legislators, and thereby allowed to bring peace by controlling the lives of the lower orders.[2] In addition, defences of 'Christian monarchy' and 'Catholic manners' abounded in the latter half of the 1790s, with de Maistre, de Bonald and Barruel developing Lefranc's idea of the Revolution as a Masonic plot and international *philosophe* conspiracy against priests and kings.[3] As writers who continued to support 'the Revolution and philosophy' initiated a defence, the manners controversy saw its final flowering before Napoleon's ascent to power.[4] This was the immediate context of the formulation of Say's political economy.

Attacks on revolutionary manners were from the first a major concern of the leading members of the post-Thermidor Convention. On 30 October 1794 (9 Brumaire, an III) the *école normale de Paris* was created as the vanguard project of the Committee of Public Instruction as a training-ground for revolutionary teachers. The eminent first professors of the *école normale de Paris* included Vandermonde in the chair of political economy and Garat in the chair of the analysis of sensations.[5] In his capacity as Minister of the Interior, the latter was also responsible for the distribution of thousands of free copies of Condorcet's *Esquisse*, as a manifesto for the renewed attempt to create a modern republic in France. The Directors who made up the executive council in accordance with the constitution ratified on 23 September 1795 (1 Vendémiaire, an IV) were equally concerned with continuing the debate about the origins and nature of manners, as the 'Daunou law' of 25–6 October 1795 (3–4 Brumaire, an IV) underlined. This ensured that 'republican morality' was taught to boys and girls in *écoles primaires* and provided legislative sanction for the creation of an *Institut national des sciences et des arts*, under whose auspices republican manners were discussed and propagated.[6] The *Institut* was divided into three classes, 'Physical and Mathematical Sciences', 'Moral and Political Sciences', and 'Literature and the Fine Arts'. Its aim was to unite the best minds in a variety of disciplines for the furtherance of truth and the support of the French republic. The second class, of Moral and Political Sciences, was unlike any other educational establishment in Europe, with sections for 'The Analysis of Sensations and Ideas', 'Morals', 'Social Science and Legislation', 'Political Economy', 'History', and 'Geography and Statistics'. Many of Say's friends and colleagues from the *Courier de Provence*, *La Décade*, and Madame Helvétius' Auteuil salon were members of the second class of the *Institut*, including Pierre-Jacques-Georges Cabanis, Constantin-François Chassebeuf de Volney, and Pierre-Louis Ginguené in 'The Analysis of Sensations', with Sieyès, Rœderer, and Dupont de Nemours in 'Political Economy'. The five volumes of papers published by the class between 1798 and 1802, and the innumerable newspaper articles they inspired, reveal an intense quarrel concerning the earlier insights of Condorcet, Sieyès, and Rœderer.[7]

One response to attacks on revolutionary manners that flourished after the Terror was popular in part because it acknowledged the verity of Necker and Rivarol's criticisms. It was associated with the movement termed 'Theophilanthropy' and derived from the view that the errors of the Revolution could be traced to a failure to replace Catholicism with a new religion for modern republics, allowing demagogues and mobs to thrive as a result. Several members of the *Institut* were attracted by this argument, but the leading figures were J. H. Bernardin de Saint-Pierre and Dupont de Nemours.[8] The latter's *Philosophie de l'univers*, written while awaiting execution in June 1793 but only published in 1796, maintained that 'Philosophy is a Religion' and attempted to sketch a natural faith from the common elements of existing religions. Founding his doctrine on instinct rather than faith, Dupont claimed he was attacking 'the puerile impertinence of modern Christians, Cabalists, Illuminists, Musulmans and Magis', and that he could not, therefore, be counted 'a Molinist, Jansenist, Confucian, Zoroastran, Platonist or Thomist'. Rather, he believed a pacifist and austere moral code could be deduced from the design of the universe, the lessons of experience, and the injunctions of the heart. A benevolent deity had created the world to grant happiness to good and moral persons, as he believed had been proved by 'the deservedly horrific deaths of Robespierre and Danton, Marat and the Duc d'Orléans'.[9] It was essential for this natural religion to be fostered in the republic, and to this end he sought to institute churches of adherents. The necessary separation of religious beliefs and virtuous civil practices was defended by a far greater number of *Institut* members. Volney was probably the most famous exponent of this view, and he had been accused of atheism by Joseph Priestley in the *Letters to the Philosophers and Politicians of France on the Subject of Religion* (1793). The materialism of the *Voyage en Syrie* had caused a sensation in 1787, and this was maintained after the publication in 1791 of *Les Ruines, ou méditations sur les révolutions des empires*, which sought to prove that 'Christianity was born a heretic in Egyptian temples', that all theological opinions were 'chimerical and allegorical', and that priests were 'impostors who opened the floodgates of falsehood and iniquity'.[10] The work was indebted to Condorcet for its central argument, that moral rules would only be followed if they were based on reason rather than instinct or faith. The pursuit of harmful passions would be avoided only when men realized that happiness was synonymous with a virtuous life. By contrast, those who lived a criminal life, embraced luxury or libertinism, would learn from the sad consequences and either moderate their behaviour or die. As Volney put it, 'Since the evils of society flow from IGNORANCE and INORDINATE DESIRE, men will never cease to be tormented until they shall become intelligent and wise; till they shall practice the art of justice, founded on a knowledge of their own organization.' The process would be hastened by the progress of civilization, as increasing sociability made habits more gentle. Thus from knowledge of the laws of nature, men would become moral in order to preserve themselves, practising charity, clemency, generosity, patriotism, frugality, and moderation.[11] Volney made another contribution to the manners controversy in 1793 when, from his Parisian prison cell, he wrote what was intended to be the second part of *Les Ruines*, entitled *La Loi naturelle, ou Catéchisme du citoyen François*. Once more Condorcet was the inspiration for the work, as Volney demanded that every citizen be taught to reason independently, by means of a rational catechism explaining the origins of moral action and the need for a life based on 'temperance, chastity, courage, activity, cleanliness, economy, and justice'. Volney saw no need for cults or festivals in the process of reforming national manners. He had an absolute faith in the capacity of every individual to reason, and his experience of the upheavals of the Revolution did nothing to alter this view. In 1798 a second edition of *Les Ruines* was issued; *La loi naturelle* was appended with the new title, *La Loi naturelle, ou principes physiques de la morale déduits de l'organisation de l'homme et de l'univers*. Here Volney claimed that 'the education of our mind and the moderation of our passions are two duties deriving from the first law of self-preservation'. Ignorance, he declared, was 'the true original sin'.

Volney's friend and colleague at the *Institut*, Cabanis, developed a perspective on manners in the late 1790s that owed more to Rœderer's lectures than to any other work. A leading figure in the Auteuil salon, Cabanis was the physician who had tended Mirabeau during his final illness and had reputedly given Condorcet the poison with which he ended his life. He was also close to Sophie Grouchy, Condorcet's widow and the author of the translation of Smith's *Theory of Moral Sentiments* (1798). Cabanis came to prominence under the Directory as the author of a 'new base for the moral sciences . . . to ensure they progress as rapidly as the physical sciences'.[12] Presented in a series of lectures to the *Institut* in 1796 and 1797, Cabanis published the book which realized this intention in 1798 with the title *Rapports du physique et du moral de l'homme*. Proclaiming that 'the study of the physical nature of man is equally interesting for the physician and the moralist', Cabanis claimed to be writing in the tradition of 'Aristotle, Democritus, Epicurus, Bacon, Hobbes, and Locke, Helvétius and Condillac', and that he sought to reveal the physiological springs of human action. These, he declared, were based on a knowledge of 'general facts'. This linguistic distinction was used to contrast chemical methods of *analysis*—associated with Condillac—with Cabanis' preferred model of physical science, moving from observed experience to general laws, seeking to group particular phenomena and to capture their movements. He argued that general laws allowed deduction and verification of hypotheses by further physical studies of the mechanical nature of human action. Cabanis called this physics of humanity *physiologie*, claiming that by *physiologically* defining fundamental need the coercion of individuals by the state could be justified or made compatible with liberty. Liberty was safe so long as the interests that the legislator promoted accorded with essential needs.[13]

In common with every member of the *Institut*, Cabanis was convinced that 'the most precious enjoyments in life are obtained only by the practice of morality', and that 'by a happy necessity, the interest of each individual can never be truly distinguished from the interest of other men'.[14] However, following Rœderer against Condorcet and Volney, Cabanis was certain that a moral society would not be secured by public instruction alone, because of the overwhelming influence of the passions and custom in human life. As a result, it was essential for a 'natural history of man' to be constructed, revealing the influence of different environmental forces and physical factors on behaviour, with the aim of providing the legislator with information to direct and guide manners towards virtue. Cabanis believed he was reviving the ancients' approach to morals by examining the effects of gender, age, health, climate, and dietary regime, and also in his ideal of the 'mixed character'. Dividing the work into sections examining each of these factors, Cabanis marshalled evidence to support several claims of importance to the manners debate. One of the most important justified the role of women as mothers and carers rather than politicians and heads of households. He believed he had physiologically proved that 'while the perfection of man is vigour and audacity, that of woman is grace and deftness.'[15] Cabanis was fascinated by hygiene and diet and argued that a good legislator would promote modes of living that underpinned the exercise of republican virtues. Once more in agreement with Rœderer, he argued that 'labour is not only a source of all wealth, but also of commonsense and order.' Above all, Cabanis claimed that climate had the greatest effect upon moral habits because it directly shaped character. Cold climates produced excessively forceful individuals, while hot countries favoured excessive sensitivity. Only temperate climes facilitated 'people happy and free'. The merits of these approaches to modern republican manners were debated in a series of essay competitions promoted by the *Institut*. They also inspired Say to develop the republican ideas to which he had been introduced by Clavière and the *Courier* coterie in the different context of the post-Terror Revolution.

2   GINGUENÉ AND *LA DÉCADE PHILOSOPHIQUE*

Military service had prevented Say from seeing Clavière's frustrated final attempts to regenerate popular manners. This was a stroke of luck because he remained beyond the grasp of the Jacobins who contrived the arrest of Girondin deputies and their acolytes in the Spring and Summer of 1793. On returning in May 1793, Say's service in the military wing of the republic placed him beyond the suspicions of the Parisian demagogues. He was consequently safely married to Julie Gourdel de Loche, the daughter of a Calvados lawyer. Despite Say's Calvinist family and his wife's Catholic faith, there is no evidence that the ceremony was religious, and no subsequent attempt was made, in more peaceful times, to sanctify the union.[16] Their initial intention was to leave Paris to set up a private school teaching philosophy and republican duties, hoping thereby to serve both country and Revolution. Before this project was realized Say was approached by the poet F.-G.-J.-S. Andrieux, a member of his battalion, and Ginguené, editor of *La Feuille villageoise* and a close friend of Clavière's associate, the recently deceased Chamfort, whom Say had known at the *Courier*.[17] They asked him to join them in creating a journal to promote republicanism through the development and popularization of the physical and moral sciences, hoping thereby to protect the *philosophe* legacy from the obloquy of the Terror.[18] With three other co-proprietors, the former lawyer Amaury Duval, the former priest Joachim Le Breton, and Georges Toscan, *La Décade philosophique, politique et littéraire* was launched at the height of the Jacobin-inspired massacres, on the 10 Floréal, an II (29 April, 1794), a few days after the closure of Ginguené's *La Feuille villageoise*.[19] Named in accordance with the division of the revolutionary calendar replacing the *semaine* of the Gregorian system, *La Décade* proclaimed itself to be the product of 'a society of republicans' who were fearful because, 'in the midst of the revolutionary crises, reason and philosophy are meditating in silence.'[20] Convinced that empirical sciences of the natural and social worlds ought to be guiding revolutionary legislators in unique circumstances (the Revolution was described as 'the first *true* experience of any large state'), the journal planned to provide a commentary on political events alongside studies of contemporary developments in 'metaphysics, logic, morals, mathematics, physics, public economy, or the social art ... public instruction, rural economy, and agriculture'. Cabanis's dictum was taken to be a universal truth: 'The progress of the sciences and the arts is the true thermometer, and the most sure guarantee, of the progress of civil society.'[21] The authors of the journal reiterated the popular clichés that the maintenance of a republic and the development of the arts were mutually sustaining. As Say himself put it in March 1798, 'political revolution has been favourable to the arts because they are the fruit of genius, and genius wishes to be independent.'[22] In addition the editors expressed the view that a successful republic ultimately depended upon the virtuous manners of its populace. The epigraph of the first edition of *La Décade* was revealing on this score: 'enlightenment and morality are as essential for the survival of the Republic as courage is for conquest'. The desired outcome of the Revolution begun in 1789 was perceived to be a republic in which the moral and political faculties of all citizens were to be fully developed. Although a new epigraph was adopted in the Autumn of 1796, enjoining the combination of the useful and the agreeable through the Horatian ode *utile dulci*, and despite the replacement of 'a Society of Republicans' with 'a Society of men of letters' early in 1797, the central aim of the journal remained to foster republican virtues and make them habitual. The republican credentials of the journal were impeccable, but the particular nature of the republic supported by *La Décade* shifted in tune with revolutionary politics. Early issues were full of praise for the existing political order that, the editors argued, had regenerated the manners of France and thereby sustained the Revolution. Although science, arts, literature, philosophy, and morals, were covered, most of the paper was taken up with political reporting, supporting the decrees of the Convention, the Jacobin Club, and the Committee of Public Safety, including Robespierre's festival of the Supreme Being. However, after the Thermidor coup *La Décade* promoted a republic distinct from that associated with the Jacobins. On 10 Thermidor the editors proclaimed that 'the country is saved', and accused Robespierre, 'the new Cromwell', of despotism while praising his victorious adversaries. From this time the authors of the journal held fast to Rœderer's claim that the ideas of the *philosophes* remained of fundamental importance to the project of creating a modern republic in France.

Although he was arrested as a Girondin sympathizer soon after *La Décade* appeared, and imprisoned for several months in Saint-Lazare, Ginguené's influence determined the early republicanism of the paper. As might have been expected from a former editor of *La Feuille villageoise*, articles abounded on 'moral botany' and the positive effect of republican government on 'rural economy'. Maintaining that 'rural economy has been exhausted by the sect of physiocrats', Ginguené believed an opportunity existed for the creation of a republic governed by 'the empire of the philosophical spirit'.[23] His conception of this 'spirit' owed a great deal to reflection upon the writings of English rebels and regicides of the seventeenth and early eighteenth centuries, and adulatory reviews were made of the works of Thomas Gordon, Algernon Sidney, James Harrington, and John Milton, with the latter's *Pro populo anglicano defensio* being described as 'an eternal manual for republicans'. Equal attention was paid to Machiavelli, Helvétius, and Paine. Reviewing the recently published *Œuvres de Machiavel*, Ginguené agreed that it was necessary to create a republic in which liberty and virtue were mutually sustaining.[24] This could only be achieved by focusing upon Helvétius' insight:

It has been said of Descartes that he created man; one can say of Helvétius that he understood him. He is the first to have founded morality on the unshakeable basis of personal interest . . . His book [*de l'Esprit*] is the product of a soul touched by the evils which afflict large societies. No one has better sensed the principles from which a government can be established.[25]

Ginguené's perspective on these writers was shaped by a prior commitment to Condorcet's republicanism, and particularly by his view of public instruction as the best means of making self-interest accord with virtue; Condorcet was described as 'the illustrious martyr of philosophy and liberty'.[26] In consequence, while Duval and Andrieux were demanding the republicanization of art and literature, Ginguené and his follower Le Breton campaigned tirelessly in the pages of *La Décade* for a popular education in rural economy and other technical arts deemed essential to a vibrant commercial republic. *La Décade* supported Garat's promotion to *commissaire de l'instruction publique*, the opening of the *écoles normales* and the *écoles primaires* (between 7 Frimaire and 27 Brumaire an II), and the institution of 'elementary instruction in republican morals'. Joseph Lakanal's inaugural lecture to the *école normale de Paris* was given prominence, in which he outlined the goals of the new government, and explained his aim of using the *philosophes*' writings to found a truly moral republic by means of an educational revolution. Guinguené wholeheartedly endorsed such sentiments: 'Men must be taught to accept absolutely that morality is the first need of all Constitutions: it is therefore necessary not only to engrave [morals] on all hearts by the voice of sentiment and conscience, but also to teach it as a real science, whose principles are evident to the reason of all men and of persons of all ages.'[27] Condorcet thereby inspired the teaching of virtuous manners in the pages of *La Décade*, through the educational institutions erected by the first Directors, and the moral catechisms popularized by such contemporary publishing successes as Saint-Lambert's *Principes des mœurs*.

3   ASSESSING THE REVOLUTION

Say's first writings for *La Décade* are difficult to identify as the majority of articles remained anonymous during the first year of the journal's existence. It was only in the summer of 1795 that writings began to appear with the abbreviation 'S.', 'J.-B. S.', or Say's pseudonyms 'Atticus' and 'Boniface Veridick'. The founding of the journal did coincide, however, with the publication of Say's second work, an edition of Benjamin Franklin's popular moral philosophy from the *Pennsylvania Almanac* articles, entitled *Poor Richard Saunders*, which had appeared in London as *The Way to Wealth or Poor Richard Improved*. Say adopted the title *La Science du bonhomme Richard*, and added a brief sketch of Franklin's life, from which it is possible to glean ideas about Say's intellectual commitments. In the preface Say claimed that the revolution in America, and specifically its republican constitution, had inspired the French to follow them and restore their liberty. But he was most interested in Franklin's life, being that of a man who 'had done only good in the world', as a model for republican manners. Franklin was praised for refusing to wear a wig, for speaking only when necessary, for his simple habits, and the apparel 'of an old peasant with a noble air'. According to Say, Franklin had discovered that 'constant happiness' could only be maintained by the adoption of 'the simplicity of ancient morals'. This entailed a life of frugality and industriousness, dedicated to the public good, in the secure belief that this was the surest means to self-help as well as the interest of the republic. There was no better proof of this than Franklin's rise from candle-maker to foreign ambassador:

Franklin, a candle-maker, who had been an apprentice printer in Philadelphia, without home or privileged origin, ate a morsel of dry bread in the street while seeking employment. This important example is one of the greatest triumphs of Equality; it is one that has opened our eyes, and prepared the establishment of our august Republic.

As to the means by which a government might encourage such manners, Say was silent, with one important exception. He signified his support for Clavière's policy of using paper money for the reformation of popular manners by praising the related American scheme.[28] But Franklin's book was first and foremost to be used as a source of 'profound observations on morality' and 'useful reflections' for the private individual seeking to live a more worthy and happy republican life. In the review which appeared in *La Décade* the virtues of frugality, industry, and moderation were highlighted, and the book was praised as 'a masterpiece of good sense, concision, and simplicity; one could add finesse, if such a discredited word could be applied to the most sublime, the most useful notions of public and private economy.' Lazy individuals, and those who lived from credit or usury, were described as slaves unworthy of a republic. It is highly probable that Say was reviewing his own edition in this instance, and favouring Condorcet's approach to the inculcation of republican manners.[29]

Say's writings in *La Décade* before 1798 covered a wide range of subjects, from the theatre, architecture, and modern poetry, to the importance of China and America for modern France. From time to time he also covered debates in the *Conseil des Cinq-Cents* and was the resident reviewer of books written in English. His first signed article appeared at the end of Ventôse, an III (March, 1795); it reviewed a Paris street concert, as Say put it, 'while our fourteen armies dictate the conditions of peace to all the powers of Europe and to the rebels of the interior'.[30] As this comment indicates, the piece emphasized Say's patriotism; it also underlined his republicanism, as he touchily noted that the music did little 'for the honour of the first Republic in the world'. The best he had to say about the vaudeville sketches was that they were 'peppered with bright sarcasm against the revolutionary nobility of the Jacobins.' Say was, however, most concerned with the effects of the concert on republican manners, proclaiming, 'If it is true that the theatre is a school, we are angry when bad lessons are taught'. In particular, he believed the theatrical verses to be dangerous for political economy, which was worrying because 'nothing is indifferent in this subject, since a single prejudice is deadly to national prosperity.' In criticizing those who hoarded money the authors shifted blame for France's economic malaise from the government to private individuals; in Say's review the root cause was described as a lack of private saving combined with the excessive buying and selling of *assignats* encouraged by ignorant politicians. A second error committed in verse was to suppose that 'ostentation vivifies commerce'. All too often in France, Say claimed, the useful commodity was sacrificed for an extravagant alternative, ignoring the fact that 'pomp always has misery as its neighbour'. What he called 'true luxury' was synonymous with 'the abundance of necessities', with 'goods of high quality', and 'cleanliness'. An excellent example of such a mistake was the librettists' condemnation of Jacobins as people who wore their hair without powder; Say attacked this portrait, arguing in favour of 'the least disguised coiffure', a taste for simplicity he was certain he shared with 'artists, philosophers, Pericles, and Virgil', none of whom had ever shown Jacobin tendencies. These ideas were characteristic of all of Say's political economy and marked him out as a republican of a particular kind. The importance of moral commerce and moderate wealth had been gleaned from Clavière, and Say never doubted his perspective. Such themes were reiterated in subsequent book and theatre reviews, short essays, moral tales, and pieces of political and cultural reporting. Say was hostile to Robespierre, whose government he called 'a fierce and distrustful . . . tyranny', and the members of the Jacobin Club, 'the French *décemvirs*', because he held them responsible for maintaining the 'Old Regime tradition of egoism'. The inevitable result of such a culture was the perpetuation of 'absurd barbarism'.[31] The Jacobins had perverted the Revolution, the great achievement of which had been to give French citizens more security, liberty, and knowledge than any society in history.[32] The key term in Say's analysis was 'corruption', the product of the 'egoism, vanity, and deceit' that continued to pollute France despite the events of 1789. Thus Say traced the collapse of the constitution of 1791 to the cultural legacy of the Old Regime, as he made clear in his commentary on the Convention's proposals for a new constitution in 1795, led by Boissy d'Anglas and Daunou, published as 'Quelques idées sur le projet de constitution de la Commission des Onze' in the Summer of 1795.[33] Say's article was intended to follow that of his friend and colleague Amaury Duval, who, as 'Polyscope', had composed a

Plan de constitution very critical of the constitutions of 1791 and 1793. The problem, according to Duval, was the excessive influence of Montesquieu, whose notion of the separation of legislative and executive powers instituted a war between these branches of government that could only be resolved by the corruption of each. Duval's aim was to replace this with a constitution based on the analogy between the human body or 'animal machine' and government or the 'political machine'. In practice this entailed a new division of functions to replace the separation of powers, with an administrative body charged with the execution of the law, a discursive body of orators charged with proposing laws, and a legislative charged with power to pass laws. Renewed every three years by a suffrage of literate men over twenty-three years of age who were able to prove their *honnêteté* and 'means of subsistence', the laws of this Senate would in turn be sanctioned by a national Assembly of representatives of each *departement*, who would assess the conduct of the members of the Senate and, without discussion, accept or reject the laws of the past three years.[34]

Say was heavily influenced by Duval's attempt to combat corruption by revised constitutional means. He followed to the letter Duval's critique of Montesquieu, arguing that the separation of deliberative and decision-making functions would prevent vanity and *amour-propre* from favouring intemperate legislation. In following the traditional notion of the balance of legislative powers between a *Conseil des Anciens* and *Conseil des Cinq-Cents*, Say expressed fears that the Constitution Committee's plan would result in civil war. It would be better, he advised, to separate rhetoric and decision-making, with decisions registered not by a show of hands or a simple yes–no ballot, but by means of coloured ivory balls indicating 'approval, rejection, adjournment, continued discussion, etc'. Say was also critical of any declaration of rights on the grounds that every constitution necessarily constrained rights, and that 'Robespierre was never impeded by such things'. Rousseau too was attacked for making a spurious distinction between the particular and general acts of government, which in practice became a mask for tyranny.[35] Having experienced the collapse of the Constitution of 1791 and the Terror, Say had become a republican fearful of 'excessively popular decrees', 'corps of aristocrats', and 'monarchical prejudices'. In addition to Duval's scheme's to combat corruption he advised that the *Conseil des Anciens* be given powers 'to nominate, for a fixed term, a committee of Public Safety' with dictatorial powers during periods of 'perpetual insurrections' or when '*la patrie* is considered to be in danger'. Say also favoured the institution of an assembly, sitting at least fifty leagues from Paris, charged with simplifying legislation and with constitutional law, which the Committee itself had adapted from Sieyès' writings on the need for a 'Constitutional Jury'.[36] Although he supported the graduated and restricted franchise of the Committee, Say had reservations about the list system of voting in the primary assemblies that he ascribed to Condorcet. The only way of preventing the election of second-choice 'buffoons', he declared, was to follow the procedures of the single transferable vote. Despite these measures, Say warned that the new constitution would be 'a sad experience' unless the people of France were committed to it and their support became habitual. In a phrase that could have been drawn directly from Rœderer's *Cours*, Say claimed 'habit alone attaches the majority of men to institutions'. Electing republicans who would resist the temptations of demagoguery and monarchism, called by Say 'terrorism and royalism', was of such importance that he was willing to override constitutional laws to ensure such an outcome. In an important article, *Y-a-t-il des cas ou il soit permis de violer les principes?*, published in *La Décade* on 30 May 1798, Say argued that it was essential to use the old Roman maxim *salus populi suprema lex esto* to justify the violation of constitutional principles for the good of the republic. Having replaced Ginguené, who had been appointed ambassador to Turin, as the editor of *La Décade* responsible for *Affaires de l'intérieur*, Say claimed that the upheavals of the 1790s could be traced to the excessive probity of revolutionaries faced with constitutional or legal constraints. Respect for 'hereditary royalty' had allowed a court faction to remain 'at the head of state in 1791', thereby ruining the first French constitution. Respect for the principle of an independent judiciary in March 1793 had allowed 'the Commission of Twelve to acquit Marat and his accomplices'. Say wished that 'the French had acted like Cicero against Catiline . . . and bayonetted the conspirators the next day'. By such action he was sure that 'perhaps 200,000 victims of the Terror would have lived, including Bailly and Roucher.' He was delighted that the leaders of the Directory had 'used the canon' to 'push back the *sections* in Vendémiaire [when Bonaparte crushed a rising in the west of Paris on 5 October, 1796], and the *faubourgs* in Germinal.' The lesson was that wise republicans would have supported the decision of the *Conseil des Cinq-Cents* on 11 May (22 Floréal, an VI) to invalidate the election of deputies with reputed royalist sympathies.[37] As in the case of Clavière's justification of war against the enemies of the Revolution, Say did not believe his ideas could with justice be labelled reason-of-state because in his eyes they were fully compatible with republican morality and absolutely essential for the maintenance of republican liberty. Say proved himself to be far removed from liberal or democratic approaches to politics and continued to defend the extreme actions first justified by the Girondins in 1791–2. 'The great drama of the French Revolution', Say contended, would continue until 'a well-intentioned government unites everyone, and is supported by the people of France'. Until that time it was necessary to use executive powers to 'expel the anarchists and *sauver la patrie*'.[38] He continued to be loyal to the Directory until at least March 1799, when he gave unqualified support to the published list of government candidates for the coming elections.[39] The problem which Say recognized in all of his writings at this time was that the powers of government to influence public opinion were limited, and that other means had to be discovered for influencing the popular culture: means that would ultimately determine the success or failure of the French republican experiment.

4   SECULAR MANNERS AND THE PROBLEM OF RELIGION

Popular habits or customs were of fundamental importance to Say. Republican constitutions and politics were perceived to be only the first step towards the creation of a successful republican nation. Of far greater consequence was the regeneration of French culture, a view he had undoubtedly been introduced to in Clavière's circle, and shared with Sieyès and Rœderer, as well as Condorcet before his death. It was essential to promote republicanism in France by making the populace more virtuous, an end which Say believed depended upon the permanent entrenchment of certain manners in French popular culture. The conclusion he stated time after time in the first years of *La Décade's* existence was that stable, virtuous manners were vital for France; as he put it, 'the perfection of the civilization necessitates the softening of manners'.[40] This would ensure that France was led by men 'who have not enriched themselves through public office . . . and are moderate in their habits and desires'. It was a fact that 'it is in the middle state between luxury and indigence that enlightenment and virtues are found.'[41] The French had to learn from the Chinese, whom Say called 'a phenomenon in morals and in politics', having the greatest of civilizations when judged by population, territory and the mechanical and commercial arts. Montesquieu had been mistaken, Say contended, when arguing that the Chinese polity was based on fear and submission. It was based on the most secure foundation conceivable: stable popular manners.[42] Say's perception of manners in his comments on China are striking. He underlined the fact that manners and morals were not synonymous. Rather, 'in China, as everywhere, cupidity is the sole God; there the laws and customs tolerate abominable practices, such as castration and infanticide'. What Say understood by manners were 'habits and ways of living, the principles which direct each individual in his public and private conduct'. The most important fact in Chinese history was the constancy of civil and religious belief, despite invasions, natural disasters, and the rise and fall of dynasties. Chinese attitudes derived from a 'national egoism', entailing 'an absolute lack of curiosity which might lead them out of their country, no love of glory which might make them risk hazardous enterprises, no affection, and no resentments which might compromise their tranquillity.' It was essential for France to establish a similarly permanent culture. But Say did not believe it was possible for the French to adopt manners identical to those of the Chinese; the societies were fundamentally different, as evinced by the fact that China had never experienced revolution. Rather, Say believed French manners should become secular and moral in specific ways that his writings sought to define. For Say, religion and virtue were antithetical words. Although he retained a sense of loyalty towards the Calvinist religion in which he had been educated, considering it more suited to commercial republics than Catholicism, his conception of the social world was profoundly anti-religious.[43] His attitude was heavily influenced by Gibbon, with whom he agreed that the Bible contained 'a complete system of morals adapted to every condition of life', but was also 'one of the the most scandalous books ever made'. In an obituary written after Gibbon's death in January 1794, he praised the historian's combination of an 'absolute rejection of Christianity' and hostility towards religious sects, with a positive view of the utility of certain Christian ethical maxims.[44] In his review of Macartney's *Voyages*, Say noted that the antiquity of the Chinese civilization 'disproved all the fables of Genesis'. He claimed to be unsurprised at the immoral alliance of William Pitt and the Pope against France, which showed that religions were also subject to reason-of-state.[45] Commenting on the early editions of the *Bibliothèque britannique*, Say associated Britain's 'mad ambition to dominate all the seas' with 'passive obedience to the dogmas of priests'.[46] More importantly, Say likened 'the furies of revolutionary government' to the 'arch-Machiavellian *gouvernement devôt* of the age of Louis XV'. Claiming that 'religious terrorism has been exercised by priests of every denomination in almost every century', he condemned Catholicism as 'the religion most opposed to healthy morals and the most contrary to the establishment and maintenance of liberty.'[47] Although the Terror was described as 'another kind of religious fanaticism', Say contended that 'political fanaticism, as awful as it is, is something less horrific, and less ferocious, than religious fanaticism'.[48] Joanna Kitchin has written that 'hostility towards Christianity is a fundamental disposition, perhaps the most important, of the philosophy professed in *La Décade*'; Say's opposition was exemplary, and it was shared with his brother Horace.[49]

Say wanted to place philosophy where religion had stood in the culture of previous societies. In his writings of this time he detailed a canon of 'men of reason', for the most part French and anticlerical, ranging from Cicero to Gibbon, but giving honourable mention to Seneca, Montaigne, Descartes, Fénelon, Voltaire, Hume, Franklin, Rousseau, and Diderot. In his eyes, an intellectual line linked the oppressed *philosophes* of all ages and the republican martyrs of 1793–4, 'La Rochefoucauld, Condorcet, Lavoisier, Bailly, and Malesberbes'. By reflecting on the writings of such men, Say held that a republican morality could be forged. It would replace Catholicism and sustain a republic which 'almost alone in the world enjoys the envied liberty of thought, speech, and writing'. Other nations, preeminently Britain and the United States of America, believed their citizens enjoyed similar liberties, but Say was convinced that in such states 'prejudice and hypocrisy . . . work like an Inquisition', as shown by the criticism of Gibbon for his anticlericalism.[50] The most important *philosophe* in Say's view was Diderot. In an extensive review of J.-A. Naigeon's edition of the *Œuvres de Diderot*, Say claimed that in a society where 'discontent, ignorance, stupidity, and bad faith support the evils which are inseparable from a great revolution', and where it was necessary to 'refashion popular attitudes with philosophical principles', Diderot was 'the most vigorous athlete . . . the best antidote against the reactionary poison of superstition and servitude.' Diderot's *œuvres* proved that he had been 'a republican under the monarchy', and also that if he had lived beyond 1784 he would 'never have been complicit in the stupid furies of vandalism'. Diderot had never underestimated the difficulty of 'making people free who were so long accustomed to slavery'; he manifested 'an enthusiasm for virtue, and the most profound indignation against tyranny'. Above all Say recommended the *Vie de Sénèque* as 'the best lecture ever made to counsel republicans or those who wish to become republicans'.[51] The ethics of a stable republican life that Say drew from such sources were austere, entailing an absolute probity and honesty in public and private life. In addition they taught the value of industry, economy, propriety, and moderation.[52] Society was no longer divided between *les honnêtes gens et la canaille*, making it essential to establish a nation without ranks 'in peace, where reciprocal confidence, and a general benevolence, unites all its citizens'.[53] A willingness to sacrifice self for the good of the republic was essential, and the living of a dutiful life of dedication to the *patrie*.[54] Say's sole, but significant, criticism of Gibbon was that he had failed to consider the public good in supporting George III in the war with the American colonies. Say quoted Fox's satirical verdict on *The Decline and Fall* as a warning to erstwhile patriots:

His book well describes,
How corruption and bribes,
Overthrew the great empire of Rome.
And his writings declare,
A degeneracy there,
Which his conduct exhibits at home.[55]

Similar criticism was directed against anything that resembled the culture of the Old Regime. Public behaviour in the *Théatre du vaudeville* was attacked for replicating 'the galleries of the old *Palais-Royal*' frequented by women 'in search of a meal or a lover'.[56] The moral *contes* penned by Say warned of the dangers of the consumption of luxury goods and the disasters ultimately in store for the *homme oisif* or the dueller who imitated the aristocrats of the Old Regime.[57] He agreed with the verses of a play written by Picard, enjoining the rich man to 'pay his debt to society', as in the case of the 'honest money-lender' who lived by thrift and hard work, avoiding 'idleness, vice, and necessity'.[58] Worthy public idols were men such as Descartes, who, in rejecting offers of patronage, had 'valued his liberty so high that no king on earth could buy him.'[59]

The model for Say was not, as it was for many anglophiles in the post-Terror era, an idealized British 'commonweal', which Say called 'a tyranny', unjustly oppressive of 'true republics' such as Ireland.[60] He cast repeated aspersions on the presumed advantages of British life, from toleration and enlightenment, to political liberty and imperial power.[61] There were more *dévots* in England, Say declared in the Gibbon obituary, than any other country in Europe. Although he admired 'the flourishing state of the sciences, arts, agriculture, and letters' manifest in the pages of the *Bibliothèque britannique*, he believed that Britain was dominated by an idle elite of property owners, who controlled the House of Commons by corrupt means, and were responsible for the 'atrocious conduct' of British merchants and politicians towards other nations. France in particular had been treated 'cruelly' by the successive administrations of 'the tyrant Pitt', who favoured the policy of 'burning our towns and starving our citizens, bribing Austria to enter the Coalition, murdering our fishermen, and killing our prisoners of war.' Say was delighted at the progress of the war in March 1798 and contended that 'France her rival has never been led by a government so firm, strong, and enterprising.'[62] He wholeheartedly supported the projected invasion of England, predicting a speedy victory over a nation brought 'by our political principles to the edge of the precipice'. Once the British empire had been defeated, the 'imbecile King' deposed and the 'rabid ministers' dispersed, Say foresaw that Europe would become 'independent of America', gaining sugar and coffee from Africa, thus ensuring that 'the vile traffic in slaves would cease naturally'. It would be better for all if the British people 'chased the corrupt ministers from power', but he agreed with Helen-Maria Williams that this was unlikely given the corruption of the state and the extent of anti-French feeling.[63] Say was certain of the outcome: 'It is the character of the French Republic not to be hindered by any obstacle: she marches obstinately to her goal and attains it.'[64] Like Rœderer, Say was also critical of examples of ancient republics being applied to modern France, holding that 'everything has changed' since the times when 'a numerous class of idle citizens, especially in towns, needed to be distracted by circuses and popular spectacles in order not to form cabals.' In ancient Greece and Rome citizens were a noble class, while the slaves formed what Say termed 'the third-estate, the industrious class of society'. Factors such as 'modern manners, our northern position, the size of our states, the breadth of our civilization, the inventions of paper and printing, the progress of the sciences, navigation, commerce, and communication' had created a wholly modern world in which any 'envy and hope of making our fellow-citizens into Greeks and Romans' had to be abandoned.[65] Commerce and technology were facts of life that Say welcomed, and which he was ready to acknowledge made him a republican of the moderns rather than the ancients.[66] He demanded that governments promote the use of machines of all kinds to better satisfy needs and that citizens be encouraged to join the *Société libre de commerce et de manufactures* 'to cultivate knowledge and to spread it'. He envisaged a society where 'agriculture and all kinds of industry are in brilliant activity, sea-ports are full of ships, canals and rivers are full of boats, where there are proper and well-provisioned markets, all of which provide an impression of abundant activity.'[67] Such commerce would create a nation whose people lived 'in ease rather than in opulence, where everyone knew how to read . . . where there are no unproductive individuals who are a burden on society, and no poor men who cannot, with labour and good conduct, win an easy subsistence, and lead the kind of life which the English call *comfortable.*' Say recommended that this word, signifying 'something commodious but without luxury', be added to every French dictionary. His only reservation, reminiscent of Clavière and Brissot's argument of the mid-1780s, was that commercial practices be made compatible with rigid republican morals, so that the *honnête homme* rather than the 'speculator and usurer' would be rewarded.[68]

Regarding the means of establishing this conception of a stable republic, Say was explicit. He rejected the approach of his friends and colleagues, Andrieux and Duval, for whom steps had to be taken to republicanize popular customs by means of public festivals and spectacles such as national theatres. In Say's view this was a utopian pipe dream of ancient republicans in contemporary garb, and he advised people 'to cultivate the land, perfect the useful arts, hold to a well-ordered conduct, and rarely, very rarely, visit the theatre.'[69] In addition he expressed reservations about certain educational practices widely canvassed under the Directory, such as republican catechisms and the spreading of knowledge of the constitution and the declaration of rights.[70] At this time Say considered the only successful means of promoting republican manners to be the practice of republican duties in every home of the republic, by husbands and wives devoted to France, dedicated to passing on such duties, by example as well as by instruction, to the children of the 1790s. As he said, 'the best education is that of the father in the home'. It was for this reason that Say was so impressed by François de Neufchâteau's attempt to aid the parents of the republic through the publication of moral songs and verses which would be understood by republican children.[71] The best education a school could provide was one that was practical and useful, rather than esoteric and over-ambitious. This was one reason to avoid catechisms and embrace the technical arts. Say argued that since three-quarters of French people could not read, it was essential to teach them whatever would be useful in their daily lives, since 'the more they undertake labour, the more their work will be perfected, the more they will be at ease with themselves and in their family, and the more the nation will be enriched by their toil.'[72] Only after such arts had been mastered was it necessary to learn to 'read, write, count, and order our affairs'. But the 'good conduct' so essential to the republic would only ever be learned 'within the society of fathers, brothers, wives, children, and friends ... [because] virtue lies in the household.' Say was certain that this was the enduring lesson of the success of China, where, despite 'the most absolute despotism', good manners were taught within the family and thereby 'sustained the Empire'.[73]

While the Directory was successfully prosecuting the war against England, display-ing a firm opposition towards supporters of monarchy and Jacobinism, and throwing up popular heroes loyal to the republic, such as Bonaparte, Say was among the most patriotic of public writers.[74] He was as impressed as any patriot with the feats of the young General, and was confident that the parents of the republic were gradually being moralized by the forces of republican constitutionalism and able governance.[75] He declared himself 'filled with national pride' at having a relative, his brother Horace, among the invaders of Egypt and Syria, and expected Bonaparte's glorious victories to 'be the first step towards a revolution in the commercial system and political balance of the world'.[76] The destiny of France was to turn the despotisms of the East, where 'manners are corrupted, seditious, ignorant, and violent', into nations of 'liberty and free government', which would in turn make them 'centres of world commerce.'[77] It was in this state of optimism and confidence in French republicanism that Say wrote his first major work of political economy in 1798.

5   REPUBLICAN POLITICAL ECONOMY

On 8 July 1797 (20 Messidor, an V) Say informed the readers of La Décade of recent events in the Moral and Political Sciences Class of the Institut, welcoming Talleyrand's analysis of ancient and modern colonies, and Rœderer's criticisms of the responses to an essay competition sponsored by the Political Economy Section of the Institut in an V, addressing the question Pour quels objets et à quels condition convient-il à un état républicain d'ouvrir des emprunts publics? Say also reported on the new questions set by the Second Class for an VI, to be completed by 15 Germinal, an VI, with prizes to be announced on 15 Messidor. The question sponsored by the Morals Section asked Quels sont les moyens les plus propre à fonder la morale chez un peuple?[78] In guidelines provided for competitors in a subsequent public séance Rœderer announced that this question had been mistakenly issued, and was considered too broad by the leaders of the Institut. The revised question asked Quelles sont les institutions les plus propres à fonder la morale d'un peuple?[79] Almost a year later, La Décade reported that no responses worthy of a prize had been received and that the Institut had decided to continue the competition into an VII, with answers expected by 15 Vendémiaire.[80] Say's interest in this second competition was underlined by his account of the séance and comment on Rœderer's revised advice to respondents, which he called 'an excellent sketch, perhaps a narrow route though sure [to good morals].'[81] In what was largely a compressed restatement of some of the themes of the Cours of 1793, Rœderer advised competitors to describe secular moral institutions (as opposed to those 'civil, political, or religious') to direct public habits, such as schools, clubs, public spectacles, and monuments, and enunciate the principles behind them. 'Ancient legislators', including 'Moses, Lycurgus, and Confucius', were cited as possible sources for relevant ideas because of their attempts to regulate domestic manners, from language and clothing to rites and sexual practices. One issue that needed to be addressed was the reconciliation of legislation to determine manners with political and civil liberty, although Rœderer implied that in matters of state survival the 'general interest' overriding liberty was easy to perceive. He was less circumspect about the republican manners he favoured, expressing the wish that several answers would assess his own view, that institutions which encouraged all individuals to work hard and labour long were the surest foundation for private morals and the well-being of a large commercial republic:

By addressing this subject, perhaps we will discover that the great determinant of domestic manners, the great tutor of private morals, is the full and complete institution of labour, which, to be established in France, requires only a total public respect for liberty and for property.[82]

Say's *Olbie, ou essai sur les moyens d'améliorer les mœurs d'une nation* was one of the competition essays of 1798 written in response to Rœderer's plea, and like him integrated the science of political economy with the inculcation of republican manners.[83]

Say divided his vision of a morally reformed nation into two parts. The first formulated the principles by which legislators ought to be guided in order to improve manners peacefully. The second gave a practical example of these principles, and applied them to an imaginary state called Olbie, a term signifying 'happiness' in ancient Greek. The citizens of this state, the Olbiens, lived in the aftermath of a successful political revolution.[84] They had thrown off the yoke of absolute monarchy through the experience of fifty years of 'good' laws but had recognized that the only way to banish corruption was to renew or perfect the manners of the people. They therefore initiated legislation for virtuous manners concurrent with political change, with the ultimate intention of making such manners habitual. The laws and schemes of the republican legislators of Olbie were directed at two groups of people. First, corrupted adults, and especially women, who had been degraded by the manners of the Old Regime, and particularly by the vices of luxury, idleness, and poverty. Second, children whose manners were independent of monarchy and whom it was crucially important to influence for the future success of the republic. Although he referred to *Olbie* as a dream world, the product of 'the philanthropic imagination', Say was addressing the circumstances of the Directory:

My task is to seek means to obtain the commitment of a people, entrenched in their vicious customs and with long-standing deadly prejudices, to follow these rules, the observation of which, would undoubtedly result in contentment.

He was firm in the view that 'to reform the morals of a people, there is no better institution than a Republic.'

Rather than analysing labour, Say developed his argument through a critique of the contemporary and historical manners of nations. His most emphatic point was that the manners of *exclusively* commercial societies, such as Venice or Carthage, were a dangerous model to follow because they encouraged luxury and idleness:

The Olbiens knew the love of gain to be a sin almost as dangerous as idleness. When this passion is strong it becomes, like all others, exclusive. It extinguishes a mass of noble and disinterested sentiments that must be part of the perfect human soul. It is thus that among certain peoples, or even among the inhabitants of certain towns too much involved with commerce, any idea, other than that of self-enrichment, is regarded as folly, and any sacrifice of money, of time or of ability, is considered trickery.[85]

Commerce had to be made compatible with austere morals and with the industry of the many rather than the few. A distinction had to be made between commercial societies, characterized by luxury and corruption, and industrious societies, characterized by equal ranks:

In industrious and rich nations, I accept whatever contributes to the well-being of the citizens, and thereby excuses the otherwise contemptible seeking after sensuality. After having thus limited the number of things which are strictly related to luxury, I am not afraid to proclaim that luxury is deadly to small and large states, and that the country where there is the least luxury, will be the richest and the happiest.[86]

Luxury encouraged transient satisfactions, the 'fleeting pleasure' of libertinism and moral laxity rather than constant pleasure or *jouissance*. Real happiness was to be found in the exercise of industry, frugality, honesty, courage, temperance, wisdom, benevolence, and mutual respect. For women Say added chastity and gentleness, which he considered essential for successful family life. The experiences of the other major commercial republic, Holland, underlined these points, proving that excessive reliance upon commerce would result in moral corruption and ultimately international war. Say warned modern republics, and especially America, that if they modelled themselves upon historic republics they would suffer the loss of virtue and decline: 'United States of America, guard against the general tendency of the minds of your beautiful republic. If what is said is true, you will become rich but you will not remain virtuous; and then you will not long remain independent and free.' Britain was described as a typical commercial society in that trade was controlled by over-powerful merchants. In making this argument Say stated that he was relying on the *Wealth of Nations*, his sole reference to Smith.[87] While Say praised America he made clear that this 'new' nation, with a predominantly agricultural economy, a small population, and no experience of a socially dominant nobility or an administratively powerful monarch, was no model for France. France had to forge a new path, combining a free republic with an industrious civilization. He believed that the key was to utilize the 'good books' of the French enlightenment to articulate those manners that would make the French people the best and most happy in history. If France comprised a majority of *honnêtes gens*, Say had hopes that 'this nation would be the happiest on earth; it would not be difficult to prove that it would also be the most rich and the most powerful.'

It is evident that this argument developed points made in Say's journalism. This was also the case in the view taken of China as being full of lessons for French republicans and particularly the practice of drawing up books of merit and blame for all citizens, tests in science and morals for all public servants, and the example of the Emperor's working of the plough.[88] Say maintained his opposition to the idea of faith as a virtue, arguing that faith entailed the institution of what would only ever be signs, rather than facts, of religiosity, and would thereby become a source of hypocrisy, fear, and superstition. He ridiculed those who favoured a civil religion, believed in miracles, or justified the institution of religious inquisitions in order to coerce the practice of virtue. History had shown that periods of great devotion were usually accompanied by great ferocity, while the most tolerant and philosophical nation, China, was also the least religious.[89] Furthermore, religious orders encouraged idleness, the Bible was full of examples of immorality, and religious fear rendered the soul timid and weak. In questions of morality it was far better to rely on 'the philosophical spirit'. Say expressed this view in stating that the goal of the legislator was to reduce the attractions of ephemeral gratifications, from idleness and profligacy to evangelical worship, and to encourage the 'real' happiness that came from living according to a code that exalted the secular virtues. One new note was Say's praise for Spartan institutions, including public censors and austere national fêtes. Lycurgus was praised for instigating a moral revolution in rendering vice deadly and virtue profitable through the use of civil law; the result was the civic courage which led three hundred citizens gladly to choose self sacrifice for the public good at Thermopylae; willingness to sacrifice the self for the public good was once more described as the touchstone of healthy manners.[90] Another new claim was that Rousseau had provided a textbook for popular instruction in *Emile*, which contained the kinds of republican arguments that would make virtue habitual if practised.[91] For those who had been corrupted by monarchical living a code of civil laws was outlined. These included the public declaration of each citizens' income, forbidding games which encouraged idleness, cupidity, and perversity (Say gave gambling as an example), and the provision of censors to register the virtue of public officials and private citizens. In addition Say favoured the institution of 'societies for relaxation' in which citizens could discuss issues of general interest, work in gardens, read, write, or simply rest; he also advocated special 'societies for women' to encourage labour and chastity before marriage. Beccaria received particular praise for his scheme of prizes for virtuous actions, banks for the poor to encourage saving, and support for the suppression of lotteries and gambling. A 'nobility of the enlightened would encourage men and women, young and old, to unite in the practice of virtue.[92]

The necessity of a broader distribution of wealth for the creation of a successful republic was given particular emphasis. Say's ideal for wealth distribution restated the argument of 'Boniface Véridick' in *La Décade*, being what Say once more called a 'comfortable medium':

Good education, and instruction, of which affluence (*l'aisance*) is the source, and of which good manners are the consequence, originates only in the affluence of the people. It is with this that we must first be concerned . . . the majority of citizens, with too little to live a life of continuous pleasure, but affluent enough to be spared attacks of discouragement or the anguish of bare need, undertake a moderate toil which leaves the soul full of spirit; little by little they became accustomed to seeking their dearest pleasures in the company of their family and a small number of friends; they cease to know idleness, boredom, and the cortège of vices which accompany them: living more soberly, with a more equal spirit, their souls became more disposed to justice and to benevolence, which are the mothers of all the other virtues.

The only means to this desired end was to educate all citizens in the science of political economy, the subject which enunciated the republican truths Say was advocating. Political economy would show individuals their 'enlightened self-interest'. It was a branch of the social art that guided legislators in their governance and citizens in their duties. The science would guide citizens to virtuous practices in their business lives and would develop their love of labour. The truly tragic nation, Say claimed, was one in which these truths were recognized but where their practical effect was nugatory because the majority of the citizens lived in ignorance. This was the state of France under the Directory, with good books and bad morals, making the spread of literacy and learning imperative:

A nation which has bad morals and good books must do its utmost to favour the spread of literacy. The indigent man, assailed by all his needs, considers the black signs printed on white pages to be irrelevant. He ignores the fact that the most sublime knowledge, the most useful ideas of political economy, for example, which are the source of prosperity and happiness in nations, are hidden under the printed symbols he despises, and that if his ancestors had been able to lift their veil, he would not be reduced to sharing with his coarse family a piece of black bread in the hut of a savage.[93]

Having learned the lesson that 'the more gold is considered useful the more virtue is sacrificed to it', the leaders of *Olbie* would set an example by adopting simple clothes and frugal habits, by displays of public fasting and other virtuous actions. Such virtuous morals would trickle down to the ordinary citizens, enlightening them as to the true route to happiness, and in the process creating a genuine moral republic.

6   THE RECEPTION OF *OLBIE*

According to Say, the Terror could be explained not by reference to the Revolution itself but solely because of monarchical manners. These continued to manifest themselves in popular preferences for monarchical or Jacobin factions, and could only be countered by waging war on inequality and by encouraging what Say perceived to be *republican* virtues; no other *Institut* essay gave such prominence to this republican conception of political economy. Say's critique of purely legislative solutions to social division was equally at odds with majority opinion. For example, Say's competitor Destutt de Tracy, whose essay was published with the title *Quels sont les moyens de fonder la morale chez un peuple?*, clung to the narrower definition of self-interest and sociability associated with Jansenism, basing his whole argument upon the necessity of coercive laws. This is not to claim that Say's arguments were original. This becomes clear when *Olbie* is examined alongside the works of leading members of the *Institut*, and particularly Rœderer, who undoubtedly was a major source for Say's text. Both men believed a form of political economy that addressed the problem of manners to be a solution to the impasse of the Directory. By 1798 this had become one of the leading themes of argument under the Directory. One source was J.-A. Creuzé Latouche in the Convention of 1794, who had argued that the study of political economy was 'the unique means of restoring abundance, and making it compatible with liberty.' He then demanded the creation of a chair of political economy at the *École normale de Paris*, and the promotion of basic works in political economy to instruct the populace: 'elementary books which particularly study the relations between laws and social institutions with the arts and industry.' He advised the incumbent of the chair to follow Condillac, since 'the progress of the sciences depends essentially on the perfection of languages.'[94] In the Second Class of the *Institut* attempts were made by the abbé Grégoire and Cambacérès to sketch out plans for a specifically 'republican' political economy, justifying republican government and measures to improve the morals of the populace. Cambacérès *Discours sur la science sociale* of 1796 praised agriculture as the means to prosperity and industrious manners, and sought to lay the foundations for a unification of political economy, morals and politics, derived from the insight: 'Without morals the legislator will find only slaves . . . Political economy forms, through the arts, the bonds of society; the legislator maintains them by his power, and morals confirm them through the exercise of duties; from this comes the happiness and goal of society and social science.'[95]

An altogether more considered plan for a republican political economy was produced by Grégoire. He argued that despotism had consciously suppressed attempts to develop 'the science of government' including political economy, but that the French republic now promised to reverse this process, since the Directory had recognized that: 'The philosophers are the legislators of principles, and the more these principles are recognized, the less reliance needs to be placed on laws . . . The republic of letters will give birth to [political] republics.'[96] Grégoire's advice to philosophers of government was twofold: first, to focus upon the project of creating republican manners and second to promote the study of statistics (in the broadest sense) as the means to the former goal. He belaboured the lack of research necessary to theoretical innovations in political economy. Grégoire was convinced that without legislation for improved manners at the centre of the new science the republican vision would soon wane, because 'the majority of governments occupy themselves more with wealth than with manners, with frivolous enjoyments than with useful knowledge.' As he said:

the *élan* of a people for liberty is only ever short-lived if it is not sustained in the mind by conviction, and in the heart by sentiment. Without enlightenment no one knows how to be free, and without virtue no one deserves to be . . . Law protects the sciences, and the sciences protect liberty.

The important point for Say's *Olbie* is that it was perceived to be a contribution to the broader projects of Grégoire and Rœderer, and was reviewed as such in *La Décade* by a fellow journalist, Charles Theremin, who called it an important work of 'public economy' for 'the perfection of the social art'.[97] This positive assessment of Say's work was not shared by his colleague Ginguené, who was chosen by the *Institut* to assess the answers to the Morals Section competition. The *Olbie* was one of three works that received commendation, and placed second in order of merit. Ginguené recognized that the work's distinctive argument was that the republic could be led to virtue through political economy. However, he argued that the substance of this political economy, other than the litany of the republican virtues, was singularly unclear. Having described the foundations of the science of manners as self-interest, Say had not explained how this was related to political economy, or how it might lead to practical measures. The most interesting part of Say's work was therefore the most unconvincing and ill-conceived:

It presents pictures rather than reasons, and gives action to what others have presented as theories and systems; but it is precisely a system and a theory that is wanted; it is clear that this vast and complex subject could not be studied in depth by this method, which considers everything superficially.

It was Guingené's criticism which Say took to heart, defending himself against it in the preface to the published edition of *Olbie*, which appeared early in 1800, where he claimed that his ideas were derived from 'a sentiment of justice supported by genuine reasoning.' However, Say did not consider this response to be adequate. The preface to the *Traité d'économie politique* of 1803 contained a detailed exposition of the method of political economy, described as a science of 'general facts', which was intended to specify the theoretical foundations of a political economy for a modern nation. Several problems are therefore raised by this reading of *Olbie*. What is the relationship between the 'republican economy' of *Olbie* and that of the first *Traité*? Did Say abandon his belief that the inculcation of the republican virtues was the most important function of the legislator, justifying intervention in the lives of the citizens? Was Say converted from republicanism to laissez-faire liberalism? If the latter is the case a study must be made of the rapid change in Say's ideas towards what is now termed classical political economy. If, as is more likely, there is a more complex relationship between the *Olbie* and the *Traité* then our view of the origin and nature of political economy in nineteenth-century France requires reassessment.

NOTES TO CHAPTER 6

1. J. Lachapelle, *Considérations philosophiques sur la révolution française* (Paris, 1797); J.-F. La Harpe, *Du fanatisme dans la langue révolutionnaire* (Liege, 1797).
2. *De l'importance des opinions religieuses*, (orig. 1788), *Œuvres complètes*, xii, 1–18, 197–9; also *Cours de morale religieuse* (orig. 1800), xiii, 409–33, xiv, 328–63.
3. See François Lefranc, *Le voile levé pour les curieux ou le secret de la révolution révélé à l'aide de la Franc-Maçonnerie* (1791), *Conjuration contre la religion catholique et les souverains* (1792).
4. Rœderer, *D'un grand moyen de perfectionner la morale du peuple*, *ŒdR*, v, 151–2.
5. See the lectures published in the *Séances des écoles normales* (Paris, 1800) 10 vols., especially Vandermonde's, ii, 233–9.
6. On the *Institut* see Jules Simon, *Une académie sous le directoire* (Paris, 1885), pp. 58–76.
7. Grégoire, *Réflexions extraites d'un ouvrage sur les moyens de perfectionner les sciences politiques*, *MdIN*, i, 556–66; Forbonnais, *Mémoire sur le genre de questions dont la science de l'économie politique comporte la solution exacte*, *MdIN*, ii, 481; Cambacérès, *Discours sur la science sociale*, *MdIN*, iii, 14; for commentary see M. Staum's 'The Class of Moral and Political Sciences, 1795–1803', *French Historical Studies*, xi (1978), 371–97; 'Individual Rights and Social Control: Political Science in the French Institute', *Journal of the History of Ideas* (1987), 411–30; 'The Institute Economists: from Physiocracy to Entrepreneurial Capitalism', *History of Political Economy*, 19 (1987), 525–51.

8. See Bernardin de Saint-Pierre's *Études de la nature* (Paris, 1796), 'Introduction'.

9. *Philosophie de l'univers* (Paris, fructidor, an IV [August–September 1796]), pp. 11, 43, 94–8, 133–7, 208–9.

10. Quotations are from the London translation of 1841 entitled, *The Ruins, or a Survey of the Revolutions of Empires*, ch. 20–2.

11. *The Ruins*, pp. 29, 44.

12. *Rapports du physique et du moral de l'homme* (Paris, 1824), preface. For commentary, M. Staum, *Cabanis: Enlightenment and Medical Philosophy in the French Revolution* (New Jersey, 1980).

13. Cabanis, *Rapports*, in MIN, 1798–1804: i, 149, 141 f., 151.

14. *Rapports du physique et du moral de l'homme* (Paris, 1824), 23–4.

15. *Ibid.*, 6th memoir, section 7.

16. Valynseele, *Les Say et leurs alliances*, pp. 29–31, 39–51.

17. For Chamfort's role in the creation of the journal see *Les Auteurs propriétaires de La Décade au public et à leurs abonnés*, LDP, xxvi, 513.

18. Say's responsibilities are clear from a letter to his aunt of 23 Prairial, an II (11 June, 1794): 'Je suis assez satisfait de ma position actuelle. Je me trouve directeur en chef d'une maison d'imprimerie avec un traitement de mille écus, plus un sixième d'intérêt promis. J'ai toujours ambitionné d'être à la tête d'une manufacture, et il en est peu de plus agréable.' *Say Papers*, BN Microfilm 6333, 29–30. See also the sketch of Say's life noting 'the execution of the Girondins', 38–40.

19. On the origins, contributors, and contents of the journal see J. Kitchin's excellent *Un journal 'philosophique': La Décade (1794–1807)* (Paris, 1965) and M. Regaldo's *Un milieu intellectuel. La Décade* (Paris, 1976), 4 vols. Many individuals contributed articles to the journal, including Say's brother Horace, a professional engineer and polymath, whose lengthy writings were prominent in *La Décade* before 1798.

20. 'Prospectus', published in M. Regaldo's *Un milieu intellectuel*, iv, 607–18.

21. *Œuvres philosophiques* (Paris, 1956), p. 481.

22. Review of P. Chaussard, *Essai sur la dignité des arts*, LDP no. 20, 20 Germinal, an VI (30 March, 1798), pp. 87–93.

23. *Économie rurale: Effet de l'action du gouvernement républicain sur l'économie rurale*, LDP, i, 332.

24. Review of Guiraudet, ed., *Œuvres de Machiavel*, LDP, 10 Messidor an IV, 52–3; xxi, 534, xxii, 25.

25. Review of *Œuvres complètes d'Helvétius*, LDP, 20 Thermidor, an V, xiv, 284.

26. Review of Condorcet's *Esquisse*, LDP, v, 475–88; *Notice sur la vie et les ouvrages de Condorcet*, LDP, xxi, 418.

27. Review of Talleyrand and Condorcet on public instruction, LDP, ix, 15–28.

28. *La Science du bonhomme Richard de Benjamin Franklin* (Paris, an II), pp. lx, lxi, xliii.

29. LDP, ii, 150–7, 10 Thermidor, an II.

30. Review of *Le Concert de la rue Feydeau, ou l'agrément du jour'*, LDP, iv, 488–91.

31. Review of *Campagne du duc de Brunswick contre les Français . . .*, LDP no. 40, 10 Prairial, an III, pp. 412–14; Review of *Les Suspects*, LDP no. 40, 10 Prairial, an III, pp. 429–30.

32. Review of Rulhière's *Histoire, ou anecdotes sur la révolution de Russie en 1762*, LDP no. 12, 20 Ventôse, an V (10 March 1797), pp. 469–78.

33. *Quelques idées sur le projet de constitution de la commission des onze*, LDP, vi, 79–90.

34. *Plan de constitution par Polyscope*, LDP, vi, 21–33.

35. *Quelques idées sur le projet de constitution de la commission des onze*, LDP, vi, 82–6.

36. *Opinion de Sieyès sur les attributions et l'organisation du jury constitutionnaire, Débats constitution-nels de l'an II, 2 & 18 Thermidor*, in P. Bastid, *Sieyès et sa pensée* (Paris, 1939), appendix, pp. 44–7. There is a hint here as to why Say was attracted to Bentham.

37. *Y-a-t-il des cas ou il soit permis de violer les principes?*, LDP no. 25, 10 Floréal, an VI, pp. 377–84.

38. Report on *Affaires étrangères*, LDP no. 28, 10 Messidor, an VI, pp. 53–7.

39. *Conseils de Leptomènes sur les élections, LDP* no. 16, 10 Ventôse, an VII, pp. 415–20.

40. Review of Chauvet's *Essai sur la propreté de Paris, LDP* no. 21, 30 Germinal, an V (19 April, 1797), pp. 147–52.

41. *Conseils de Leptomènes sur les Élections, LDP* no. 16, 10 Ventôse, an VII, pp. 415–20.

42. Review of Æneas Anderson's *Relation de l'Ambassade du Lord Macartney à la Chine dans les années 1792, 1793 et 1794, LDP* no. 5, 20 Brumaire, an V, pp. 284–291, no. 6, 30 Brumaire, an V (20 November, 1796), pp. 350–6.

43. Review of William Guthrie, *Nouvelle géographie universelle, descriptive, historique, industrielle et commerciale des quatres parties du monde, LDP* no. 27, 30 Prairial, an VII, pp. 522–33; review of the sermons of the ex-*Courier de Provence* journalist and Calvinist pastor, Samuel Reybaz, *LDP* no. 90, 20 nivôse, an X.

44. Obituary of Gibbon, *LDP* no. 54, 30 Vendémaire, an IV, pp. 147–52.

45. Review of *Le Brigand, LDP* no. 47, 20 Thermidor, an III, pp. 300–3.

46. Review of *Bibliothèque britannique, ou receuil extrait des ouvrages anglais . . ., LDP* no. 78, 30 Prairial, an IV (18 June, 1796), pp. 524–35.

47. Review of L.-M. Réveillère-Lépeaux's *Réflexions sur le culte, sur les cérémonies civiles et sur les fêtes nationales, LDP* no. 25, 10 Prairial, an V (29 May, 1797), pp. 405–11.

48. Review of J. A. Creuzé-Latouche, *De l'intolérance philosophique et de l'intolérance religieuse, LDP* no. 35, 20 Fructidor, an V (6 September, 1797), pp. 461–7.

49. *Notice sur Horace Say, chef de l'état-major du génie, mort en Syrie, LDP* no. 8, 20 Frimaire, an VIII, pp. 462–73.

50. Review of La Réveillère-Lépeaux, *Réflexions sur le culte.*

51. Review of Jacques-André Naigeon, ed., *Œuvres de Diderot, LDP* no. 15, 30 Pluviôse, an VI (18 February, 1798), pp. 332–44.

52. Review of François de Neufchâteau, *l'Institution des enfans, ou conseils d'un père à son fils imités des vers que Muret a écrits en latin pour l'usage de son neveu, et qui peuvent servir à tous les jeunes écoliers, LDP* no. 21, 30 Germinal, an VI, pp. 163–5.

53. Review of Chauvet's *Essai sur la propreté de Paris, LDP* no. 21, 30 Germinal, an V (19 April, 1797), pp. 147–52; *Boniface Véridick à Polyscope, sur son projet de théatre pourle peuple, LDP* no. 10, 10 Germinal, an IV (30 March, 1797), pp. 38–44.

54. Review of Thiébault's *De l'Enseignement dans les écoles centrales, LDP* no. 11, 20 Nivôse, an V (9 January, 1797), pp. 75–80.

55. Obituary of Gibbon, p. 148.

56. Review of *Le Chat perdu ou les fausses conjectures, LDP* no. 54, 30 Vendémaire, an IV, pp. 173–5.

57. *Les Enrichis, allégorie, LDP* no. 84, 30 Thermidor, an IV (17 August, 1796), pp. 358–64; *Le Duel, anecdote, LDP* no. 24, 30 Floréal, an V (19 May, 1797), pp. 350–8.

58. Review of Picard's *Les Amis de collège, ou l'homme oisif et l'artisan, LDP* no. 60, 30 Frimaire, an IV, pp. 560–3.

59. Review of *René Descartes, LDP* no. 1, 10 Vendémaire, an V (1 October, 1796), pp. 39–41.

60. Report on *Affaires Étrangères, LDP* no. 28, 10 Messidor, an VI, pp. 53–7.

61. Review of *Correspondance de l'armée française en Egypte, interceptée par l'escadre de Nelson, LDP* no. 13, 10 Pluviôse, an VII, pp. 227–32.

62. Review of P.-F. Tardieu, *Notice historique des descentes qui ont été faites dans les Iies brittaniques depuis Guillaume jusqu'à l'an VI de la République française, LDP* no 17, 20 Ventôse, an VI (10 March, 1798), pp. 461–6.

63. Say was in contact with Williams at this time as her letter to him reveals, published in *LDP* no. 22, 10 Floréal, an VII, pp. 299–335. For Say's sympathy with her view of Britain see the introduction to his translation of her travel writings, *Nouveau voyages en Suisse* (Paris, 1798), favourably reviewed by Amaury Duval in *LDP* no. 23, 20 Floréal, an VI, pp. 283–9.

64.	Review of Tardieu, *Notice historique*, p. 466.
65.	*Boniface Véridick à Polyscope, sur son projet de théatre pour le peuple*, LDP no. 10, 10 Germinal, an IV, pp. 38–44. See also *Lettre sur l'harmonie des vers, dans quelques langues modernes, et sur celle que les vers français pourraient emprunter de ces langues*, LDP no. 35, 20 Fructidor, an V (6 September, 1797), pp. 473–80.
66.	Report on the *Lycée des arts, Séance publique* du 20 Prairial, *LDP* no. 42, 30 Prairial, an III, pp. 531–4; report on the *Lycées des arts, Séance* du 20 Thermidor, LDP no. 48, 30 Thermidor, an III, pp. 334–7.
67.	*Boniface Véridick à Polyscope, sur son projet de théatre pour le peuple*, pp. 38–44.
68.	Report on *Affaires de l'Intérieure*, LDP no. 26, 20 Prairial, an VI, pp. 504–12.
69.	*Boniface Véridick à Polyscope, sur son projet de théatre pour le peuple*, LDP no. 10, 10 Germinal, an IV (30 March, 1796), pp. 38–44.
70.	*Lettre de Boniface Véridick, sur son voisin le maître d'école*, LDP no. 39, 30 Floréal, an III, pp. 356–60.
71.	Review of François de Neufchâteau, *l'Institution des enfans, ou conseils d'un père à son fils imités des vers que Muret a écrits en latin pour l'usage de son neveu, et qui peuvent servir à tous les jeunes écoliers*, LDP no. 21, 30 Germinal, an VI, pp. 163–5.
72.	*Lettre de Boniface Véridick à Polyscope*, p. 39.
73.	Review of Lord Macartney, *Voyages dans l'intérieur de la Chine et en Tartarie, fait dans les années 1792–4*, LDP no. 24, 30 Floréal, an VI, pp. 338–42; also LDP no. 25, 10 Prairial, an VI, pp. 402–8.
74.	Review of P. Chaussard, *Essai sur la dignité des arts*, LDP no. 20, 20 Germinal, an VI (30 March, 1798), pp. 87–93.
75.	Report on *Affaire de l'Intérieur*, LDP no. 25, 10 Prairial, an VI, pp. 444–8.
76.	*De l'Egypte*, LDP no. 2, 20 Vendémiaire, an VII, pp. 91–100.
77.	*Suite de l'article intitulé De l'Egypte*, LDP no. 3, 30 Vendemiaire, an VII, pp. 156–67.
78.	*Nouvelles littéraires, faits remarquables, etc.*, LDP no. 29, 20 Messidor, an V, pp. 104–6.
79.	*Nouvelles littéraires, faits remarquables, etc.*, LDP no. 2, 20 Vendémiaire, an VI, pp. 107–10.
80.	*Classe des sciences morales et politiques*, LDP no. 30, 30 Messidor, an VI, pp. 149–52. Sixteen answers were received addressing the first question. Eight responses were received for the second competition, including Say's. See Martin Staum, 'The Enlightenment Transformed: The Institute Prize Contests', *Eighteenth Century Studies*, 19 (1985–6), 153–79.
81.	*Nouvelles intéressant à la littérature, les sciences ou les arts: Observations critiques*, LDP no. 2, 20 Vendémiaire, an VII, pp. 107–10.
82.	*Précis des observations sur la question proposée par l'institut national pour le sujet du premier prix de la classe des sciences morale et politique, lues dans la séance du 15 vendémière an 6, ŒdR*, v, 366. Rœderer recalled in his old age that he had worked out one hundred and eighteen different ways to answer the question: see *ŒdR*, v, 373–6, *Ce que c'est que la section de morale de l'académie des sciences morales et politiques* (1833).
83.	Two versions of *Olbie* have been examined, the first edition of 1800 (*OlbA*) and the Daire edition of 1848 (*OlbB*). The Daire edition omits Say's copious notes which were appended to the first edition.
84.	*OlbB*, 592.
85.	*Ibid.*, 596.
86.	*OlbA*, 122.
87.	*OlbA*, 107, from *Wealth of Nations* (Indianapolis, 1981), Bk. I, ch.10, p. 145; Bk. IV, ch. 6, p. 170. It is important to note that Say used the term *libérale* to denote a life of civic responsibility.
88.	*OlbB*, 609; *OlbA*, 104, 111.
89.	*OlbA*, 83.

90. *OlbB*, 606. Say was probably influenced by P.-C. Lévesque's *Mémoire sur la constitution de la république de Sparte, MdIN*, iii, 347.

91. This section was indebted to Horace Say's proposed republican school 'to form the soul for virtue' printed in 1792–3 as *Plan d'éducation dans les principes de J.-J. Rousseau*. A copy is in Say's papers, BN Microfilm 7689, 52–9.

92. *OlbB.*, 597–9.

93. *Ibid.*, 588.

94. J.-A. Creuzé Latouche, *Discours sur la nécessité d'ajouter à l'école normale un professeur d'économie politique* (Paris 1794) p. 10.

95. Cambacérès, *Discours sur la science sociale, MdIN*, iii, 14. See also the unilluminating Véron-Forbonnais' *Mémoire sur le genre de questions dont la science de l'économie politique comporte la solution exacte, MdIN*, ii, 481.

96. Grégoire, *Réflexions extraites d'un ouvrage sur les moyens de perfectionner les sciences politiques, MdIN*, i, 556–66.

97. *LDP*, xxiv, 476.

7

The Idea of a *Traité d'économie politique*

I SAY AND THE CONSULATE

The published version of Say's *Olbie* appeared in the first months of 1800, and included a preface making clear the author's enthusiastic support for the new regime which had been instituted since the work had been written. Although intended to address the problems of the Directory (the 'fifty years of stability' which the Olbiens moral reformation was based upon was held to be the product of the constitution of 1795), Say argued that *Olbie* was still more suited to the Consulate. There was 'no better time for a public work on the manners of a nation' than when 'two men, whose extraordinary talents and morality are not contested even by their greatest enemies, have conceived the project of founding the stability of the Republic on the observation of moral rules, and have been chosen by their fellow-citizens as first magistrates.'[1] The two men were Napoleon Bonaparte and Emmanuel Sieyès, and Say undoubtedly wrote the preface at a time when he was expecting Sieyès to play as great a role in the new republic as the first consul. Say later denied that he had played an active role in the Brumaire coup of November 1799, but this was coloured by his subsequent aversion to Napoleon—he had called Bonaparte a 'hero' in *La Décade* in March 1798, and became close enough to furnish the general with a list of books to read during the Egyptian campaign—and the need, during the Restoration, to distance himself from the Revolution. Say's particular task in 1799 might have been to ensure the support of *La Décade*, which was one of only thirteen journals not to be suppressed by the press law of 27 Nivôse, an VIII. Say was immediately honoured by the new government and nominated to the Tribunate by Sieyès in November 1799 (Frimaire, an IX). Say's political commitment was clear from his resignation from editorial duties (though he continued to write articles) at *La Décade* on his entry to the Tribunate. Furthermore, there is evidence that he was favourably disposed towards Bonaparte until 1802, despite Napoleon's opposition to those at *La Décade* and the *Institut* whom he termed *Idéologues*, after the failed assassination attempt of 24 December 1800.[2] At the bar of the Tribunate in January 1801 his first speech supported the 'armies of the Orient', whom he congratulated for having 'carried civilization to replace barbarism'; he also praised the restoration of peace in Europe 'by the genius of Bonaparte and the Republic'.[3] In the same year he attacked Clavière's friend and latterly apologist for Britain, François D'Ivernois, who had called the first consul a 'Cromwell preparing the return of the Bourbons'.[4] Nor was there any significant reduction in Say's faith in the imperial ambitions of the revolutionary armies in the years after 1799. As late as 1802 he was expounding his belief that Britain was the real source of international strife, through the artifice of a mercantile ministry seeking greater control over trade.[5] By creating trade routes to supply Europe with primary goods from Russia, through the Dardanelles and the Black Sea, and via Egypt, resurrecting what he called 'the old Levant route', Say was sure that France could undermine British commercial supremacy.[6]

Allegiance to the Directory only waned in the summer of 1799, when it was becoming clear that instead of creating the stability Say had anticipated, the regime was contributing to national disunity. Having given support to government candidates in the elections of March–April 1799 (1–30 Germinal, an VII), Say was disappointed that the result was the fragmentation of opinion in the *Conseils* and the Directory, and still greater antagonism between the two constitutional bodies, which led to the coup of 30 Prairial (18 June) when the Directors Merlin de Douai and La Révellière-Lepeaux were forced to resign. A royalist insurrection commenced in the Midi in August (18 Thermidor), while the Jacobins under Barras in the *Conseils* attempted to restore their power from July. Leading figures in the *Institut*, including Rœderer, Volney, Talleyrand, Destutt de Tracy, and Cabanis, were also beginning to blame the political system for this state of affairs, and conspired to create a new constitution after Sieyès replaced Reubell as Director on 16 May (27 Floréal, an VII). Say was probably aware of such activity through his visits to the Auteuil salon of Madame Helvétius, which united the members of the Second Class of the *Institut* and the editors of *La Décade*. Another source was Say's colleague Andrieux, a leading conspirator who was a friend of the rising star of the *Conseil des Cinq-Cents*, Lucien Bonaparte. Sieyès had concluded at this time that a leading republican general must be persuaded to display sufficient executive force to quell the disputatious legislative *Conseils* while rallying the people to a new convention. After Joubert's death at Novi on 15 August (28 Thermidor, an VII) he was inclined to favour Moreau, but Bonaparte's return to Fréjus from Egypt on 9 October (17 Vendémiaire, an VIII) and the rapturous reception he received from the populace on his entry into Paris on 16 October, convinced Sieyès that this was the man for the coup. In negotiations conducted via Talleyrand and Lucien Bonaparte, Sieyès agreed to Napoleon's demand that rather than a national convention the aftermath of the coup would be a constitutional committee selected from the existing *Conseils*, presided over by three consuls. The coup itself was carried out on 9–10 November (18–19 Brumaire) when the *Conseil des Anciens* voted in favour of a transfer of the legislature to Saint-Cloud on the pretext of an anarchist plot, and military muscle ultimately persuaded both *Conseils* to accept the creation of new constitutional commissions.

In his commentary on the Brumaire coup in *La Décade* written in January 1800 (15 Nivôse, an VIII) Say followed his fellow editors by portraying the Consulate as a new dawn for enlightenment and republicanism. The opportunity to express his views came in a review of Cabanis' defence of the new regime, *Quelques considérations sur l'organisation sociale en général et particulièrement sur la nouvelle constitution*. Cabanis here argued that 'la bonne démocratie' had become a possibility in a large state like France because the Consulate would 'fortify the empire of virtue', in part by promoting elementary books on morals for 'the indigent class'.[7] Say was full of praise for Cabanis' work, contending that it truly reflected the Consular constitution, which was based not on 'rights anterior to societies' or the 'pure fiction of the state of nature', but rather on 'the science of the social organization' which justified 'the two great discoveries of the moderns: the separation of powers and the representative system'.[8] According to Say, a government founded on these principles united the best elements of 'theocracy, democracy, monarchy, and aristocracy', by instituting popular sovereignty while ensuring that only the educated and the capable would be elected. Say quoted Garat's flattering summation and added an adage of his own: 'Although no one is excluded, it is difficult for anyone to be ill-chosen . . . Everything is done for the people and in the name of the people; nothing is done by the people or because of its unreflecting will.' Once more Say praised Sieyès and Bonaparte's role in the creation of the constitution, arguing that 'the union of men of wisdom and men of action . . . men of philosophy by taste and temperament' had conceived the project of 'restoring the Revolution to its greatest days'. A return was being made to what Say called les *principes libéraux* of 1789, when 'enlightened men, generous souls . . . the elite of the nation' had 'destroyed the influence of the privileged, and sought to place it in the hands of talented men of probity and good sense to carry France to a high point of splendour and prosperity.' The tragedy, which had been identified in many of Say's writings before this date, was that 'the profound corruption nourished by the monarchical regime and the court', and 'the obstacles with which they hindered the reformation', had caused:

the noble *élan* towards liberty to become a party affair; hatred between men became a hatred of institutions; the triumph of the good was less sought after than the triumph of the self; the means used became a matter of indifference; the men for whom humanity and public and private virtues are not vain words, withdrew one after another from a field they would have wished to cultivate, but which had in reality become an arena.

Say expected the Consular constitution, which he portrayed as a product of the union of Socrates and Caesar, to restore the principles of 1789; to protect the liberty of individuals without recourse to oppression, to provide a stable government, essential because 'time improves all good institutions' and to allow 'the perfection of men, of industry, and of talent'. He countered those who felt that the executive was too strong with the argument that 'civil and foreign war has been ended with honour', and that a 'powerful leader' was necessary to transform manners from an acceptance of servitude to the enjoyment of liberty. Say went so far as to acknowledge that any violence had been justified on the grounds that 'the evil that it combated was a greater threat [to society]'. In the new regime 'capitalists, land-owners, and entrepreneurs' would flourish because their property was fully protected. With such public support 'great civic virtues' and 'the cultivation of benevolence' would begin to characterize French culture; the creation of 'democracy purged of all inconveniences such as popular clubs or an ignorant class' signified 'the last act of the Revolution.' Say had returned to Sieyès's conception of the constitution of 1789, purged as it would have been of monarchical involvement in the legislative branch of government. By contrast with Clavière and Brissot's republicanism, he had been converted to the view that restrictions on citizenship were vital for stability. The difference between the early years of the Revolution and Say's consular concerns was the focus on manners as the key to the defence of the state and success of the republican nation. This was, of course, Clavière's legacy.

2 *IDÉOLOGUE* REPUBLICANISM

As Say's perspective indicates, the Consulate was not conceived as a break with the past but rather as a final reflection on the events of the 1790s, to institute and defend the best elements of the Revolution, which lay between a society dominated by monarchy and that characterized by Terror. As a result there was a striking continuity with the republicanism espoused in the intellectual citadels of the Directory, a fact underscored by the unhindered publication in 1800 of the third volume of the papers of the Moral and Political Class of the *Institut*. An active republican legislator, forcing citizens to be free in the certain knowledge of their general interest, remained an integral element of political thinking. Thus the project enunciated by *Olbie* and innumerable republican political economists' tracts was not abandoned but acquired still greater momentum between 1799 and 1802, seeking to educate the lower reaches of the populace in the duties of citizenship. The Moral and Political Sciences Class of the *Institut* continued to search for elementary works to explain the need for republican manners and to outline the best means for their inculcation. Concurrently the works of old and new philosophers were being published, such as Antoine Lasalle's *Traduction complète des œuvres de Bacon* (1800), J.-B. Salaville's *De la perfectibilité* (1800), on the benefits of universal education, and Anthelme Richeraud's *Nouveaux éléments de philosophie* (1800). Works of political economy, social science, physiology, metaphysics, and the new *idéologie* were written for use in the *écoles*, and for the education of the general populace. The hope of an educational revolution for the menial and the elevated had inspired Condorcet, and continued to animate such figures as Cabanis, Destutt de Tracy, Charles Dumas, Philippe Pinel, Maine de Biran, Xavier Bichat, and Rœderer. They cherished the belief that liberty would never be imperilled if legislation respected the *facts* of human nature; if legislation promoted *essential* needs there would be no danger to liberty. The functions of government could, it was argued, be specified and the role of the state in education monitored and rendered legitimate. Cabanis' *Rapports* of 1798 was based on these suppositions, as was Destutt de Tracy's *Idéologie* of 1801, and Rœderer's *Mémoires sur quelques points d'économie publique* of 1800–1.

As the building blocks of a republican legislative science were perceived to be human sensations, the foremost philosophical inspiration behind these projects was Condillac, whose twenty-two volume *œuvres* had been republished at Paris in 1798. The *savant* priest was lauded as the founder of an empirical approach to human science, called the 'science of man', based on the 'sensations' which established the 'facts' of human nature as a bulwark against scepticism.[9] Condillac had famously claimed that if language was analysed into component elements identifying the fundamental sensations by which men functioned in society the result would be foundational ideas defining human nature. His hope was that these core elements of the human mind could be recombined to illustrate the functioning of *healthy* human faculties. The linchpin in this argument was the identification of 'enlightened self-interest' with 'uncorrupted sensations'. The union of these ideas defined the morally healthy adult whose reason was sufficient to abjure corruption and thereby unhappiness. In articulating this vision Condillac proved the need for on all-embracing science of legislation, the function of which was to define precisely the nature of human well-being and determine the best possible politics and laws. Although Condillac attempted to prove the usefulness of this method in *Le commerce et le gouvernement: Considérés relativement l'un à l'autre* (Amsterdam, 1776), he believed that he had only sketched the philosophical foundations of a new kind of jurisprudence, and left its development and practical application to others, such as d'Alembert, Lacretelle, and Condorcet. The intellectuals of the late-1790s, and particularly those involved in the *Institut*, perceived Condillac's objective to be unrealized. Rœderer, for example, praised Condillac for revealing the means to human flourishing by 'enlightening reason through perfecting the language of moral and political ideas'.[10] Once more following Condillac, he believed that the moral and political sciences ought to imitate chemistry, and explore modern languages to discover the fundamental elements that could be distinguished and recombined for human use. Human science had to 'become positive' and find 'a Lavoisier'. The possibility of governing human conduct through the analysis of sensations caused the Second Class of the *Institut* in 1797 to sponsor a competition to address the question, *Determiner l'influence des signes sur la formation des idées*. The prize was ultimately awarded to Joseph Marie de Gérando, but it also gave Destutt de Tracy the opportunity to develop the revelations that had come to him on 5 Thermidor, an II (23 July, 1794), while imprisoned before trial, namely that 'virtue is happiness' and that 'liberty entails philanthropy'. In a paper read to the *Institut* in 1796 he had announced his intention of developing a science of virtuous manners using Condillac's investigation of language and sensations as a guide. Destutt promised that the correct methodological approach would reveal the unity of the human sciences, and declared that there was no limit to the application of his insights. He was seeking 'to create the theory of moral and political sciences, which have languished to this day in deadly uncertainty . . . knowledge of the process of human understanding is the unique science . . . The truths it comprises are susceptible to the same degree of certitude as the truths of the mathematical sciences.'[11] Destutt called his application of Condillac's method *idéologie*, signifying the study of the communication and combination of ideas, and seeking to work out the logical structure of the act of 'understanding', in the hope of revealing the art of judging ideas, the best mode of teaching them, and, most importantly of all, ways of influencing individuals' moral habits. It would become possible to make the direction of habits compatible with liberty by ensuring that they conformed to essential human faculties and desires, what Destutt called the 'true will' as opposed to the 'arbitrary will of narrow passion'. Destutt's research led to the publication of the *Projet d'éléments d'idéologie à l'usage des écoles centrales*, which promised to develop 'a human algebra' to address moral problems and the *Observations sur le système actuel de l'instruction publique*, which proclaimed, 'If the great nations do not wish to have masters, they must be enlightened.'[12] Destutt's educational programme aimed to 'defeat centuries of despotism' by creating *écoles primaires* for the *classes ouvrières* and more specialist schools (*écoles centrales*) for *savants*. All individuals were to be taught mathematics and physics, as well as moral and political science. He argued that this combination would cope with the need of the division of labour for a flexible work force while ensuring that all individuals were capable of fulfilling the obligations of republican citizenship.

An approach to moral and political science critical of Condillac and Destutt also flourished under the Consulate. It was led by Cabanis, who argued that analogies between analyses of language and mathematics or chemistry would ultimately be vacuous if they failed to define language physiologically, the only route to the empirical validation of theories of human behaviour.[13] In consequence, Cabanis called himself a 'student of the physics of humanity', and entitled the science *physiologie*. Condillac's analysis of human understanding had not isolated the motive forces of the mind, the faculties and instincts that consciously and unconsciously acted upon sensations. By contrast to chemical methods of *analysis,* Cabanis lauded physical science, moving from observed experience to general laws, seeking to group particular phenomena and to capture their movements. He claimed that by physiologically defining fundamental need the coercion of individuals by the state could be justified or made compatible with liberty. Once the passions were understood physiologically they could be combated, controlled, or harnessed. Although critical of Destutt's *idéologie*, Cabanis' approach to human science was part of the same project, accepting the view that 'the most precious enjoyments in life can only be obtained by the practice of morality'. Both men were republicans, believing that it was only in such states that a general interest that created law had a chance of remaining uncorrupted by privilege and passion. They further agreed that it was necessary to create a science that made this general interest clear.[14] Cabanis argued, however, that although progress had been made since Bacon, and most notably by Condillac, the *Institut* had to complete the work by unifying all the human sciences under the banner of physiology. This was now a possibility, because he had discovered physiological *faits généraux* (general facts) that proved that all human sciences derived from the same root. The most important of all was that 'since all moral and physiological phenomena are always uniquely linked, in the last resort, to physical sensibility (*sensibilité physique*) . . . Physical sensibility is the general fact of living nature.'

3   THE 'GENERAL FACT' APPROACH TO POLITICAL ECONOMY

The term 'general fact' originated in Scottish moral philosophy, although it was not used by Smith or Hume.[15] It was adopted by Condorcet in his most influential work, the *Esquisse*. It was written to reveal the general fact that the human species was morally perfectible, by which he meant that individuals were capable of living at peace with each other in communities of material and legal equality in which all adults participated in politics. In the republican state of the future advocates of monarchy, privilege, the hierarchy of ranks, and luxury would all be vanquished. These claims rested upon the universal truth that intellectual capacities were determined by social conditions: the consequence was that with the improvement of society both scientists and the general populace were becoming increasingly enlightened. The 'general' fact of perfectibility was general because it could be seen at work in every kind of society in history, and in every individual during the course of their lives. It was a 'fact' because there was empirical proof of progress in the works of the great philosophers throughout history. History became the key human science: it was no longer a conjectural enterprise but the fount of certain information about the creation of the ideal republic. It could teach legislators and citizens the means to perfectibility: 'for as facts accumulate men learn to classify them, to reduce them to more general facts: at the same time as the instruments and methods which were used to observe them, and to measure them with exactitude, acquired at the same time a new precision.' One of the most important examples of a general fact was the value of free trade. Condorcet argued that 'more liberal rules of commerce' were a force making for human perfectibility, regardless of the politics or conditions of particular societies.[16] Where the benefits of economic liberty were recognized, political liberty was promoted, and manners became more sociable and less corrupt. Equally, where political liberty reigned, economic liberty would inevitably follow. These species of liberty were mutually reinforcing, and had been beneficial in every kind of state. The only contemporary journal to focus on the *Esquisse's* use of the term was *La Décade*, in a review by Ginguené, who wholeheartedly agreed with Condorcet's view of the future of republicanism.[17]

In 1799 it was Cabanis' colleague and friend at the *Institut*, Talleyrand, who applied the method of seeking general facts to the branch of physiology called political economy.[18] Talleyrand used the term 'general fact' in papers to the Moral and Political Science Class of the *Institut* which addressed the thorny problem of why France had not developed closer commercial relations with America, despite the successes of the wars of the 1770s and 1780s, and widespread American antipathy towards the English. The central goal of his first paper was to justify the general fact that commerce developed between nations whose manners and politics were similar. This had never ceased to be the case with Britain and America, and therefore explained the continual increase of Anglo-American trade under adverse political conditions.[19] The populace of Britain and America shared commercial manners. The political cultures of the two states were at one in their vigorous pursuit of pecuniary gain. He concluded that if France wanted to develop as a commercial nation with an extensive export trade it would have to promote a commercial culture that approached that of Britain and America. The task of the French revolutionaries was thus not only to secure civil and commercial liberty but to foster the commercial manners which would become the basis for trade between the new republics. A second paper underlined this conclusion, arguing that only the fusion of a republican constitution with civil, economic, and political liberty (entailing the renunciation of colonial slavery) would revive the French economy and bring wealth to all classes.[20] The crucial point raised by Talleyrand's writings was that, for participants in the intellectual life of the *Institut* around 1800, general facts would have been recognized to be the empirical foundation for a perspective on political economy conceived as a branch of a broader republican human science. In this variety of political economy, the manners of the populace and the republican form of government played a crucial role. For Talleyrand, as for Cabanis and Condorcet, general facts constituted information about the behaviour of human beings within the framework of a broad investigation seeking to create the ideal modern republic in France. General facts were certain and universal aggregations of information about human nature that could be used to justify and formulate republican laws intended to improve moral, political, and economic conditions. It is significant that Say reviewed Talleyrand's work for *La Décade* and applauded Cabanis' work at the beginning of the Consular era.

4   UNITING VIRTUE WITH SELF-INTEREST

After the publication of *Olbie* Say was convinced that he could make a contribution to these projects. It was important for France, he believed, to become aware of the dangers of empire, 'which menaces the constitution of England' since 'the larger the state the less the patriotism of the people', and the greater the risk of administrative corruption.[21] Say felt that such problems could only be combated by means of schemes to promote civic responsibility and became interested in directing individuals to the public good, by enlightening self-interest using a variety of incentives and punishments. A proposal dear to Say's heart, and one which he would support many times in later life, was to increase the number of canals in France. In an adulatory review of Robert Fulton's work, Say once more used China as a bench-mark, arguing that 'the astonishing uniformity of their customs and manners' and 'stability of government in such a vast state', could be traced to the network of canals which united the nation. Admiring the Languedoc canal, which 'honours Louis XIV far more than the wars born of his pride', and the Duke of Bridgewater's Liverpool canal, Say claimed that the costs of building a canal system in France could be covered by the sale of wood by the side of waterways and a consumption tax on their use; this would put to work 'a million unemployed or ill-employed men' over a seventeen-year period of construction. Anticipated problems of demobilization could be addressed by such measures, so that 'the defender of the Republic becomes the founder of prosperity'. Above all it would contribute to the goal of creating a republic in a large state by creating a force for the communication of manners and their unification.[22] For similar reasons Say was favourably disposed towards La Rochefoucauld-Liancourt's study of experiments with different kinds of prison regime then being undertaken in Philadelphia. Rather than seeing the goal of the prison to be solely coercive, attempts to 'correct' felons by means of an incentive-based scheme of rewards and punishments aimed to 'improve the social order' of North American society. The basic regime was one of silence, frugality, cleanliness, and industry, with opportunities to earn in accordance with individual skill, to teach the less able, to be educated, and to enjoy a humane regime in which the worst punishment was solitary confinement rather than chains and beatings. Breaking the rules of the institution, which included avoiding idleness, was met first with a warning and subsequently with isolation. Say was particularly attracted by the fact that such prisons were said to pay for themselves through the labour of their inmates, making nails or cleaning cotton, thereby refuting Howard's concern that the work would never be sufficient to cover costs. The 'motivating force of fear and hope' had been ignored by Howard and Say expected the 'new government which opens a constitutional door to all reforms' to introduce this humane and moral regime in Parisian institutions, so that *idées libérales* would prove their worth.[23] Identical principles were to be applied to the hospitals and hospices of Paris. Administrative action would ensure that the sick or orphaned were neither too well treated—'so that their number increases'—nor shamed into crime or idleness by accident, misfortune, or neglect. The solution was the introduction of an austere regime in which 'all the able-bodied, whatever their age, must be subjected to work in proportion to their capacity.' Some of the costs of the hospitals would be met by such measures, while improving the skills of the patients. 'Harshness', but not cruelty, was necessary to guarantee the 'reformation of manners'.[24]

These ideas were inspired, Say's friend Augustin-Pyramus de Candolle tells us in his *Mémoires*, by a model reformer in Say's eyes, and the greatest influence upon him at this time: Benjamin Rumford, the soldier and inventor who had been made a count in Bavaria after experimenting with 'houses of industry', savings banks, and soup kitchens (*soupes économiques*), for the poor.[25] Rumford argued that virtue and self-interest could be made synonymous by means of practical schemes combining philanthropy with the encouragement of the learning of skills to remove the industrious poor from poverty. In a review of Candolle's translation of Rumford's *Essays*, which appeared in *La Décade* in the Autumn of 1799, Say fulsomely praised his mentor, likening his work to that of Sieyès because both men recognized that in modern societies 'the strength of man's foresight, the extent of his communication, the utility of his occupations, and the skill of his labour, contracts or extends his empire relative to his needs, and by consequence the sphere of his liberty.' To increase liberty while improving 'the social organization' it was necessary 'to direct the faculties towards a useful employment'. The 'duty and necessity of labour' was Rumford's great insight into the life of 'free peoples' and Say particularly applauded the combination of 'gardens of repose' with 'houses of industry'.[26] In a later review Say argued that *honnête industrie* was the key to Rumford's proposals, and the force that united virtue and self-interest. Rumford was developing ideas that had first been canvassed by numerous revolutionaries and most forcefully by Rœderer's *Cours*; the prominence of the term 'social organization' in Say's journalism at this time reveals the direct influence of Rœderer's writings. The point of importance is that Say was attracted to such writers because they offered means of making a corrupt populace more virtuous and thereby more republican. This was what he understood Bentham to be seeking to do and explains his veneration of the English sage from 1815 as a latter day Rumford. Say's commentary on Rumford is also important because it revealed his interest in the work of Adam Smith, whom he considered another source of useful projects for modern governments seeking to unite virtue with self-interest. Say cited Smith alongside Rumford as an example of an author who had recognized that political economy was concerned with manners as well as wealth:

Can all our readers have sensed from the depths of their hearts the truth of this reflection of Smith, that the study of Public Economy is at once the source of patriotism and its sustenance; and can the rapid progress of this interesting subject proclaim the return of the most noble affections to the heart of man, and the regeneration of labour, as well as opinion and manners?[27]

This perspective on Smith is important because it shows the development of an interest in Smith since the completion of *Olbie*. By 1800 Say was becoming convinced that Rumford's attack on 'unproductive professions', such as soldiers who remained idle while waiting for war, was derived from Smith. Say agreed that this view of soldiery was 'the most deadly in political economy, since it absorbs the most [production] while producing nothing.' He made the point that 'modern peoples have a false view of independence' because of their obsession with the practice of arms.[28] Smith was being perceived as a source for ideas that would transform manners away from military virtue towards the social benefits of industriousness and 'honest commerce'. In short, Say understood Smith in the light of the republicanism of the late 1790s which sought to address the problems of a divided and impoverished France.

Some time between 1799 and 1801 Say reread the *Wealth of Nations*. We are fortunate that Say's copy, the fifth London edition of 1789, has survived with copious annotations in the margins.[29] References to *mon ouvrage* show that some of Say's comments were made concurrently with the writing of the *Traité*. It is therefore unsurprising that some of Say's annotations prefigure the arguments and interests of his work of 1803, notably criticisms of Smith's labour theory of value, his view of the costs of employing slaves, support for machines which replaced labour, the distinction between productive and unproductive labour, and the critique of the physiocratic doctrine of the 'sterile labour of the artisan class'.[30] But the most important aspect of Say's comments is evidence that Say understood Smith as a fellow-traveller in the search for 'the general interest of humanity', which Say perceived to be synonymous with 'the natural order', guiding virtuous individuals operating outside the corruptions of politics or the particularities of culture. He focused upon Smith's search for social conditions in which labour would be rewarded, where each could rely upon his industry and be guaranteed a reward consonant with each individual's effort, expressed by 'the just idea of the natural price'. Say underlined what he saw as Smith's insights into the working of human nature: 'in the human body, there is a principle of life that seeks to balance the ill-effects of an unhealthy regimen; this principle is personal interest. It can make men prosper even in the face of threats to their well-being.' He also supported Smith's conclusion that 'the interest of the producer is the same as that of the people.' Unlike many readers of the 1790s, Say read Smith as an author seeking to define the interests which united humanity. As such, he understood Smith's writings as supportive of the French republicans in their search for means to create a united and just nation. Smith was also recognized to be a 'modern', an advocate of a commercial society more egalitarian than any comparable society in history: 'The progress of the arts and of commerce have caused the power of the clergy to vanish as well as the power of the nobility. It has rendered the different classes of society independent.' He thus emerged as an advocate of the revolutionary attempt to promote commerce by removing the clerical and aristocratic elements of the Old Regime. Such a reading would have been alien to Smith's Scottish disciples, such as Dugald Stewart, and was almost the opposite of Burke's interpretation. It can only be understood by reference to the intellectual traditions that developed in France from the late 1780s.

5   THE AIMS AND METHOD OF THE FIRST *TRAITÉ*

In his annotations to the *Wealth of Nations* Say was critical of Smith, and declared himself to be astonished that 'so excellent a mind as Smith's was so just yet also so disordered in his ideas.'[31] At some point he decided that a reassessment of this book would be his contribution to the manners controversy. Given that Guinguené had identified the lack of philosophical rigour to be the fundamental lacuna in *Olbie*, Say's first step in writing an elementary work on political economy was to become involved in the controversy over the nature of human science then dominating the *Institut*.[32] The product of Say's labours was published three years later as the *Traité d'économie politique* and divided into five books. Book I examined the nature of wealth and the causes of production. Books II and III, of money and of value, comprised a critique of mercantile and physiocratic political economy. Book IV, of revenue, investigated the distribution of wealth between social groups. The final book analysed consumption and its role in a healthy economy. The first and last books were the most original of the *Traité*, containing Say's critique of Smith and his strategy for the improvement of the economic position of France in the prevailing international climate. Behind the titles and cutting across the chapters, Say continued *Olbie* by developing an argument about the precise manners which would create a more egalitarian society in France, vanquishing poverty in the process. Hints at Say's overall intentions were revealed in the sixty-page *Discours préliminaire*. At the outset this proclaimed that the *Traité* was a restatement of Smith's views, which had been misunderstood since 1776, and therefore amounted to a new approach to political economy in the Revolutionary era. The first step was, in order to avoid errors, to provide a precise definition of political economy. By errors Say meant false or exaggerated connections between '*vérités*', the latter term referring to statements supported by empirical evidence.[33]

The reason why definition was so crucial was made clear at the end of the *Discours*, where Say acknowledged that Europe was richer than at any previous time in history or in any prior state of society. Against excessive optimism with regard to progress, however, he issued a warning: the vast majority of the people, even in the richest state in Europe, continued to live in conditions of acute poverty, making stability and opulence utopian pipe dreams:

if one considers that in *the most prosperous countries* there is not one individual in a hundred thousand who is able to satisfy all these needs, that everywhere we see great indigence next to gross opulence, the forced labour of some set against the idleness of others, huts next to porticos, the rags of poverty mixed with the signs of luxury, in a word, the most valuable abundance amidst the most urgent needs, one will be unable to regard as superfluous any research conducted with the aim of understanding the causes of such evils, and any means of remedying them.[34]

The outstanding goal of the science of political economy, therefore, was to ameliorate the harsh inequality and dire poverty that plagued modern societies. Say maintained that to meet this goal political economy had to model itself on those natural sciences that eschewed all claims not founded upon the hardest of empirical evidence. His preferred model was physics, which his late brother Horace had expounded in the pages of *La Décade*. Facts, Say contended, *bien observés*, were the foundation of political economy:

In Political Economy as in physics, as in everything, systems have been made before establishing truths, for it is easier to build a system than to discover a truth. But this science has profited from the excellent methods that have contributed so much to the progress of other sciences. It has only accepted *rigorous consequences of well-observed facts* and has altogether refuted the prejudices and the dogmas that, in science as well as in morals, in literature as well as in administration, have always put obstacles between man and the truth.

The majority of political economists of the period asserted that their ideas were derived from empirical reality. Say was distinctive, however, in arguing that facts were of different types, and that the kinds of facts pursued by a particular human science distinguished it from others. Political economy was distinct from statistics, the former being based upon 'general facts', and the latter upon 'particular facts'. The different orders of facts allowed the focus of each science to be demarcated:

In the subject with which we are concerned, the knowledge of these two types of facts forms two distinct sciences: Political Economy and Statistics. The first shows how wealth is created, distributed and destroyed; the causes that favour its accumulation and those that lead to its decline; the necessary relationship with population, the power of states, and the happiness or the misery of peoples. The second reveals the state of production and of consumption in one or in several nations, during a given era, or in successive eras, as well as the condition of the population, its strengths and the events which occur in it and which can be the subject of mathematical analysis. It is a form of detailed geography. The difference between Political Economy and Statistics is the same as the difference between Politics and History.

Say described particular facts as the observed outcome of specific actions in definite circumstances. Particular facts were therefore certain but simple, in that they occurred in the unique conditions which they described. By contrast, general facts were identifiable by their relation to an anterior law that explained the operation of phenomena—and the relations between phenomena—in the human world; they were *general* because they revealed the essential and universal regularities of the moral world. Whereas particular facts were compilations of evidence, general facts were the next stage in the process of acquiring knowledge: they allowed the deduction of laws that illustrated the optimum conditions of human existence, and could therefore be used to educate and influence wayward humanity. His conception of general facts was illustrated with an example drawn from physics: the discovery of the property of mass in a physical body was the foundation for general facts that explained the behaviour of an object with mass in all conditions. It was a general fact that a body with a mass greater than that of air would always fall to earth:

But it has not been noticed enough that there are two types of facts. There are *general* or *constant facts*, and *particular* or *variable facts*. The *general facts* are the product of the actions of the laws of nature in identical circumstances. Particular facts are equally the result of one or several actions that modify each other, in a specific case. The former are no less certain than the latter, even when they appear to be in contradiction; in physics it is a general fact that heavy bodies fall towards the earth; however, our jets of water contradict this. The particular fact of a jet of water is a case in which the laws of equilibrium combine with that of gravity, without disproving either of them.

Say argued that knowledge of general facts would explain expected behaviour as well as aberrations from anticipated behaviour. The latter case was particularly important because the operations of particular facts often appeared to contradict the general fact. In political economy it was a general fact, Say argued, that a direct relationship existed between the rate of interest payable on borrowed capital and the risk of the venture. Equally, it was not a contradiction to say that in some circumstances this rule might be overshadowed by other factors. The crucial point was that the general fact was always true, even when obscured by local circumstance.

The search for general facts had two immediate consequences. First, those who identified political economy with the encyclopaedic exposition of statistics about wealth were not political economists in the proper sense. Proponents of political arithmetic and statistics, Say argued, were incapable of resolving the economic problems facing Europe because their evidence was never certain; it shifted with circumstance and could give different results in different conditions. Say did not believe a science of political arithmetic to be possible, since it necessarily rested upon particular phenomena conditioned by the uncertainty of evidence, lack of information, inexactitude, ill-will, and the antagonism of governments, 'which makes truth last for only an instant'. He undoubtedly had in mind Joseph Peuchet's recently published dictionary of commerce and Nicolas Canard's statement of the principles of political economy in the form of political arithmetic.[35] Smith, he believed quite correctly, had never had any faith in such enterprises. The second consequence was that political economy was a 'natural science' in the sense that the principles governing the creation and distribution of wealth were universal, and independent of the particularities of social and political relations and structures. Say held that it was only by moving from particular facts to general facts and thence to principles that political economy would attain scientific status. The real problem was that the policies of European citizens, subjects, and legislators would continue to be imperfect until the task of making an independent and certain empirical science had been achieved. Even Smith's work failed the tests of properly defining political economy and pursuing the correct method:

The work of Smith is nothing more than a confused assemblage of the soundest principles of Political Economy supported by illuminating examples, and of the most curious elements of Statistics combined with instructive reflections; but it is a complete treatise neither of the one nor of the other. His book is a vast chaos of just ideas, mixed haphazardly with positive ideas.[36]

6   POLITICAL ECONOMY ANCIENT AND MODERN

The first general fact that the *Traité* identified was very surprising for a republican of Say's stamp. It expressed Say's intention of distinguishing his political economy from the republican approaches that had developed since 1792, and especially from *Idéologie*. On the first page of the *Discours* he declared without qualification that an absolute monarchy was equally as likely to be economically successful as a popular republic:

Wealth is independent of the nature of government. Under all forms of government a state can prosper if it is well administered. We have seen absolute monarchs enrich their country, and popular councils ruin theirs. The structure of public administration itself only indirectly and accidentally influences the formation of wealth, which is almost entirely the work of individuals.[37]

One of the most important of all the claims of the *Traité* was that forms of government only indirectly influenced the creation of wealth. To political economists like Cabanis, Destutt de Tracy, Talleyrand, and, more especially, Condorcet, this amounted to heresy. Say was aligning himself with those who believed that specifying laws independently of forms of government and states of society was possible, and moving against the republican writers who had argued since 1792 that laws could not be conceived outside of a particular political context. Informed and enlightened administration rather than the messy business of governance was proclaimed to be Say's ideal. The scientific administrator was contrasted with the self-interested and unscrupulous politician: an image that recurred in all of Say's subsequent writings on political economy. Say believed that confusing political economy with politics had above all else retarded political economy before 1776. The root cause lay in the misleading legacy of historical experience. The ancients had lived in a very different social and political world in which 'economy' was a branch of the household, reflecting the extent to which the individual was conceived of only as a member of a republic with civic duties. Thus when the term 'political economy' was coined it referred to the governance of the household or city state. The ancient world had passed down to the modern world a belief that 'private economies', be they those of a state or an individual, did not exist. This was the source of the confusion:

Until Smith's work, Politics, which ought to be understood as the science of government, was confused with Political Economy, which shows how wealth is created, distributed, and consumed. This confusion was perhaps uniquely caused by the name that has inappropriately been given to research of this kind. Since the word *economy* signifies the laws which regulate the household or home affairs, and the word *politics* appears to apply this idea to the political family or city, some have desired that political economy takes charge of all the laws which regulate the affairs of the political family. It was therefore not necessary to involve research into the creation of wealth.[38]

The problem with the ancient linkage of politics and political economy was twofold. First, it was a general fact that forms of government were independent of wealth; this was the message that the experience of the French Revolution had made clear. Second, enlightened commentators upon the modern world had discovered the general fact that commerce, including manufactures and agriculture, were, in the words of Sully, 'the twin breasts of state'. This fact had been unknown to the Romans and the Greeks, whose backward economies were based upon slave labour in agriculture alone. Uniting political economy with governance, Say contended, had obscured this truth, by focusing the interests of political economists upon the security and liberty of the individual before they considered the creation of wealth. The error had led ministers and theorists to associate the successful creation of wealth with the stability or prosperity of the existing form of government of a state, or of groups of individuals within it. Examples of such solecisms were abundant in modern French history. Louis XIV had gone to war because he had linked the security of his state with the acquisition of wealth by conquest. Likewise, the regency after 1715 had made a system from the claim that luxury enriches states in the mistaken belief that successful politics and political economy were one and the same. The result was bankruptcy and a political culture in which 'moderation and economy became terms of ridicule'. Say believed he could trace the same mistakes in the work of political economists who had ignored two of the most significant general facts of the modern world. Montesquieu had 'sowed brilliant errors' in the political economy of *L'Esprit des lois*.[39] The physiocrats and Voltaire, in their virulent disputation over the merits of the freedom of the grain trade in the 1760s, had been fighting in the dark. The former had fallen into the worst kinds of errors in their political economy because they had refused to follow the method of the physical sciences of the period, by making general facts the touchstone of their analyses. Regarding Quesnay and Mirabeau's *Physiocratie*, Say argued:

Instead of first observing the nature of things, of ordering their observations, and of deducing general truths, they began by stating generalisations, and sought to organize all the particular facts around them, and to draw consequences from them; this engaged them in the defence of maxims evidently contrary to common sense and to centuries of experience.[40]

Despite their severe morals, their 'love of the public good', their advocacy of free trade and civic duty, the physiocrats' methods were those of the worst human scientists. The tragedy was that their method had been so popular that the works of Condillac, Raynal, and even Condorcet had been infected by their gratuitous suppositions. Say decried as equally mistaken those who mixed politics with political economy to oppose the physiocrats during the 1750s and 1760s. He included Rousseau and James Steuart in his litany of the ignorant: the latter for being too obsessive a disciple of Colbert. Say concluded:

The study of the causes of public and private prosperity is therefore independent of purely political considerations; in combining them we have confused ideas rather than enlightening them. This reproach can be levelled at Steuart, who entitled his first chapter, *Of the Government of Humanity*; it is a reproach that can be levelled against the sect of Physiocrats, and at J. J. Rousseau in the *Encyclopaedia*.

Only Turgot had avoided these errors, but even his independence of mind had not led him to remake the science of political economy on the sure foundation of *vérité fondamentale*. The modern science of political economy was only twenty-seven years old. Say unreservedly credited Smith with overturning the alchemical fallacies that had obscured political economy before 1776. The *Wealth of Nations* represented an intellectual revolution deserving fulsome praise:

When one reads this work, it becomes clear that Political Economy did not exist before Smith. I do not doubt that the writings of the Physiocrats were very useful to him . . . but, between the doctrine of the Physiocrats and his, there is the same distance that separates the system of Tycho Brahe and the physics of Newton. Several times before Smith true principles had been advanced; but he was the first to show the connections between them, and that they are necessary consequences of the nature of things . . . He has done more than establish truths: he has given the true method of signalling errors. He does not permit himself a single assertion, or a sole supposition, which does not accord with the most uniform facts.[41]

Political economy had been like chemistry, a species of alchemy with adepts who promised to turn metal into gold. Smith had reinvented the science with the first work of political economy to be based upon facts. The problem was that Smith's political economy had become unrecognizable in the hands of many interpreters. For example, although Say accepted that the best translation of the *Wealth of Nations* was that of Garnier in 1802, the author had repeated the errors of the physiocrats in his treatment of Smith. The reason for this misunderstanding was Smith's methodological inexactitude and disorganization in formulating the science. Say declared he would avoid the long digressions and expositions of particular facts that had so marred the *Wealth of Nations*.

Having been so generous about his debt to Smith, Say immediately began to differentiate his own conception of political economy. He made it clear that it was definitely not a branch of 'the science of a statesman or legislator'. His political economy was distinctive in its object: to alter the culture of nations by revealing to citizens the role they played in the creation of wealth, thereby influencing their behaviour in order to make it more enlightened:

Almost always, the principal function of Political Economy has been deemed to be that of answering the questions of a small number of men concerned with affairs of state; insufficient account has been taken of the fact that, since virtually everybody contributes to the creation of wealth, and that everyone, without exception, contributes to their own consumption, there is nobody whose conduct does not influence, to a lesser or greater extent, their own or the general wealth, and, in consequence, their particular fate and the fortune of the state; Political Economy has not been seen for what it truly is—even among people subject to an arbitrary power: everybody's business.[42]

He had discovered the general fact that, to be a successful science, political economy had to address all citizens. This perspective on political economy might be called 'republican' in that Say was arguing that the people at large was potentially important to the creation of wealth and had to be informed and enlightened about their role. Say reasoned that unless all of the people were convinced of the benefits which would accrue to them in pursuing the behaviour recommended by a political economist, and recognized its social prescriptions as being true, then any law would either be impeded by popular resistance or defeated by a failure to act in accordance with it. This had certainly been the cause of the failures of the liberalization of the grain trade in the 1760s and 1770s:

Finally, suppose that all those who take part in the management of public affairs, of all ranks, were skilled in Political Economy, while the nation was not . . . what resistance would the realization of their surest plans not face? . . . In order for a nation to benefit from a good economic system, it is not enough for the leaders to adopt the best policies of every kind; it is necessary that the nation is in a state to receive them.[43]

The best example of the necessity for this approach was the experience of the British state. Although British policy had handicapped the advance of wealth creation by centring on foreign trade to the detriment of domestic markets, huge rewards had been reaped because the policy had been stable and, above all, popular. The British people had been educated to believe in mercantile practices and this had been conducive to social stability and economic prosperity. The pattern of French policy had, by contrast, been altogether less constant and consequently far less successful. The root problem was that France lacked a culture that would sustain the effects of good laws. Say used a distinctive term for this in his analysis of the history of economic policy in France: 'she has advanced haphazardly because the nation has not had *fixed opinions* concerning the causes of public prosperity.' Only when the ideas for an economically successful culture were widespread, becoming 'common parlance', would France fulfil her economic potential: 'When the most sound principles of Political Economy are professed among the various orders of society, by the farmer, by the merchant, and by the magistrate . . .

then we will have a general plan of administration, which can be followed whatever revolutions are undergone.'[44] Say's ideal was to establish a set of easily understood principles or maxims that would be beyond the pale of popular dispute and political faction. He believed that such ideological stability would, by its very nature, be conducive to increased opulence. Say was not a utopian and did not expect such a culture to be speedily formed. Like Clavière and Brissot a decade earlier, Say placed his faith in the middling ranks of nations, those who were not tempted by luxury and were unthreatened by the spectre of poverty, and therefore able to recognize truth and to administer the laws founded upon general facts:

can powerful individuals themselves be truly wise, when the ordinary individuals are not? This difficult question is worth considering. It is among the middle class (*la classe mitoyenne*), far from the worries and the pleasures of grandeur; far from the anguish of destitution; it is in the class where honest fortunes are found, where leisure is combined with the habit of toil, and where one finds the free communication of friendship, the taste for reading and travel; it is in this class, I say, that enlightenment is born; and it is from them that it spreads among the nobility and among the people; because the nobility and the people have not the time to think; they make truths their own only when they are presented in the form of axioms, and have no more need of proof. And even when a monarch and his principal ministers have become familiar with the principles on which the prosperity of nations is founded, what would they do with their knowledge, if they were not supported, in all the grades of administration, by men capable of understanding these principles, of adopting these ideas, and of putting them into practice? The prosperity of a town, even of a province, often depends upon the work of an office, and the head of a very small administration, in taking an important decision, can often have an influence superior to that of the legislator himself.[45]

7   SAY'S CRITIQUE OF CONSULAR REPUBLICANISMS

It should now be clear that Say was using Adam Smith in 1803 to demarcate political economy from specific features of the republican legislative sciences of the 1790s. Say had witnessed the failures of successive revolutionary governments to solve the economic problems of France. Having experienced another loss of confidence with the rapid subversion of the Consulate into a monarchy bolstered by the Catholic church, Say declared himself willing to abandon elements of the political project initiated in September 1792; he was no longer an orthodox republican. The conclusion he drew from recent French history was that political economy had to precede constitution building. A new political economy had to be formulated, independent of republican government, but intimately concerned with the encouragement of an industrious and frugal culture. Such a culture would in turn produce a more even distribution of wealth, and independent citizens averse to luxury while being free from poverty. Say was convinced that Smith had been the first to recognize the need for such a culture in modern states. However, he did not cite any textual evidence from the *Wealth of Nations* and no author at this time shared Say's view of Smith. Furthermore, in making political economy a popular science, Say was moving in a direction Smith never contemplated.

It must be emphasized that Say's idea of liberty was far removed from the liberalisms of the nineteenth century in which the goal of political economy was to defend each citizen in the pursuit of well being against government intervention. He believed that most of the mistakes of human behaviour were caused by ignorance and not by the tyranny of excessive government. Rather than allowing individuals to pursue their own conception of happiness it was vital for them to understand their role in 'the social mechanism'. Only then would they would become industrious and useful citizens. The legislator had to be concerned with encouraging a virtuous culture and the 'real' interests that the industrious and enlightened citizenry, rich and poor, shared. The general fact method revealed this interest. It was the source of certain laws, independent of political faction and egoistic prejudice, which would increase wealth and social cohesion. As such, it was premised upon an evident unity of interest that was the antithesis of hidden-hand conceptions of social harmony relying on unintended consequences. One major difference between the *Traité* and the *Wealth of Nations* was the lack of historical analysis. In part this was because Say did not want to cover ground which he believed might mask his central arguments, as he was sure the long historical digressions had in Smith's book. Another reason was the almost universal acceptance of commercial society by the revolutionaries, obviating any need for discussion of the four states theory of stadial change. More importantly, however, Say disagreed with Smith's view of history, giving prominence as it did to the role of accident and the hidden hand of self-interest. Condorcet's greater influence showed at this point, with its optimism about human rationality and the progress of the human mind once general facts had been identified. The *Traité* was therefore, unlike the *Wealth of Nations*, a work pitched at the ill-educated, for the dual reason that the lowliest citizens were important economic functionaries and capable of rational adherence to virtuous manners. In short, the general fact method was ultimately intended to put an end to the upheavals of the Revolution without abandoning the republican ideas of progress and happiness that it embodied.

NOTES TO CHAPTER 7

1. *OlbA*, ix.
2. Joanna Kitchin, having examined Say's letters of this period to Amaury Duval (whose papers can be found at the Société Éduenne, Musée Rollin, Autun), concludes that Say's 'absolute hostility' to Bonaparte's regime dates from September 1804. However, Say's fears are clear from his counsel to Duval to suppress the *Politique intérieure* section of *La Décade* in a letter of 4 February, 1801 (15 Pluviôse, an IX), and his opposition is evident from the tone of his journalism during the next year.
3. *Discours prononcé au corps législatif par le citoyen J.-B. Say, Tribun: Pour appuyer le projet de loi tendant à déclarer que l'armée d'orient a bien mérite de la patrie. Séance du 23 Nivôse, an IX.*
4. Comment on D'Ivernois', *Des causes qui ont amené l'usurpation de Bonaparte et qui préparent sa chûte,* in a review of Helen-Maria Williams, *Aperçus de l'état, des mœurs et des opinions dans la République française, vers la fin du XVIIIe siècle*, LDP no. v. 28, pp. 222, 278.
5. Review of *Lettres politique, commerciales et littéraires sur l'Inde, ou vues et intérêts de Angleterre, relativement à la Russie, à l'Indostan, et à l'Egypte, par Lieutenant-Colonel Taylor*, LDP no. v. 30, pp. 7–14.

6. Review of *L'Europe conquise avec une plume et du cotton, ou Court exposé de la puissance du commerce anglais*, LDP no. v. 28, pp. 261.

7. *Quelques considérations sur l'organisation sociale en général et particulièrement sur la nouvelle constitution* (Paris, 25 Frimaire, an VIII (16 December 1799)), published in *Œuvres philosophiques* (Paris, 1956), p. 465.

8. Review of Cabanis, *Quelques considérations sur l'organisation sociale en général et particulièrement sur la nouvelle constitution*, LDP no. I, 15 Nivôse, an VIII, pp. 9–16.

9. See especially Condillac's *Extrait raisonnée du Traité des sensations* (Paris, 1764).

10. *D'un grand moyen de perfectionner la morale du peuple*, ŒdR, v, 151–2; *De l'imitation et de l'habitude*, ŒdR, v, 258–71; ŒdR, v, 391; ŒdR, iv, 154.

11. Destutt de Tracy *Mémoire sur la faculté de penser*, MdIN, i, 283–450, 285, 288.

12. *Éléments d'Idéologie* (Paris, 1801), p. 322.

13. Cabanis, *Rapports du physique et du morale de l'homme* (Paris, 1844) pp. 20–3, 43–4, 95, 493.

14. Cabanis, *Considérations générales sur l'étude de l'homme, et sur les rapports de son organisation physique avec ses facultés intellectuelles et morales*, MdIN i, 37–8, 149, 141 n., 151.

15. The term appears to have originated in John Bruce's *Elements of the Science of Ethics, on the Principles of Natural Philosophy* (London, 1786), which included a section entitled 'Preliminary Sketch of the General History of the Human Mind'; it was translated into French at Paris in the 1790s. I am indebted to Michael Sonenscher for this reference.

16. *Esquisse d'un tableau historique*, pp. 2, 51, 58, 132, 217–18.

17. *LDP*, no. v, 475–88.

18. *Mémoire sur les rélations commerciales des Étas-Unis avec l'Angleterre*, MdIN, ii, 86.

19. *Mémoire sur les rélations commerciales des Étas-Unis avec l'Angleterre*, MdIN, ii, 92.

20. *Essai sur les avantages à retirer de colonies nouvelles dans les circonstances présentes*, MdIN, ii, 288.

21. Review of William Guthrie, *Nouvelle géographie universelle*, LDP no. 27, 30 Prairial, an VII, pp. 522–33.

22. Review of Robert Fulton, *Recherches sur les moyens de perfectionner les canaux de navigation*, LDP no. 20, pp. 462–6, 525–31.

23. *Économie sociale: Des prisons de Philadelphie*, LDP no. v. 24, pp. 73–80.

24. *Des hôpitaux et des hospices de Paris*, LDP no. v. 30, pp. 260–6.

25. Candolle, *Mémoires et souvenirs* (Geneva, 1862), pp. 106–15.

26. *LDP*, xxii, 276–85, 467–77, review of Rumford's *Essais politiques, économiques et philosophiques*; see also *Bibliothèque britannique: Littérature* (Geneva, 1796), i, 499.

27. *LDP*, xxii, 276–85, 467–77, review of Rumford's *Essais politiques*.

28. Review of *Précis des événements militaires*, LDP no. 5, 20 Brumaire, an VIII, pp. 276–85.

29. *Notes inédites de J.-B. Say qui couvrent les marges de la Richesse des Nations et qui critiquent: rédigées avec une introduction*, Kyoto Sangyo University Economic and Business Review, vii (1980), 53–81; *Notes inédites de J-B Say qui couvrent les marges de la richesse des nations et qui la résume*, Kyoto Sangyo University Economic and Business Review, ix (1982), 31–133. I am grateful to Professor Hashimoto for supplying copies of these articles.

30. *Kyoto Sangyo University Economic and Business Review*, vii, 70.

31. *Ibid.*, vii, 71.

32. Letter to Joseph Peuchet, [undated, probably spring 1803], in Hashimoto, *Les lettres inédites de Jean-Baptiste Say*, Treatises 20 (1971), p. 84.

33. *TE*, i, i.

34. *Ibid.*, i, xliii.

35. Canard, *Principes de l'économie politique, ouvrage couronné par l'Institut dans sa séance du 15 nivôse l'an 9, et depuis revu, corrigée et augmentée par l'auteur* (Paris, 1801); Peuchet, *Dictionnaire de la géographie commerçante* (Paris, 1799, 1800).

36. *TE*, i, xii.
37. *Ibid.*, i, ii.
38. *Ibid.*, i, i.
39. *Ibid.*, i, xv–xvi.
40. *Ibid.*, xvi.
41. *TE*, i, xx.
42. *Ibid.*, i, xviii.
43. *Ibid.*, i, xxix.
44. *Ibid.*, i, xxxi.
45. *Ibid.*, i, xxviii–xxix.

8

Defending Republican Manners

The *Discours préliminaire* of the *Traité* began with a radical and, to an observer of revolutionary politics, a breathtaking claim: that politics and political economy were distinct subjects with different concerns, laws, and objectives. The body of the *Traité* underlined another difference with orthodox republican political economy. Say renounced his faith in public instruction as a means of inculcating virtue in the citizenry:

> The only important study which does not appear to me to be worthy of being the object of public instruction is the study of morality. Is it necessary to have a master to tell us our duties towards our brothers and sisters, and towards our friends? Morals must everywhere be learned and nowhere be taught. The parents of a child and those who care for it are the teachers of his morals, because they alone can direct his habits. If they fulfil this noble task badly, it is a misfortune without doubt, but who could replace them? I have never seen a civic education that sufficed to make men virtuous, and the only honest men I have ever seen are those who have been brought up with good habits.[1]

The rejection was explicit and followed from Say's journalism, particularly the critique of Duval and Ginguené's revival of Condorcet's civic projects in the late 1790s.[2] In opposing the teaching of morals, Say nevertheless made clear his belief in the need for a moral culture. Equally, morals had to be 'learned'. This was only possible if parents inculcated moral maxims, establishing 'good habits' which would be followed for life. Morals were not rational axioms independent of everyday experience. Rather, they accorded with enlightened self-interest, the product of personal experience or knowledge of the experience of others. Approaching morality from this perspective meant that Say was being somewhat disingenuous in his distinction between the learned and the taught. His intention was to show that morals could be taught if they were associated with everyday experience and directly linked to self-interest. Say was therefore condemning the forms of republican instruction advocated by the early republicans and contemporary *idéologues*. He was not repudiating central threads of *Olbie* or turning his back on the republican virtues and concern about the distribution of wealth.

The aim of this chapter is to reveal the sense in which Say remained a revolutionary republican, untypical perhaps, but nevertheless maintaining several orthodox strands of the tradition which had placed such a major role in the intellectual movements of the previous decade. Following Clavière's view of the means of transforming corrupt societies, Say continued to focus on national manners as the central element of political economy. The *Traité* sought to justify specific manners that accorded with what he held to be universally valid ideas about enlightened self-interest. In doing so he leaned on the authority of Adam Smith. Although Smith was the most frequently cited author in discussions of manners, Say approached Smith from a perspective first formed by Condorcet, Sieyès, and particularly Rœderer, in the mid 1790s. After the failure of the Directory, Say was rejecting republican constitutionalism but affirming republican manners. Although he had lost his faith in the success of the former, Say was extremely optimistic about the possibility of fostering republican manners in France. French greatness would ultimately be restored because Britain would remain, he was sure, a society characterized by inequality with—as a consequence—far weaker subjects than the united and patriotic citizens of her neighbour. How Say used Smith in his strategy for the defeat of Britain is the subject of the next chapter. This chapter concerns Say's use of Smith to support ideas that the enlightened Scot would have found inconceivable— Say made Smith into the patron saint of a revolutionary and republican moral code.

2 INDUSTRIOUS MANNERS AND EGALITARIAN RANKS

In the Preliminary Discourse, Say had stated that he was setting himself two central goals. The first was to reveal to citizens their contribution to the wealth of society. This, Say contended at the beginning of Book II, had been achieved in his analysis of production:

In the preceding Book I have explained as clearly as it is possible for me to do, the principal elements of production. The intellectual, the businessman, the labourer, the man who exercises whatever talent, the capitalist, the land-owner, and finally even the government, have been able to see what share they contribute to this mass of activity, through which society draws its needs and draws its pleasures.[3]

Say's second aim was to assess and specify measures capable of combating the poverty which continued to ravage Europe, and which appeared immune to the wealth generated by commercial societies. The condition of Europe, Say persistently asserted, provided certain evidence of the extent of poverty and the dangers it represented for modern states. For Say poverty was a symbol of malign civilization: 'In our Europe, the most idle workers are those who are closest to the habits of the savage.' Solutions were possible, however, if it was realized that making the poor industrious would make the state economically successful and thereby internally more stable:

The ease of the lower classes is not incompatible with the existence of the social body, although it has been said all too often . . . Even the most wealthy of our European nations are once more impoverished, since there is not a single nation in which the majority of families are able to enjoy the basic satisfactions of life; in short, where they are safe from exposure to cruel want.[4]

Say argued, as he had in *Olbie*, that unless modern states discovered means of combating poverty, then all schemes for political and moral reform would come to nothing. The solutions that Say developed spanned the five books of the *Traité*.

In Book I Say's discussion of poverty commenced with the clarification of one of his most firmly held beliefs: only in a society where the citizens were industrious could poverty ever be remedied. Although he had a far more productive and egalitarian society in mind, Say repeated Smith's famous claim that because of the industriousness of the moderns the condition of the poorest labourer was superior to that of the greatest king of a savage state: 'Thanks to his industry, the most lowly inhabitant of our towns enjoys an infinity of comforts which a king of savages is obliged to do without.' The example Say gave was of the state of Malta, which, although built upon the most infertile soil, had yet been able to sustain a large population because of the industrious manners of Maltese citizens. Industrious activity geared to the creation of a useful product could, Say argued, be divided into three functions: the conceptualization of the product by the innovative thinker; the organization of production through the application of this knowledge by the farmer, manufacturer, or merchant; and the fashioning of the product by the manual labourer. This categorization of industriousness led Say to the conclusion that a state would never be fully industrious unless its inhabitants thrived in all three branches of production. Say underlined his conviction that if the imaginative classes, the thinkers and the writers, were neglected, because they were considered to be unproductive, then the creation of national wealth would be impeded:

Everywhere industry comprises theory, application, and execution. It is only so far as a nation excels in all three kinds of operation that it is truly industrious. If it is unskilled in one or another, it cannot produce goods that result from all three. Therefore one realizes the utility of sciences which at first glance appear destined to assuage only a useless curiosity.

Say's next action was to specify the most important of all the actions of the industrious citizen, and the key to the creation of a prosperous society: the use of industry to create productive capital. Productive capital, from simple tools to complex machines and the infrastructure of production, was, Say argued, the stimulus to further industry and the source of ever-cheaper subsistence goods for the mass of the population. The sign of the successful capitalization of the economy was a reduction in the ratio of tangible productive capital to that embodied in circulating metal monies: 'What is true of one individual, of two, of three or four, is true of society as a whole. The capital of a nation consists of the capitals of all individuals, and the more a nation is industrious and prosperous, the more its capital in money is small relative to the sum-total of all its capitals.'[5] The wealth of every state was limited only by the extent of its capital. For example, Geneva produced only enough agricultural products to satisfy a tenth of its population, but its citizens lived in abundance by virtue of their use of capital. The problems of state size and the limits upon natural resources, Say maintained, could be overcome by increasing the amount of productive capital in an economy. To this end it was vital that each individual recognize his contribution to the wealth of society through industrious activity:

Thus the labour of the scholar, who experiments and writes books, is productive; that of the entrepreneur is productive, although he does not put his hand directly to labour. Finally, the toil of the worker, from the day-labourer who digs the land to the sailor who mans a ship, is also productive.[6]

The direct relationship between economic welfare and capital was proved, Say was sure, by the recent case of Egypt, which had faced economic paralysis when the import of capital from France had been suspended by the British navy. Say repeated his argument at the beginning of Book IV. Here he added that an industrious citizenry was a prerequisite for the property created by the labours of the different members of society to be respected. If labour of any sort was not rewarded, and not deemed sacred by society, then the productive capacity of the state was in jeopardy:

The qualities that I call industrious, and which are the product of the skills and talents of the industrious man, are as sacred as any other. They are the fruit, as we have seen in Book I (ch. 43), of a labour of variable duration and of an accumulated capital; an origin which is common to many mobile forms of property. It is by means of this labour and these advances that a man acquires the means to produce what we call industry. His right to this property has the same basis as the right of the owner of capital to his capital; and the fruits owed to him in return are like the interest on capital to the capitalist. Thus a country where industrious talents, as with land and capital, are not guaranteed from all forms of attack, is a country where properties are not entirely secure.[7]

Say's claim that an industrious citizenry creating capital goods was the source of wealth was directly related to his formulation of what has become known as 'Say's Law'. The fervour of his belief in industrious labour, and the greater production that he believed would be its consequence, led Say to ponder the effects of the ever-increasing creation of useful goods. The question was whether this would lead to gluts, unemployment, and wasted labour. Say concluded that industrious manners were no danger to a state because they stimulated the demand for goods by an amount equal to any increase in production. It was crucial for Say to prove that the physiocrats were wholly mistaken in taking increased consumption to be the motor of a productive economy. Say argued that production ultimately determined future economic welfare. This was the essential message of one of the most famous passages of the *Traité*:

The *extent of the demand for the means of production in general* does not depend, as too many people have imagined, on the *extent of consumption*. Consumption is not a cause: it is an effect. To consume, it is necessary to buy; now, you can only buy with what you have produced. Is the quantity of products demanded therefore determined by the quantity of products generated? Without any doubt; everyone can as they wish consume what they have produced; or with their produce buy another product. The demand for products in general is therefore always equal to the sum of products.[8]

'Say's Law' was not only intended as a refutation of what he believed to be the central tenet of the physiocractic creed by asserting the power of industriousness. In addition, as Charles Comte recognized, the law defined a general interest which non-corrupt and non-criminal citizens shared, thereby underlining Say's faith in a clear sense of the public good. Say intended the law to play an educational role in society, teaching citizens to believe in the unity of national interest and the possibility of addressing social problems without recourse to violent divisions between the citizenry along class lines. Rather than underlining the hidden hand of egoism, Say conceived of the law as a statement of enlightened self-interest and as such something which had to be learned by those playing an economic role in society. The operation of the law was not automatic and the relationship it described was not conceived of as a mathematical identity valid in all conditions. Say was not a conservative in any sense of the term. Nor was he a Pangloss in his optimism. If Say's first statement of the law is placed in the context of Say's discussion of the importance of industriousness in the *Traité* as a whole (and alongside his view of poverty in contemporary Europe), it will be seen that he was arguing for the promotion of industrious manners and emphasizing their social worth. In short, Say's law would only operate to alleviate poverty in conditions where specific republican manners had come to characterize national character. Industrious and additional virtues had to have been adopted by the citizenry before the law could be said to have any validity.

In later years, historiographical attention, particularly in British circles, centred on Say's criticism of Smith's claim that the labour of the slave was dearer than that of the free labourer, an argument which can be traced to his notes in the margins of the *Wealth of Nations*.[9] There was, however, a more explicit recognition of differences between their approaches to political economy, one that would figure prominently in English responses to Say. While historians have recognized Say's attack on Smith they have generally failed to understand its import. The dispute stemmed from a statement early in the *Traité* that Smith had been mistaken about the fundamental causes of national wealth. The effects of the introduction of the division of labour had been exaggerated, while underestimating the productivity of nature in fashioning goods. Say's further point was that Smith would have better understood the nature of value if he had recognized the overriding importance of what Say called 'utility'. Labour was not a quantity with a fixed value that could be discerned in any product. Experience showed that the value of a good fluctuated in accordance with its perceived utility, the worth of the natural resources embodied in it, and the quality of the labour involved in fashioning it. The individual agent's assessment of the usefulness of a good was intended to replace Smith's search for an objective standard of value, measured by labour-time or corn prices. Say argued that Smith's theory of value had been over-influenced by 'physiocratic prejudices', which led him to underestimate the contribution of particular social groups to wealth creation. Where Smith called the labour of those not involved in the creation of tangible products unproductive, Say praised all activities 'productive of utility', and rejected Smith's terminology. According to Say, the services of the musician or the lawyer were potentially as productive of utility as any other labour; what, he asked, 'does manufacturing labour produce? Only utility, a value in the thing worked upon, and, as a result, a purely immaterial quality.' Smith had consequently mistaken the importance of what Say called 'the imaginative classes' to the creation of wealth, among whom he included intellectuals and entrepreneurs. Say's idea of utility is crucial to understanding the difference between the political economy of Smith and Say. In using the term utility, Say was not replacing Smith's theory of value with a more individualistic conception of society or an increasing faith in the 'hidden hand'. By 'productive of utility', Say included actions which satisfied what he called 'real needs'. These could be specified by social function; the activity of the intellectual, the businessman or merchant, and the labourer, could all be considered useful because they were essential to production. Other activities could also be considered useful as far as they did not waste natural resources, encourage idleness, luxury or sensuality, or involve either pain or ultimate hardship. The magistrate and the musician were useful only in so far as they did not violate this negative moral code. Utility was therefore a term explicable only in a secular moral discourse. It underlined Say's opposition to hidden hand explanations of wealth, and his support for enlightened self-interest explanations. He was clearly not in any meaningful sense a precursor of ideas about marginal utility, as some have supposed.[10] Say's moral perspective upon utility had no parallel in Smith. It signified his republican faith in a society of non-hierarchical ranks, an idea that Smith had never accepted as practically realizable in modern states.

3   FRUGALITY

The second part of Book I of the *Traité* sought to place frugality beside industriousness as the founding virtues of a modern society:

As the industry of a nation always expands in proportion with its productive capital, the more productive capital there is, and the more there are people who can earn a living, that is to say, contribute to production and consume their part of the product they have created, all savings, and every accumulation of capital, yields an annual gain, not only for those who collect interest from it, but for all the people whose industry is put in motion by this portion of capital.[11]

One of the reasons why Smith was a great political economist, in Say's eyes, was his recognition of the fundamental importance of frugality to the prosperity of modern societies:

Thus the celebrated Adam Smith compares a frugal man who augments his productive funds . . . and a prodigal who wastes part of his capital, with the dishonest administrator who squanders the funds of a religious foundation, and leaves without resources, not only those whose survival depended upon it, but all those who would have done so in future. He does not hesitate to name the dissipator a public menace, and any frugal and sober man a benefactor of society.[12]

Smith's chief error, Say argued, was to have placed the virtue of frugality above that of industriousness in his explanation of the wealth of nations. He ought rather to have recognized that the operation of each of these virtues was essential to the prosperity of every state:

Smith also believed that the wealth of the moderns is rather due to the extent of their savings than to any growth of production. I know full well that certain exceptional [feudal] destructions are no longer seen as they once were, but one must pay attention to the small number of people to whom such profusions were permitted, and take the trouble to consider how much the benefits of a more abundant and varied consumption have become more widespread, especially among the middle class of society; one will find, it seems to me, that the consumptions and savings have accrued simultaneously; this is not contradictory—how many entrepreneurs in all kinds of industry produce enough in prosperous times to augment at the same time their spending and their saving? What is true of a particular enterprise can be true of the majority of enterprises in a nation.

According to Say, the frugality and industriousness of the general population of France in the seventeenth century explained the increase in the wealth of the state in spite of the dissipations of the court in the later years of the reign of Louis XIV. The proof of this was that after the death of Colbert saving and industrious activity were depressed while the court continued its frivolous consumption; the result was the rapid decline of the French economy in the early eighteenth century. In the long fourteenth chapter of Book I, Say was concerned to underline the importance of frugality to modern citizens:

'The art of saving is due to the progress of industry, which on one hand has discovered a great number of efficient methods, and which, on the other, has everywhere demanded capital and offered to capitalists, small and large, better conditions and more secure opportunities.' Say returned to the theme of manners in the nineteenth chapter of the *Traité*, in which he sought to explain the superiority of Britain's capacity to produce goods. The 'genius' of the British people, Say argued, was to be frugal and simple in their tastes, and flexible and active in their labours. Such qualities had led them to apply the inventions of other nations, such as those of the French chemists Berthollet and Laplace, with a speed and efficiency that could not be matched by the scientists' mother country. British manners ensured a vast domestic market for commonly-used products, the demand for which ensured the success of new products aimed at improving the conditions of the mass of the population. By contrast, the diversity of French tastes and the inferior activity of the French populace inhibited French emulation. The success of Britain's strategy of undercutting the prices of French goods in international markets, while maintaining a higher standard of living for the general populace, was due, Say held, to the domestic market secured by the manners of the British people.[13] Quesnay had therefore been mistaken in ascribing Britain's wealth to its agricultural sector just as Law and others had wrongly traced it to its national bank and rules for public credit. In Say's eyes the key was Britain's national character, with its decidedly republican bent.

The point of greatest importance in this perspective was that national character could be reformed because it could be directed by an enlightened legislator. Far from seeing Britain as a utopia, Say believed that the republican element of national character was being eroded and that the state was gradually approaching its nadir. His intention was to persuade the French to learn from Britain's mistakes, and in particular to over-come the poverty which characterized failed or declining societies. In envisaging means of putting his plan into practice he returned to Clavière's emphasis on the commercial-ization of the populace. Say's solution was not to recreate the *assignats* but to enlighten more directly the self-interest of the labouring poor by teaching them that the optimal means to the betterment of their condition was to save and to toil. The genius of Benjamin Franklin had been to recognize and act upon this truth, not only by being a living model of the advantages of an industrious life, but also by preaching the benefits of saving and frugality, and acting upon this maxim by lending his own money to lowly but industrious labourers.[14] One of the most important inventions of the modern world was therefore the savings bank, which offered to the poor a means to better their condition by honest and regular industry, with the ultimate rewards of economic secu-rity in old age, the improvement of the wealth of a family, or the opportunity to invest in productive capital.

4   MODERATE WEALTH

It was in the final book of the *Traité* that Say most explicitly described the model citizen and the practices which individuals and nations seeking to ameliorate poverty ought to pursue. Book V also responded to what Say recognized to be a common critique of his justification of industrious and frugal manners. First, that such manners countered equality by increasing the wealth and power of the rich while keeping the mass of the people imprisoned by poverty and dependent upon a minimal subsistence. Second, that industrious manners, in promoting the division of labour, would create a society of individuals dependent upon, and brutalized by, the introduction of machines by entrepreneurs. Thirdly, that in practice self-interested actions were never frugal and industrious. Rather, they were egoistic and self-indulgent, favouring pleasure and idleness rather than moderation and self-control. Advocates of this pessimistic view argued that the warlike and idle characteristics of human nature necessitated dependence of the poor upon the rich. Say ascribed the first of these arguments to the physiocrats, the second to 'popular prejudices', and the third to advocates of the control of trade by a mercantile state. He collected these disparate ideas together, and condemned them for justifying the poverty, the immorality, and the violence that continued to characterize societies that were commercialized. Say sought to undermine such pessimistic assessments of the consequences of industriousness and frugality. He first acknowledged the depth of the problems facing Europe. The division of labour, he made clear in the first book, was far from being an unequivocal boon to the modern world. Rather, it could be a force for the degeneration and degradation of the moral and economic health of the mass of the populace:

A man who, throughout his life, has undertaken one single task can be sure of executing it better and more quickly than another man; but, at the same time, he becomes less capable of any other task, be it physical or moral. His other abilities fade away, and this results in the degeneration of the man considered as an individual. It is a sad epitaph to have only ever made the eighteenth part of a pin.[15]

The consequences of the overzealous introduction of the division of labour, Say claimed, departing from the argument of the *Wealth of Nations*, could be seen all too clearly in the experiences of England, where the wages of labour had fallen drastically with mechanization. The response of local communities had been to supplement the income of the poor by taxing the entrepreneurs who, Say believed, paid the poor rate (unbeknown to Say, it was in fact the landowners). This view was in contrast to Smith, who, in the second chapter of Book II of the *Wealth of Nations*, had been more optimistic about the introduction of machinery. In Say's eyes the tragedy was that enforced benevolence by means of higher taxation could not address the fundamental cause of impoverishment: the lack of capital and production to employ labour at reasonable levels of subsistence. Taxing the organizers of wealth creation further limited the production of goods and was therefore self-defeating. In the last analysis well-intentioned benevolence did even more damage to the common labourer than the harshest conditions of employment:

In the labouring class, this incapacity for more than one employment renders the condition of the workers harsh, more dull, and less lucrative. They are less able to demand an equitable part of the total value of the product. The worker who carries in his arms a complete trade can go anywhere to exercise his trade and find the means to subsist; the other is only an accessory who, separated from his fellow-workers, has neither capacity nor independence, and finds himself forced to accept whatever law is imposed upon him. It is in England that this misfortune has particularly been felt, first of all because the laws of this country are obstructive, but also because the division of labour has been pushed further there than elsewhere. One reads in the reports of the Charitable Societies of this country that in certain counties a day-labourer with a family can no longer subsist from his work. The entrepreneur, and the government which taxes the entrepreneur, take in general in England too large a proportion of the mass of products of society: this then obliges them to return considerable amounts to the labouring class in the form of relief, which is for many reasons a bad distribution of the annual product.

Such passages were a damning indictment of commercialization. Yet Say's response to these problems was not to condemn modern societies but to posit a very different vision of an economically healthy nation. Once laws such as primogeniture had been abolished, Say believed that industrious activity would generate enough wealth to ensure that the lowly labourer could enjoy the benefits of modern productivity. As in *Olbie* Say used the term *aisance* to describe the economic conditions of the realization of his ideal of a society of responsible and educated artisans:

Comfort permits leisure, and leisure is always filled with activities other than habitual work. The worker could thus give time to education and to the pleasures of understanding; for the same reason the man of letters often does things foreign to his state—he cultivates his garden, exercises his body, and seeks distraction in the study of art . . . It is not rare to see, in rich factories, lowly workers in possession of a library of ten or twelve books. If a means could be found to expel from the worker's library irrelevancies and stupidities, and introduce one or two good works concerning the skills of the worker, or the arts which more directly affect him, such as those to maintain health, and the education of children, who can doubt the immense influence these ten or twelve volumes would exercise upon the moral faculties of a nation?[16]

Say argued that the culture he was defending had become a practical possibility for nation states only in the modern world. Commerce, he argued in Book I, had created a new class of people who did not own land or property, but who were unlike the plebs of the cities of ancient republics. The latter had been mercenaries in thrall to demagogic emperors such as Augustus and Nero, and wholly dependent upon crusts from the tables of the patrician class which owned the land and subsidized the army. In contrast, the new class of citizens without land were free labourers who directly exchanged their labour to meet their basic needs and could thereby remain beyond the control of the more wealthy classes above them. The great advantage that the modern citizen had over his ancient forbear was that he could realize his aspirations to independence and social mobility by the simple practice of frugality and industriousness. The lesson was that happiness and economic security in commercial societies were to be found not in serving the great, or in military service to the state, but in the practice of manners that generated this independence. This was what Say meant in his chapter identifying *l'indépendance née chez les modernes des revenus industriels*:

the revenues of industry have benefited, for the moderns, a numerous class in any society: those who possess neither land nor capital . . . whatever our forms of government, every man who has an industrious skill is independent. The nobility in each state are no longer the richest, because they no longer have the same powers as the chiefs of ancient nations. The latter, after having conquered a country, divided the land, the mobile property and even the inhabitants: but one can no longer destroy the peoples by such means; governments can be changed and nothing more.

Admittedly, the new government draws tributes from a country it has conquered; but, after some time, these tributes hardly cover the costs of administration and the defence of the conquered country, which are much greater than before. In a parallel case, the masses of the nation find that there is little advantage to be found in serving the nobility, and that there is a lot to be found in serving the public, that is to say, to draw on a part of its industry. Henceforth, no more clientage; the poorest citizen can do without a patron; he puts himself under the protection of his talent in order to subsist, and the governments draw from the people the assistance that they formerly provided. Thus modern nations can exist by the same means when their governments are overturned.[17]

Such passages amounted to a summary statement of the central ideas of French republican political economy, as it had been developed by d'Holbach, Diderot, Clavière and Brissot, Rœderer, Sieyès, and Condorcet. Say was reiterating their attacks on nobility, their faith in natural forms of commerce that increased equality, their demand for a new system of ranks and their faith in a republican moral code.

5   MORAL COMMERCE

In the ideal society Say envisaged, individuals would be enlightened about the nature of genuine happiness, and therefore be able to recognise and avoid the temptations of luxury and prodigality. The second chapter of Book V, *Des consommations bien ou mal entendu*, sketched an education intended to encourage *aisance* by specifying the kinds of consumption and activity conducive to 'real' happiness, and the forms of luxury and dissipation that were its most deadly foes. The first form of legitimate production was of goods that satisfied fundamental and universal needs as opposed to those that provided fleeting sensual pleasures:

I understand as real needs those that ensure our existence, our health, and signify contentment to the majority of men. They are the opposite of those that arise from an affected sensuality, opinion, and caprice. Thus the consumptions of a nation are sensible if they comprise things convenient rather than grand, much more linen than lace, abundant and wholesome foodstuffs rather than fine stews, and good clothes without embellishments. In such a nation, public institutions would function with the minimum of pomp and the maximum usefulness. The needy would not see sumptuous infirmaries but would find certain assistance, roads would not be twice as large as necessary, and inns would be well-furnished; towns would not perhaps present so many beautiful palaces, but walking on the footpaths would be safe. Ostentatious luxury grants only an empty satisfaction; convenient luxury, if I can call it this, brings a genuine satisfaction. The latter is less expensive and as a consequence entails less consumption. By contrast, the former is limitless; . . . 'Pride', Franklin has said, 'is a beggar who cries as loudly as need; but is infinitely more insatiable'.[18]

Say's second demand was for durable products that were used regularly and could be consumed over long periods of time. The danger was that if goods consumed by the general populace did not have these characteristics, then people would be seduced by luxury and refined tastes, and fall prey to gambling, intemperance, and a litany of other vices. Equally, the consumption of common but useful products secured the domestic market for goods whose production employed the mass of the poor. Say added that he expected consumption to conform to the standards of an austere morality:

A nation and individuals will give proof of their wisdom, if they seek goods whose consumption is slow and whose use is frequent. It is for this reason that they will have a house and furnishings that are convenient and functional . . . the rapid succession of fashions impoverishes a state through what it consumes and what it fails to consume . . . sensible consumption conforms to the laws of sound morality. If individuals cannot abide by its maxims, this is more true of the nation as a whole.

Say concluded that it was crucial for governments to direct the populace towards what he considered to be 'sensible consumption':

In every country the government greatly influences consumption, not only because it decides on public consumption, but because its example and authority directs much private consumption. If the government is the friend of pomp and ostentation, a flock of imitators will follow it . . . a prince who senses the prodigious influence of his conduct on his fellow-citizens, and the prodigious influence of their conduct on prosperity and national manners, must have a high idea of his duties.[19]

The evidence of French history supported his claims. Villages that preferred to institute gambling dens and promote trivial public fêtes, rather than to invest in such communal projects as water-courses, were more likely to succumb to poverty and unhappiness. Equally, the disastrous wars of Louis XIV could be ascribed to the corrupting effects of luxury and idleness that made individuals intemperate and states foolish. Louis' wars against the Dutch and the British had been inspired by vengeance. Luxury was a cause of the impoverishment of states, especially monarchies, and a fundamental cause of greater inequality between citizens.[20]

Say was particularly concerned to respond to the argument that maintained it was the luxury of the rich that was responsible for the employment of the poor. Although the argument played a prominent role in numerous writings from Mandeville to Necker, Say ascribed its popularity to Montesquieu and was withering in his assessment of the consequences of the doctrine. The spending of the rich on useless products led directly to greater inequality. The resulting lack of capital in the economy prevented governments from finding resources that could protect the poor against the threat of famine. This increased taxes, further damaging the prospects for saving and the accumulation of capital:

It is an oft-repeated mistake that the profusions of the rich allow the poor to live. In fact, they exhaust one of the sources of the wealth of society. Wealth begets wealth; and every time it is destroyed, one does not simply lose what is consumed, but all that could have been procured with wealth . . . Montesquieu, ending the chapter where he wishes to show that luxury suits monarchies and large states, contradicts, in a word, the evidence of his argument: 'Republics collapse through luxury; monarchies through poverty.' This is a permanent truth that proves that frugality enriches all states while luxury ruins them.[21]

Little was new in Say's arguments. He was simply more systematic in his statement of republican political economy, at least by comparison with previous theorists such as Diderot or d'Holbach, because he believed in the necessity of providing a text-book for the people who would thereby learn the central doctrines which defined the interest which all citizens shared.

6   REPUBLICANISM REVISED

In 1803 Say repudiated the legislative inculcation of manners through moral catechisms. He also broke with the past in arguing that a republican constitution was no longer essential to foster industrious manners. Nevertheless, Say adhered to the republicanism of *Olbie* in three respects. First, he continued to believe that inequality was the greatest threat to the peace and prosperity of modern societies. Second, that poverty and luxury could not be alleviated without consideration of the social consequences of the distribution of wealth. Third, a society of independent citizens had to be created whose mode of life was characterized by industriousness and frugality. This would stimulate the production of capital and grant to all toiling citizens an adequate, but not excessive, level of income. His vision was articulated in greatest detail towards the end of Book V, in which Say summed up his view of manners. He attacked the evils of luxury, advocated moderation in everyday passions, and argued that all citizens should aspire to become independent. The latter term was used not in the liberal sense of being alone and in control of one's own destiny but in Rousseau's sense of being a member of a moral community and willingly adhering to certain codes for living. Say's notion of independence was utopian because he believed that such a moral community could be created outside government:

What leads a nation into luxury or restrains it within the limits of moderation? Its customs. The rich man satisfies his needs as he pleases: the manners of his country, of the class to which he belongs, ensure this in turn. There is only a very small number of men, reasonably firm of spirit, and with a fairly independent fortune, who can act according to their principles, and who only have models in their own conduct. From this comes the prodigious influence of manners upon the wealth and happiness of societies. I say happiness, because the sad satisfaction that luxury grants to the affluent does not match the ill that it does to society. Those who seek happiness in ostentation know well that it cannot be found there. It is not necessary to have much philosophy to understand that once the reasonable needs of life are satisfied, one can find happiness in the moderate exercise of the faculties of our body and of our spirit, and in the sentiments of our soul.

Say's emphasis on self-interest as the driving force of modern society, and his focus upon the wealth of the individual, must be understood as a product of his view of virtuous manners. Say did not associate self-interest with egoism or slavery to the passions. Rather, he was attempting to construct a picture of a society in which perceived interests were informed, independent, and the product of reflection. Interests were not to be influenced by lust for excessive wealth, and he envisaged them as being immune from the pressure of poverty. When Say used the term 'self-interest' in the *Traité*, he was clearly referring to what he had called in *Olbie* 'enlightened self-interest'. He argued that this kind of individual self-interest could be trusted to operate in the interest of society as a whole. It was more effective than direct government action because individuals were more independent and better informed than politicians. This was far from the idea of self-interest embodied in Smith's notion of the autonomous hidden hand. Say never abandoned the belief that governments had to encourage scholars, like himself, to reveal the 'real interest' of society to the general populace. It was only within such a culture that personal interest would accord with the interest of society:

It is fortunate that personal interest tends continuously to the conservation of the capital of individuals; it can at no time divert capital from a productive employment, without the loss of a proportionate profit. The conservation of capitals belonging to the public is guaranteed only by laws; thus they are much more frequently dissipated; in truth, they are continuously maintained by new taxes upon the income of individuals; nevertheless, capitals formed in this manner are always more widespread than those which would have been created by individuals for themselves with the total of these taxes. It is therefore better that in each nation the capital belonging to the public in common is the least possible; less will be lost and its maintenance will be less onerous.[22]

Fortunately for the public interest, personal interest is, in the majority of cases, the first to be warned, and the most affected, by superfluous consumption. Thereby suffering warns our limbs of the injuries against which they need to be protected, and often preserves us from the privations which would result from their loss. If the inept consumer were not the first to be punished by the losses which he himself causes, we would see much more frequently cases of factories being established, and speculations being undertaken, which would consume more products than they would create.[23]

Say's focus on manners allowed him to explain the superiority of British wealth and arms since the Seven Years War. France under the Old Regime had been seduced by luxury; even the physiocrats had not recognized the latent dangers of excessive consumption. Although the Revolution could be praised for ending this state of affairs, rather than seeking a new culture through which commerce could flourish, French legislators had been seduced by the chimerical glories of empire and mercantile trade. As a result the natural superiority of the French over the British, in terms of natural resources, inventiveness, geographical size, and population, remained obscured by misleading perceptions of national interest and an ignorant commercial culture.

NOTES TO CHAPTER 8

1. *TE*, ii, 438.
2. *Boniface Véridick à Polyscope, sur son projet de théatre pour le peuple*, *LDP* no. 10, 10 Germinal, an IV (30 March, 1796), pp. 38–44.
3. *TE*, i, 413.
4. *Ibid.*, ii, 382–3.
5. *Ibid.*, i, 10–15.
6. *Ibid.*, i, 38.
7. *Ibid.*, ii, 148.
8. *Ibid.*, ii, 175.
9. Hashimoto, 'Notes inédites de J-B Say', pp. 67–74. In the third edition of the *Traité* (1817) Say acccepted that he had been mistaken on this issue.
10. See the articles by T. W. Hutchison and N. B. de Marchi in R. D. Collison Black, A. W. Coats, C. D. W. Goodwin, eds., *The Marginal Revolution in Economics. Interpretation and Evaluation* (Durham N.C., 1973), pp. 79, 182.
11. *TE*, i, 95.
12. *Ibid.*, i, 96 f., citing *Wealth of Nations*, Bk. II, ch. 3, p. 341.
13. *Ibid.*, i, 131–7, ii, 95–9.
14. *Ibid.*, ii, 182.

15. *TE*, i, 78.
16. *Ibid.*, i, 81–2 f.
17. *Ibid.*, i, 262–4.
18. *Ibid.*, ii, 349–50.
19. *Ibid.*, ii, 351, 354, 356.
20. *Ibid.*, ii, 377–8.
21. *TE*, ii, 379–81.
22. *Ibid.*, i, 96.
23. *Ibid.*, ii, 345.

9

Restoring French Glory

I BRITAIN'S WEAKNESS

According to the *Traité*, Britain's successes in commerce and in war could be traced to three factors. First, 'several acts of public administration', in which case Say was probably referring to the lack of internal customs barriers and the laws protecting civil liberty. Second, 'the genius of the nation', meaning the republican national character so suited to industriousness and frugality. Third, the 'concordance of accidental circumstances'. The final factor, Say made clear, had played a major role in recent British history and it is to be speculated that Say meant by this that Britain had thrived because the legacy of the failed republican revolution of the seventeenth century had been a national character singularly suited to virtue and trade. The irony was that Britain's wealth had failed to contribute to 'the happiness and the glory of the British nation in general.'[1] By this Say did not merely mean that wealth had been wasted in war. He was making the more significant point that British legislators had not planned for the future and resolved the problem of poverty that was both dividing and weakening the nation. This in turn was due to Britain's social hierarchy and corrupt constitution, both of which contributed to the mercantile policy of the control of trade. This policy engendered a culture of luxury and immorality, and Say was sure that the resulting pollution of Britain's national character was creating a nation whose republican character was being lost and whose luck was running out. Like many Frenchmen of this time, and despite his opinion of Bonaparte, he remained a patriot who believed Britain to be a more corrupt and despotic state than post-revolutionary France could ever be. He must have relished the letter from his friend Daunou in the aftermath of the *Traité*'s publication, 'You make war on the British, in writing a better book than any of them.'[2]

In writing the *Traité*, Say was not only seeking to respond to critics of republican political economy while refuting the political economy of the *Idéologues* and other contemporaries. In many respects his overriding ambition was to restore French glory, by analysing Smith's criticism of Britain's commercial laws and practices and developing from them a strategy for the restoration of French glory. Despite Smith's influence, Say's study of Britain's weaknesses was typically republican, focusing as it did on the moral corruption of the politicians and the populace, the excessive material inequality and social hierarchy, and the waste of production in luxury, needless expenditures, and unproductive labour. Part of Say's strategy was, as should now be clear, the affirmation of certain republican manners in the French populace by means of the education of self-interest. The second part was more subtle, involving as it did a series of laws and policies, most of which were gleaned from Smith, which were intended to increase wealth in ways compatible with republican virtue and moderation. The aim of this chapter is to explain this second part of Say's strategy. In addition, it seeks to show Say's continued defence of what was originally Clavière's republican perspective on Smith, at a time when such an approach was being abandoned by numerous political economists.

2 PERSPECTIVES ON SMITH IN CONSULAR ARGUMENT

During the early years of the French republic political economists had three objectives, in descending order of priority. First, safeguarding the liberty of the citizen by maintaining the republican constitution and defending it from external attack. Second, inculcating the republican manners which were deemed to be the embodiment of liberty, and therefore compatible with legal coercion. Third, making laws for economic prosperity compatible with republican liberty and manners. Such ideas were vindicated by Say in *Olbie*, in Rœderer's *Cours*, by Sieyès, Cabanis, Grégoire, and numerous other luminaries of the *Institut*. As was noted in the first chapter, interest in transforming the manners of the general populace meant that Smith's *Theory of Moral Sentiments* attracted more notice than the *Wealth of Nations*; it was deemed to be a book singularly suited to the issues of the time, as Sophie Grouchy-Condorcet explained in her *Lettres sur la sympathie*. From the establishment of the Consulate conceptions began to alter. For the first time in a decade political economy was described beyond the confines of a republican and representative constitution, which had hitherto defined its legitimate range of action and concern. Investigations were once more initiated into what the best form of government for France, and the natural answer was no longer a popular republic. C.-H. de Saint-Simon's vision of progress was significant, for example, because it described a class of brilliant scientists creating laws to direct politicians and legislators.[3] A second development centred on the fact that the active inculcation of popular republican manners was also gradually being abandoned as an objective, because ardent, patriotic manners were being blamed for the instability that had destroyed the Directory. 'Principles of politics' continued to be sought by writers such as Constant, even after his ejection from the Tribunate, but he too began to demand revision of the republican ideas of the 1790s.[4] This was also the command of Necker's last work, the *Dernières vues de politique et de finance, offertes à la nation française*, which appeared in 1802.[5] Another indication of this movement was the use of Smith to reflect on the course of the Revolution since 1789, and to draw practical consequences for the future. Rœderer and Garnier utilized Smith in their published responses to the collapse of revolutionary optimism in the early years of the Consulate. Constant's close friend Sismondi's work, inspired by Smith, was published concurrently with the *Traité*. All of these writings shared the view that modern states could only be maintained by increasing wealth rather than by means of republican patriotism or the *levée en masse*. They were divided, however, on the surest way to define the general good which they believed had been Smith's first aim in the *Wealth of Nations*. An additional disagreement concerned the nature of the general good Smith was seen to have defended.

Garnier's masterly translation and critique of the *Wealth of Nations* was published early in 1802. The preface, comprising the critique of Smith and the application of his political economy to France, was begun in 1794 when Garnier was in exile, and completed when he entered the *Institut* as an associate member.[6] Until the Directory Garnier had been a supporter of Dupont's political and moral solutions to the problems of the Revolution; he advocated the immediate dismantling of economic controls, a single tax upon the net product of agriculture, and an economic strategy based on high agricultural prices. He was also one of the most strident supporters of a republican constitution based on the enfranchisement of the landed interest, which he believed would counter the unstable democratic turn of the Revolution after 1792.[7] By 1802, however, Garnier was arguing that the rigid physiocracy expounded by Dupont should be tempered. He believed it to be overly critical of commerce, and demanded that some of Smith's arguments be incorporated into physiocracy to redress the balance. As he put it, 'The distinction between the labour of agricultural workers and other forms of labour is an abstraction almost always useless.'[8] Almost paraphrasing Smith, he advanced the division of labour and capital created by saving as the most important sources of wealth and announced support for indirect taxes.[9] Garnier did not picture Smith as Dupont had: as a supporter of a constitution based on the rule of industrious property owners. Rather, he maintained his belief that the landed class were the best representatives of popular sovereignty, and argued that Smith concurred in this through his support for the British constitution, which Garnier believed to be based upon a landed aristocracy. Wealth creation in a state depended in the first instance upon political structures. Political economy therefore remained a branch of the 'art of governing men'. The physiocrats, in trying to make a rigid science of certain laws, had ignored both theoretical and practical evidence, necessitating focus on Smith's insights: 'While this sect of philosophers occupied Europe with its speculations, a more profound and more perceptive observer carried his researches into the same issues, and worked to establish the fundamental elements of the true doctrine of political economy.'

Smith was used to justify a different conception of political economy in Rœderer's *Mémoires sur quelques points d'économie publique* of 1800, a reassessment of his *Cours* of 1793.[10] It articulated a political economy addressing the problems of the Consular state, as with Garnier in the form of a critique of physiocracy. Rœderer rejected the demand that political participation be confined to the class of landowners. Following the *Cours*, mobile property was described as more necessary to society, but it was now used to justify the enfranchisement of a class of citizens who deserved to represent the nation because of their interest in property.[11] Support for a plutocratic constitution was in stark contrast to the democratic republicanism of the *Cours*. Instead of favouring the legislative inculcation of industrious manners in the entire populace, Rœderer argued that property was indicative of the manners conducive to social stability. Revised constitutionalism derived from an altered perspective on Smith. In the *Cours* Smith's *Theory of Moral Sentiments* had provided philosophical foundations for the transformation of popular manners by an active legislator. In 1800 Rœderer turned to Smith for arguments to support his plutocratic constitutional prescriptions. The *Wealth of Nations* was praised because it revealed the means of creating laws regulating opulence within the framework of a constitution in which the propertied represented the general interest.[12] Rœderer's interpretation of a constitution that would be a prerequisite of wealth creation was, as a consequence, very different from Garnier's.

The third example of the intellectual shift that paralleled the waning of the Consulate was distinctive in being the product of a Genevan writer (a French citizen since the republican annexation) who retained faith in the project of establishing republics in large states and as a consequence maintained the reading of Smith as a defender of republican manners. Sismondi's *De la richesse commerciale* shared Say's view that Smith had created a new science. Rather than viewing Smith from the perspective of defending a specific form of government, however, he followed more closely the argument and structure of the *Wealth of Nations*. Political economy was described as 'the science of the legislator'. If wealth was not scrutinized from the multiple perspectives supplied by this broad science 'it runs the risk of being contradicted by the laws of the progress of national prosperity.'[13] It was a branch of an all-encompassing science, called 'the science of government', embracing 'everything that matters to us, our laws, manners, property, religion, our liberty, and sometimes even our existence.' In the context of the post-1790s, this can be described as a republican reading of Smith because it sought to establish the welfare of every member of a society without ranks: 'The science of Government is therefore the science of making men happy; and since happiness comprises diverse elements, it can be redefined as knowledge of the means of giving Peoples the greatest amount of liberty, of security, of tranquillity, and of virtue; of wealth, of health, and of forces which can be enjoyed simultaneously.' Sismondi's political economy must be understood as one part of an investigation encompassing a series of books, which included the discussion of the manners most conducive to political liberty and the constitution that would best protect political liberty:

In 1796 I commenced my research into the constitutions of free peoples. This work, which has never been finished, but on which Benjamin Constant sought to obtain an assessment from the *Institut*, has occupied me for five years . . . My work on the constitutions of the Italian republics obliged me to study their history, and it was at this time, in 1798, that my efforts began to study this subject and, soon after, my decision to write about them.[14]

The specific objective of Sismondi's *De la richesse commerciale* was to persuade the French administrators who had annexed Switzerland in 1798 of the impolicy of imposing Napoleon's mercantile system upon the cantons. One direct difference with Say was that political economy was not to be a popular subject. Although he acknowledged that an individual's life might be improved by the study of political economy, he believed the science of the legislator to be too vast and too difficult for popular civic instruction. Sismondi's vision of a republican legislator seeking the happiness of the citizenry was different from Rœderer's and Garnier's more limited conception of a legislator, making laws for wealth creation within a specific constitutional apparatus. While the French interpreters Rœderer and Garnier envisaged the abandonment of a popular form of government and focussed on Smith's view of such a government, Sismondi sought to establish rules of policy that described a certain form of state. He consequently made the figure of an ideal republican law-maker, the all-seeing legislator, the centrepiece of his political economy.

3 FALSE GODS AND NATURAL LIBERTY

Say, by contrast with Rœderer and Garnier, rejected the association of Smith with a non-republican form of government, portraying him, like Sismondi, as an author who had sought to define the public good for the best possible form of state. Both authors followed what might be termed a 'Genevan' interpretation of the *Wealth of Nations*, centring on the policies to purify manners. They were also interested in the concrete proposals Smith offered for the reform of modern states by the restoration of natural liberty, perceived by Say and Sismondi to be a realm of moral and transparent commerce. The *Traité* followed Smith in associating the natural progress of opulence with the introduction of machinery, the application of the division of labour, and increased wealth in general, by comparison with economic conditions in the feudal or ancient worlds. Yet the most important role of Smith's work was to have provided solutions to the genuine evils of the present age. Like Sismondi, Say read Smith as the thinker who had squarely faced the dangers of inequality, and of moral and physical degeneration, but who had reconciled them with a broader vision of a commercial society in which the industrious element of the population received a fair and adequate reward for their labour. He believed that Smith had been led to this vision by discovering ways of combating poverty and agreed with Smith that it was necessary to liberalize the economy by abandoning national aspirations to mercantile empire. The *Wealth of Nations* supplied a critique of British economic policy and the blueprint of a legislative strategy to restore French glory. Smith's work defined a public interest that united all individuals, regardless of their rank or station. As long as manners were pure and privileges illegal, all citizens were consumers and this interest defined that of society.[15] This perspective was the basis of a critique of conceptions of societies and nations as states at war, necessitating the control of the economy in the service of the higher goal of victory over foreign rivals. Following Smith, Say called this 'system' that of the 'mercantile legislator'. His intention was to contrast the experience of such an empire with the regime of natural liberty. Although he used examples drawn from the experience of numerous states, the example of Britain as the model mercantile empire was never far from his mind and he believed that he was drawing from the *Wealth of Nations* Smith's critique of his own state. The obvious lesson was that France should embrace natural liberty and thereby distinguish itself from its rival. Say's particular hope was that by establishing legislation to restore the French economy to conditions of natural liberty, in circumstances characterized by a political culture of republican manners, French glory would be re-established. The five fulcra of a mercantile empire were condemned outright; the balance of trade or control of bullion flows, trading companies, colonies, the control of markets, and war. The recent experience of France was evidence of the purposelessness of the pursuit of precious metals; before the Revolution there had been far more silver in the economy, but this bore a relation neither to the general price level nor to the mass of wealth in the state. Once it was recognized that precious metals were commodities, the futility of attempts by governments to control the levels of money in the economy would become manifest. Say drew his example directly from Smith; the attempt by the Scottish parliament to control the money supply had been self-defeating because precious metals flowed to London where they were more highly valued. Another example supplied by Smith was that the companies of Sweden and Denmark had wasted the capital that could have stimulated their languishing domestic markets. The general rule was that the further away from the domestic market that trade occurred the less profits would be of benefit to the citizenry. The further danger was that companies and governments would take advantage of their market powers to maintain high prices and exploit foreign markets and domestic consumers to raise revenues for war. The state that had recognized these facts was Portugal, with no privileged companies in the Indies, but which had generated the most wealth from its colonies. Say contrasted the free commerce of Portugal with the privileges accorded by France, arguing that only a policy of 'commerce abandoned to itself' suited 'political circumstances, the capital of the nation and of the individual'. Privileges of any kind 'drained the public purse and wasted capital and labour'.[16]

These claims were also applied to France by Garnier, Rœderer, and Sismondi, but Say was distinctive in his use of Smith to attack mercantile empire. Modern colonists were described as buccaneers who sucked dry the wealth of the foreign possession, subjugated native populations and left them barren, before returning to their own land for glory and idle lives. Say condemned practices in Brazil, Peru, Mexico, and the Antilles:

Population had been devoted to the development of the land, and large capitals have been required for this to occur. Yet always they [the colonists] have sought to return to their country of origin loaded with immense riches, rather than seeking to live a life of ease, with a happy family and a spotless reputation; the former motive has caused the introduction of violent measures to foster development, in the vanguard of which is slavery.

By contrast, he commended the ancient Greek system that saw colonies as solutions to problems of overpopulation and therefore led to permanent colonization, entailing consideration for the welfare of native populations, improvements in the land, and the extension of citizenship and civilization. Once capital had been transferred to the colony its prosperity and progress would be assured, just as France had hoped for Egypt. The only modern attempt at ancient colonial practice was America, which he praised for the manners of its citizens and minimal government: 'It appears that when the colonists abandoned their native land, they also left behind a part of their vices.' This did not mean that he favoured British-style colonization in America; he argued that all modern colonies were too costly to defend, a burden on domestic tax payers, and, following Smith again, hardly ever worth the meagre commerce generated by monopoly. In any case, such wealth inevitably flowed to merchant cabals rather than the general populace:

The power that the metropolis exercises over its colonies obliges them to sell only to her, which is to say at a lower price, and only to buy what she sells, entailing a high price. This is simply a monopoly, for the seller or the buyer, in favour of the metropolis and to the detriment of the colonists. It is a tax on the colony to enrich imperial merchants; it is to take silver from one section of the nation to give it to another. Note that I say that only the *merchants* and not the *consumers* of the metropolis profit from the [low] prices at which the colonists are forced to sell their goods.[17]

Franklin's 'proof' was cited, that Parisians and Londoners paid more for sugar supplied direct from their colonies than the Viennese who lived six hundred miles from a sea port. The policy of free trade was superior, since the argument that France would become open to blockade and ransom was a myth: Germany and Italy had no colonies and had not suffered such threats. Commercial alliances were a superior means to prosperity. Following Talleyrand at the *Institut*, he noted that no one now doubted that the loss of America had been a boon to Britain. Say was certain that external commerce should supplement rather than supplant domestic trade, and be fostered only when domestic commerce was flourishing. He condemned both the mercantile assumption that an export strategy would best increase wealth, and the physiocratic argument that prosperous agricultural markets were the foundation of all wealth. Josiah Child's *Treatise on Commerce* was named as one source for the argument that subsidies and other legislative encouragement to industry was 'more miserable than useful'.[18] It was a general fact that governments were dupes in all markets. The Gobelin tapestries were a loss to the nation, an albatross to trade and a source of corruption. Internal and external liberty of trade ought to be left to the dictates of the market:

Steuart, whose system has almost always been followed by his government, supports an opinion diametrically opposed to the physiocrats. 'Export', he advises, 'manufactured goods which have little intrinsic value, and receive in exchange primary goods which will stimulate your industry, and with which you will make new profits'. It seems to me that enlightened reason will leave these two systems to do battle together, and say 'Export the goods you are able to; import those you lack; but prefer first to cultivate, make, and sell as much as possible in your own country. It is better not to have to rely on foreigners for profits or for goods.[19]

Say also used Smith to oppose war as a tool of increasing trade, stating that: 'the more a state is industrious the more war is deadly and destructive to it.' He was nevertheless optimistic because of the redeeming fact that in future the most commercial of states would be those best able to defend themselves: 'power will probably in future be on the side of civilization and enlightenment; civilized nations alone can produce enough goods to sustain the burdens of military force. The future threat of those upheavals that fill history, of barbarians overthrowing civilized peoples, has been removed.' The surest evidence of this was Rome, which, had it pursued commerce rather than war, would never have fallen: 'If Romans had pursued another system with the same vigour, in seeking to spread civilization among the barbarians, and if they had established relations of mutual need with them, it is probable that Roman power would have continued to this day.'[20] The message was that the modern Romans, the French, if they established the commercial form of state advised by Smith, would surpass the Britain that remained wedded to a mercantile empire characterized by corruption and doomed to decline. Say was also concerned to follow Smith in combating the prominent rival vision, which hinged upon the enactment of physiocratic laws. Against Dupont, he defended nations in which manufactures and commerce were prominent, denying that such states were less prosperous or secure. The indisputable proof of this was that Holland was more opulent and stable than Poland, despite the importance of agriculture to the Polish economy. Furthermore, if land sufficed for the production of wealth why was so much of the globe fertile but unpopulated, and why were prices so high in a vast agricultural nation like America?[21] Say was similarly critical of Dupont's support for a high-price strategy for agricultural products:

In one of the most esteemed works of his sect, Dupont de Nemours says 'do not believe that cheap primary goods are profitable for ordinary people, because the low price of primary goods reduces their wages, which in turn reduces their standard of living, gives them less work to do, fewer lucrative employments, and destroys the revenue of the nation.'

Raising agricultural prices would in practice increase the costs of goods in secondary and tertiary production, including commerce and manufactures; it would also reduce the real income of all consumers, and thereby adversely affect the labouring class. The immediate consequence would be weaker non-agricultural sectors and a poorer populace. This would in turn limit the production of commercial and manufactured goods, which Say believed would then reduce demand for agricultural production itself. Thus the strategy pursued by the physiocratic legislator was as self-defeating as that pursued by the mercantile legislator: 'the exchange value of goods follows a path opposite to the exchange of productive services, and as a result any operations which raise the prices of primary goods (which means that less of a good is purchased relative to the productive service undertaken) are deadly from every perspective, and only more deadly when this is general.'[22] The false assumption that agriculture was the determinant of national prosperity was the root problem of the taxation policy of the physiocratic legislator. Say opposed a single tax because he did not believe that taxes necessarily fell upon the landed proprietor. All individuals sought to avoid taxes. Taxes fell upon those who could not pass the costs on to others. This was the case for producers who feared increases in the prices of their products. It was also the lot of the consumer in a market for a popular good in constant demand. There were no general principles of taxation that could be laid down for a state or an economy. Who paid which tax ultimately depended upon competition and popular manners, neither of which were predictable: 'It falls on those who cannot avoid it, because it is an onerous charge which everyone does their best to avoid; but the means of avoiding it vary to infinity following the different kinds of tax, and are also affected by the role of the person in the social machine.'[23]

4 NATURAL LIBERTY IN FRANCE

Say's work was not intended to be merely critical. It aimed to describe what he held to be the genuine functions of legislators who had accepted the general facts of political economy, and were seeking to promote the general interest of a society without ranks. Necessitating the concrete definition of a society characterized by natural liberty, Say once again closely followed Smith. The first function of the legislator in a regime of natural liberty was the security of property, which was a prerequisite for stable social life: 'the question that occupies us can be reduced to this: is it useful for the prosperity of a nation for property to be secure? The reply is beyond doubt. Self-love is dominant in man, and nothing stimulates the means to well-being more than the certitude of enjoying the benefits of property.'[24] A fundamental cause of the problems of modern states was that labour was not rewarded for its industriousness. The solution was legal protection of labour from interference by more powerful groups: 'The right to this property has the same foundation as the right of an owner of capital over his capital; the fruits must be returned to him, just as the interest on capital returns to the capitalist. Therefore a country where industrial talents are not secure from all kinds of attack is a country where property is not entirely safe.' An instance of injustice that fascinated Say was the failure of legislators in France to secure literary property and grant authors greater financial reward for their writings. This explained the lack of enlightenment among the general populace, and impeded the progress of all sciences. He demanded that France follow the British example by granting writers and their families more secure literary rights that would continue a decade beyond the writer's demise. In general, however, Say believed that a fair reward for labour could only be guaranteed in a free market, in which wages matched effort. He applauded the actions of 4 August 1789, when the National Assembly had swept away the feudal rights and privileges which explained the economic backwardness and injustices of the Old Regime. The feudal system was 'an injury to industrial property'. Industrious activity required the free production, distribution, and consumption of goods; this was the most practical lesson of Say's attack on the mercantile legislator. 'Individuals', he declared, 'are more immediately interested in production'. Every public authority should 'leave to the individual a free disposition in the choice and the manner of production.'[25] It was essential for economic development to establish the impartial administration of justice. As Say put it: 'The surest manner of maintaining and attracting men is to be just and fair to all, and to ensure for all the enjoyment of the rights which they consider the most precious: the free use of the person and of their goods, the ability to go, to come, to remain, to speak, to read, and to write, in conditions of absolute safety.'[26] Justice demanded that laws be abandoned which favoured the eldest male child of a family above his brothers when inheriting property. Primogeniture was a source of inequality that diminished the positive effects of free commerce. Justice also demanded that all administrators be selected by open competition and granted adequate salaries for their labour, responsibility, and expertise. Say praised Smith for these ideas and also for recognizing the need for payment by results: 'Public services are never better carried out than when the reward is a result of their execution, and in proportion to its quality.'[27] The competitive system of nation states set limits on the legislator's plans for free commerce. Say's legislator accepted the need for a professional army. In hunting and pastoral societies defence was the activity of all the populace. In agricultural societies the free citizen could spend half of the year at war. In commercial societies, however, war had become a profession because of the progress of the division of labour.[28] Ever sceptical of public credit, Say argued that only in times of acute crisis could such dangerous methods be employed for the survival of the state.[29] This was the area in which he most completely abandoned Clavière's political economy, founded as it had been on the opportunities provided by the existence of a national debt.

Say translated large sections of the *Wealth of Nations* in his description of the natural growth path of modern states. He was equally impressed by Smith's warnings concerning the difficulty of establishing a regime of natural liberty by legislative action. No system of policy was perfect or to be applied to the letter because the human world was corrupted and full of unique circumstances which defied the application of general laws. Necessity and history had both to be taken in account. For example, Smith had argued in the second chapter of Book IV that general rules of policy could be overridden when they clashed with security and Say reiterated his ideas. Active interference in the exercise of property rights was essential in the case of individuals or groups of individuals violating the rights of others to become a threat to civil peace. The interesting example Say gave was in the case of slavery, showing a departure from Smith's condemnation on purely economic grounds.[30] The second case was where 'public safety demands, sometimes urgently, the sacrifice of private property.' The example Say gave showed how seriously he took the urgency of order. Once more against Smith, he accepted that in times of scarcity the grain trade ought not to be free because popular uprisings had to be countered:

In spite of the arguments of the partisans of unlimited liberty, I believe that the special properties which distinguish grain, and commodities which supply essential nourishment, justify forbidding exports when prices exceed a level designated in advance, or at least submit exports to a heavy tax, since it is better that those who are determined to smuggle pay an insurance premium to the state rather than to their insurers . . . however, when the remedy is in itself an evil, it is necessary to employ it only in times of unavoidable necessity.[31]

Defence was a priority for his legislator as for Smith's. A permanent defence was essential for France because of the threat posed by the British. He justified legislative promotion of the grain trade on land which might be more profitably used to grow the vine on the grounds that the British might cut off the international supply in times of war. Navigation acts were necessary in order to ensure a supply of trained sailors and ships that could be called upon in national emergency. The production of certain goods essential for war, such as the armaments industry, had to be regulated by the legislator. France simply could not afford to abandon the controls that regulated her foreign commerce, because the British were actively subsidizing their goods in order to undercut French markets: she would be 'at a real disadvantage relative to British goods'. After taking into consideration 'the rarity of capital in France', Say concluded that import taxes were 'only equivalent to [British] burdens.'[32] The discussion of defence reveals the extent to which Say's legislator was prudent and flexible, uninhibited by rules, rights or laws. Even if a legislator had recognized that free commerce ought to be introduced into a state, Say advised him to pause and consider the effects of excessive change: 'An able statesman, having conceived an eminently sensible plan, is often restrained by the vices which steal into its execution . . . Despite the inconveniences associated with prohibiting foreign goods, it would undoubtedly be rash to abolish them abruptly. An ill does not cure itself in a day.'[33] Say therefore did not believe in general laws of policy that could be applied in all circumstances. Apart from security, the existing manners of the state had to be considered. Following Smith, his legislator operated in an imperfect world in which speedily introducing a regime of perfect liberty would, in the short term, worsen rather than ameliorate the injustices of the mercantile system. Therefore, 'second-best' laws and policies had to be pursued by necessity:

Every absolute system is an excess. Every excess is an evil. I have only sought to ensure a just appreciation, and to make clear the advantages and disadvantages which result, in order that policies are not lightly adopted, because only their benefits are perceived, and prescriptions are not made without appeal, through measures in which only the faults are recognized.[34]

This was most clear in questions of taxation, which could not be resolved by assuming or seeking laws to explain how the flow of national wealth would be influenced. Nicolas Canard and the physiocrats were fools because they had never considered the particular manners that ultimately determined the effects of specific taxes. Say's rules for taxation were therefore prudent. He accepted that the wealthy ought to pay proportionately more than the poor. He attacked lotteries as a tax on the poor and a stimulant to idleness. The most maligned yet most useful taxes were consumption taxes, which left choice to the individual. In matters of taxation Say undermined established icons rather than erecting his own theory. Such considerations led Say to justify active legislative involvement in the lives of the citizens for defence, for justice, and when necessity dictated. The last case included the stimulation of new industry by the use of subsidies and patents. He applauded Colbert's support for the introduction of fine cloth and silk industries into France, which he affirmed had become the best in the world. It was also essential for the legislator to organize the production of goods that were beyond the means of private capital, or where there would be a risk to a state of creating a private monopoly. Roads and canals were prime examples. Say advised that when France faced demobilization, or any slump in trade, the unemployed men should be employed at public expense in the improvement of routes of communication.[35]

In his critique of the mercantile legislator, Say had argued that it was imperative that France renounce the aspiration to universal monarchy and self-sufficient empire which had inspired statesmen since Colbert, and which caused Louis XIV's disastrous wars. He believed that once peace in Europe was secured the French could develop commercial alliances based upon mutual advantage. He expected this to ensure the development of extensive commercial and manufacturing export markets for France. This strategy alone would defeat the British domination of world commerce. Navigation acts had to be countered by out-producing Britain's commercial trade by a long-term free trade strategy between nations not allied to or controlled by the British:

Against such a measure other peoples can only take similar action against Britain, in forbidding her the facilities of commerce and transport. If between them they abolished all barriers to trade, the power [Britain] that will continue to allow them to maintain these relationships would soon be punished, because commerce takes the principal route where, with equal security, it finds fewer hindrances. This power [Britain] will find world commerce escaping it, by the very means it uses to attempt to control it.[36]

This strategy for the foreign relations of France was matched by detailed schemes to develop her internal markets. He considered the domestic market to be the key to France becoming what he called *une nation industrieuse*.[37] It was vital that France commercialize her agricultural sectors, since he believed that the profits generated in this manner would stimulate manufactures in the towns and generate a beneficial commerce between these sectors. It was therefore vital to place domestic commerce before foreign. The proof of this was China, which had benefited from avoidance of empire, colonies and foreign trade. The natural order of economic activity was clear:

It is pleasing that the natural tendency of things carries capital to the most preferable ends, not where it would make the highest profit, but to whatever action is of most benefit to society. Preferred employments are first the improvement of land, next domestic manufactures and commerce, and, after all the rest, foreign commerce, transport, and long-distance trade ... Only by the lure of forced gains and monopoly profits does a nation, whose industry stands in need of capital, become engaged in the Indies trade or colonial commerce.[38]

The success of the French domestic economy depended upon creating wider markets for commonly-used products which would be cheap and popular. This necessitated the mechanization of production wherever possible, the creation of private banks to encourage saving in local economies, and the introduction of competition into all walks of life. This would create a virtuous spiral of capital accumulation and rising production, which in turn would increase the size of the French domestic market and the wealth of the consumers within it. This, Say believed, was the secret of Britain's success; their products were useful and well made, and therefore able to undercut the high quality but expensive French products catering for more specialist markets. Gradual liberalization of the French economy would stimulate each of the three branches of industry and create an integrated productive machine.[39]

Say's legislator was interested in the promotion of the manners essential to productive commerce. He argued against the physiocrats that small farms ought to be promoted against vast agricultural factories, not because they were necessarily more efficient or productive, but because 'small cultivation is more fine, and more pleasant, than any other'. Frugality and industry would be stimulated in small farms far better than elsewhere. Say's legislator was also active in the education of the populace. He made it clear that he was not seeking to coerce the population into a specific moral code, and acknowledged that he had seen all such schemes fail; the moral education of the populace had to be left to parents. However, he argued that it was vital for the prosperity of a state that all its inhabitants be able to read, write and count: and that they be aware of new technologies, particularly in agriculture:

The position of the ordinary labourer in the productive machine of society reduces his profits almost to the level of his subsistence. At the very most he can afford to raise his children; but he will not be able to give them the degree of instruction that we consider necessary for the well being of the social order. If society wishes to enjoy the advantages of such a level of instruction in this class, it must therefore cover the costs. This aim is achieved by means of instruction carried out in small schools, where reading, writing, and arithmetic are learned. Such knowledge is the foundation of all others, and is sufficient to civilize the most ordinary labourer.

Governments were advised to subsidize the writing of elementary books that would teach the populace about the modern sciences. Such provision did not extend to open hospices and hospitals for the sick and the needy. The poor had a right to public succour so far as their poverty was caused by society. For this reason some hospices ought to be provided on a means-tested basis for the industrious sick. However, he believed that universally free institutions would simply reduce the wages of labour and ultimately increase the number in poverty:

Considering other hospices, perhaps the only measures capable of reducing the excessive numbers of the needy, which conform to the principles of humanity, is to maintain an equitable but severe discipline, which makes the indigent equate the institution with a form of religious terror. The great improvement in the condition of the poor in the hospices and hospitals of Paris since the revolution have probably increased the number of persons supported, even more than the evils of war and our intestine civil dissensions.[40]

Workhouses were a better means to protect and aid ailing citizens. Echoing Rumford, these were to be centres of labour, where the industrious could earn a minimum wage while adhering to a rigid discipline. He hoped they would ultimately pay for their own upkeep and enable those who used them to save in order to re-enter the world of free labour. The legislator would ensure that all public organizations, including prisons, inculcated the skills and manners that would make them more valuable to a productive society.

The ideal French legislator was expected to help stimulate industry in the manner Say had described. It was particularly important to aid the development of the scientific community, which he considered superior to that of Britain and a potential source of innovation. The result would be a society in which the mass of the population were skilled, constantly employed, and in receipt of adequate wages:

As wealth increases in a society, which is to say that as its capital grows, the wages of labour increase and the profits of capital diminish. The reason is straightforward. The more capital there is in a nation, the more there is in circulation, the greater the demand for industry. Capital is in greater supply, and industry in greater demand. Competition between capitalists leads them to accept an average profit, and the progressive demand for industrial labour ensures a higher wage. But when capital becomes rare, industrial wages fall.[41]

He was convinced that he was following Smith in arguing in favour of a well-fed, -housed and -clothed work-force as a means to greater production in general. In his exposition of the 'art of legislation' Say was following Book V of the *Wealth of Nations* and applying its ideas to France. Two lengthy reviews that recognized both the economic strategy of the *Traité* for France and Say's use of Smith, appeared in *La Décade* towards the end of 1803. The first, by Say's colleague Joachim Le Breton, praised the book as the greatest work of political economy since the *Wealth of Nations*; while making clear that Say had gone beyond Smith in his justification of a political economy which was 'everybody's business'.[42] Say's close friend Augustin-Pyramus de Candolle, in the guise of a member of the *Société pour l'encouragement de l'industrie nationale*, argued that the *Traité* surpassed Smith in revealing the path to a flourishing society by promoting industrious and frugal manners among the entire populace.[43]

Say's legislator in 1803 clearly differed from the one envisaged by his fellow political economists. By contrast with Garnier, Sismondi, and Rœderer, Say divorced the legislator from political or constitutional considerations. The ideas of the *Traité* were radical because they were in principle equally applicable to despotisms or democracies. This was one reason why Napoleon was initially intrigued by Say's work and attempted to seduce him into an administrative position. Say refused because he considered Napoleon to be the archetypal mercantile legislator and in consequence an advocate of a society of established ranks, particularly those associated with Catholicism. In his formulation of economic strategy Say's legislator was more aware of the need to adjust laws to manners. A legislative strategy had to be popular to be successful. The most distinctive feature of Say's legislator in 1803 was, however, his obsession with the problem that had first been sketched in *Olbie*. States would only succeed if they alleviated the endemic poverty of commercial societies. Manners and wealth ultimately depended upon an egalitarian distribution of wealth, which enabled citizens to live above the level of poverty and below that of excessive affluence. A life characterized by ease generated by toil was Say's ideal. His perception of this problem and its solution underlined a continuing fraternity with the radical republican creeds of the 1790s. Say concluded from revolutionary experience that these republican values could not be encouraged by traditional methods but had to be inculcated by the forces of free trade made safe from the interventions of legislators, and by the propagation of enlightened self-interest among the citizens. The transformation of society towards a more egalitarian, sociable and moral order was to be achieved with only the minimal activity of the legislator. Therefore Say combined an original interpretation of Smith with a peculiar faith in republican values and manners. He held that the *Wealth of Nations* was a manual for laws to encourage republican manners.

5 THE FATE OF THE FIRST *TRAITÉ*

The laudatory reception of the *Traité* was short lived. In 1804 Say was part of the second wave of ejections from the Tribunate after declining Napoleon's request that he rewrite the *Traité* as a defence of Napoleon's regime.[44] The book became one of the first works to suffer the disapprobation of the life Consul; Say was prevented from publishing further as long as Bonaparte held onto the reins of power. His response, after exploring the idea of emigration to America in correspondence with Jefferson, was to enter the entrepreneurial world as a cotton-mill owner at the village of Aulchy in the Pas-de-Calais. According to Say's son-in-law, Charles Comte, it was this experience which confirmed his belief in the ideas expressed in the first *Traité*. He later claimed that Say had seen at first hand that it was possible, without the legislative direction of lives and prices, to take a 'a malign village' and create a manufacturing centre of four hundred workers, mostly women and children, where, according to Comte, Say 'had the satisfaction of seeing industry and ease animate a countryside in which, for several centuries, a feudal and monkish regime had only been able to entrench poverty and misery.' Say's project was described as 'Owenite before Owen'.[45] This was the essence of Say's a-constitutional republicanism, reflecting a similar optimism about the progress of popular culture and morality.

NOTES TO CHAPTER 9

1. *TE*, i, 181.
2. Letter to Say from Daunou, 7 Thermidor an XI, Say papers, BN Microfilm 5786, 146.

3. *Lettres d'un habitant de Genève à ses contemporains* (Paris, 1803), p. 15.
4. *Fragmens d'un ouvrage abandonné sur la possibilité d'une constitution républicaine dans un grand pays*, ed., Henri Grange (Paris, 1991), pp. 217–19, 226. The work remained in manuscript.
5. *Dernières vues* (Geneva, 1802), *Œuvres complètes de Necker*, xi, 196–236.
6. *Recherches sur la nature et les causes de la richesse des nations; par Adam Smith. Traduction nouvelle, avec des notes et observations; par Germain Garnier de l'institut national* (Paris, 1802).
7. *Abrégé élémentaire des principes de l'économie politique* (Paris, 1796).
8. *Recherches*, p. vi.
9. *Ibid.*, xl, from *Wealth of Nations*, Bk. II, ch. 3, pp. 337–9.
10. *Mémoires sur quelques points d'économie publique, lus au Lycée, en 1800 et 1801, ŒdR*, viii, 41–97.
11. *ŒdR*, viii, 60, 62. In a footnote Rœderer was more circumspect about the practical application of his views on political participation: 'il ne suffit pas d'avoir établi que les capitalistes ont autant d'intérêt à l'ordre que les propriétaires fonciers pour en conclure qu'on peut leur confier de même la plénitude des droits politiques, et particulièrement l'éligibilité aux grandes magistratures. Il faudrait aussi établir qu'ils y ont une même aptitude.'
12. *Ibid.*, viii, 67.
13. *De la richesse commerciale, ou principes d'économie politique, appliqués à la législation du commerce* (Geneva, 1803), i, i–xiii, 13.
14. *Tableau de l'agriculture Toscan* (Geneva, 1801), p. 263.
15. *TE*, ii, 91.
16. *Ibid.*, i, 181, 194–8, ii, 30, 116.
17. *Ibid.*, i, 214, 230.
18. *Ibid.*, i, 239, 326.
19. *Ibid.*, i, 160.
20. *Ibid.*, i, 349, ii, 425.
21. *Ibid.*, i, 128.
22. *Ibid.*, ii, 83, 89.
23. *Ibid.*, ii, 489.
24. *Ibid.*, ii, 142.
25. *Ibid.*, i, 242.
26. *Ibid.*, i, 189–90.
27. *Ibid.*, ii, 413–14, from *Wealth of Nations*, Book V, ch. 1, pp. 810–11.
28. *Ibid.*, ii, 418, from *Wealth of Nations*, Book V, ch. 1, p. 697.
29. *Ibid.*, ii, 519–26.
30. *Ibid.*, ii, 143–4.
31. *Ibid.*, i, 311.
32. *Ibid.*, i, 285, 250–2.
33. *Ibid.*, i, 261, 289, 292.
34. *Ibid.*, i, 330.
35. *Ibid.*, i, 474, 509, 259, 333.
36. *Ibid.*, i, 172.
37. *Ibid.*, i, 353, 398–402.
38. *Ibid.*, ii, 332.
39. *Ibid.*, ii, 80.
40. *Ibid.*, ii, 434–45.
41. *Ibid.*, ii, 183–4, citing *Wealth of Nations*, Book I, ch. 8, p. 97.
42. *LDP*, xxxviii, 328.
43. *Sur le nouveau Traité d'économie politique du citoyen Say, LDP*, xxxix, 143–53; *Seconde lettre aux Auteurs de la Décade philosophique sur le Traité d'économie politique du citoyen Say, LDP*, xxxix,

198–208; *Dernière lettre aux Auteurs de la Décade philosophique sur le Traité d'économie politique du Citoyen Say, LDP*, xxxix, 265–73.

44. Say later described this episode in a letter to Dupont of 5 April 1814: 'Durant ma fonction de Tribun, ne voulant pas pérorer en faveur de l'usurpateur, et n'ayant pas la permission de parler contre lui, je rédigeai et publiai mon Traité d'économie politique. Bonaparte me fit venir auprès de lui et m'offrit 40 mille francs par an si je voulai écrire dans son sens; je refusai, et fus compris dans l'élimination de 1804.': cited by P. Steiner, *Politique et économie politique.*

45. *Le Censeur Européen, ou examen de diverses questions de droit public, et des divers ouvrages littéraires et scientifiques, considérés dans leurs rapports avec les progrès de la civilisation* (Paris 1817), i, 172.

PART FOUR

REPUBLICAN POLITICAL ECONOMY IN CONDITIONS OF MONARCHY

10

Rejecting the Post-War Settlement

1 THE RETURN OF THE BOURBONS AND BRITISH CONSTITUTIONALISM

The end of Napoleon's control over France, after military defeat at Leipzig and a speedy abdication to Elba in April 1814, was a clarion call to many intellectuals to address the question 'whither France?' It was universally accepted that there would be no return to 1799; the republic of letters created in the 1790s had been sliced in two by attitudes to the First Empire. Committed *philosophes* such as Rœderer, Garnier, and Cabanis, took a decision to follow the imperial standard, and were amply rewarded for their change of face.[1] The institutions of republican intellectual discourse were no more. The second class of the *Institut* had been closed down at Napoleon's behest in 1806, and replaced by the *Académie des inscriptions et belles lettres*. As Say later noted, in one of many tirades against Bonaparte, the *Institut* became an appendage of the court, reminiscent of the sycophantic *Académie* of Louis XIV.[2] Above all, the reintroduction of Catholicism as the state religion, and the promotion of clerical control over education, dealt blows to the revolutionary *philosophe* movement. Probably the most successful political idiom of the Empire was that of Chateaubriand, celebrating *Le Génie du Christianisme* while castigating the 1790s as a secular hell worthy of divine wrath.[3] Such themes were reiterated in a multitude of journals including, ironically, that into which *La Décade* was incorporated, *Le Mercure de France*.[4] Given the nature of Napoleon's defeat and the ascendancy of Britain in Europe, it is not surprising that a return was made to prominent political languages of the late 1770s and 1780s. Once more, models of Britain's constitution and social structures became the focus of attention. The difference was that the Comte de Provence, soon to be crowned Louis XVIII, promoted the discussion rather than perceiving it to be a threat to his authority. Landing at Saint-Ouen on May 2 1814, he promised 'a liberal constitution'. The *Chartre constitutionelle*, largely his own work, was presented to Napoleon's Senate and Chamber of Deputies on June 4. Its acceptance instituted civil equality and a restricted representative system in which the king held legislative and executive powers tempered by a hereditary Chamber of Peers and a property-owning Chamber of Deputies with control over the national purse. Although Catholicism remained the established religion and a preamble dated the constitution 'the nineteenth year of our reign', there was no immediate attempt to restore the institutions, attitudes, and social structures of the Old Regime. Rather, it was as if the Bourbons had chosen to move France towards a British constitutional model over the past twenty-five years, having accepted the social and political changes associated with commercialization. Even after the Hundred Days and a second restoration, Louis XVIII clung to British-style constitutionalism, going so far as to dissolve the reactionary *Chambre introuvable* in September 1816. He was praised for his attitude in Chateaubriand's *De la monarchie selon la charte* (1816), which wholly welcomed the turn towards Britain.[5] Although the journey they had taken was very different from that of Louis XVIII, many ex-revolutionaries accepted that Britain now provided the best model for France. Germaine de Staël, having been converted to modern republicanism in the mid-1790s, returned to the views of her father's *Du pouvoir exécutif dans les grands états* (1792). In her posthumously published *Considérations sur les principaux événemens de la révolution française* (1818), she argued that Louis XVIII should follow the example of 1688 since 'up to the fall of Bonaparte, the French Revolution greatly resembles that of England'; the work ended with a detailed study of British history and the lessons it presented to France.[6] Her old friend Benjamin Constant had become equally convinced of the impossibility of a republic in a large state. 'The more popular the government we wished to create in France', he contended, 'the deeper were her wounds.'[7] Returning from England in 1816, after the success of *De la doctrine politique qui peut réunir les partis en France*, Constant became a keen advocate of Britain's constitutional example, as his lectures at the *Athénée Royale* reveal. The lesson of the Revolution was that the 'liberty of the ancients' could not be resurrected in modern states, a truth exemplified by Britain's successful combination of civil equality in a commercial society with limited political liberty.

The question to be resolved was the nature of the constitution perceived to be behind Britain's wealth and stability. At one extreme, Chateaubriand emphasized the importance of Britain's hereditary aristocracy, adding that France ought to be able to imitate her rival successfully because Catholicism ensured the greater placidity of the lower orders than in Britain.[8] This view greatly influenced the upper echelons of French society in the early Restoration, who favoured a compromise between the aristocracy of the Old Regime and the commercial ranks of the new Europe. Against this stood Constant, for whom commercial society signified 'a social organization essentially homogeneous', necessitating the absolute entrenchment of civil freedoms. As he put it in *De la liberté des anciens comparées à celles des modernes,* it was vital for aristocracies to be gradually dissolved by commerce, a process which he believed would end the threat presented to liberty by tyranny; otherwise an oppressive feudal–commercial state would result: 'Let us mistrust this admiration for certain ancient memories . . . I humbly beg these monarchies not to borrow from the ancient republics the means to oppress us.'[9] Once a commercial society without hierarchical ranks had been established, Constant argued against defining or prescribing modes of living or moral codes by legislative means, which was one of the reasons why he was an early critic of Bentham.[10] His interest in Say's political economy, manifested in several works from this time, was due to Say's claim that an industrious society, which to Constant was synonymous with a commercial society, need not be inegalitarian in social structure, or entail the impoverishment of the ordinary labourer.

The political arena of Restoration France was equally characterized by the writings of Saint-Simon, who shared the dominant view of Britain's greatness, but for different reasons. Writing in 1815 with his secretary Augustin Thierry, he agreed that 'history from 1688 has confirmed [the British constitution] to be the best form of government possible'.[11] However, he added that to 'direct society towards the public good' the creation of an Anglo-French parliament was essential, with powers to foster a new 'positive' religion to replace Christianity. His intention was to combat 'today's monstrous situation in which all particular interests are directed by those skilled in science and industry while general interests are still subject to theology and feudal principles.'[12] The secret of Britain's success was not a particular political architecture, but rather a *culture* opposed to feudalism and dedicated to science and industry: the impoverished masses were not rebelling against the feudal political elite because they recognized that their own prosperity was being secured by the social progress of industry. These ideas attracted attention with the launch of the journal *L'Industrie* in 1817, in which Saint-Simon undertook a critical evaluation of Say's political economy, which fascinated him for obvious reasons. The aim of this chapter is to assess Say's writings of the period 1814–1825 against this intellectual landscape, to discover the fate of the carefully modified republicanism of the first *Traité* in wholly altered political conditions.

2   THE SECOND *TRAITÉ*

With the achievement of peace in 1814 Say was able to publish the second edition of the *Traité* which appeared in July of that year. The revised title and advertisement claimed the work to have been 'entirely recast'.[13] The five books of the first edition (production, money, value, revenue, and consumption) were reduced to three, conforming to Say's definition of political economy as 'the production of wealth, the consumption of wealth, and its distribution.' An *Épitome des principes fondamentaux de l'économie politique* was added, presenting the themes of the second *Traité* in rigorous deductive form. When revising the work in 1812, Say had written to his cousin Michel Delaroche that he was gaining confidence in the originality of his ideas about political economy and moving away from Smith.[14] In a letter of July 1814 to his friend de Candolle—enclosing a copy of the work—Say claimed it to be 'an entirely new work, refashioned over eleven years, during which time I believe I have established the principles of this science . . .'.[15] Some reviewers shared this view, accepting that the first edition was henceforth to be put aside in favour of a book that was 'less a new edition than a new *Traité*'.[16] The dedication of the work to Tsar Alexander I was certainly distinctive, and underlines Say's utter contempt for 'the dictator' Napoleon. In not mentioning the Emperor's other opponents in the dedication it might also have signalled a recurrence of his antagonism towards Britain. He stated that he had been 'obliged for ten years to hide as if it was a crime, a book that seems to me to supply useful ideas to Princes and to Nations'. Alexander was praised as a 'friend of enlightenment' who had 'broken the shackles which chained all liberal thought and pushed back the barbarism whose rapid progress we observed with terror'.[17] Since a good prince necessarily sought the public good, Say was convinced that the Tsar would be interested in an investigation of 'the causes of public prosperity'. The mention of 'ideas useful to Princes' was of fundamental importance, because it hinted that the focus of the second *Traité* in fact differed little from the first regarding the political strategy for the increase of national wealth that Say had gleaned from Smith. This was indeed the case. Although more critical of Smith on the role of labour in the production of wealth, the extent of the division of labour, and unproductive labour, Say maintained the view that 'there was no political economy before Smith', significantly adding 'if Smith is read as he deserves to be read'.[18] Chapters dealing with the role of the prudent legislator, the necessity of a gradual transition to free trade, the abandonment of empire, public credit, the need for free public instruction, and the evils of international rivalry, emerged unscathed from 1803, largely because of Say's belief that experience of Napoleon's continental blockade gave force to his contentions.[19] The most striking addition to the work was the support Say found for his views from his reading of the Italian political economists—after Pietro Custodi's 1804 publication of the *Scrittori classici italiani di economia politica*, and particularly Pietro Verri, Beccaria, and Filangieri. That this is the case should not be surprising given the extent of Say's business and family commitments during the final years of the Empire, which are amply documented in his private correspondence.[20]

Reference to 'ideas useful to Nations' indicated that Say continued to believe in political economy as a force for popular enlightenment. Although he now stated that the work was directed towards 'all those who fulfil with an enlightened spirit the diverse professions of society', he declared the book to be *un Traité populaire*.[21] The science remained 'everybody's business', as was clear from the addition of the *Épitome* and the publication in 1815 of the first edition of Say's popular *Catéchisme d'économie politique*. The *Épitome* sought to explain how each 'class of producers' shared an interest in the creation of wealth and its fair distribution. 'Productive and industrious' classes were listed in accordance with their multiplication of knowledge, application of knowledge to human use, and practical execution of useful ideas. Say listed the diverse members of an industrious society who contributed to wealth creation, and who deserved to reap its rewards: 'intellectual, industrial entrepreneur, cultivator, farmer, manufacturer, merchant, retailer, labourer, capitalist, landed proprietor'. Discussion of these classes is important, because it shows that Say maintained his view of a definitive interest which united an industrious society, and his belief in a diverse but egalitarian social order which would make it prosperous and stable. The *Catéchisme* sought to show the united interest of the nation in increasing the numbers of 'industrious persons', and particularly the 'labourers, capitalists, and landed proprietors.' He believed that as these groups increased poverty would be reduced across the nation, which was one of the reasons why he wanted to make the science as popular as possible.[22] As he wrote to Ricardo, 'I am persuaded that ultimately all [these truths] will be known in the cottages, and the consequences will be immense.'[23] Confidence in an empirical approach founded on 'general facts' was as absolute and as strident as in the edition of 1803.[24] In the letter to de Candolle, Say stated that 'The new school of scientists recognize that moral events are connected, just as physical events . . . since there is no effect without a cause.'[25] Once more he expressed the hope that the work would 'contribute to the amelioration of the social order.' Say's view of poverty as the greatest threat facing Europe was maintained; his faith in the 'middle class' as the source of enlightenment, his opposition to feudalism, and conception of political economy as a force for 'peace and civilization', were as prominent as hitherto. The second *Traité* equally affirmed Say's critique of the republican legislative strategies of the 1790s, as J.-B. Biot recognized in his review of the work.[26] In a response to Dupont's critique of the second edition, Say confirmed that his intention was to put an end to attempts to consider the right form of government alongside the laws which he believed made political economy an independent science, because all attempts to establish 'the rights of man' became embroiled in endless controversy and had never prevented tyranny.[27] He did, however, convincingly defend himself against Dupont's claim that he had made political economy a science of reason-of-state and was overly impressed by British approaches. The view of human nature behind each edition of the *Traité*, and indeed all of Say's writings, derived from a belief in the possibility and necessity of enlightened self-interest shared by *every* industrious member of society, rather than egoism, altruism, or the benign operation of the hidden hand of private self-interest.

What I have claimed to be the most important element of the first *Traité*, the articulation of the republican manners to create a society without hierarchical ranks, was equally prominent in 1814. Although the language was refined and supporting evidence added, Say retained extensive discussion of the necessity of labour, frugality, and probity, to industrial success in agriculture, commerce, and manufactures. As a note in his private papers responding to criticisms of the second *Traité* makes clear, rather than being a restatement of Smith, Say believed he was breaking new ground in revealing 'the links between the diverse professions and the laws and manners of a well-constituted society, which can alone allow us to resolve the problems which present themselves when one wishes to govern a family or state well.'[28] These claims were recognized and reaffirmed by his two disciples, Charles Dunoyer, and Say's son-in-law, Charles Comte, in their extensive review of the second and third editions of the *Traité* published in the first two volumes of their journal, the *Censeur Européen*, in 1817.[29] Say's texts were described as being opposed to reason-of-state approaches to politics and political economy, exemplified by Louis XIV, Robespierre, and Bonaparte's amassing of bullion and support for blockade and colonial crimes, and the British state's propagation of violent wars to destroy French industry. Comte and Dunoyer brought Say's criticisms of existing political theory to the fore in underlining his opposition to the ancients' approach to politics. His was a study not of the best form of government but of the means to cultural enlightenment.[30] Say was portrayed as an innovator rather than Smith's disciple: 'Adam Smith developed with great wisdom a large number of truths in this matter; but it is only in the hands of M. Say that political economy has become a true science.' The *Censeur* argued that Say's views amounted to a moral vision, portraying a society in which fraternity rather than cupidity predominated. They welcomed Say's support for 'real needs ... gradual consumption rather than spontaneous consumption, and consumptions which result in a preference for goods of superior quality, the consumption of popular goods ... and the consumption of goods compatible with healthy morals.' As might be expected from writers who knew Say intimately, and who shared his views at this time, their perspective rightly underlines Say's opposition to avarice and prodigality, and his faith in economy and industry as the foundational virtues of the modern world: 'Economy is the daughter of wisdom and enlightened reason ... nothing is more fecund in happy consequences.' In their eyes,

Say's political economy represented a new approach to social improvement that addressed the faults the Revolution had exposed in traditional perspectives on morals and politics. It articulated a general interest that could be made plain to all individuals and become a force for social peace and stability:

Political economy shows the common interests shared by men; it destroys jealousies, and the hates which render men enemies of each other; it unites the diverse classes of society and disposes them to mutually support each other . . . Moralists have said that idleness is the mother of all vices; political economy has shown that it is also the source of poverty, just as labour is the source of all wealth, as well as a large number of virtues. Moralists teach men to put their duties before their interests; the economists reveal how men can conciliate their interests and their duties. The first teaches men to fight against natural needs, while political economy teaches the satisfaction of needs, not only without harming anyone, but while doing good to other men.[31]

Comte and Dunoyer therefore interpreted Say's thought in the context of the breakdown of 1790s republicanism, and the need to shift the focus of debate towards enlightening the nation. French audiences in the early years of the Restoration had little difficulty discerning exactly what was Say's goal, as Saint-Simon showed in the journal *L'Industrie*:

It is clear that M. *Say* makes two distinct and separate subjects of politics and political economy . . . *Smith* . . . presented it [political economy] as a means by which *governments* could enrich themselves; he announced it only as a secondary science, as auxiliary to and dependent upon *politics*. M.*Say* went one step further than *Smith* from the *philosophical* point of view: he established, as the main argument of his work, that *political economy* is distinct from and independent of *politics*; he stated that it has its own foundation, quite different from the one upon which the science which deals with the organization of *nations* is based.[32]

What this project meant in the political context of the Restoration was made clear by Say in his most revealing work of this time, *De l'Angleterre et des Anglais*.

3   SAY'S VIEW OF BRITAIN

Say remained a republican despite the broad acceptance of the Empire by his colleagues at *La Décade* and his friends at the *Institut*. So firm was his faith that even in a light-hearted letter to Michel Delaroche, whom he had called 'a king among men', he confessed 'to desire nothing from royalty, either for their happiness or for ours.'[33] J.-A. Blanqui recalled that he had been astonished on meeting Say in the early years of the Restoration that the political economist 'had very revolutionary ideas for the times; he detested both the Bourbons and Bonaparte'.[34] The experience of the Empire was of definitive importance in the formation of Say's views, and he continued to reflect on its consequences for the rest of his life. After what he called 'the nightmare of the Hundred Days', very few of his private letters and none of his public writings failed to condemn 'the usurper and tyrant' who was 'worse than Caesar or Cromwell'. Charles Prinsep was arraigned in 1821 for suggesting, in the first English translation of the *Traité*, that Say had been over-critical of Napoleon because of 'personal provocation'.[35] In a long letter Say attacked Napoleon for being a warmonger, for restoring ranks and political corruption, for 're-establishing the influence of priests and the intervention of the Pope', and for fostering an egoistic culture which had made France 'one of the weakest and most dominated powers in Europe.' The message of Napoleon's defeat was that active legislators were incapable of controlling the culture and practices of modern populations. This reflection did not, however, convert Say to a positive view of Britain's laws and constitution.

In the early months of the Restoration Say had high hopes of public office. It is likely that by soliciting Dupont de Nemours, who continued to be close to the then leading French minister Talleyrand, Say was given a secret mission to examine on behalf of the government the condition of the British economy after twenty-five years of war.[36] In mid-September 1814 Say travelled to England, and spent one month in London and one month in Glasgow, before returning to Paris at the end of December.[37] After paying a visit to Place with a letter of introduction from Godwin, he was introduced to Bentham and James Mill at Ford Abbey and Ricardo at Gatcombe Park.[38] Having submitted a report to the government, which has been lost, Say published an account of his assessment of Britain, which proved popular, being twice reprinted before the end of 1816.[39] As was the case in the majority of Say's writings, he made his central line of argument clear at the beginning of the text. Britain's power was not to be explained by her military or maritime strength, her gold reserves, or her political structures. Rather, the 'economic system as a whole' provided 'wealth and credit'; by this he meant the culture of the entire nation, which he believed had embraced industry of all kinds.[40] Furthermore, he claimed that the 'economic system' was beyond the control of politicians who sought to increase trade by means of taxes and bounties. Britain had flourished during the wars not because of the wisdom of her statesmen, but because of 'the stupidity of Bonaparte', who, in a comment which betrayed Say's republican sympathies, 'had made an enemy of the people of Europe where the French republic had only made enemies of Kings'. Bonaparte's wars across Europe had distorted national capacities to become involved in trade, resulting in relatively cheap British goods flooding the markets of the continent despite the blockade. Say's second point was equally controversial, claiming as it did that the successes of British industry during the war years had given the nation an impression of economic strength that was in fact superficial. The industries that had risen to prominence had enriched 'speculators and fat entrepreneurs at the expense of the people'. As a result the domestic market was not extensive enough to support British production in the context of European competition. 'Taxes and debts' had carried away too much capital, and weakened future productive capacity. What Say called 'the "ancient abuses" of the political system' had been exacerbated by 'new abuses which accompanied the new expenditures'. As a consequence, 'the ministers' friends have grown more numerous.' Higher taxes had caused prices to escalate, which Say claimed did not concern the owners of large amounts of land but obliged the general populace 'to undertake persistent labour, and enjoy no rest'. The 'labouring class' were in such distress that 'the parish supports a third of the nation'. It was ironic that workers had begun to emigrate to war-torn Europe rather than remain in their victorious country of origin; as Say put it 'the condition of labour is now worse there than it is in France'. 'Deplorable effects' were perceived to have followed from these conditions. The 'country of Bacon, Newton, and Locke' was no longer as enlightened as it had been in the past. Deleterious economic circumstances were 'making philosophy decline' while the nation 'moved rapidly towards barbarism'. People no longer had time to read. Books were in any case too expensive and 'fell upon an exhausted soil'. The quality of goods had also suffered. Say was struck by the falling reputation of British products: 'the people who have been called the richest in the world are condemned to drink, under the name of wine, the most dangerous poisons.' Against those who traced Britain's problems to the decline of religion, Say argued that 'there is no country more religious than Britain, as the rise of Methodism shows.' His experiences led him to conclude that 'civil and religious liberty, liberty of the press, the security of property, and the dominion of the seas' were of little consequence when measured against the effects of the poverty of the people as a whole.[41] Even the machines 'which render production so cheap' could not outweigh the costs associated with higher taxes. Governments had mismanaged the economy to the extent that commerce and manufactures were being ruined by the grain price support system, while landowners claimed they would be ruined if it collapsed. Say anticipated a bankruptcy, although he expected 'the political system to crumble' if such a step was taken. The only alternative in his view was the speedy renunciation of empire, while also reducing costs through severe restrictions on domestic spending.[42] First hand experience of British conditions led Say to reiterate the critique of mercantile empire in the first and second *Traité*. He prophesied a bleak future for such states.

By contrast with the majority of his contemporaries, Say considered Britain to be no model for France, and that the end-point of the liberty of the moderns was not to be found in such a nation. The fundamental problem was Britain's social structure, which was too unequal and divided to create the systems of exchange and the large domestic markets necessary for economic success. Instead, 'egoistic superiors' and 'wretched villains' robbed the poor of the fruits of their labour. The 'scientific education' Say considered so important to wealth creation simply could not be established. Just as in France, the government had ruined the nation, which had become too corrupted to survive. The French republican perspective on Britain was reclothed for a post-Empire world.

4 SAY'S VIEW OF FRANCE

If the condition of the French nation was seen by Say to be little better than that of Britain, he was still more sceptical about the prospects of the Bourbon government. Horace Say was advised by his father to expect further revolutions: 'France will be malgoverned . . . [the administration] is weaker and more timid than that of Bonaparte. These poor Bourbons have neither the troops nor the money. Soldiers have not once cried "Vive le Roi" . . . the King himself is surrounded by ravenous wolves.'[43] Say's pessimism was so great that he raised once more the issue of emigration to North America. As he put it, 'If we could establish a business together I would be very content. Your sisters would be able to marry more easily than here.' In a letter to Ricardo of 2 August 1815 Say revealed that his hopes of public office on his return from Britain had been dashed, 'because of the impossibility of doing any good'. He added that he expected to die 'before my ideas become popular in France'.[44] A letter to Bentham, written on the same day, argued 'they are trying to build here a rotten throne; it cannot stand.'[45] Three years later he spoke in similar terms of 'the sacrifices that the people make to royalty.' Once more the blame was ascribed to Bonaparte: 'In fourteen years Bonaparte managed to set aside all that was pure and honourable; and when the Allies came there was not a single public man to plead for the citizens. The Bourbons had the matter of corruption ripe and ready in their hands. Beware of French reputations. You would be astonished at the stuff out of which they are made.'[46] Corrupt and corrupting men could be found everywhere: the ex-physiocrat 'Garnier, made a Count by Bonaparte, has been made a Marquis by the Bourbons'. Press restrictions ensured that 'the abettors of abuse alone are privileged to speak'. The ghosts of the Old Regime had returned to haunt the present in the form of vast sums expended 'buying the creatures of the court': 'Having no real control from the self-proclaimed representatives of the nation, the public authorities pay out of the public purse a host of vampires who, far from rendering services to the State, are, for the most part, horribly pernicious to it.' Although there is no evidence that Say was directly affected by the 'White Terror' which followed the second restoration, his friend de Candolle was a victim of what he referred to in his *Mémoires* as 'the Bourbons with their priests and nobles, and their hostility towards Protestants and the sciences'. In late 1815 he was forced to abandon his post as rector of the Imperial University at Montpellier and to return to Geneva, where he became Professor of Natural History. Say's letters to him into the 1820s show no abatement of opposition to monarchical government. Both men attempted to maintain their faith. In a letter recalled by Candolle's son, Say reported 'one must cease to be a republican as late as one can'. Any alternative was inconceivable. In a letter to Sarah Austin of April 1826, he commented 'The truth is, kings, nobles, and priests are doing their best to make themselves obnoxious, and are succeeding admirably.'[47]

The question is, of course, what the republicanism attested to by so many of his friends meant to Say in the Restoration context. It was clearly not simply a disgruntled allegiance to past ideas. Say passionately believed that the science of political economy he espoused could combat the political and economic malaise of France (and indeed Europe) by enlightening nations about their real interests, thereby creating the ideal republican societies he imagined, without corrupt politicians, overlarge capitalists, or mercantile legislators. He had come to doubt whether, in creating such republics, governments should be of much concern. As he put it in a letter to Bentham, he wanted to question whether 'governments are such a necessary part of society at all'.[48] This did not mean that Say was attracted by anarchism or had ceased to believe in the ultimate possibility or efficacy of the virtuous legislator at whom so many chapters of successive editions of the *Traité* were directed. Rather, modern governments were so malign in character, and monarchy was so entrenched in Europe, that it became necessary to address the 'nation' directly before politics could be made republican. In short, it was necessary to expound and propagate a republican morality that would be the first step towards the restoration of natural liberty in France by showing the positive effects of living in accord with the virtues of industriousness, frugality, and moderation. This aim lay behind one of Say's works that at first glance might not be considered to be concerned with political economy, the *Petit volume* of 1818. In fact it described a branch of political economy that Say was beginning to believe to be of overriding importance. Reversing his judgment of Duval in the 1790s and his comments on public instruction in the first *Traité*, Say now argued that the teaching of morality was essential. The best means of doing so was by publishing tracts for the masses that included advice and maxims for enlightening self-interest. The *Petit volume* was a moral catechism intended to stand beside the political economy catechisms repeatedly published from 1815. The two subjects were only distinguished for educational purposes. The issues they dealt with were broadly similar. Thus the *Petit volume* contained a defence of the republican manners Say pressed on the French in all of his writings. Following *De l'Angleterre* he attacked the governments of Europe for generating war and corruption where they should have been extinguishing it: 'All governments, without exception, the good as well as the bad, affect the purest intentions . . . yet they squander while speaking of economy, make war while protesting a love of peace, and take arbitrary actions in the name of the laws.'[49] The cynical tone of this comment was tempered by a sense of cultural progress in France that infused the work, called by Say 'the growth of enlightenment'. He argued 'It is no longer necessary for each man to master everything; [man] has a better sense of his true interests [than hitherto], and of how far it is possible to contribute to happiness in life.' Once more Say claimed that this happiness was synonymous with the regular labour of every citizen, which would 'destroy hostilities between men and harmonize the interest of each with the interest of the whole'. Such an interest would only be recognized when individuals pursued wisdom for themselves, 'making themselves virtuous through the development of their intellectual faculties'. Civilization would be attained when nations were 'free, industrious, and pacific.'[50] Echoing Say's writings of the Restoration and Empire, critiques of courts, kings, aristocracies, and established religions, were barely veiled. The subjects of Restoration France had to be made to recognize that governments would never make them virtuous, because in trying to direct society politicians were acting, as Dunoyer put it in his illuminating review of the book, 'like flies on coaches'.[51] Dunoyer claimed that Say's book 'influenced politics greatly' in attacking 'the military and mercantile systems, and especially the regulatory regime which tends to dominate and paralyse everything.' Since Say had shown that 'society determines its own destination, and propels itself', it was essential to oppose 'those governments seeking to make a sovereign people in a conquering country, or a *dévot* populace'. The means to this end were, first, the liberty of the press, and, second, an education in political economy, 'the voice of civilization'. Once these were established the functions of government could be limited to the protection of property of all kinds. Rather than being a species of liberalism, Say's opposition to governments—although more vitriolic than in his earlier writings— restated his republican morality, which was now intended to stand alone.

Frustrated with contemporary political and intellectual life, Say at this time broadened his intellectual objectives, through the writing of a *Traité de morale* and a *Traité de politique pratique*, intended to stand with the *Traité de l'économie politique* to provide a complete education for modern citizens.[52] His private papers reveal the amassing of

notes for these books, particularly the *Politique pratique*. Although they must be treated
with caution, as they remain largely disjointed fragments, the notes give a good idea of
Say's broader attitudes after 1810. Draft sections of the *Politique pratique* include discussions of 'despotism', 'moral diplomacy', 'of political corruption and public spoilation',
'of political crimes', 'of the principal causes of war', and 'of the lack of instruction and
enlightenment among populations'. Notes headed 'the representative system', 'federal
states', 'that large states can only be well administered', 'inconveniences of democracy',
and 'advantages and inconveniences of the separation of powers', reveal Say to have
maintained his view of Britain as a corrupt monarchy with an overpowerful aristocracy.
Restating several themes of 1790s republicanism, they also show an interest in North
American experiments with federalism and other techniques for decentralizing
power.[53] Although he clearly still believed in the project of creating a republic in a large
state, arguing that it was not the excessive size of France which had led to the collapse of
the republics of the 1790s, Say acknowledged the problem to be an awesome one: that of
making old world politics more like those of the new. Drawing on James Mill's *History of
British India* and 'the example of China', he sought to show that the central problem
facing modern states was the corruption of manners. It is evident, however, that he had
shifted position, maintaining 'That the manners of nations govern the governors'. The
problem with France was that Napoleon had 'de-moralized the nation'.[54]

Continuing to adhere to Clavière's views of the early 1790s, Say expressed no faith in
declarations of rights or constitutional guarantees without the foundation of virtuous
manners. Establishing these manners by political means in the Restoration context
would have been Say's most distinctive contribution to intellectual debate, seeking as he
did to find areas of political and moral 'certainty' to counter corruption and egoism,
and to define the public good for those who wished to remain virtuous in the face of a
corrupting monarchy. Had they been published, it would be clear that Say—in moving
away from the republican legislator he had perceived Smith to have addressed—was not
following Constant because his faith in representative government, civil liberty, and a
British-style commercial society was limited, while his faith in the specification of
useful industrious manners was infinitely greater. They would also have affirmed the
differences between Say and Saint-Simon, who had altogether renounced the large-state
republicanism based on civil equality and the universal recognition of secular virtuous
manners. Say's sole hope was to be found in the belief that 'nations march by themselves, and not by the impulse of government, which is only one part of society.' The
Politique pratique was never completed because Say had no purely political solution to
the regeneration of virtue in the populace, and he became too sceptical about the possibility of establishing political certainty. It was therefore incumbent upon political economy to 'form opinions by enlightenment', and to combat the lack of 'public instruction'
which always corresponded to 'the poverty and bad governance of the people.'

5   POLITICAL ECONOMY AS CIVIC EDUCATION

The opportunity to put these ideas into practice came from the very government that
Say so often castigated in his private correspondence. It is a mistake to assume that Say

cut himself off from French political life after 1815; there is evidence in his papers of contacts with various ministries and the provision of advice on numerous projects.[55] This was partly because Say was becoming famous through the popularity of the second and third editions of the *Traité*, and partly because of the successful *Cours de l'économie politique* which Say taught at the private *Athénée Royale* from 1815–1819, during which time one of Say's colleagues was Constant and one of his students was Saint-Simon.[56]

In 1818 Baron Thénard, a member of the *Académie des sciences*, requested Say's thoughts on 'a special school for industry'. Say took the opportunity to apprise Thénard of his view that the lack of education in political economy had caused 'in France, probably more than elsewhere, a zeal to indulge in enterprises which cannot succeed, while rejecting processes which we will soon see enriching foreign rivals.' France had 'stimulated the spirit of enterprise without enlightening it', something 'deadly to public prosperity'. By contrast, the broader knowledge and acceptance of political economy in Britain 'make them more advanced'; something Say now acknowledged, although he asked Thénard to keep this to himself, perhaps because of the contradiction with *De l'Angleterre*. The solution was 'to destroy the mass of prejudices, and spread ideas [about political economy] further than they currently are'. The aim of 'a truly manufacturing nation', Say contended, would only be created by educating the country's leading entrepreneurs. Say restated the view of the second *Traité*, that it was no longer necessary to educate 'ordinary workers' by such methods, since a basic instruction at the workplace would suffice for the success of their working lives.[57] Thénard had influence at the ministerial level. Government fears about the economic prosperity of France led to Say's appointment to the Chair of *Économie industrielle* at the *Conservatoire des arts et métiers* in 1820. The course he taught from this year until his death followed that of the *Athénée*, the notes for which of 1819 have recently been published. These confirm the view that at this time Say conceived of political economy as a means of educating the nation in its true interests. This is why Say took pains in his course to prove that 'political economy is a branch of the moral and political sciences', a 'positive science', based on the indisputable facts of 'the nature of things'.[58]

One of the most important elements of the *Cours* was Say's discussion of the role of government. Conforming to the position of the *Petit volume*, the second and third *Traités*, and the *Traité de politique pratique*, he argued that 'government is not an essential part of the social organization'. 'Public authority', he declared, 'is an accident; an accident rendered necessary by our imprudence, and the injustice which leads us to violate the rights of fellow individuals.' Proof was to be found in the fact that government had collapsed 'four or five times during the past thirty years', while the people discovered 'more order than there had been before'. The example of Kentucky was also cited as evidence because it was not yet part of the North-American federal union but was being peaceably civilized without political involvement. Say concluded that 'all productive enterprises are the conception of the governed'. Distinguishing between the industriousness of society and the purely administrative functions of political institutions, he attacked 'the idea of the State as a family and the head of the administration as a father.'[59] France had suffered from adherence to such ideas, which made her 'too much governed, either by the councils of the *communes*, or the Committee of Public Safety, either by the *Préfets*, or by a centralized and military authority.' It was essential to turn away from the example of Britain and towards that of the United States to understand that 'the perfection of the social organization is not a vain theory but can be practically realized.' The federal government of North America secured the internal liberty of trade, levied modest external duties, protected property, and established the absolute right to free labour. Say's advice to French governments was to take similar measures, and to improve things still further by renouncing the policy of initiating any war: 'The State that does not attack another is never attacked, so long as the courage of the nation is recognized . . . If the government is national, and respects the interests of the nation, it will seek only to defend itself.'[60] History proved that states which declined were those whose governments failed to tolerate different religious and cultural practices within the nation, thereby destroying the productive energies of minority groups. Say asked Frenchmen to look to the collapse of Portugal and Spain because of the Catholic Inquisition and the expulsion of the Jews and the Moors. He also advised French governments to begin decentralizing the administration of public liberties, once more in the manner of the American republic. If the government did this while the leaders of industry were educated in political economy he was sure that the result would be an extraordinary increase in French wealth and power, which would encompass all of the industrious classes of the nation. In his *Discours d'ouverture* at the *Conservatoire* on 2 December 1820, he asked his students to recall that 'in cultivating industry, you labour for yourself and at the same time for morality and happiness; for the public good and the private good.'[61] The new republicans were not politicians; they were citizens who invested their capital in enterprises, such as canal building, which brought wealth to all sections of French society and unified national culture. Their modest personal wants and moral uprightness made them the epitome of virtuous manners. Such citizens patriotically believed that 'the public good is everything', and recognized the science of political economy to be the fount of this form of patriotism.[62]

NOTES TO CHAPTER 10

1. There is a nice anecdote about Rœderer's conversion in Candolle's *Mémoires et souvenirs*, pp. 82–3; see also Rœderer's *Mémoires sur la révolution, le consulat, et l'empire*, ed., O. Aubry (Paris, 1942), pp. 185–200.
2. Letter to C. R. Prinsep, May 1821, *ŒD*, pp. 429–38.
3. *Le Génie du Christianisme* (Paris, 1802), *Œuvres complètes de Chateaubriand* (Paris, 1867), ii, 140–5.
4. Kitchin, *La Décade*, pp. 89–79.
5. On Chateabriand's view see J.-P. Clément's excellent introduction to *Chateabriand: Grands écrits politiques* (Paris, 1993), 2 vols., ii, 303–16.
6. *Œuvres complètes de Mme. la Baronne de Staël* (Paris, 1820), xiv, 5th part, 24; 6th part, chs. 2–9.
7. *Principes de politique applicables à tous les gouvernements* (Paris, 1816), ed., E. Hoffman (Geneva, 1980), p. 37.
8. *De la monarchie selon la charte*, op. cit., ii, 336–9, 432–5, 447–53.
9. *De la liberté des anciens . . .*, tr. B. Fontana, *Constant's Political Writings* (Cambridge, 1988),

      pp. 313, 322–3, from *Collection complète des ouvrages publiées sur le gouvernement représentatif et la constitution* (Paris and Rouen, 1820), 4 vols., 238–74.

10. *Principes de politique*, op. cit., pp. 58–61.

11. *De la réorganisation de la société européen*, pp. 132–4.

12. *Aux anglais et aux français qui sont zélés pour le bien public* (1815), pp. 145–6.

13. *TT2*, i, ii.

14. Letter of 16 May 1820, Say papers, BN Microfilm 6333, 18–20.

15. *Mémoires et souvenirs*, p. 558.

16. *Le Moniteur universel* (1814), p. 1013.

17. *TT2*, i, viii.

18. *Ibid.*, i, xlviii.

19. This is confirmed by letters to members of the Delaroche family, 1807–12, Say papers, BN Microfilm 6333, 4–28; Charles Schmidt, 'Jean-Baptiste Say et le blocus continental', *Revue historique des doctrines économiques et sociales* (1911), 148–54.

20. *Mes lettres particulières du 1 Fevrier 1811–26 Juillet 1812*, Say papers, BN Microfilm 6333, 37–74.

21. *TT2*, i, lix–lx.

22. *Catéchisme*, *ŒD*, 65–72, 89–92. The extended edition of 1821 has recently been republished in Philippe Steiner's *Cours d'économie politique*.

23. Letter of 2 August 1815, *The Works and Correspondence of David Ricardo*, vi, 245–6.

24. *TT2*, i, xlv–xlviii.

25. Letter to Candolle, p. 558.

26. *Journal des savats* (1817), 397.

27. Letter to Dupont, 15 November 1815, *ŒD*, p. 388.

28. Say papers, Mss. F375.2: cited by E. Schoorl, *J.-B. Say*, p. 159.

29. *Le Censeur Européen*, i, 159–227; ii, 169–221.

30. *Ibid.*, i, 166, 187, 207.

31. *Ibid.*, i, 187, 189; ii, 213–14.

32. *L'industrie littéraire et scientifique liguée avec l'industrie commerciale et manufacturière* (Paris, 1817), in *Œuvres de Claude-Henri de Saint-Simon* (Paris, 1868–9), 6 vols., i, 185; ii, 155–6. The translation is based on G. Ionescu's *The Political Thought of Saint-Simon* (Oxford, 1976), pp. 106, 123. The passage continued: 'Cette contradiction prouve que l'auteur a senti vaguement, et comme malgré lui, que l'économie politique est le véritable et unique fondement de la politique, mais qu'il ne l'a pas vu d'une manière assez sûre, puisqu'il le fait entendre, il est vrai, dans les détails de son ouvrage, mais qu'il le nie dans ses considérations générales. Quoi qu'il en soit, son travail a rendu les plus grands services. Son ouvrage renfermé tout ce que l'économie politique a découvert et démontré jusqu'ici; c'est, présentement, le nec plus ultra de cette science en Europe.' On Saint-Simon's relationship with the Revolution see H. Gouhier, *La Jeunesse d'Auguste Comte* (Paris, 1941), 3 vols., iii, 144–57; R. Wokler, 'Saint-Simon and the Passage from Political to Social Science', in A. Pagden, ed., *The Languages of Political Theory in Early-Modern Europe* (Cambridge, 1987), pp. 325–38 and 'The Enlightenment and the French Revolutionary Birth Pangs of Modernity', in *The Rise of Social Science* (Sociology of the Sciences Yearbook, 1998); K. M. Baker, 'Closing the French Revolution: Saint-Simon and Comte', *The French Revolution and the Creation of Modern Political Culture: The Transformation of Political Culture 1789–1848*, eds., Furet and Ozouf, (Oxford, 1990), pp. 323–39.

33. Letter of 25 February 1812, Say papers, BN Microfilm 6333, 10–11.

34. Cited by E. Teilhac, *L'Œuvre économique de J.-B. Say* (Paris, 1927), p. 51.

35. Letter of May 1821, *ŒD*, pp. 429–38.

36. Letter to Dupont, 5 April, 1814, Dupont Papers, Hagley Museum, Philadelphia. Talleyrand received a copy of the second *Traité* on its publication in July 1814; see Say papers, BN

Microfilm 5786, 393. In July 1815 Say wrote to Talleyrand requesting a position in the ministry dealing with the reduction of customs duties. Talleyrand immediately replied, politely advising that no positions were available: BN Microfilm 7690, 293–5.

37. Say confessed in numerous subsequent lectures that he had been enraptured by sitting in Smith's professorial chair in Glasgow. A number of prominent writers tried to meet Say during his visit and many, such as Dugald Stewart, were unsuccessful. Say's papers reveal the extensive correspondence he maintained with British intellectuals from this time, including Bowring, John Sinclair, Robert Hamilton, Grote, Tooke, and Napier: BN N.Acq.F. R97418.

38. Place papers, BL Add. Mss 35152.

39. A further edition followed in 1824, and the essay was translated into English in 1816 and German in 1818. For the controversy it inspired see Simon Gray, *All Classes Productive, or National Wealth, with Four Letters to the Celebrated French Economist M. Say on his De l'Angleterre* . . . (London, 1840).

40. *De l'Angleterre et des Anglais* (Paris, 1816), pp. 1–2.

41. *Ibid.*, pp. 11, 18–28.

42. *Ibid.*, pp. 53–61. Sismondi recognised Say's originality in a letter to his mother of April 10 1815: 'I have just read a pamphlet from M. Say, which was published on his return from England, which is altogether in agreement with what I believe concerning their finances and their disastrous economic predicament because of their customs barriers.': quoted by H. O. Pappe, *Sismondi's Werggenossen* (Geneva, 1963), p. 30.

43. Letter of 26 May 1814, cited in G. Michel, *Léon Say* (Paris, 1899), p. 15.

44. *The Works and Correspondence of David Ricardo*, op. cit., vi, 245–6.

45. *The Correspondence of Jeremy Bentham* (Oxford, 1988–90), 4 vols., ed. F. S. Conway, viii, 491–2.

46. Letter to Bentham, 3 May 1818, op. cit., ix, pp. 193–4.

47. Candolle, *Mémoires et souvenirs*, op. cit., pp. 124, 251–4, 563; J. Ross, *Three Generations of Englishwomen*, pp. 46–8.

48. Letter of 2 August 1815, *Correspondence of Bentham*, vii, 491–2.

49. *Petit volume, contenant quelques aperçus des hommes et de la société* (Paris, 1818), *ŒD*, p. 691.

50. *Ibid.*, p. 667.

51. Review of the second edition, *Censeur Européen*, 7 (1818), 80–126. See also the review of the first edition, *Censeur*, 6 (1818), 247–54.

52. The notes can be found in BN N. Aq. F. R. 111917, R. 111919, R. 106316. When dates are signified they are from the period 1818–20, a point confirmed by Charles Comte, *Notice sur la vie et les ouvrages de J.-B. Say*, ix. In a fragment probably written in the early 1820s, as Say refers to himself solely as 'the author of the *Traité* . . .', he expresses the intention to complete a *Traité ou essais de politique pratique*, a collection of *Essais de morale pratique*, and a *Traité de l'utilité morale des religions*: BN Microfilm 6739, 214–16.

53. Say papers, Microfilm 9095, 33–4, 270–92, 293–308, 309–15, 316–25, 324–9; Microfilm 7269, 93–100, 280–314.

54. Say papers, Microfilm 9096, 199–212. Cf. letter to Sismondi, 8 February 1807: 'C'est la nature des governements qui fait les nations ce qu'elles sont.' P. Roggi, 'Sette lettere di J.-B. Say a J. C. L. Sismondi'.

55. P. Steiner, *Politique et économie politique*. Say's papers show that he was involved in the establishment of a distillery at this time and was active in the *Société d'encouragement pour l'industrie nationale* and *Société pour l'instruction elémentaire*: BN Microfilm 7690, 11–46.

56. Constant referred to Say as his 'friend and colleague' in a letter of 30 June 1820, requesting the writings which traced Say's dispute with Malthus and Sismondi: Say papers, BN Microfilm 5786, 132–3.

57. Letter of 1818, *ŒD*, pp. 520–5.

58. *Cours à l'Athénée* (1819), ed. P. Steiner, *Cours d'économie politique*, pp. 83–6. Sets of notes for different years of teaching at the *Athénée, Conservatoire,* and *Collège de France* can be found in BN. N.Aq.F. R. 97419, R. 103780, R. 103781.

59. *Ibid.*, pp. 148–56. See further Say's *De l'économie politique moderne, esquisse générale de cette science, de sa nomenclature, de son histoire et de sa bibliographie, Encyclopédie progressive,* i, 217–304.

60. *Cours à l'Athénée,* op. cit., pp. 83–6.

61. *Discours d'ouverture du Cours d'économie industrielle, ŒD,* pp. 145–7.

62. *Des canaux de navigation dans l'état actuel de la France* (Paris, 1818), *ŒD,* 232–3.

11

'Social Science in its Entirety'

1   RICARDO, MALTHUS, SISMONDI

Say's writings between 1816 and 1822 underline an interest in North American society as a model for Europe, in the face of James Madison's contention that Say was exaggerating the republic's assets.[1] They also affirm a faith in the capacity of reason-induced virtue to create a society characterized by civil equality. Furthermore, Say's work makes clear an increasing scepticism about legislators, and the resulting need to present indisputable facts about social behaviour to the nation, so that the public good everyone shared would be gradually realized. Say's confidence in his views was growing stronger, as evinced by a request to his students to dispute with him on any issue in political economy, in order to achieve the unity of opinion he believed to be essential to progress.[2] The approval he anticipated was not forthcoming. Ricardo, Malthus, and Sismondi, between 1815 and 1821, attacked Say's notion of utility as incapable of supporting a conception of the public good powerful enough to satisfy the diverse elements of a modern nation.

As early as August 1815, Ricardo recognized ambiguities in Say's identification of 'value' and 'utility' in the second edition of the *Traité*. His major point was that Say had not made clear whether social usefulness was expressed in the price of a product in a free market. Ricardo plainly did not believe this to be the case: 'A commodity must be useful to have value but the difficulty of its production is the true measure of value. For this reason iron, though more useful, is of less value than gold.'[3] In an exchange of letters up to 1820, Say held fast to the view that although utility was not the sole cause of value it was the most important determinant, the costs of production being overwhelmed by social desire manifested by the forces of supply and demand. Since 'all value is relative, and wealth, being only value, is also relative', it was more important to establish the unhindered exchange of goods, the increase of all kinds of industry and the reduction of taxes, to engender thereby the movement of prices to their lowest possible level in order to increase the real income of the lowest paid workers.[4] Ricardo persisted in his criticisms, maintaining in his public and private works that Say had confused 'use value' and 'exchange value'. For Ricardo the term 'value in exchange' had to be tied to a concrete quality, such as the comparative quantity of labour necessary to production, in order to be useful in evaluations of wealth.[5] By 1821 Say inexplicably believed that the dispute was drawing to a close, yet continued to hold that 'to create utility is to create wealth, but that we have no other measure of utility than the greater or lesser quantity of a product, the quantity which forms the *exchange value* or *current price*.'[6] Until his death in 1822 Ricardo continued to believe that the weakest element of Say's theory was his attempt to combine an assessment of social usefulness with the far more arbitrary determination of price; he caused Say to recognize that he was sounding like a stoic with a theory of value resting on the forces of supply and demand but which in addition sought to counter luxury and superficial needs.[7] Say's problem was that his idea of a free market was defined by the necessary exercise of the enlightened republican virtues; this would not have been obvious to Ricardo, who identified a problem in the compatibility of attempts to promote 'liberty' with strictures about how to live in accordance with the public good. For Say, the major problem with Ricardo's attempt to clarify the problem was its abstract nature; this violated the key tenet of Say's perspective: the need for absolute clarity in order to convince the general populace of the certainty and practicality of political economy, in order to reform their behaviour. This criticism of Ricardo was repeated in Say's notes to the French translation of the *Principles of Political Economy* (1821) and in his *Examen critique du discours de M. MacCulloch sur l'économie politique* (1825).

The attacks of Malthus and Sismondi were more serious than Ricardo's in that they questioned the possibility of articulating an interest shared by every member of society. The commercial crises following the end of war in Europe had spread from Britain to Brazil; it led these authors to adopt the view that excessive production was responsible for the distress of the working classes. Demand had been outstripped and a 'general glut' or 'the choking-up of markets' had produced bankruptcies and unemployment.[8] The commercial system itself was the cause of the malaise. Sismondi, by contrast with his earlier *De la richesse*, confessed to having few solutions to the problem, while Malthus considered it necessary to justify the consumption of luxuries by aristocratic ranks in order to build a bulwark against economic collapse.[9] Say's response to these claims, in his *Lettres à Malthus*, was to restate his view that goods were being produced in an imperfect world of ignorance, social hierarchy, and political corruption. In the longer term, general gluts would be overcome. Say traced the existence of impoverished classes in Britain to two factors. First, laws 'framed upon the absurd idea of the balance of commerce', which increased taxes and national jealousies; second, 'the customs which are the result of a vicious political system', favouring 'the progress of luxury and large emoluments'.[10] As was the case in the majority of modern states 'the efforts of citizens are paralysed by the Administration'. France was suffering because of cultural prejudices against living in the countryside, which caused large proprietors to neglect their businesses. Thus 'the vices of the social community' were the root cause of national poverty—unproductive consumption, the hoarding of money, and the sacrifice of future production 'to the pleasures of the moment'—this directly led to 'the labourer being continually forced to work at any price, even when the production no longer affords him the wherewithal to live.'[11] Say argued that his law of markets remained unchallenged by current economic problems, the only solutions to which were a war on ignorance and corruption. Flexible prices and ever-greater production would then 'open a market to the sale of produce', and guarantee the ordinary worker and the largest landowner a fair return on their capital; the associated increase of real wages would then protect the weakest elements of the community. Four years later, writing in the *Revue encyclopédique*, Say claimed that 'there is no nation where we find overproduction', because 'even in the most flourishing, 7/8 of the population lack necessities'.[12]

Furthermore, social equality was gaining in the richest nations relative to the poorest, a process which could be seen in 'Britain, the United States, Belgium, Germany, and France' because of the progress of industry. Against Sismondi, he contended that mechanized industries paid the highest wages, once initial fluctuations accompanying the introduction of machines had been overcome; this was now evident from the experience of cotton manufacture. Low prices 'have come not at the expense of the working class but because of the progress of the sciences and the arts.' The fundamental problem was 'the bad calculations of the entrepreneurs' who had, in consequence, 'to be educated in social economy'. This science would improve the real conditions of the working class rather than relying, as Say believed Malthus did, 'only on the wisdom of Providence'. It would teach nations to abandon laws of primogeniture and entail which, in creating hierarchical ranks, were a major source of poverty.[13]

Despite such confident rhetoric it was clear by the mid-1820s that Say was concerned about the success of his attempt to educate nations in republican manners. The arguments of successive editions of the *Traité*, he believed, had been misunderstood by 'some of the most eminent men in Europe'. Letters to Sismondi reveal that Say genuinely expected his 'dear *concitoyen*' to agree ultimately with him about the nature of modern nations, and to 'arrive by different routes to the same end'; as Say put it: 'if I have argued particularly against you, it is because I regard you as the most worthy interpreter of the opinions I don't share'.[14] Although Sismondi believed his perspective was closer to Say's than that of any British political economist (and shared the aim of ultimate agreement) this was not forthcoming.[15] Faced by seemingly endless epistolary disputation, Say decided to undertake a final reassessment of his ideas in the hope of achieving his long-standing goal of specifying for the public, and for fellow political economists, what was valuable in the republican project of creating a virtuous society. He believed that he could take what was convincing in the work of his fellow writers—such as Ricardo on money, and Malthus on the principle of population—and integrate their ideas into a coherent scientific manual.[16] In fulfilling this goal Say turned to Bentham's idea of utility as a means of achieving clarity and precision. It was to be 'a social science in its entirety'.[17]

2   THE INFLUENCE OF BENTHAM

Say undoubtedly became aware of Bentham between 1789 and 1792, when the *Courrier de Provence* published synopses and translations of Bentham's thoughts on rights in general, and the procedures to be followed in the National Assembly in particular. As a reviewer of the journal for *La Décade*, he would have read Bentham's writings in early editions of the *Bibliothèque britannique*. It was in this journal that his friend Dumont published letters explaining his commitment to Bentham's approach to social problems and why he was willing to devote so much of his life to explaining it to a wider audience.[18] Bentham was not, however, cited in the first *Traité* of 1803 and it is unlikely that Say drew from Bentham his theory of value based on utility. Bentham was cited from the third edition of 1817, not for any specific ideas about political economy, but rather for identifying 'the abuses from which Britain suffers'. Say's letters from this time underscore an allegiance to Bentham's demand that modern intellectuals seek what was most useful to society, by specifying, justifying, and practically realizing the greatest good of the greatest number; it was also Bentham who had written to Say on 11 April 1818: 'Every European that can should now fly to United America.'[19] Like Dumont, what Say was interested in was Bentham's promise to justify projects conforming with the good of humanity. He perceived Bentham to be a republican. Like Clavière and Brissot before him, he believed Bentham to have launched a republican critique of British society, politics and laws, and to have formulated a modern republican doctrine to resolve its ills. Bentham was described as an opponent of the traditional hierarchical social order. Of particular interest to Say was Bentham's focus on manners as more important than, as Dumont put it, 'the study of different forms of government'.[20] In a review of the *Tactique des assemblées legislatives*, Say said that, despite an excessive regard for the procedures of the British Parliament, Bentham's work was 'excellent in matters of the general interest'. It showed how to 'gradually perfect the details of the social organization' in the face of established prejudices, and particularly those of the nobility.[21] Say's interest in the 'science of utility' Bentham expounded can be traced to the early Restoration period, after Ricardo had been critical of Say's use of the term in the third *Traité* of 1817, and when the republicanization of French society was perceived to be most necessary.

On meeting Bentham during his visit to Britain in 1815, Say was distinctly impressed. As Place related to Ricardo after Say's departure: 'He spoke with rapture of you all, Mr. Bentham's philosophy, and, as M. Say expressed it "his heart full of benevolence in everything", made his eyes sparkle as he pronounced the words: "You and Mr. Ricardo are", he says, "profound economists"; from both of you, he says, "he has learnt much that will be useful." ' [22] From this time onwards Say received copies of all of Bentham's published writings, and a constant stream of miscellaneous papers and manuscripts. In a letter of 3 May 1818, after the burning of the St Petersburg Panopticon prison, he sketched his attitude to Bentham's writings in flattering terms that were unquestionably sincere:

When you are no more, Panopticons will be built in hundreds. Your bust will be in each; but in the meantime, the original will be persecuted. This is the order of things; Chamfort was right in saying that 'our moral world is the result of the caprices of a devil run mad'. But for a few men like you, there would be nothing for it but drowning.[23]

In his *Cours à l'Athénée* Say spoke of 'the celebrated Bentham' as 'my friend, or rather, my master'. He used the example of the Panopticon as proof of the existence of a positive science of morals and politics. Bentham had done a great service to humanity through his 'profound knowledge of the morals of men, and of the principle that one becomes habituated not to do ill from the moment when it is recognized that no advantage comes from it, and that one does good when one becomes accustomed to it by strong motives'. In applying this principle to prisoners they received 'the habit of order and labour'. Despite the ruining of the project by 'ministerial intrigue and private interests', Say was convinced it would 'render to society honest men in the place of felons.'[24]

It is unclear at what date Say decided that it would be necessary to explain why he considered his political economy to be, as he put it to Dumont, 'an extended application of the principle of utility'.[25] An undated fragment in his papers discloses the intention:

To write a short work entitled *Of the principle of utility* or simply *Utility*. I will first define utility in the broadest terms, as a proficiency in being able to serve mankind. I will show that in their affairs all men who do not have utility as a goal, are ignorant, misled, demented. [I will show] that to lead men to live by the principle of utility is to lead them to the proper use of their reason, and to the greatest happiness possible. [The principle will be] applied to politics, to political economy, to all the sciences and all the arts. Allow this to appear only after my other works. It will be the key to them all.[26]

It is impossible to know when Say wrote this, but it is likely that it dates from 1819–1822, because it was at this time that Say's use of the term *utilité* was under the greatest scrutiny from Ricardo, while his plans for future works were then at their broadest. Furthermore, later fragments are concerned with the refutation of accusations of egoism, sensuality, materialism, and atheism, which Say does not refer to in this instance. When attacks on the principle of utility reached a crescendo in the mid-1820s, Say was goaded into constructing a defence. He perceived his opponents to be the French branch of what he called 'the germanic–scholastic sect', who based their arguments 'on the *truths of sentiment*', inspired by Staël's *De l'Allemagne* and Necker's *De l'importance des opinions religieuses*. In Say's eyes the latter's ideas were taken up in Constant's *Essais philosophiques* and Victor Cousin's *Cours de philosophie* in the 1820s, and necessitated refutation 'to make clear that we understand by *principle of utility* neither personal nor national egoism . . . not through a polemic, but by showing all the young people of Europe how to form just ideas about the interests of society and the nature of things'.[27] Historical examples would show that men, such as George Washington, who had lived according to the greatest good of the greatest number, were rewarded by 'glory and tranquillity'. Those who lived for themselves, 'seeking their happiness in doing evil to others', suffered in consequence, just as Bonaparte had 'died of chagrin at Saint-Helena'.

The *Essai sur le principe de l'utilité* was appended to the sixth volume of the *Cours complet* and published in 1829, although it had been completed at an earlier date. Say was dissatisfied with the result, which was one of the reasons why he exchanged so many letters with Dumont, in the hope (which was initially successful) of persuading the latter to write it anew. Dumont wrote to Say in July 1829 with the news that attacks of apoplexy, which were to kill him within months, would prevent him from undertaking the piece, particularly as he was burdened by prior commitments: 'to supervise the printing of our second *Projet de code pénal*', the completion of the *Projet de code de police*, and diverse articles for the *Bibliothèque universelle* and Cherbuliez's journal *L'Utilitaire*. Despite its author's view of it, Say's *Essai* is revealing, because it illustrates his perspective on political economy as a force for 'the felicity of men and the true honour of nations.' Say distinguished between 'utility' as a means of assessing the value of a good, and the 'principle of utility', which measured the value of actions to society as a whole. The last point was crucial, because he believed that experience proved 'egoism . . . and national egoism or exclusive patriotism . . . constitute at the same time a vice and a bad calculation.' By contrast, the man (or the nation) who 'measured his esteem according to the greatest good of the greatest number, is eminently virtuous . . . conducting men to the most real and most durable good, for humanity, his nation, and himself.' Utility in this sense was synonymous with 'everything that contributes to the well-being of man.'[28] The ally of the principle of utility was reason, which gave it power 'to enlighten ignorance and dementia'; the man who sought to 'submit the passions to the empire of reason is a benefactor of humanity and works efficaciously for the happiness of mankind.' Using examples from Mitford's popular *History of Greece* and Marie-Joseph Chénier's poetry, Say sought to prove what he recognized to be Cicero's claim: that what was *utile* was also *honnête*, making duty, self-interest, and virtue synonymous. As a result he launched an attack on Staël's *Corinne* and *De l'Allemagne*, which had attacked the principle of utility as a force for epicureanism, and expounding the view that 'what is useless can be useful'. The evidence Say used in countering Staël is interesting, because it shows that he remained firm in his anticlericalism. Drawing on Sismondi's *Histoire des républiques d'Italie*, Say argued that 'superstition and the sacerdotal system', which Staël had praised, were responsible for the destruction of enlightenment and morals in Italy, and had made 'people, who were supposed to be the most pious, in practice the most corrupt.'[29] It was essential that modern individuals did not follow Bossuet, who had preached 'that we are nothing', but rather to recognize, with 'the citizen of the world and friend of all humanity, Jeremy Bentham', that 'you are men, and the condition of humanity is in your hands: Oh! you are great when you are enlightened.' Thus the republican project of specifying the interests of humanity and fostering virtue had been saved by Bentham after the Revolution, and was being applied by Say to the problems of poverty and national flourishing.

3   THE COURS COMPLET

The *Essai sur le principe d'utilité* was intended to provide a philosophical foundation for the book that Say had devoted his energies to between 1825 and 1828, which was published in six volumes as the *Cours complet d'économie politique pratique* between 1828 and 1829. Say considered it to be his greatest work. In a letter to Malthus of July 1827 he advised him of 'the most complete work that I have yet made', and of the hopes he had that it would 'enlighten the points of political economy which can leave doubts in good minds'.[30] When Sismondi received one of the volumes in August 1828 Say confessed to being 'happily exhausted' because his book was 'full of truths of great force—you will find many more developments and applications which have much more weight than my *Traité*.'[31] As the title of the work indicated, it was intended to be the most practical work of political economy yet published. It was also intended to be the most popular. As Say wrote to Thomas Tooke, 'you will easily recognize that I wished to popularize this science and to extend it to the young people, who begin to be so occupied with it in the world.' He added, 'every man endowed with an ordinary intelligence will be able to confirm for himself, in his daily observations, all of the truths that the work professes.'[32] If the body of the text proved too taxing for the reader, the *Catéchisme d'économie politique* was appended. The text proper was organized to cover every issue in political economy; nine sections covered the nature of wealth and production, exchange and money, the influence of institutions on the economy, revenues and their distribution, population and poverty, consumption, public finance, and political arithmetic. An

Histoire abrégé des progrès de l'économie politique was also added, to underscore the quality of the intellectual developments which revealed an abyss between the ancients and the moderns, and emphasize the particular progress from Smith's foundation of the science of political economy to what Say believed was his own lasting contribution: 'the theory of markets . . . which in showing that the interests of men and nations are not mutually opposed, has spread the seeds of concord and peace, which in time will germinate.'[33]

It is not my intention to outline the details of Say's theories about the working of the economy in the *Cours*, and the concessions he made to Sismondi in a chapter recognizing 'the limits of production', to Ricardo on value and on money, and to Alexander Everett on population.[34] It is necessary merely to signal that the majority of Say's chapters were based on those which could be found in the *Traité* of 1803; Adam Smith's legislator was no longer directly addressed but the economic strategy Say had derived from Smith remained largely intact, with the rider that it was now the job of nations rather than governments to ensure progress. Rather than go over such ground, my aim is rather to explain Say's conception of political economy at this late stage of his life. As might be expected from a man who remained a republican and who clung to the same fundamental ideas for a period of almost thirty years, there was little that was new in Say's characterization of the science. There was, however, a change in Say's language. The aim expressed in the book was to define 'civilization'—to specify the aspects of the modern world which contributed to it and those which impeded or destroyed it. Mercantile legislators who favoured economic strategies based on the balance of trade, and who fostered social hierarchy, were now described as 'barbaric', being cases of 'governments and peoples ignorant of their true interests, and persecuting themselves in the name of absurd and insignificant dogmas.' Say's attack on war was more strident than hitherto, and he condemned 'warmongering inspired by jealousy and the persuasion that the prosperity of a neighbour was an obstacle to your felicity.'[35] The great aim of political economy was to spread civilization, 'making more general the progress of enlightenment', through 'instruction in the art of living in society'. The rewards of increasing civilization were believed by Say to be immense, because 'we are all, every day, victims of the prejudices of the past':

If enlightenment had been more generally widespread at Rome [in the time of Caesar] and in France [under Bonaparte], rather than depending on the cupidity of a small number of men of state, and the warlike bent of the people, [these states] would have founded institutions according to the greatest good of the greatest number, and established the prosperity of the country for a long time to come.[36]

Promoting civilization entailed the creation of enlightened and industrious peoples, where the moral qualities and intellectual faculties of individuals were valued because 'industry renders good relations between men indispensable, teaches them to help each other . . . makes manners more gentle, and procures ease for all'. General and popular instruction had to replace 'the economists of the eighteenth century who believed themselves to have been called to direct the government of nations'. While Say recognized that 'political liberty is of all regimes, the most favourable to a nation', and believed that representative government would one day become universal, he held that such matters were only of secondary importance when compared with the need 'to instruct all peoples in their true interests'. As long as the form of government was not despotic, and the administration uncorrupted, it was possible to create a successful state by 'placing enlightened and honourable men in positions of power'. Social structures were more important than politics. A 'regime of equality' had to be established in which 'men are classed according to merit'; systems of 'castes and privileged bodies' had to be outlawed. The interest that united rich and poor equally in Say's view could only be recognized in regimes without social hierarchy, and North America remained a model in this respect. This interest was to be taught to all in the form of 'social economy', the branch of 'social science' that taught that politics and government were 'accidental organs', and revealed to individuals the means to bring peace and prosperity to their own communities, of any size or condition.[37] Manifest optimism about promoting civilization did not lead Say to underestimate the dangers presented by what he called 'an ignorant people' or 'malign governments'. A major source of ignorance Say believed to be the writings of Rousseau that indicted civilization; the eloquence of these writings had created a passion for savage life without recognition of the poverty, ferocity, ignorance, and loneliness that accompanied it.[38] Rather than respecting savage peoples, Say advised modern nations to seek out such cultures and 'civilize' them, as he believed the North American government to have been doing since Jefferson's presidency. 'Men', he declared, 'are richer and better provided for when they are more sociable and better instructed'. As he put it, 'Society follows on the heels of enlightenment and industry'. The Pacific islanders who had massacred Captain Cook were a guide to this process: 'despite the passage of only fifty years, they already provide an example of civilized European industry among a people once barely human.' It was necessary to initiate similar forces of change among 'ignorant and brutal savages across the world'.[39] An opposite but equally grave threat to civilization came from Britain, whose social structures Say continued to condemn because he believed they encouraged a passion for empire.[40] Empire was the institution that had to be banished from the modern world. Napoleon had been entranced by it, and created a state in the image of Britain; this brought war, superstition, and poverty, to a Europe in the throes of a successful social revolution. Repeating the ideas of an earlier essay based on Mill's *History of British India*, Say argued that empire had brought no profit to Britain and served only to increase corruption and maintain aristocracy. The causes of wealth were rather to be sought: 'in the midst of the people themselves. It is the active and judicious industry of the British, the spirit of order and economy of their merchants, and the protection enjoyed by everyone from equal laws, which are the sources of wealth; sources that are equally open to other nations.'[41] Say's advice was not to abandon European influence over colonial races since he believed that: 'The people of Asia resemble their flocks, who scarcely think it possible to live without a master'. Rather, educational institutions ought to be introduced and free commerce encouraged, until—and here he included the native Americans—'these peoples have seen their native religions collapse with the march of progress', and were 'ready for national, independent and good political institutions'.[42]

4 THE FINAL WRITINGS

Although Say had hopes of completing the intellectual edifice he had once planned, in the form of the *Politique pratique* and *Traité de morale*, recurring nervous attacks—particularly after the death of his wife in January 1830—put an end to this labour. As early as March 1820 Say had written to Ricardo that he had had 'a warning of mortality'.[43] In the last years of his life, according to Charles Comte, bouts of madness 'considerably weakened his constitution'.[44] With the publication of the *Cours*, Say's activities in society, other than his lectures, were severely curtailed. In a letter to Dumont of May 1829, Say related that he 'did not see Comte any more . . . [I] work a lot and go little into the world'.[45] He was pleased with what he had achieved. In an application to the Académie des Sciences in 1828 Say claimed 'to have contributed to making political economy a positive science, founded solely on experience and observation'.[46]

Until the Revolution of 1830, Say's view of French government was unchanged. Noting British improvement in 1828, he stated: 'It is the opposite in France. The government is detestable. They wish to make us into a monastery, but happily there was never a people less suited to such a regime. Our superior is a Jesuit imbecile, whose principal concern is salvation in the next world.'[47] Hostility was mutual. Reports of the Prefet de Police monitoring Say's lectures at the *Conservatoire* between 1824–5 presented their author as 'a danger to monarchy', 'an advocate of liberty and equality', and 'hostile to nobility'.[48] Leading figures opposed to the Bourbons, the *Doctrinaires* Guizot and Royer-Collard, welcomed complementary copies of Say's *Cours* in 1828–9; the former acknowledged 'the excellent influence which has been done by all of your writings.'[49] Say certainly felt more content with the state of France with their ascent to power. It was apposite that his final work received a prize from the Class of Moral and Political Sciences of the newly formed *Institut Royal*, which sought to imitate the republican *Institut national* that Say had so much revered. Aged ex-revolutionaries, including Rœderer and Say's *Décade* colleague, Andrieux, were actively involved in raising Directorial republicanism from the dead for employment in the service of the July Monarchy. Although touching letters were exchanged with Andrieux, Say was too ill to attend.[50] Another unexpected prize came after Guizot had ensured Say's promotion to the Chair of Political Economy at the *Collège de France* on 16 March 1831. Although bad health prevented Say from giving many lectures, his *Discours d'ouverture* reveals optimism about the spread of social economy and the progress of industry and industrious manners. Political economy was described as 'the science that combats ignorance'. A 'profound knowledge of political economy' explained why Bentham's works remained 'the most sure guides which can be consulted in civil and political legislation.' The science was a 'branch of moral and political science' that proved:

our intellectual and moral faculties have marched in step with the perfection of the useful arts. Production has civilized us, and caused us to learn that resources are secured by more sure means than the brigandage of conquest and the theft of other goods . . . it remains for us to see how goods can be equitably distributed, and consumed for the greatest benefit of society. I ask you, Sirs, what is more favourable to good conduct, and to the moral perfection of nations?[51]

At a time to come, he argued, 'pure politics and the constitutional organization' would be included in political economy. Given the imperfect state of current knowledge it was necessary 'as Montaigne says of the soul, to circumscribe in order to perfect'. The ideal republic Say had imagined in the 1790s would return, but only after political economy had civilized nations. Using careful language more fitting to monarchical times, Say noted that groups of men governing a state were always more enlightened in republics. The problem, he admitted, was making a broad political elite compatible with egalitarian social structures. Fortunately, nineteenth-century political economists had discovered that:

> The constitution is a secondary influence [on prosperity], similar to the effects of the climate, religion, and language, which vary between states, and are in no way essential to the existence of societies . . . Political economy is concerned with the vital organs which nature has made a condition of existence for civil society.[52]

In a lecture of 1832, weeks before his death, Say talked of the progress made by secular studies since the time of Smith, whom he continued to call 'the founder of a true science'. He expressed confidence in 'the improvements that have been made since the abominations of Cato, who favoured usury and had slaves, and Lycurgus, who advised idleness and justified theft, and the terrible fêtes of animals and men enjoyed by Trajan.' In the modern world there was 'much less hate, more peace, and more happiness'. Say believed that the idea of the state 'as the key to prosperity' was in decline. Such 'political sheep-pens' were not suited to 'a century attaining its maturity'.[53] His general perspective on the world remained virulently anticlerical. Towards the end of his life many people tried to persuade Say to recognize the importance of religious beliefs and to convert him to the practice of Christianity. When the Protestant minister Théophile Abauzit made an attempt through letters in 1830 Say confessed that he believed in a God revealed 'in nature and in the laws of the natural world'. But he defended an absolutely secular conception of political economy, arguing that 'religious motives are not as great as commonly thought' and that 'many deplorable actions have come from religion.' Eternal damnation he described as one of the most pernicious and false ideas ever conceived.[54] When, again just weeks before his death, Say's cousin Rosine de Chabaud sent him a Bible, he said he would accept it 'for the use of my grandchildren, as it will instruct and console them'. In a final reference to Bonaparte, he expressed the wish that religion had saved such a man from killing two million men, and claimed to have no great fears for his own salvation.[55] These correspondents were unaware of Say's plan to prove that 'religions are more dangerous than useful' and his belief that 'religions will be replaced by industry as a centrifugal force in society'.[56] If Say died a deist, his political economy was intended for the inculcation of virtue in a society of atheists.

NOTES TO CHAPTER 11

1. Letter from Madison, May 14 1816, Say papers BN Microfilm 5786, 254–5. See also the review of *Lettre de M. Jean-Baptiste Say à M. Martelly, sur le commerce d'Haïti* (Port-au-Prince, 1822), *Revue Encyclopédique*, xv (1822), 122–3.
2. Some of these letters are to be found in Say's papers, BN N. Acq. F. 97419.

3. Letter of 18 August 1815, *Works and Correspondence of David Ricardo*, vi, 246–9.

4. Letter of 10 August 1820, *Ibid.*, vi, 270–5.

5. Letter of 11 January 1820, *Ibid.*, viii, 149–50.

6. Letter of 19 July 1821, *Ibid.*, ix, 31–6.

7. Draft letter to Ricardo, *ŒD*, pp. 411–3.

8. Sismondi, *Nouveaux principes d'économie politique, ou de la richesse dans ses rapports avec la population* (Paris, 1819), pp. iv–vi, 9–11, ; also, 'Examen de cette question: Le pouvoir de consommer s'accroît-il toujours dans la société, avec le pouvoir de produire', *Annales de législation et de jurisprudence*, 1820, 111–44; Malthus, *Principles of Political Economy* (Cambridge, 1989), 2 vols., ed., J. Pullen, i, 353–67, 497.

9. Winch, *Riches and Poverty*, pp. 352–67.

10. *Lettres à Malthus* (Paris, 1820), pp. 8, 42–4.

11. *Ibid.*, p. 49.

12. 'Sur la balance des consommations avec des productions', *Revue encyclopédique*, xxiii (July 1824), *ŒD*, 250–60.

13. 'De la crise commerciale de l'Angleterre', *Revue encyclopédique*, xxxii (1826), 40–5.

14. Letters of 16 August 1820 and 28 April 1823, published in P. Roggi.

15. Letters to Say, 3 September 1820, 18 May 1823, Say papers, BN Microfilm 5786, 382–4.

16. 'Compte rendu de Malthus', *Revue encyclopédique*, xxxii (1827), 494–9.

17. *Three Generations of Englishwomen*, pp. 58–9.

18. 'Lettre aux Rédacteurs de la Bibliothèque britannique sur les ouvrages de Bentham', v (1797), 155–64.

19. *Correspondence*, op. cit., ix, 189–90.

20. See Bentham's wonderful letter to Say of 9 September 1828 in which he recounts the story of his request for a letter of introduction from Dumont to Lafayette on behalf of Leicester Stanhope, while mentioning in passing how unfortunate the young man was to be of such birth. Rather than recognizing this as a reference to eminent lineage, Dumont 'had taken him for a bastard': BN Microfilm 5786, 73–7.

21. Review of *Tactique des assemblées legislatives, suivie d'un traité des sophismes politiques, Censeur Européen*, iv (1817), 74–96.

22. Letter to James Mill, 15 January 1815, Place papers, BL Mss. Add. 35.152 fol. 128, cited in *Works and Correspondence of David Ricardo*, vi, 161.

23. *Correspondence of Jeremy Bentham*, ix, 193–4. On the first page of a copy of the prospectus for Robert Owen's *New View of Society*, Say wrote *Panoptique*; he believed Owen to have drawn his political ideas directly from Bentham's plans for penal reform: BN Microfilm 7269, 544.

24. *Cour à l'Athénée*, op. cit., pp. 92–5.

25. Letter to Dumont, 5 March 1829, *ŒD*, pp. 556–7.

26. Say Papers, BN Microfilm 8713, 240.

27. Letter to Dumont, 10 May 1829, *ŒD*, pp. 557–60.

28. *Essai sur le principe de l'utilité, CdPp* (Paris, 1837), p. 665.

29. *Ibid.*, pp. 672–4.

30. *CdPp*, (Paris, 1837), pp. 644–5.

31. Letter of 29 August 1828, in Roggi.

32. Letter of 15 April 1828, *CdPp*, pp. 646–7.

33. *CdPp*, 572.

34. Letter to Everett, 10 January 1824, letter from Everett, 18 February 1824, letter to George Grote, 11 May 1827, *ŒD*, pp. 546–9, 571–2; see also the fifth edition of the *Traité* (1826), ii, 291. Sismondi recorded in his diary of September 26 1826, 'I had this morning a visit from Say who said to me that his friendship for M. Ricardo and his school has very often cramped him, but

that in truth he finds they have injured the science by the abstraction into which they have thrown it, and that he shall be obliged in the new edition he is preparing absolutely to oppose them.', M. Mignet, ed., *Political Economy and the Philosophy of Government; A Series of Essays Selected from the Works of M. de Sismondi* (London, 1847), p. 449.

35. *CdPp*, p. 14.

36. *Ibid.*, p. 15.

37. *Ibid.*, pp. 16–17, 25–8, 247, 555; see further *Notions sur la Grèce, pour l'intelligence des événemens qui se préparent dans cette portion de l'Europe, Revue Encyclopédique*, xxiv (1824), 257–74.

38. *CdPp.*, pp. 29–30.

39. *Ibid.*, pp. 238–40. Say supported North American attempts to 'civilize' ex-slaves at the same time as the tribes in their continent of origin by establishing industrious colonies in 'Liberia': 'De la première colonie formée par les Américains en Afrique', *Revue encyclopédique*, xxiv (1824), 5–18.

40. Review of William Blake, *Observations sur les effets produits par les dépenses du gouvernement* (London, 1823), *Revue Encyclopédique*, xv (1824), 125–7.

41. *Ibid.*, pp. 125–7, drawing on the *Essai historique sur l'origine, des progrès, et des résultats probables de la souveraineté des Anglais aux Indes* (Paris, 1824).

42. 'De l'influence des futurs progrès des connaissances économiques sur le sort des nations', *Revue Encyclopédique*, xxxvii (1828), 14–34.

43. *Works and Correspondence of David Ricardo*, viii, 161–2.

44. *Notice historique sur la vie et les ouvrages de J.-B. Say*, *CdPp*, p. xi.

45. Letter of 10 May 1829, *ŒD*, pp. 557–60.

46. Say papers, BN Mss F375.13: cited by P. Steiner, *Politique et économie politique chez Jean-Baptiste Say*.

47. Letter to George Grote, 11 May 1827, *ŒD*, pp. 571–2.

48. Say papers, BN Microfilm 7693, 297–308.

49. Undated letter (from Guizot), and letter from Royer-Collard of 24 November 1829, Say papers, BN Microfilm 5786, 195, 363.

50. Letters of 12 July 1830 and 1 January 1832, Say papers, BN Microfilm 5786, 13–18.

51. *Discours d'ouverture d'économie politique, de l'année scholaire 1831–2*, *ŒD*, pp. 162–5.

52. *Discours d'ouverture prononcé le 4 juin 1831 au Collège de France*, BN Microfilm 6648, 12–13.

53. *Discours d'ouverture d'économie politique, de l'année scholaire 1832–3*, *ŒD*, pp. 190–3.

54. Letter of February 1830, *ŒD*, pp. 572–6.

55. Letter of 26 October 1832, *ŒD*, pp. 577–8.

56. Say papers, BN Microfilm 9096, 174; 6739, 214–16; see also 322–33, *Morceaux de 1800 à 1808 et qui ne doivent pas être imprimés*, which question ideas about final causes and the immortality of the soul.

12

Conclusion

In the preface to the sixth edition of the *Traité d'économie politique* published in 1838, Horace Say claimed that his father 'had professed liberal doctrines' from the time that 'he fulfilled the role of Tribune'. This view was understandable in a country which had, in the mid-1830s, showed the first symptoms of a civil war between capital and labour, and which was facing anew the question of political legitimacy with the declining fortunes of the Orléans constitutional monarchy. Nevertheless, it is a mistake. Along with contemporaries of every shade of political opinion, Jean-Baptiste Say used the term 'liberal' as an adjective and, in later life, as a noun. As I have argued earlier, using 'liberal' to signify a party grouping or philosophical standpoint makes no sense in France before the Restoration.[1] Although he had more in common with Saint-Simon than Constant, and was closer to Charles Comte and Dunoyer than any other contemporaries, Say's perspective was distinctive. It must be understood in the light of the failure of modern republicanism with the rise of Napoleon, and continuing reflection upon the nature and relevance to France of the British and American models of state and society.

Clavière converted Say to a belief in modern republicanism in large states, in the possibility of virtuous manners and the creation of a society without hierarchical ranks. Rœderer was undoubtedly the greatest influence on Say's reflections on these themes in the 1790s.[2] Although with the writing of the first *Traité* Say changed his view of modern republicanism, he maintained a republican perspective on manners and ranks. This made him a vitriolic critic of Britain's constitutional and social example throughout his life.[3] It also explains why Dupont de Nemours wholly misunderstood Say's work in 1814. What is best termed Say's political moralism distinguished him from the majority of his fellow political economists; those who shared his concern with national manners—such as Malthus and his Chritian followers—could never have appreciated Say's anti-religious conception of the social world. Nor can Say be classed with British republicans in the tradition of Catherine Macaulay and William Godwin, which was sceptical of commerce, or that of Price, Priestley and David Williams, which opposed the creation of republics in large European monarchies.[4] The French republican tradition of Diderot and Clavière was indebted to the writings of certain British radicals, especially Price, but their philosophies were very different. A distinction must therefore be made between the French attempt to create a new kind of republican state and British radicals' concern with extending liberty within a mixed government. Say intended to address the problems of post-revolutionary France, and was never understood by writers across the channel who had conflicting intentions. In consequence, it is equally misleading to group him with exponents of classical political economy in Britain, as many historians

of economic thought continue to do. Say's conception of utility must be seen as a product of a French discussion about public virtue rather than a partially-formed building
block of a new science. Say's 'Law', by contrast with the use made of it by British
Ricardians, was intended to combat fears of 'general gluts' by the introduction of
specific ranks and manners.

The anti-religious views Say inherited from the French *philosophes* are also an important part of his intellectual make-up, as he was one of the few French writers who
refused to consider political economy from anything but a secular perspective after 1815.
He rejected arguments based on the utility of a 'civil' religion just as he had had no truck
with theophilanthropy in the 1790s. The 'industrious society' or 'social republic', whose
virtues he expounded during the Restoration, was based on an assumption that a public
interest could be defined which was shared by capitalists, land-owners, entrepreneurs,
and labourers. Industry, he believed, required civil equality and would bring greater
material equality while reducing poverty. It would also bring international peace, when
nation states recognized their real interests. Many political economists saw the utopian
content of these views during Say's lifetime.[5] Those of his generation who lived beyond
him, notably Sismondi and J.-A. Blanqui, acknowledged the formation of a wholly new
political and social landscape during the 1830s and 1840s.[6] Say was too much a child of the
Revolution to have taken a more cautious, or liberal, attitude to the problems of industrial and international unrest. His political economy simply made no sense once the
assumptions that underpinned his world collapsed, as Marx rudely recognized in attacks
on 'the insipid Say'.[7] This is why his works were rarely published except for polemical
purpose after the revolutions of 1848. The era of republican optimism had ended.

In explaining Say's ideas by reference to the intellectual context of the Revolution
my intention is not to belittle them. Say never considered himself an innovator in the
manner of Rœderer or Sieyès, but rather as a writer who brought clarity and precision
to an important subject for modern citizens.[8] That he was successful is beyond doubt,
and he remained the most widely read political economist before John Stuart Mill
published his *Principles* in 1848.[9] This achievement makes Say an important source for
intellectual historians, and it is worth pointing out some of the ways in which a knowledge of the development of Say's ideas alters our perspective on the French intellectual
movements of his time. The most important concerns the relationship between the
French Enlightenment and the Revolution. Say's generation was fully aware of the practical import of enlightenment political and economic thought. In particular, they recognized the limits of *philosophe* conceptions of political change in France; why, for
example, writers as radical as Helvétius and d'Holbach could not conceive of a society
without ranks, or why Rousseau considered the *Contrat Social* as workable only in
prescribed conditions.[10] Say believed that the only *philosophe* who had conceived of
modern republicanism in France before the mid-1780s was Diderot, whose work was
important because it revealed the extent of the problem of manners facing such large
and civilized states. Two lessons can be drawn from this. The first is that historians using
terms such as 'Rousseauism' or 'radical enlightenment' have to be careful about what
they mean.[11] *Philosophes* who might have expressed radical ideas on a number of
subjects under the Old Regime were not necessarily revolutionaries, as many (such as

the abbé Morellet) realized in the early 1790s. French politics had faced a crisis between the late 1770s and mid 1780s, during which time the British constitutional model was rejected by men such as Clavière and Rœderer in favour of an amalgam of an American-inspired society without ranks and a French version of an industrious civilization. The battle between these perspectives, made more difficult by the uncertain role of Louis XVI and the continuing need to create public finances extensive enough to challenge Britain in war, ensured the turbulence of the National Assembly and the ultimate collapse of the constitution of 1791. After this time, the intellectual controversies of the Revolution were governed by the need to create republican manners and make them popular, as Clavière and Diderot had foreseen.

The Terror was an extreme, rather than a necessary, development of this intellectual movement. This is the second point that Say's writings underscore: the importance of the manners question after 1792. Many historians have failed to recognize the importance of this debate, which shows how futile it is to define the Revolution by reference to the presumed rise of the bourgeoisie, or constitution building outside competing national cultures.[12] Responses to the problem of manners after the Terror sustained revolutionary intellectual life until the creation of the Empire, in the face of the critiques of Burke, La Harpe, de Maistre and de Bonald. This perspective on the 1790s enables us to recognize the extent to which the Revolution was an on-going intellectual event, and the precise ways in which revolutionaries sought to break away from the republicanisms of the past.[13] Unsurprisingly, Tocqueville recognized the importance of the manners issue and as a consequence had an interest in the intellectual movements of the Directory. His view of its relevance for the future of France was one of the reasons why he and Beaumont read and discussed Say's *Cours complet* on the boat that took them to America in 1831. In focussing on the centralization of governmental powers as a process of modern-state formation rather than the intellectual aspirations of the revolutionary generation, however, Tocqueville underestimated many of the qualities of 1790s' argument.

Say remained a *philosophe* in his opposition to established religious practices in any form. For him the Revolution could only have been successful in so far as it was a secular phenomenon. Those least likely to grasp the significance of the social transformation promised in the 1790s were *dévots* of any creed. Say would have been very surprised at attempts to find the intellectual origins of the Revolution in Jansenism or other religious movements of the pre-revolutionary era. His view of enlightenment philosophy leads to the conclusion that seeking a purportedly radical public sphere in late eighteenth-century French thought is ultimately a white elephant. Such a project cannot capture the real divisions between *philosophes*, revolutionaries, and their antagonists, concerning small and large states, forms of government, ancient and modern republicanism, the nature of civilization, the merits of commerce and industry, the kinds of ranks which characterize a modern social order, the civil value of different religions, and the merits of the political and social cultures offered by other nations, particularly Britain, Switzerland, China, and North America. Say believed in a Revolution, the product of a critique of *philosophe* projects for restoring French glory, which was among the most radical intellectual experiments in modern history: the creation of a republic without social hierarchy in conditions of advanced civilization.

NOTES TO CHAPTER 12

1. The best recent writer on 'liberal' ideas in eighteenth-century France and America tentatively makes this point: Bernard Manin, *Les deux libéralismes: la règle et la balance*, in *La Famille, la loi, l'état: De la révolution au code civil* (Paris, 1989); 'Checks, balances and boundaries: the separation of powers in the constitutional debate of 1787', in B. Fontana, ed., *The Invention of the Modern Republic* (Cambridge, 1994), pp. 27–62.

2. Say continued to read Rœderer's writings to the end of life: his papers reveal notes on Rœderer's justification of *aisance* in his *Mémoires sur Louis XII* (Paris, 1825), p. 318: BN Microfilm 8713, 269.

3. Review of William Jacob, *Second rapport sur l'état de l'agriculture et des subsistances d'une grande partie de l'Europe* (London, 1828), *Revue Encyclopédique*, xxxix (1828), 84–94.

4. R. Whatmore, 'A Gigantic Manliness: Paine's Republicanism in the 1790s', *Economy, Polity and Society: Essays on British Intellectual History*, eds., S. Collini, R. Whatmore, B. Young (Cambridge, 2000).

5. Friedrich List, *Systems of National Economy* (London, 1840), ch. 32.

6. Sismondi, 'L'Avenir', *Revue encyclopédique*, 47 (Sept. 1830), 524–49; 'Les espérences et les réalités', *Revue encyclopédique*, 51 (July 1831), 5–29; *Études sur les sciences sociales* (Paris, 1836–8), 3 vols. Blanqui, *Histoire de l'économie politique*, ch. 43.

7. *Capital*, volume I (Harmondsworth, 1976), pp. 209–10; volume III (Harmondsworth, 1981), p. 980.

8. This is brought out in Comte and 'D.D.''s reviews of Say's *Cours* in the *Revue encyclopédique*, xxxviii (1828), 623–39; xl (1828), 359–67; xlii (1829), 84–92; xlv (1830), 288–97.

9. The world-wide esteem in which Say was held is evident from the exchange of letters between Jefferson and Madison on 30 November and 3 December 1824: *The Republic of Letters: The Correspondence between Thomas Jefferson and James Madison, 1776–1826* (New York, 1995), 3 vols., iii, 310–11.

10. Roberto Romani, 'All Montesquieu's Sons: the Place of *esprit général*, *caratère national*, and *mœurs* in French Political Philosophy, 1748–89', *SVC*, 362 (1998), 189–235.

11. Robert Darnton anachronistically calls Clavière and Brissot 'Rousseauistes' in *L'Idéolgie à la bourse, Gens de lettres gens du livre* (Paris, 1991), pp. 85–98; *The Literary Underground of the Old Regime* (Cambridge Mass., 1982), pp. 41–70. The problem with Darnton's work is that he fails to give intellectual content to the *mentalités* he believes to be so important in explaining the movement of public opinion towards revolutionary ideals; for example what is 'Rousseauism as a cultural framework for finding meaning in life'?: *The Forbidden Best-Sellers of Pre-Revolutionary France* (New York and London, 1995), chs. 6–7.

12. Marxist categories of explanation have rightly been rejected in recent decades but historians continue to be influenced by Marx's notion of the relationship between constitution-building and social structure in nascent capitalist societies. This is why historians such as François Furet neglected the relationship between different conceptions of republican culture and French politics, and wrongly assume the Terror to have been a logical development of 1789: 'L'Idée de république et l'histoire de France au XIXe siècle', *Le Siècle de l'avenement républicain* (Paris, 1994), pp. 287–312.

13. James Livesey, 'Virtue, Commerce, and Farming: Agrarian Ideology and Commercial Republicanism during the French Revolution', *Past and Present*, 157 (1997), 94–121; *Inventing Democracy in the French Revolution* (forthcoming, Harvard, 2001).

Bibliography

1 MANUSCRIPT SOURCES

British Library, Place papers, Add. MSS 37949–37950.

Bibliothèque Nationale, Say papers, Microfilms 7690, 7689, 6333, 5787, 6648, 8713, 8714, 5786, 6739, 9095–6, 7269.

2 PRIMARY SOURCES

(i) Printed Books

BACHAUMONT, L. P., *Mémoires secrets* (London, 1780–89), 37 vols.

BAUDEAU, abbé Nicolas, *Première introduction à la philosophie économique ou analyse des états policés* (Paris, 1767).

—— *Lettres d'un citoyen à un magistrat sur les vingtièmes et autres impôts* (Paris, 1767).

BELGODÈRE, Joseph Marie, *Supplément aux éclaircissements, pour servir de base à l'opinion qu'on doit avoir sur le citoyen LAMARCHE, directeur de la consection des assignats, & sur les ministres Clavière qui en à la surveillance* (Paris, 1793).

BENTHAM, Jeremy, *The Correspondence of Jeremy Bentham* eds. J. H. Burns, J. R. Dinwiddy, F. S. Conway (Oxford, 1968–94), 10 vols.

BERNARDIN DE SAINT PIERRE, Jacques Henri, *Études de la nature* (Paris, 1799).

BLANQUI, Jérôme-Adolphe, *Histoire d'économie politique en Europe, depuis les ancien jusqu'à nos jours* (Paris, 1860), 2 vols.

BRISSOT, Jacques-Pierre, *Correspondance et papiers 1776–1793*, ed. C. Perroud (Picard, 1912).

—— *De la France et des Étas-Unis, ou de l'importance de la révolution de l'Amérique pour le bonheur de la France* (Paris, 1791).

—— *Dénonciation au public du nouveau projet d'agiotage* (Paris, 1786).

—— *Mémoires 1754–1793*, ed., C. Perroud (Picard, 1910), 2 vols.

—— *Observations d'un républican sur les diverses systêmes d'administrations provinciales* (Lausanne, 1788).

—— *Point de banqueroute, ou lettre à un créancier d'état, sur l'impossibilité de la banqueroute nationale, & sur les moyens de ramener le crédit & la paix* (London, 1787).

—— *Seconde lettre contre la Compagnie d'Assurances* (Paris, 1786).

—— *Sur un nouveau projet de Compagnie d'Assurances contre les incendies à Paris* (London, 1786).

CABANIS, Pierre-Jacques-Georges, *Œuvres philosophiques* (Paris, 1956), 2 vols.

—— *Quelques considérations sur l'organisation sociale en générale et paticulièrement sur la nouvelle constitution* (Paris, 1799).

—— *Rapports du physique et du morale de l'homme* (Paris, 1798 and 1824).

CANARD, Nicolas, *Principes de l'économie politique* (Paris, 1801).

CANDOLLE, Augustin Pyramus de, *Mémoires et souvenirs* (Paris, 1862).

CANTILLON, Richard, *Essai sur la nature du commerce en général* (Paris, 1952).

CÉRUTTI, Joseph Antoine Joachim, *Idées simples et précises sur le papier monnoie, les assignats forcés, et les biens ecclésiastiques* (Paris, 1790).

CHAMFORT, *Œuvres de Chamfort*, ed., P. L. Ginguené (Paris, 1795), 4 vols.

CHASTELLUX, François Jean, Marquis de, *De la félicité publique, ou considérations sur le sort des hommes dans les différentes époques de l'histoire* (Paris, 1776).

—— *Voyages dans l'Amérique Septrionale* (Paris, 1783).

CHATEAUBRIAND, F. R., *Grands écrits politiques*, ed., J.-P. Clément (Paris, 1993), 2 vols.

CLAVIÈRE, Etienne, *Adresse de la Société des Amis des Noirs à l'Assemblée Nationale, à toutes les villes de commerce, à toutes les manufactures, aux colonies, à toutes les Sociétés des Amis de la Constitution* (Paris, 1791).

—— *Clavière, ex-ministre des contributions publiques, à la convention nationale. Réponse à A. G. J. Ducher Des deux hémisphères* (Paris, 1793).

—— *Correspondance du ministre Clavière et du général Montesquiou, servant de réponse au libelle du général contre le ministre* (Paris, 1792).

—— *Coup d'œil sur les monnoies; Sur leur administration, et sur le ministre des contributions publiques* (Paris, 1793).

—— *Coupons d'assignats. Pétition proposée aux quarante-huit sections de Paris* (Paris, 1790).

—— *De ce qu'il faut faire dans l'état actuel des finances* (Paris, 1791).

—— *De la conjuration contre les finances et des mesures à prendre pour en arrêter les effets* (Paris, 1792).

—— *Discours de M. Clavière, ministre des contributions publiques, À la Société des Amis de la Constitution, séance aux Jacobins Saint Honoré, le 4 April 1792* (Paris, 1792).

—— *Du numéraire métalique* (Paris, 1792).

—— *Lettre de la Société des Amis des Noirs, à M. Necker, avec la réponse de ce ministre* (Paris, 1789).

—— *Etienne Clavière à l'Assemblée Nationale, sur les finances* (Paris, 1791).

—— *L'État actuel de nos finances; Avec la critique du compte rendu par M. Montesquiou et celle du mémoire de M. Bergasse* (Paris, 1791).

—— *Lettre de M. Clavière à M. Beaumez, Sur l'organisation du trésor public* (Paris, 1790).

—— *Lettres écrites à M. Cerutti, par M. Clavière, Sur les prochains arrangemens de finance* (Paris, 1791).

—— *Mémoire envoyé par le ministre des contributions publiques à l'Assemblée Nationale, le 9 Mai 1792* (Paris, 1792).

—— *Mémoire par le citoyen Clavière, ministre des contributions publiques, à la Convention Nationale* (Paris, 1792).

—— *Mémoire sur le Cadastre de la France* (Paris, 1792).

—— *Opinions d'un créancier de l'état, sur quelques matières de finance importantes dans le moment actuel* (Paris and London, 1789).

—— *Pétition faite à l'Assemblée Nationale par E Clavière, député suppléant de Paris. Sur le remboursement des créances publiques non vérifiées, & sur le paiement des domaines nationaux en assignats & espèces effectives* (Paris, 1791).

—— *Proclamation du conseil-exécutif provisoire, relative aux subsistances* (Paris, 1792).

—— *Réflexions addressées à l'Assemblée Nationale, sur les moyens de concilier l'impôt du tabac avec la liberté du commerce, et les rapports que la France doit entretenir avec les Américains libre* (Paris, 1790).

—— *Réflexions sur les formes et les principes auxquels une nation libre doit assujétir l'administration des finances; avec des observations sur le dernier rapport fait à l'Assemblée Nationale par M. Rœderer, dans la même matière, et suivies d'une lettre à M. Baumez, sur l'organisation du trésor public, où l'auteur discute les avantages et la nécessité d'une caisse publique* (Paris, 1791).

—— *Réponse au mémoire du M. Necker, concernant les assignats, et à d'autres objections contre une création qui les porte à deux milliards* (Paris, 1790).

—— *Réponse de M. Clavière à la lettre de M. Montesquiou, sur un écrit intitulé De la Conjuration contre les finances de l'état, & des mesures à prendre pour en arrêter les effets* (Paris, 1792).

—— *Supplément à la correspondance du ministre Clavière et du général Montesquiou* (Paris, 1792).

—— *Sur l'état actuel des manufactures des poudres et salpêtres du royaume* (Paris, 1792).

—— and BRISSOT, Jacques-Pierre, *De la France et des Étas-Unis ou de l'importance de l'Étas-Unis pour le bonheur de la France* (Paris, 1791).

—— —— *Le Philadelphien à Genève, ou lettres d'un Américain sur la dernière révolution de Genève, sa constitution nouvelle, l'émigration en Irlande, etc, pouvant servir de tableau politique de Genève jusqu'en 1784* (Dublin, 1783).

CONDILLAC, Etienne Bonnot de, *Le commerce et le gouvernement: Considérés relativement l'un à l'autre* (Amsterdam, 1776).

—— *Œuvres philosophiques*, ed., Georges Le Roy (Paris, 1947), 3 vols.

CONDORCET, Marie Jean Antoine Nicolas Caritat, Marquis de, *Éloge de Turgot* (Paris, 1786).

—— *Esquisse d'un tableau historique des progrès de l'esprit humain*, ed., O. Prior (Paris, 1970).

—— *Œuvres*, ed., A. Condorcet O'Connor (Paris, 1847–9), 12 vols.

CONSTANT, Benjamin, *Fragmens d'un ouvrage abandonné sur la possibilité d'une constitution républicaine dans un grand pays*, ed. H. Grange (Paris, 1991).

—— *Political Writings*, ed. B. Fontana (Cambridge, 1988).

—— *Principes de politique applicables à tous les gouvernements* (Geneva, 1980), ed. E. Hoffmann.

COYER, abbé Gabriel François, *La Noblesse commerçante* (n.p. 1756).

—— *Développement et défense du système de la noblesse commerçante ou militaire* (Amsterdam and Paris, 1757), 2 vols.

—— *Nouvelles observations sur l'Angleterre, par un voyageur* (Paris, 1779).

CREUZÉ LATOUCHE, Jacques-Antoine, *Discours sur la nécessité d'ajouter à l'école normale un professeur d'économie politique* (Paris, 1794).

D'HOLBACH, Paul-Henri, Baron, *Ethocratie, ou le gouvernement fondé sur la morale* (Amsterdam, 1776).

—— *La Morale universelle, ou les devoirs de l'homme fondés sur sa nature* (Paris, 1820), 3 vols.

—— *La Politique naturelle, ou Discours sur les vrais principes du gouvernement* (London, 1773), 2 vols.

—— *Le Christianisme dévoilé, ou Examen des principes et des effets de la religion Chretienne* (London, 1790).

—— *Système de la nature ou des lois du monde physique et du monde moral* (Paris, 1821), 2 vols.

—— *Système social, ou principes naturels de la morale et de la politique, avec un examen de l'influence du gouvernement sur les mœurs* (London, 1773), 3 vols.

DAVENANT, Charles, *The Political and Commercial Works* (London, 1770), 5 vols.

DESTUTT DE TRACY, Antoine Claude Louis, *Projet d'élemens d'idéologie à l'usage des écoles centrales* (Paris, 1801).

—— *Quels sont les moyens de fonder la morale chez un peuple?* (Paris, 1798).

DIDEROT, Denis, *Œuvres complètes*, eds., J. Assézat and M. Tourneaux (Paris, 1875–7), 20 vols.

—— *Œuvres de Diderot*, ed., J.-A. Naigeon (Paris, 1797), 13 vols.

—— *Political Writings*, J. Hope Mason and R. Wokler, eds. and tr. (Cambridge, 1992).

D'IVERNOIS, François, *L'Histoire des révolutions de Genève dès la réformation* (Geneva, 1789).

DUMONT, Etienne, *Réclamation des Genevois patriotes établis à Londres, Contre la nouvelle aristocratie de Genève contenue dans deux lettres aux procureur général & aux adjoints* (Paris, 1789).

—— *Souvenirs de Mirabeau et sur les deux premières assemblées legislatives* (Paris, 1952).

DUPONT DE NEMOURS, Pierre-Samuel, *Autobiography*, tr., Elizabeth Fox-Genovese (Wilmington, Delaware, 1984).

—— *De la périodicité des Assemblées Nationales, de leur organisation, de la forme à suivre pour amener les propositions qui pourront y être faites, à devenir des loix* (Paris, 1789).

—— *De l'origine et progrès d'une science nouvelle* (London, 1768).

—— *Examen du gouvernement d'Angleterre, comparé aux constitutions des Étas-Unis, Où l'on réfute quelques assertions contenues dans l'ouvrage de M. Adams & dans celui de M. Delolme, par un cultivateur de New-Jersey* (London, 1789).

DUPONT DE NEMOURS, Pierre-Samuel, *Lettres de Dupont de Nemours écrites de la prison de la force, 5 Thermidor–8 Fructidor*, ed., G. Chinard (Paris, 1929).
—— *Mémoires sur la vie et les ouvrages de M.Turgot* (Philadelphia, 1782).
—— *Motifs de ceux qui cherchent à engager la nation à faire une incursion sur les terres de l'empire* (Paris, 1792).
—— *Philosophie de l'univers* (Paris, 1796).
—— *Vues sur l'éducation nationale par un cultivateur, ou moyens de simplifier L'INSTRUCTION, de la rendre à la fois, morale, philosophique, républicain, civile, et militaire sans déranger les travaux de L'AGRICULTURE et des ARTS, auxquels la jeunesse doit concourir* (Paris, 1796).
FLETCHER, Andrew, *Political Writings*, ed., J. Robertson (Cambridge, 1997).
FORBONNAIS, F. Verron de, *Recherches et considerations sur les finances de France, depuis l'année 1595 jusqu'à l'année 1721* (Basle, 1758) 2 vols.
GALIANI, Ferdinando, *Dialogue sur le commerce des blés*, ed., Fausto Nicolini (Milan, 1964).
GARNIER, Germain, *De la propriété dans ses rapports avec le droit politique* (Paris, 1792).
—— *Abrégé élémentaire des principes de l'économie politique* (Paris, 1796).
—— *Récherches sur la nature et les causes de la richesses des nations d'Adam Smith, traduction nouvelle avec les notes et les observations* (Paris, 1802).
GRIMM, Friedrich-Melchior, Baron, *Correspondance littéraire philosophique et critique*, ed., Maurice Tourneaux (Paris, 1877–82), 16 vols.
GROUCHY, Sophie, *Théorie des sentimens moraux et lettres sur la sympathie* (Paris, 1798).
GROUVELLE, P. A., *De l'autorité de Montesquieu dans la révolution présente* (n.p., 1789).
GUIZOT, F., *The History of Civilisation from the Fall of the Roman Empire to the French Revolution*, tr. W. Hazlitt (London, 1856), 3 vols.
HELVÉTIUS, Claude Adrien, *De l'homme, de ses facultés intellectuelles et de son éducation* (London, 1773).
—— *De l'ésprit* (Paris, 1758).
—— *Œuvres complètes d'Helvétius* (Paris, 1795), 14 vols.
HERBERT, C., *Essai sur la police générale des grains* (London, 1754).
JEFFERSON, Thomas, *The Republic of Letters: The Correspondence Between Thomas Jefferson and James Madison, 1776–1826* (New York, 1995), 3 vols.
KING, Gregory, *Natural and Political Observations & Considerations upon the State and Condition of England* (Baltimore, 1936).
LA HARPE, J. F., *Du fanatisme dans la langue révolutionnaire* (Liege, 1797).
LACHAPELLE, J., *Considérations philosophiques sur la Révolution française* (Paris, 1797).
LAFRETÉ, *Observations sur la pétition de M. Clavière* (Paris, 1791).
LAW, John, *Money and Trade Considered with A Proposal for Supplying the Nation with Money* (Edinburgh, 1705).
—— *Œuvres de Jean Law*, ed., P. Harsin (Paris, 1934), 3 vols.
LE MERCIER DE LA RIVIÈRE, P. P., *L'Ordre naturel et essentiel des sociétés politiques* (Paris and London, 1767).
LE TROSNE, Guillaume François, *De l'Administration provinciale et de la réforme de l'impôt* (Basle, 1788).
LEFRANC, F., *Le voile levé pour les curieux ou le secret de la Révolution révélé à l'aide de la Franc-Maçonnerie* (1791).
LINGUET, Simon Nicolas Henri, *Reponse aux docteurs modernes* (Paris, 1771).
—— *Théorie des lois civiles, ou principes fondamentaux de la société* (London, 1767).
LIST, Friedrich, *Systems of National Economy* (London, 1840).
MABLY, Gabriel Bonnot de, *Collection complète des œuvres de l'abbé de Mably*, ed., Arnoux (Paris, an III), 11 vols.

—— *De la législation ou principes des lois* (Amsterdam, 1776), 2 vols.

—— *Des droits et des devoirs du citoyen*, ed., J.-L. Lecercle (Paris, 1972).

—— *Entretiens de Phocion* (Amsterdam, 1765).

MIRABEAU, Honoré Gabriel Riqueti, comte de, *Considérations sur l'ordre de Cincinnatus, ou imitation d'un pamphlet anglo-americain . . . Suivies de plusieurs pièces relatives à cette institution* (London, 1784).

—— *De la constitution monétaire* (Paris, 1791).

—— *Lettres de Mirabeau à Chamfort* (Paris, 1797).

MIRABEAU, Victor Riquetti, marquis de, *Entretiens d'un jeune prince avec son gouverneur* (London, 1785), 3 vols.

—— *L'Ami des hommes* (La Haye, 1758–62), 6 vols.

—— *Lettres sur le commerce des grains* (Amsterdam, 1765).

—— *Philosophie rurale, ou Économie générale et politique de l'agriculture, reduite à l'ordre immuable des lois physiques & morales, qui assurent la prospérité des empires* (Amsterdam, 1764), 3 vols.

—— *Théorie de l'impôt* (Paris, 1760).

MONTBRON, F. de, *Préservatif contre l'anglomanie* (Minorca, 1757).

MONTCHRETIEN, Antoine de, *Traicté de l'œconomie politique* (Geneva, 1970).

MONTESQUIEU, Charles Louis de Secondat, Baron, *The Spirit of the Laws*, tr., Thomas Nugent, (New York, 1949).

MORELLET, abbé André, *Réfutation de l'ouvrage qui a pour titre dialogues sur le commerce des bleds* (London, 1770).

NECKER, Jacques, *Œuvres complètes*, ed., A. L. de Staël-Holstein (Paris, 1820), 15 vols.

PEUCHET, Joseph, *Dictionnaire universel de la géographie commerçante* (Paris, 1799–1800), 4 vols.

QUESNAY, François, *François Quesnay et la physiocratie* (Paris, 1958), 2 vols.

RAYNAL, abbé Thomas Guillaume., *A Philosophical and Political History of the Settlements and Trade of the Europeans in the East and West Indies*, tr., J. O. Justamond (London, 1798), 6 vols.

—— *Histoire philosophique et politique des établissements et du commerce des Européens dans les deux Indes* (Amsterdam, 1780), 10 vols.

—— *Tableau philosophique de la Révolution en France en 1789* (Marseille, 1790).

RICARDO, David, *The Works and Correspondence of David Ricardo* (Cambridge, 1952–73), 11 vols.

RIVAROL, Antoine de, *De la philosophie moderne* (Paris, 1799).

ROBESPIERRE, Maximillien, *Œuvres*, eds., M. Bouloiseau and A. Soboul (Paris, 1967), 10 vols.

RŒDERER, Pierre-Louis, *Mémoires sur la Révolution, le consulat, et l'empire*, ed., O. Aubry (Paris, 1942).

—— *Œuvres*, ed., A. M. Rœderer (Paris, 1853–6), 8 vols.

ROLIN, L., *The Decline of Britain* (London, 1850).

ROUSSEAU, Jean-Jacques, *Correspondance complète de J-J Rousseau*, eds., R. A. Leigh, J. Laming (Oxford, 1965–98), 51 vols.

SAINTE-FOIX, P.-A. de, chevalier d'Arcq, *La Noblesse militaire ou le patriote françois* (Paris, 1756).

SAINT-JUST, Louis Antoine, *Œuvres complètes*, ed., Michèle Duval (Paris, 1984).

SAINT-SIMON, Claude-Henri, *L'industrie littéraire et scientifique liguée avec l'industrie commerciale et manufacturière* (Paris, 1817).

—— *Œvres de Claude-Henri de Saint-Simon* (Paris, 1966), 6 vols.

SAY, Jean-Baptiste, *A Treatise on Political Economy; or the Production, Distribution, and Consumption of Wealth*, tr., C. R. Princep, ed., C. C. Biddle (Philadelphia, 1832).

—— *Cours complet d'économie politique pratique; ouvrage destiné à mettre sous les yeux des hommes d'état, des propriétaires fonciers et des capitalistes, des savants, des agriculteurs, des manufacturiers, des négociants, et en général de tous les citoyens, l'économie des sociétés* (Paris, 1828–9), 6 vols.

—— *De la liberté de la presse* (Paris, 1789).

SAY, Jean-Baptiste, *De l'Angleterre et des Anglais* (London, 1816).

—— *Discours prononcé au corps législatif par le citoyen J.-B. Say, tribun: Pour appuyer le projet de loi tendant à déclarer que l'armée d'orient a bien mérite de la patrie. Séance du 23 Nivôse, an IX.*

—— *Essai historique sur l'origine, des progrès, et des résultats probables de la souveraineté des Anglais aux Indes* (Paris, 1824).

—— *Lettres à Malthus* (Paris, 1820).

—— *Mélanges et corréspondance d'économie politique; ouvrage posthume de J.-B. Say*, ed., Charles Comte (Paris, 1833).

—— *Œuvres diverses, avec des notes par Ch. Comte, E. Daire et Horace Say* (Paris, 1848).

—— *Olbie, ou moyens d'améliorer les mœurs d'une nation* (Paris, 1800).

—— *Traité d'économie politique, ou simple exposition de la manière dont se forment, se distribuent et se consomment les richesses* (Paris, 1803, 1814, 1817, 1838), 2 vols.

SAY, Léon, and CHAILLEY, Joseph, eds., *Nouveaux dictionnaire d'économie politique* (Paris, 1891), 2 vols.

SENIOR, N. W., *Conversations with M. Thiery, M. Guizot and Other Distinguished Persons*, ed., M. C. M. Simpson (London, 1878), 2 vols.

SIEYES, Emmanuel, *Emmanuel-Joseph Sieyes: écrits politiques*, ed., Roberto Zapperi (Paris, 1985).

—— *Œuvres de Sieyes*, ed., M. Dorigny (Paris, 1990), 3 vols.

SISMONDI, J. C. L. Simonde de, *De la richesse commerciale, ou Principes d'économie politique, appliqués à la legislation du commerce* (Geneva, 1803), 2 vols.

—— *Le nouveaux principes d'économie politique* (Paris, 1821).

—— *Political Economy and the Philosophy of Government; A Series of Essays Selected from the Works of M. de Sismondi* (London, 1847).

—— *Tableau de l'agriculture Toscan* (Geneva, 1801).

SMITH, Adam, *An Inquiry into the Nature and Causes of the Wealth of Nations* (London, 1789).

—— *The correspondance of Adam Smith*, eds., E. C. Mossner and I. S. Ross (Oxford, 1977).

STAËL, Germaine de, *Œuvres complètes* (Paris, 1820) 18 vols.

STANHOPE, P. D., fourth Earl of Chesterfield, *Letters to His Son and Others*, ed., R. K. Root (London, 1929).

TOCQUEVILLE, Alexis de., *L'Ancien Regime et la Révolution* (Paris, 1856).

TURGOT, Anne-Robert Jacques, *Des administrations provinciales, Mémoire présenté au roi par feu Turgot* (Lausanne, 1788).

—— *Œuvres de Turgot et documents le concernant, avec biographie et notes par Gustave Schelle* (Paris, 1913–1923), 5 vols.

—— *Œuvres de Turgot*, ed., Dupont de Nemours (Paris, 1808–11), 8 vols.

VOLNEY, Charles-François-Chassebeuf, *La Loi naturelle, ou Principes physiques de la morale déduits de l'organisation de l'homme et de l'univers* (Paris, 1934).

—— *Les Ruines, ou Méditations sur les révolutions des empires* (Paris, 1792).

VOLTAIRE, F. M. A., *Œuvres complètes de Voltaire*, ed., L. Moland (Paris, 1877–85), 52 vols.

YOUNG, Arthur, *Travels in France During 1787, 1788 and 1789* (New York, 1969).

(ii) Contemporary Journals

Annales politiques, civiles et littéraires du dix-huitième siècle. Ouvrage périodique, ed., Simon Nicholas Henri Linguet (Paris, 1777–92), 19 vols.

Bibliothèque de l'homme public; ou Analyse raisonnée des principaux ouvrages françois et étrangers, Sur la politique en général, la législation, les finances, la police, l'agriculture, & le commerce en particulier, & le droit naturel & public. Par M. le Marquis de Condorcet, secrétaire perpétuel de l'Académie des sciences, l'un des quarante de l'Académie Françoise, de la Société Royale de Londres; M. De Peysonnel, ancien consul-général de France à Smirne; M. le Chapelier, député de l'Assemblée Nationale, & autres gens de lettres (Paris, 1790–2), 28 vols.

Encyclopédie méthodique: Économie politique et diplomatique, ed., Joseph Panckouke (Paris, 1784–8), 4 vols.

Encyclopédie ou Dictionnaire raisonné des sciences, des arts et métiers, par une société de gens de lettres, mis en ordres & publié par M. Diderot . . . quant à la partie mathématique, par M. d'Alembert (1751–65), 17 vols.

Ephémérides du citoyen, ou Chronique de l'esprit national et bibliothèque raisonnée des sciences morales et politiques, eds., Nicolas Baudeau and Victor Riquetti, Comte de Mirabeau, from May 1768 ed., Pierre-Samuel Dupont de Nemours (Paris 1767–72), 63 vols.

Journal d'instruction sociale; par les citoyens Condorcet, Sieyes et Du Hamel, nos. 1–6 (Paris, 1793).

Journal de l'agriculture, du commerce et des finances (Paris, July 1765–November 1766).

La Chronique du mois ou les cahiers patriotiques de E. Clavière, Condorcet, L. Mercier, A. Auger, J. Oswald, N. Bonneville, J. Bidderman, A. Broussonet, A. Guy, L-Kersaint, J-P. Brissot, J. Ph. Garan de Coulon, J Dussaulx, F Lanthenas, Collot d'Herbois, ed., Nicolas Bonneville (Paris 1791–3).

La Décade philosophique, littéraire et politique, par une société de républicains (after 1800 par une Société des Gens de Lettres), eds., P-L. Guinguené, J.-B. Say, F.-G.-J.-S. Andrieux, A. Pineux Duval, J. Le Breton (Paris, 1794–1807), 42 vols.

Le Censeur Européen, ou Examen de diverses questions de droit public, et des divers ouvrages littéraires et scientifiques, considérés dans leurs rapports avec les progrès de la civilisation, eds., Charles Comte and Charles Dunoyer (Paris, 1817–19).

Le Courrier de Provence. Servant de suite aux lettres du Comte de Mirabeau à ses commettans (Paris, 1789–91), 11 vols.

Le Républicain, ou Le Défenseur du gouvernement représentatif, par une société de républicains, eds., Condorcet, T. Paine, A. Du Chatelet (Paris, 1791).

Mémoires de l'Instutut National, classe des sciences morales et politiques (Paris 1796–1803), 5 vols.

Nouvelles Ephémérides économiques, ou Bibliothèque raisonnée de l'histoire, de la morale et de la politique, ed., Nicolas Baudeau (Paris, 1776).

Revue mensuelle d'économie politique, ed., Theodore Fix (Paris, 1833–7), 4 vols.

Séances des écoles normales recueillies par des sténographes, ed., D. J. Garat, (Paris, 1801), 10 vols.

3   SECONDARY WORKS

(i)   Books

ACOMB, F., *Anglophobia in France 1763–1789: An Essay in the History of Constitutionalism and Nationalism* (Durham N.C., 1950).

ALBERTONE, M. and MASOERO, A., eds., *Political Economy and National Realities* (Torino, 1994).

ALDRIDGE, A. O., *Franklin and his French Contemporaries* (New York, 1957).

AULARD, A., *The French Revolution. A Political History, 1789–1804,* tr., B. Miall (London, 1910).

BAKER, K. M., *Inventing the Revolution: Essays on French Political Culture in the Eighteenth Century,* (Cambridge, 1990).

—— ed., *The French Revolution and the Creation of Modern Political Culture. The Political Culture of the Old Regime* (Oxford, 1987).

BASTID, Paul, *Sièyes et sa pensée* (Paris, 1939).

BÉNÉTRUY, J., *L'Atelier de Mirabeau: Quatre proscrits dans la tourmente revolutionnaire* (Paris, 1962).

BOISLISLE, J., *Correspondance des contrôleurs-généraux des finances avec les intendants des provinces, 1683–1715* (Paris, 1874–97), 3 vols.

BONNEVILLE, D. A., *Diderot's Vie de Sénèque* (Florida, 1966).

BOUCHARY, J., *Les Maniers d'argent à Paris à la fin du xviiiᵉ siècle* (Paris, 1943), 3 vols.

CHAPUISAT, E., *La Prise d'armes de 1782 à Genève* (Geneva, 1932).

CHARTIER, R., *The Cultural Origins of the French Revolution* (Durham, N.C., 1991).

CLARK, T. N., *Prophets and Patrons: The French University and the Emergence of the Social Sciences* (Cambridge Mass., 1973).

COLE, C. W., *French Mercantilism, 1683–1700* (New York, 1965).

COLEMAN, D. C., *Revisions in Mercantilism* (London, 1969).

COLLISON BLACK, R. D., COATS, A. W., GOODWIN, C. D. W., eds., *The Marginal Revolution in Economics. Interpretation and Evaluation* (Durham N.C., 1973).

CROUZET, F., *Britain Ascendant: Comparative Studies in Franco-British Economic History*, tr., Martin Thom (Cambridge, 1985).

DAIRE, L. F. E., ed. *Economistes financières du 18ᵉ siècle* (Paris, 1864).

DARNTON, Robert, *The Literary Underground of the Old Regime* (Cambridge Mass., 1982).

—— *The Forbidden Best-Sellers of Pre-Revolutionary France* (New York and London, 1995).

DEDIEU, J., *Montesquieu et la tradition politique anglaise en France* (Paris, 1909).

FACCARELLO, Gilbert, and STEINER, P., eds., *L'économie politique pendant la Révolution française* (Œconomia, Paris, 1990).

FONTANA, B., *Benjamin Constant and the Post-Revolutionary Mind* (New Haven, Connecticut, 1991).

—— ed., *The Invention of the Modern Republic* (Cambridge, 1994).

FORSYTH, Murray, *Reason and Revolution: The Political Thought of the Abbé Sieyes* (Leicester, 1987).

—— *The Spirit of the Revolution of 1789* (Leicester, 1989).

FURET, F., ed., *Le Siècle de l'avenement républicain* (Paris, 1994).

—— *Revolutionary France*, tr., A. Nevill (Oxford, 1992).

FURET, François, and OZOUF, Mona, eds.,*The French Revolution and the Creation of Modern Political Culture. The Transformation of Political Culture 1789–1848* (Oxford, 1990).

GODECHOT, J., *Les Institutions de la France* (Paris, 1951).

GOODMAN, D., *The Republic of Letters: A Cultural History of the French Enlightenment* (Ithaca, N.Y., 1994).

GRIEDER, J., *Anglomania in France 1740–1789: Fact, Fiction and Political Discourse* (Geneva, 1985).

GUILLAUME, J., *Procès-verbaux du comité d'instruction publique de la Convention nationale* (Paris, 1891–1907), 6 vols.

GUILLOIS, A., *Le Salon de Madame Helvétius* (Paris, 1894).

GUSDORF, G., *La Conscience révolutionnaire: Les Idéologues* (Paris, 1978).

HAAKONSEN, Knud, *The Science of a Legislator: The Natural Jurisprudence of David Hume and Adam Smith* (Cambridge, 1981).

HARSIN, P., *Les doctrines monétaires et financières en France* (Paris, 1928).

HIGONNET, P., *Sister Republics: The Origins of French and American Republicanism* (Cambridge Mass., 1988).

HONT, I. and IGNATIEF, M., eds., *Wealth and Virtue: The Shaping of Political Economy in the Scottish Enlightenment* (Cambridge, 1983).

HORROWITZ, I. L., *Claude Helvétius: Philosopher of Democracy and Enlightenment* (New York, 1954).

HUBERT, R., *D'Holbach et ses amis* (Paris, 1928).

IONESCU, G., *The Political Thought of Saint-Simon* (Oxford, 1976).

ISRAEL, J., *Conflicts of Empires: Spain, the Low Countries and the Struggle for World Supremacy 1585–1713* (London, 1997).

JACOB, M. C., *The Radical Enlightenment: Pantheists, Freemason and Republicans* (London, 1988).

—— *Living the Enlightenment: Freemasonry and Politics in Eighteenth-Century Europe* (Oxford, 1991).

JARDIN, A., *Histoire du libéralisme politique* (Paris, 1985).

KAPLAN, S., *Bread, Politics and Political Economy in the Reign of Louis XV* (The Hague, 1976), 2 vols.

KATES, G., *The Cercle social, the Girondins, and the French Revolution* (Princeton, 1985).

KITCHIN, J., *Un journal 'philosophique': La Décade (1794–1807)* (Paris, 1965).

KORS, P., *D'Holbach's Coterie: an Enlightenment in Paris* (Princeton, 1975).

LACORNE, D., *L'Invention de la république. Le modèle américain* (Paris, 1991).

LARÈRE, C., *l'Invention de l'économie politique au XVIIIe siècle* (Paris, 1992).

LUCAS, Colin, ed., *The French Revolution and the Creation of Modern Political Culture. The Political Culture of the French Revolution* (Oxford, 1988).

—— ed., *Rewriting the French Revolution. The Andrew Browning Lectures 1989* (Oxford, 1991).

MANIN, B., *La Famille, la loi, l'État: De la Révolution au code civil* (Paris, 1989).

MARGERISON, K., *P. L. Rœderer: Political Thought and Practice During the French Revolution* (Philadelphia, 1983).

MARION, M., *Histoire financière de la Révolution française* (Paris 1919–25), 4 vols.

MEEK, R. L. and KUCZYNSKI, M., *Quesnay's Tableau économique* (London, 1972).

MEEK, R. L., *The Economics of Physiocracy* (London, 1962).

MICHEL, G., *Léon Say* (Paris, 1899).

MIZUTA, H. and SINGIYAMA, C., *Adam Smith: International Perspectives* (London, 1993).

MORNET, D., *Les origines intellectuelles de la Révolution française, 1715–1787* (Lyon, 1989).

MURPHY, A. E., *Richard Cantillon, Entrepreneur and Economist* (Oxford, 1986).

—— *John Law* (Oxford, 1997).

PAGDEN, A., *Lords of all the World: Ideologies of Empire in Spain, Britain and France c.1500–c.1800* (New Haven, Connecticut, 1995).

PALMER, R. R., *J.-B. Say: An Economist in Troubled Times* (Princeton, N.J., 1997).

PAPPE, H. O., *Sismondi's Werggenossen* (Geneva, 1963).

PERROT, Jean-Claude, *Une Histoire intellectuelle de l'économie politique* (Paris, 1992).

PETTIT, P., *Republicanism: a theory of freedom and government* (Oxford, 1997).

PICAVET, F., *Les Idéologues. Essai sur l'histoire des idées et des théories scientifiques, philosophiques, religieuses etc. en France depuis 1789* (Paris, 1891).

PICKERING, M., *Auguste Comte: An Intellectual Biography* (Cambridge, 1993).

RAWSON, E., *The Spartan Tradition in European Thought* (Oxford, 1969).

REGALDO, Marc, *Un milieu intellectuel: la décade philosophique (1794–1807)* (Paris, 1976), 4 vols.

REYNAUD, Pierre-Louis, ed., *J.-B. Say: Textes choisis* (Paris, 1953).

ROELS, J., *La notion de réprésentation chez Roederer* (Heule, 1968).

RUGGIERO, G. de, *The History of European Liberalism* (Oxford, 1927).

SAY, L., *Turgot* (Paris, 1887).

SCHOORL, E., *J-B Say* (Groningen, 1986).

SCHUMPETER, J., *A History of Economic Analysis* (George Allen and Unwin, 1952).

SKINNER, Q., *Liberty Before Liberalism* (Cambridge, 1998).

SMITH, D. W., *Helvétius: a study in persecution* (Oxford, 1965).

SOREL, A., *Europe and the French Revolution*, tr., Alfred Cobban and J. W. Hunt (London, 1969).

SOWELL, T., *Say's Law: An Historical Analysis* (Princeton, 1972).

—— *Classical Economics Reconsidered* (Princeton, 1974).

STAUM, Martin, *Cabanis: Enlightenment and Medical Philosophy in France* (Princeton, 1980).

—— *Minerva's Message. Stabilizing the French Revolution* (Montreal and Kingston, 1996).

STEINER, P., DELMAS, B. and DELMAS, T. eds., *La diffusion internationale de la physiocratie* (Grenoble, 1995).

—— *La 'science nouvelle' de l'économie politique* (Paris, 1998).

STEINER, P., *Sociologie de la connaissance économique: essai sur les rationalisations de la connaissance économique (1750–1850)* (Paris, 1998).

STRUGNELL, A., *Diderot's Politics: A Study of the Evolution of Diderot's Political Thought after the Encylopédie* (The Hague, 1973).

TEILHAC, E., *L'Œuvre économique de Jean-Baptiste Say* (Paris, 1927).

TULLY, J., *Locke in Context* (Cambridge, 1992).

VALYNSEELE, J., *Les Say et leurs alliances* (Paris, 1971).

VAN KLEY, D. K., *The Religious Origins of the French Revolution* (New Haven, Connecticut, 1996).

VIARD, J., ed., *L'Esprit républicain* (Paris, 1970).

WELCH, Cheryl, *Liberty and Utility. The French Idéologues and the Transformation of Liberalism* (New York, 1984).

WEULERSSE, Georges, *Le Mouvement physiocratique en France* (Paris, 1910), 2 vols.

WICKWAR, W. H., *Baron d'Holbach: a Prelude to the French Revolution* (London, 1935).

WINCH, D., *Riches and Poverty: an Intellectual History of Political Economy in Britain 1750–1834* (Cambridge, 1996).

WOOTTON, D., ed., *Republicanism, Liberty, and Commercial Society, 1649–1776* (Stanford, California, 1994).

WRIGHT, J. Kent, *A Classical Republican in Eighteenth-Century France: the Political Thought of Mably,* (Stanford, California, 1997).

(ii) Periodicals

ALCOUFFE, A., 'The Institutionalisation of Political Economy in French Universities 1819–1896', *History of Political Economy*, 21 (1989), 313–44.

ALLIX, E., 'J-B Say et les origines de l'industrialisme', *Revue d'économie politique*, 24 (1911), 303–13, 341–63.

—— 'La déformation de l'économie politique libérale après J.-B. Say: Charles Dunoyer', *Revue d'histoire des doctrines économiques et sociales*, 4 (1911), 114–47.

—— 'La méthode et la conception de l'économie politique dans l'œuvre de J-B Say', *Revue d'histoire économique et sociale*, 4 (1911), 321–60.

—— 'La rivalité entre la propriété foncière et la fortune mobilière sous la Révolution', *Revue d'histoire économique et sociale*, 6 (1913), 297–348.

APPLEBY, J. O., 'America as a Model for the Radical French Reformers of 1789', *William and Mary Quarterly*, 28 (1971), 267–86.

BAUMOL, W. J., 'Say's (at Least) Eight Laws, or What Say and James Mill May Really Have Meant', *Economica*, 44 (1977), 145–161.

COLEMAN, D. C., 'Mercantilism revisited', *The Historical Journal*, 23 (1980), 773–91.

DARNTON, R., 'What was Revolutionary about the French Revolution', *The New York Review of Books*, 19 January, 1989.

DIECKMANN, H., 'Les contributions de Diderot à la Correspondance littéraire et à l'Histoire des deux Indes', *Revue d'histoire littéraire de la France* (1951), 417–40.

DUCHET, M., 'Diderot collaborateur de Raynal: à propos des Fragments imprimés du fonds Vandeul', *Revue d'histoire littéraire de la France* (1960), 531–56.

DZIEMBOWSKI, E., 'Un nouveau patriotisme français, 1750–1770: La France face à la puissance anglaise à l'époque de la guerre de Sept Ans', *SVC*, 365 (1988).

FORGET, Evelyn, 'J-B Say and Adam Smith: an Essay in the Transmission of Ideas', *Canadian Journal of Economics*, 26 (1993), 121–33.

FRICK, J. P., 'Philosophie et économie politique chez J-B Say; Remarques sur les rapports entre un texte oublié de J-B Say et son œuvre', *Histoire, économie, société*, (1987), 57–66.

GROENEWEGEN, P. D., 'Turgot and Adam Smith', *Scottish Journal of Political Economy*, XVI (1969), 71–87.

HASHIMOTO, H., 'Les lettres inédites de Jean-Baptiste Say', *Treatises* 20 (1971), 74–99.

—— 'Notes inédites de J.-B. Say qui couvert les marges de la Richesse des Nations et qui critiquent: rédigées avec une introduction', *Kyoto Sangyo University Economic and Business Review*, 7 (1980), 53–81.

—— 'Notes inédites de J.-B. Say qui couvrent les marges de la richesse des nations et qui la critiquent', *Kyoto Sangyo University Economic and Business Review*, 9 (1982), 31–133.

HONT, I., 'The Permanent Crisis of a Divided Mankind: The Contemporary Crisis of the Nation State in Historical Perspective', *Political Studies*, 42 (1994), 166–231.

—— 'The Political Economy of the 'Unnatural and Retrograde Order': Adam Smith and Natural Liberty', *Politische Ökonomie und Französische Revolution* (Trèves, 1989), 122–49.

JAMES, Michael, 'Pierre-Louis Rœderer, Jean-Baptiste Say and the concept of *industrie*', *History of Political Economy*, 9 (1977), 455–75.

KAISER, T. E., 'Politics and Political Economy in the Thought of the Idéologues', *History of Political Economy*, 12 (1980), 141–61.

LEVAN-LEMESLE, A. L., 'La promotion de l'économie politique en France au XIXe siècle 1815–1881', *Revue d'histoire moderne et contemporaine* (1980), 270–94.

LIVESEY, J., 'Virtue, Commerce, and Farming: Agrarian Ideology and Commercial Republicanism during the French Revolution', *Past and Present*, 157 (1997), 94–121.

LUFTALLA, M., 'Jean-Baptiste Say et les siens: une famille d'économistes', *Revue d'économie politique*, 89 (1979), 389–407.

MAZA, S., 'Politics, Culture and the Origins of the French Revolution', *Journal of Modern History*, 61 (1989), 703–23.

ROGGI, P., 'Sette lettere di J.-B. Say a J. C. L. Sismondi', *Rivista di politica economica* (1972), 963–79.

ROMANI, R., 'All Montesquieu's Sons: the Place of '*esprit général*', '*caratère national*', and '*mœurs*' in French Political Philosophy, 1748–89', *SVC*, 362 (1998), 189–235.

ROTHSCHILD, Emma, 'Adam Smith and Conservative Economics', *Economic History Review*, 45 (1992), 74–96.

SCHMIDT, C., 'Jean-Baptiste Say et le Blocus Continental', *Revue d'histoire des doctrines économiques et sociales*, 4 (1911), 148–54.

SCHOORL, E., 'Bentham, Say and Continental Utilitarianism', *The Bentham Newsletter* 6 (1982), 8–18.

SHOUL, B., 'Karl Marx and Say's Law', *The Quarterly Journal of Economics*, 71 (1957), 611–29.

SONENSCHER, M., 'The Nation's Debt and the Birth of the Modern Republic: The French Fiscal Deficit and the Politics of the Revolution of 1789', *History of Political Thought*, 18 (1997), 64–103, 267–325.

STAUM, M., 'The Enlightenment Transformed: The Institute Prize Contests', *Eighteenth Century Studies*, 19 (1985–6), 153–79.

—— 'The Institute Economists: from Physiocracy to Entrepreneurial Capitalism', *The History of Political Economy*, 19 (1987), 525–50.

STEINER, Philippe, 'Intérêts, intérêts sinistres et intérêts éclairés: problèmes du libéralisme chez J-B Say', *Cahier d'économie politique*, (1989), 21–41.

—— 'J-B Say et l'enseignement de l'économie politique en France 1815–1832', *Œconomia*, (1987), 345–77.

—— 'Politique et économie politique chez Jean-Baptiste Say', *Revue française d'histoire des idées politiques* 5 (1997), 23–58.

—— 'The Structure of Say's Economic Writings', *The European Journal of the History of Economic Thought*, 5 (1998), 227–49.

TEICHGRAEBER, Richard F. ' "Less Abused Than I Had Reason to Expect": the reception of the Wealth of Nations in Britain, 1776–90', *Historical Journal*, 30 , 337–66.

TIRAN, A., 'Jean-Baptiste Say: Manuscrits sur la monnaie, la banque, et la finance (1767–1832)', *Cahiers monnaie et financement* (1995), 1–229.

WINCH, D., 'Science and the Legislator: Adam Smith and After', *The Economic Journal*, 93 (1983), 501–20.

—— 'The Burke-Smith Problem and Late Eighteenth Century Political and Economic Thought', *The Historical Journal*, 28 (1985), 231–47.

(iii) Unpublished Dissertations

DARNTON, R., *Trends in Radical Propaganda on the Eve of the French Revolution (1782–1788)* (Oxford, 1964).

RAMASWAMY, J., *Reconstituting the 'Liberty of the Ancients'; Public Credit, Popular Sovereignty, and the Political Theory of Terror during the French Revolution, 1789–1794* (Cambridge, 1994).

Index

Abauzit, Théophile, Protestant minister 214
Académie des inscriptions et belles lettres 189
Académie des sciences 200
Academy of Lyon 67
agriculture, and commerce 48
agronomy 50
Aix-la-Chapelle 19
d'Alembert 28, 140
Alexander I, Tsar 191
Allix, Edgard, on Say 6
Alsace, economy of 74
d'Ameilhon, editor of *Journal de l'agriculture, des arts et du commerce* 8
America 219
   colonial practices in 175
   commerce of 177
   democracy of 24
   federalism of 199
   inflation of 88
   on promoting civilization 212
   republicanism of 66, 95
   Say's attitudes towards 205, *and see* Say on America
   social equality and industry in 207
   trade relations with Britain 142
American Revolution (1776) 11, 29, 56, 61, 65
Amsterdam 18
Andrieux, F.-G.-J.-S. 115, 116, 124, 137, 213
Antilles, colonial practices of 175
Aristotle 113
Arrêt du Conseil 53
assignats 162; *see also* Clavière
Athénée Royale 190, 200
Athens 5
Aubin, St, on Smith's *Wealth of Nations* 9
Augsburg, economy of 75
Aulchy (Pas-de-Calais) 183
Austin, Sarah 197
Austria 91

Bacon 113, 141, 196
Badeau, Nicolas 49; *Principes de la science morale et politique sur le luxe et les loix somptuaires* 60 n. 84
Bailly 120, 122
Barnave 89, 90
Barras 137
Barruel, on religion 111
Bavaria 144

Beaumont 219
Beccaria 128, 192
Belgium, social equality and industry in 207
Bentham 17, 144, 190, 195, 197
   influence of on Say 6, 132 n. 36, 207–8, 210
   on America 208
   Tactique des assemblées legislatives 208
Bergasse, Nicolas 26, 79, 90
Bergerac, Cyrano de 20
Bernardin de Saint-Pierre, J. H. 112
Berthollet 162
Bertin, Controller General 46
Bibliothèque britannique 121, 123, 207
Bichat, Xavier, on an educational revolution 139
Biot, J.-B., review of Say's second edition of the *Traité* 193
Biran, Maine de, on an educational revolution 139
Bizard, abbé, 'Éloge historique de l'abbé Mably' 24
Black Sea 137
Blake, William 216 n. 40
Blanqui, Jérôme-Adolphe, 12, 218
   on Say 4, 6, 194
   professor of *Économie industrielle* 4
   Histoire de l'économie politique 4
Blavet, abbé, French translations of Smith's *Wealth of Nations* 7–8
Blenheim 19
Bodin 23
Boisguillebert, *Factum de la France . . .* 57 n. 12
Boissy d'Anglas 118
Bolingbroke, on liberty and commerce 41
Bonald, de 111, 219
Bonaparte, Lucien 137
Bonaparte: *see* Napoleon
Bonnet 100
Bonneville, Nicholas, 82
Bossuet 52, 210
Bourbon Restoration (1814) 17
Bourbons, monarchy of 19, 21, 24, 29, 40, 136, 189, 194, 213
Bourbon–Habsburg, rivalry of 18
Bowring 203 n. 37
Brazil
   colonial practices in 175
   commercial crisis of 206
Briasson, *Métaphysique de l'âme*, the French trans. of Smith's *Wealth of Nations* 7

Bridgewater, Duke of 143
Brissot 11, 12, 17, 26, 152
  co-founder of the *Société Gallo-Américain* 11
  and Clavière 78
  in London 78
  republican ideas of 78
  republican political economy of 62, 138, 165
  Patriote françois 82
Britain 219
  and France 19, 46
  as model for France after Napoleon 190
  Bank of England 86
  commercial crisis of 206
  criticisms of social structures of by Say 170,
    212
  decline of after 1780s 70
  French attitudes towards 38, 39, 42, 54, 78, 86,
    91–2
  mixed government of 21–2, 26, 27, 28, 56, 61
  non-republican nature of 66
  social equality and industry in 207
  supremacy of in first half of eighteenth
    century 19, 25, 39–40, 41, 54, 170, 189
  trade relations with America 142
Brown, John 23
Bruce, John, *Elements of the Science of Ethics, on
    the Principles of Natural Philosophy* 154 n. 15
Brumaire, coup of 136
Buchanan 5
Burke 17, 219
  on reason-of-state political economy 92
  on Smith's *Wealth of Nations* 145

Cabanis, Pierre-Jacques-Georges 5, 112, 137
  against Destutt's *idéologie* 141
  and Rœderer 113
  in praise of new Consulate 137
  in support of monarchy 189
  on educational revolution 139
  on foundation of new base for moral sciences
    113
  on importance of climate as an influence on
    behaviour 114
  on importance of labour 114
  on natural history of man in order to establish
    morality 114
  on *physiologie* 141
  on progess of society 115
  on relationship between wealth and govern-
    ment 148
  on role of women 114
  physician to Mirabeau 113
  republican political economy of 171
  using analytical methods of physical science
    113–14

*Quelques considérations sur l'organisation sociale
    en général et particulièrement sur la nouvelle
    constitution* 137
Rapports du physique et du moral de l'homme 113,
    139
Caesar 194
  Commentaries 40
Calonne 7, 11, 72, 86
Calvados 114
Calvinism 10, 114, 121
Cambacérès, *Discours sur la science sociale* 130
Camus, against Clavière's *assignats* 88
Canard, Nicolas 148, 180
Candolle, Augustin-Pyramus, de 12, 191
  translation of Rumford's *Essays* 144
  Mémoires et souvenirs 144, 197, 201 n. 1
Carthage 5, 126
Castenet, grandfather of J.-B. Say 15 n. 38
Castille, grain trade of 54
Catherine II 25
Catholic Inquisition 201
Catholicism 10, 111, 112, 114, 121, 122, 152, 189, 190
Cato 214
Censeur Européen 193
Cercle social 91
Chabaud, Rosine de 214
Chambre introuvable 190
Chamfort 76, 115
Champagne 10
Champs de Mars 89
Charlemagne 24
Charles I, king 44
Charles II, king 19
Chartre constitutionelle, of Louis XVIII 189
  favouring British-style constitutionalism
    189–90
Chassebeuf de Volney, Constantin-François 112
Chastellux, Marquis, de 28
  on division of sovereignty 21, 22
  De la félicité publique; in support of British
    mixed government 55, 56; against
    commerce 56
Chateaubriand
  De la monarchie selon la charte 190; on British
    constitution as model for France 190
  La Génie du Christianisme 189
Chénier, Marie-Joseph, poetry of 210
Cherbuliez, editior of *L'Utilitaire* 209
Chesterfield, Lord, on French crisis prior to
    Revolution 19–20
Child, Josiah, *Treatise on Commerce* 176
China 49, 199, 219; *see also* Say, J.-B. *on* China
Choiseul 53
Chronique du mois 82, 91
Cicero 122, 210

Civil Constitution of Clergy 85
Clavière, Etienne 3, 12, 17, 62, 136, 152, 199
  against aristocracy 80–1, 90, 91
  against Britain 219
  against Calonne 86
  against Necker 86
  alliance with radical Genevans to promote
    commercialization of the populace 81–2
  and Brissot 78, 79, 80; *De la France et des États-
    Unis* 79, 86; *Observations d'un républicain*
    78–9, 82 n. 7; *Nouveau voyage dans les États-
    Unis de l'Amérique septrionale, fait en 1788* 83
    n. 51; *Société Française des Amis des Noirs* 81
  and Mirabeau 89, 90
  and Montesquieu 90
  and Paine 91
  and Rousseau 80
  and Saint-Just 95
  as Minister of Public Contributions 92
  banking policies of 87–9; on commerce,
    public credit and issuing of legal tender, his
    assignats 87–8, 89, 90–1; influenced by
    Smith 86, 87, 88; on currency reform 88–9;
    principle of morality in 89, 116
  change in political philosophy as stated in his
    manifesto of 1792, *De la conjuration* 91;
    assignats linked with 'French fidelity' 91;
    against bankers 91; war against aristocracy
    91–2; financing of war 91–2; disposal of
    assignats 92; war as moral imperative 92;
    banking policies with Geneva 92; acknow-
    ledged failure of his *assignats* to produce
    republican manners 92, 93, 95; arrest and
    suicide of 92
  family history and career of 10–11
  formation of the *Société Gallo-Américain*, circle
    of friends associated with 79
  in Ireland 78
  influence of on Say 7, 12, 114, 217, *see also* J.-B.
    Say
  influence of Rousseau's *Contrat social* on 11
  on American Revolution and public virtue 80
  on a republican interpretation of Smith 170
  on Britain 81, 86, 89
  on counter-revolution 94
  on debt problem and on 'ancient liberty' 79
  on expanding commerce, industry and public
    credit 79–80
  on French Revolution 85
  on justification of war 120
  on manners 78, 114, 219
  on moral commerce and wealth 11, 118
  on national debt 178
  on popular culture 97
  on public virtues and commerce 80, 81–2
  on transforming corrupt societies 156
  overthrow of Small Council 11
  republican political economy of 31, 78, 80, 87,
    104, 138, 165
  support for civil liberty in West Indies 89–90
Clovis 24
Cocles, Horatius 101
Colbert 19, 22, 40, 53, 150, 161
  on commercial success of Dutch 48
  on fine cloth and silk industries 180
Collège de France 3, 213
Committee of Public Instruction 111
Committee of Public Safety 115, 201
Compagnie d'assurances à vie 10
Comte, Charles 183, 213, 217
  on Say 4–5, 6, 10
  review of Say's *Traité* (2nd and 3rd edn) 193–4
Condillac 100, 130
  and physiocrats 150
  as founder of 'science of man' 139
  chemical methods of analysis 113
  on science of legislation 139–40
  Le commerce et le gouvernement 60 n. 98, 140
Condolle, Augustin-Pyramus de, recognition of
  Say's debt to Smith in Say's *Traité* 182
Condorcet 5, 12, 84 n. 56, 112, 114, 122, 140, 153
  advocating changes in French constitution 62,
    66, 68
  against British constitution 67
  against Clavière's *assignats* 88, 90, 96
  and Sieyès 98
  and physiocrats 150
  and Volney 113
  disciple of Turgot 66
  from physiocracy to republicanism 66–7, 77
  his plan of rights (Autumn 1789) 65
  influence on Rœderer 103
  influenced by Clavière 95, 97
  on Cromwell 95
  on debt problem 77
  on 'general fact' approach to political
    economy 141, *and see* his *Esquisse*
  on landed proprietors 67
  on manners 95, 117
  on national education 96, 97, 139
  on relationship between wealth and
    government 148
  on separation of public functions 76
  on Smith's *Wealth of Nations* 8, 9, 157
  on state support for men of genius in *Société
    nationale* 96
  on voting in primary assemblies 119
  republican political economy of 23, 116, 165
  suicide of 113
  Éloge de François Quesnay 66

Condorcet (*cont.*):
  Esquisse d'un tableau historique des progrès de l'esprit humain 96, 111, 141–2
  Essai sur la constitution et les fonctions des assemblées provinciales 67; influenced by Turgot's *Mémoire* 67
  Vie de Turgot 23, 66, 79
Conseil des Anciens 119, 137
Conseil des Cinq-Cents 118, 119, 120, 137
Conservatoire des arts et métiers 3, 4, 200, 201
Constant, Benjamin 5, 6, 17, 173, 199, 200, 217
  against hierarchy 190
  against legislative interference 190
  in support of a commercial society 190
  influenced by Say 190
  on British constitution as model for France 190
  on 'principles of politics' 171
  De la doctrine politique qui peut réunir les partis en France 190
  De la liberté des anciens comparées à celles des modernes 190
  Essais philosophiques 209
Constituent Assembly 73, 89, 90
Constitution, collapse of (1791) 119
Consulate 152, 171, 173
Convention 93, 97, 98, 115
Cook, Captain 212
Corsica 23
Courier de Provence 6, 17, 85, 112, 114, 115, 207
Cousin, Victor, *Cours de philosophie* 209
Coyer, Gabriel, abbé 22, 46
  on depopulation thesis 42
  on problems of Britain's mixed government 55–6
  La Noblesse commerçante 42
Creuzé Latouche, J.-A. 129–30
Crèvecœur 79
Cromwell 27, 95, 136, 194
Croydon 10
Curtius 101
Custodi, Pietro, *Scrittori classici italiani di economia politica* 192

D'Ivernois, François, apologist for Britain 11, 136
Daire, Eugène 3, 57 n. 12
Danton 112
Dardanelles 137
Daunou 118
  'Daunou law' 111–12
  in praise of Say's *Traité* 170
Davenant, Charles, on liberty and commerce 41
David, Jacques-Louis 76
La Décade philosophique, politique et littéraire 10, 12, 28, 61, 85, 95, 98, 112, 115, 120, 121, 128, 136, 137, 142, 144, 146, 182, 194, 207, 213

aims of 115
anti-religious stance of 122
influences of Condorcet on 116–17
influences of Ginguené on 116
  La Mercure de France 189
relationship between arts, republic and manners 115
republican philosophy expressed in 115
Decius 101
Defoe, *Plan of English Commerce* 41
Delaroche, Michel 191, 194
Delaunay, on Clavière's *assignats* 90
Delolme, Jean, *La Constitution de l'Angleterre* 21, 55
Democritus 113
Denmark, economy of 175
depopulation thesis 42
Descartes 66, 116, 122, 123
Destutt de Tracy 137
  criticism of by Cabanis 141
  on educational revolution 139–40
  on *idéologie*, or relationship between ideas and act of understanding 140
  on relationship between wealth and government 148
  on science of virtuous manners 140
  Idéologie 139
  Observations sur le système actuel de l'instruction publique 140
  Projet d'éléments d'idéologie à l'usage des écoles centrales 140
Diderot 28, 73, 98, 122, 166, 217
  against Quesnay 54
  against British mixed government 29
  atheism of 29
  commentary on Helvétius' works 29, 31
  contributions to *Encyclopédie* 29
  on commerce 30, 31
  on manners 219
  on moral actions 30
  on revolutionary actions 31
  on sovereignty 29, 30
  praise for republican America 30, 56
  republican political economy of 165, 29, 30
  revisions to Raynal's *Histoire philosophique* 56
  additions to 3rd edn of Raynal's *Histoire philosophique des deux Indes* 30
  Aux insurgents de l'Amérique 30
  Essai sur la vie de Sénèque 30, 31
  Supplément au voyage de Bougainville 29
  Vie de Sénèque 122
Directory 124, 125, 126, 129, 130, 136, 137, 139, 157, 171, 172, 219
Douai, Merlin de 137
Du Roveray, Pierre 11, 81

Duc d'Orléans 112
Duhamel 95
Dumas, Charles, on educational revolution 139
Dumont, Etienne 17, 81, 85, 213, 215 n. 20
    and Say's *Essai sur le principe de l'utilité* 209
    contributions to the *Bibliothèque universelle* 209
    on Bentham 207, 208
    Projet de code de police 209
    Projet de code pénal 209
Dunoyer, Charles 217
    on Say 3
    on Say's *Petit volume* 198
    review of Say's *Traité* (2nd and 3rd edn) 193–4
Dupont de Nemours, Pierre-Samuel 4, 16 n. 44,
        47, 59 n. 63, 64, 72, 195
    advocate for representative government 67–8
    against British constitution 67
    against Clavière's *assignats* 88
    against commerce 176
    analysis of Say's *Traité* 37–8
    and *Institut national* 112
    as advocate of neo-physiocracy 68
    attack on Say's 'British' inclinations 38–9
    critique of Say's second edition of *Traité* 193
    disciple of Turgot 66, 67
    emphasis on moral code 66
    importance of landed proprietor 68
    influence of Quesnay on 61
    influence of Smith's *Wealth of Nations* on 9,
        172
    on philosophy of religion 112
    on reorganization of assemblies 68
    on separation of public functions 76
    on sovereignty 52
    physiocracy as the 'science of liberty' 61
    political economy of 172
    support for French constitutional reform 62,
        67
    Abrégé des principes de l'économie politique 66
    *Notice abrégée des différents écrits modernes qui
        ont concouru en France à former la science de
        l'économie politique* 56 n. 4
    Œuvres posthumes de M. Turgot 14 n.19, 82 n. 7
    Philosophie de l'univers 112
    Physiocratie 48
    *Rapports au comité d'administration de l'agricul-
        ture* 82 n. 18
    translation of *Examen du gouvernement
        d'Angleterre* 67, 68
Dutot 40, 46, 55
Duval, Amaury 115, 116, 124, 133 n. 63, 153 n. 2
    on Condorcet 156
    on division of powers 119
    on evils of Montesquieu 119
    Plan de constitution 118–19

École normale de Paris 95, 111
Écully 10
Egypt 5, 137, 158, 175
Elba 189
Encyclopédie Méthodique 7, 26, 29
Epicurus 113
Estates General, Third Estate of 73
Everett, Alexander, and Say, on population 211

Fénelon 122
Filangieri 192
Fix, Theodor, *Revue mensuelle d'économie politique*
    5
Flanders, grain trade of 55
Forbonnais, François Véron de 18, 20, 31 n. 3
    on political economy of France 41
Ford Abbey 195
Fougeret de Montbron, Louis-Charles, on *anglo-
    manie* 42
Fox, on Gibbon 122–3
Frankfurt
    economy of 75
    wealth of 55
Franklin, Benjamin 122
    on colonial practices 176
    on industry and frugality 162
    Pennsylvania Almanac 117
    Poor Richard Saunders (title of London edn: *The
        Way to Wealth of Poor Richard Improved*) 85,
        117; Say's edition and discussion of 117, *and
        see* Say, J.-B.
Frederick the Great 25
Fréjus 137
French Restoration 136, 190, 194, 195, 198, 218, 219
French Revolution (1789) 10, 17, 25–6, 53, 61, 85–6,
        111, 112, 115, 136, 139, 149, 168, 171
French Revolution (1830) 213
French Revolution (1848) 4
Fructidor, election of 95
Fulton, Robert 143

Galiani, abbé 21, 22, 28, 56
    Dialogues sur le commerce des bleds 53; attacks on
        the physiocrats 53–5; on the supremacy of
        Britain 54; understanding political econ-
        omy as a science of 'reason-of-state' 53–4
Garat 28, 111, 116
Garnier, Germain 197
    concept of the legislator 173
    influence of Smith's *Wealth of Nations* on 9
    on commerce 172, 175
    on Dupont 172
    support for monarchy 189
    translation and critique of Smith's *Wealth of
        Nations*, 171, 172, 174, 182

Gatcomb Park 195
Geneva 10–11, 76, 92, 173, 174
  as a republic 22
  constitutional revolution in 78
  economy of 54–5, 75, 158
  revolution of (1782) 11, 86
  see also Clavière
Genoa, wealth of 55
Gérando, Joseph Marie de 140
Germany
  social equality and industry in 207
  trade practices of 176
Gibbon 121, 122
  The Decline and Fall of the Roman Empire 122–3
Ginguené, Pierre-Louis 112
  and Chamfort 115
  as ambassador to Turin 120
  as editor of *La Feuille villageoise* 115, 116
  critical of Say's *Olbie* 145
  in support of English rebels and regicides 116
  on Condorcet 142, 156
  on future of republicanism 142
  on importance of morality 116
  on republic of rural economy 116
Giro, Jesuit teacher 10
Gironde 17
Girondins 12, 85, 92, 93, 95, 114, 116, 120
Glasgow 195
Glorious Revolution 39
Gobelin tapestries, sale of 176
Godwin, William 195, 217
Gorati, Jesuit teacher 10
Gordon, Thomas 27, 116
Gossec 104
Gourdel de Loche, Julie, wife of J.-B. Say 114
Gournay, Vincent de 18
Greece, ancient, colonial practices of 175
Grégoire, abbé
  republican political economy of 130, 171
Grimm, Friedrich-Melchior 28, 60 n. 86
Grivel, 'Droit naturel de l'homme', in
    *Encyclopédie méthodique: économie politique et
    diplomatique* 60 n. 83
Grote, George 215 n. 34, 203 n. 37
Grouchy-Condorcet, Sophie
  French translation of Smith's *Theory of Moral
    Sentiments* 113
  Lettres sur la sympathie 171
Guizot 5, 213
Gusdorf, Georges 107 n. 61

Hamilton, Robert 203 n. 37
Harrington, James 22, 116
Harringtonian, neo- 24, 25, 27
Helvétius 8, 27, 28, 46, 101, 102, 113, 218

influenced by Locke 33 n. 29
influences on 25
  on Britain; wealth of 25; hazards facing 43;
    supremacy of mixed government of 42
  on morality and liberty 116
  on republicanism 25–6
Helvétius, Madame, Auteuil salon of 112, 113, 137
Henri IV, king 20, 29
Herbert, Claude, *Essai sur la police générale des
    grains* 57 n. 10
Hobbes 8, 37, 102, 113
  philosophy of 27, 28–9
  De Corpore 28
d'Holbach, Baron (Paul Thierry) 10, 30, 166, 218
  against British mixed government 26, 28
  against Christianity 26, 28, 29
  articles for *Encyclopédie* 26, 28; *Représentans*
    27
  dinner associates of 28
  on commerce 27, 28, 29, 71
  on sovereignty 27–8, 29
  republican political economy of 25, 28, 165
  De la nature humaine 28
  Politique naturelle 28
Holland
  commerce of 40, 47, 127, 176
  economy of 75, 98
  trade of 54, 57 n.12
  wealth of 55, 102
Howard 143
Huguenots 11
Hume 28, 82 n. 2, 102, 122, 141
  on American Revolution 80
  on beginnings of political economy 18
  on passions 97
  Essays 67
  History 67
  Of Public Credit 79–80
Hundred Days 189, 194

idéologues 148, 156, 170
Index, the 111
India 5
Indies, French trade with 40
L'Industrie 191, 194
Institut national des sciences et des arts 112, 130, 137,
    141, 194, 213
  closure of 189
  competitions of 140
  discussions on nature of human science in
    145–6
  Moral and Political Sciences class of 112, 113,
    114, 125, 139, 142
  objectives of republican political economy
    expressed in 171

on education of populace in duties of
citizenship 139
on republican manners 139
on separation of religious beliefs and virtuous
civil practices 112
Institut Royal 4, 213
d'Invau, Mayon, Controller General 53
Italy, trade practices of 176

Jacob, William 220 n. 3
Jacobin Club 115
Jacobin Terror 85–6
Jacobins 92, 93, 95, 98, 100, 114, 115, 116, 118, 125,
129, 137
Jansenism 129, 219
Jaucourt, de 28
Jefferson, president 183, 212
Jesuits 10
Jews, expulsion of 201
Joubert 137
Journal de l'agriculture, des arts et du commerce 8, 48
Journal d'instruction sociale 95, 96
July Monarchy 213

Kentucky 200
King, Gregory 19, 39
Kornman Mesmerist lodge 12

L'Averdy, Controller General 46
La Grange 30
La Harpe 219
La Révellière-Lepeaux 137
La Rochefoucauld 102, 122
La Rochefoucauld-Liancourt, on prison reforms
in Philadelphia 143
Lacretelle 140
Lafayette 81, 215 n. 20
Lakanal, Joseph, 116
Lameth, Alexandre de, on Say 5
Languedoc, canal of 143
Laplace 162
Lasalle, Antoine, *Traduction complète des œuvres de
Bacon* 139
Lavoisier 122, 140
Law, John, 20, 46, 55
banking experiments of 39, 40, 45, 88, 162
on potential of France's political economy 40
on supremacy of Britain's political economy
39–40, 41
Le Breton, Joachim 115, 116
review of Say's *Traité*, recognition of Say's
debt to Smith in 182
Le Trosne, *De l'administration provinciale et de la
réforme de l'impôt* 66
Leipzig 189

Leonidas 101
Linnaeus 9
Liverpool, canal of 143
Livingstone 82 n. 19
Locke 33 n. 29, 74, 100, 113, 196
First Treatise on Government 75
London 18, 176, 195
Lorraine, economy of 74
Louis XIII 18
Louis XIV, 19, 20, 39, 143, 149, 161, 166, 180, 189,
193
Louis XV 18, 23, 121
Louis XVI, 12, 62, 63, 78, 90, 219
Louis XVIII, his *Chartre constitutionelle* 189
Louisiana, colony of 40
Lüthy, *La Banque protestante* 11
Lycurgus 214
Lyon 10
Archbishop of 10

Mably, Gabrel Bonnot de, abbé 27, 30, 60 n. 86
influences on 24
on mixed government in France 23–4
republicanism of 24, 26, 77
reverence for Clovis and Charlemagne 24
De la législation ou principes des lois 24
Des droits et des devoirs du citoyen 23
Doutes aux économistes, Principes de législation
98
Entretiens de Phocion 23, 24
Lettres sur les constitutions des États-Unis 9
*Observations sur le gouvernement et les lois des
États-Unis d'Amérique* 24
Macartney, *Voyages* 121
Macaulay, Catherine 217
McCulloch 6
Machiavelli 25, 38, 41, 116
Discoursi 22
Madison, James, on Say 205, 220 n. 9
Federalist 73
Maistre de 111, 219
Malesberbes 122
Malta, industrious citizens of 158
Malthus 5, 6, 210, 217
and J.-B. Say 203 n. 56
critical of Say's theory of utility 205
dispute with Say on overproduction as cause
of commercial crisis 206
in support of social hierarchy 206, 207
on principle of population 207
Mandeville 102, 166
Marat 98, 112, 120
Marius 102
Marmontel 28
Martinique (West Indies) 89

Marx 5
  on Say 6, 218
Masons 111
Maupeou 53, 55, 61
Maurepas 65
Mazarin 19
Melon, Jean-François 40, 46, 55
Mercier de la Rivière, P.-F.-J.-H. 49
La Mercure de France, formerly *La Décade* 189
Metz 74, 76
Mexico, colonial practices in 175
Mill, James 17, 195
  History of British India 199, 212
Mill, John Stuart 12
  Principles 218
Milton, John, *Pro populo anglicano defensio* 116
Mirabeau, Honoré-Gabriel Riqueti de 11, 62, 86
  Considerations on the order of the Cincinnatus . . . 82 n. 8
  Courier de Provence 12, 82
Mirabeau, Victor Riqueti de 46, 50
  criticism of the nobility 61
  on Britain 49
  on commerce 48
  on free trade and public credit 21
  on sovereignty 52
  on theocracy of Quesnay's economic policy 52
  L'Ami des hommes 49
  Bref état des moyens pour la restauration de l'autorité du Roi et de ses finances 47
  De la monarchie 52
  Lettres sur le commerce des grains 52
  Physiocratie 150
Mitford, *History of Greece* 210
Monceau, Duhamel de 50
Le Moniteur 84 n. 56, 90
Montaigne 122
Montchrétien, Antoyne de, *Traicté de l'œconomie politique* 18, 57 n. 12
Montesquieu 12, 19, 51, 55, 56, 75–6, 119, 121
  against universal rules of national economy 53
  comparison of political economies of France and Britain 43–6, 49
  on aristocracy 80, 166
  on commerce, esp. economic commerce 44–6
  on hazards facing Britain 43, 46
  on honour 72
  on liberty 9, 44
  on liberty of trade 93
  on manners 62
  on republicanism 22, 26, 77
  on sovereignty of France 4 3–4
  praise of Britain 25, 43
  L'Esprit des lois 25, 43, 149

Montesquiou 92
Moors, expulsion of 201
Moreau 137
Morellet, Antoine, abbé, 28, 55, 219
Morelly, *Code de la nature* 98
Mounier 12, 72

Naigeon, J.-A. 28
  Œuvres de Diderot 122
Napier 203 n. 37
Naples 53
  economic problems of 55
  famine of 54
Napoleon 9, 38, 111, 120, 125, 136, 170, 173, 191, 192, 193, 194–5, 209, 212, 214, 217
  abdication of 189
  and Say 17; *see also* Say on Napoleon
  and the *Institut* and *La Décade* 136
  on the creation of a new constitution 137, 138
Napoleonic Wars 6
National Assembly 73, 76, 78, 87, 88, 89, 178, 207, 219
Necker, Jacques 11, 12, 21, 22, 56, 76
  against revolutionary manners 112
  against need for social reform in France 68, 79
  banking system of 86–7
  fall from power of 87, 88
  in support of the rich 166
  on British form of government 86
  on political economy as 'reason-of-state' 55
  on religion as foundation for manners 111
  on taxation and sovereignty 68
  opposition to Genevan revolution 86
  political economy of 68
  Administration des finances 79
  De l'importance des opinions religieuses 209
  Dernières vues de politique et de finance 171
Netherlands 8
Neuchâtel 78
Neufchâteau, François de, on education in the family 124
Newton 196
Normandy, grain trade of 55

Octavian 102
Olbie: *see* J.-B. Say's *Olbie, ou essai sur les moyens d'améliorer les mœurs d'une nation* 126
Orient, French trade with 40
Oudenarde 19
Owen, Robert, *New View of Society* 215 n. 23

Pacific Islands 212
Paine, Thomas 17, 91, 116
  on wealth and manners 80
Panchaud, Isaac 12

Paris 10, 11, 12, 17, 39, 53, 76, 93, 98, 143, 176, 195
    Treaty of (1763) 39, 46
Pas-de-Calais 17
penal reforms 143, 208
Peru, colonial practices in 175
Petty, William 39
Peuchet, Joseph 148, 154 n. 32
Philadelphia, penal reforms of 143
Philippe, Louis, his *Institut Royal* 4
philosophes 218, 219
    decline of movement of 189
    on republicanism 75, 77
physiocracy 7, 8, 21, 22, 24, 27, 37, 47, 48, 100, 116,
        149–50, 159, 160, 163, 168, 176, 180, 197
    and liberalism 9
    assessment of by Sieyès 68–9
    attacks on by Galiani 53; *see also* Galiani
    criticisms of 70, 74
    decline of 56
    defined as 'science of liberty' 61
    desiring national regeneration without consti-
        tutional change 52–3
    in support of small farms 181
    interpretation of Smith 172
    land as source of wealth for 50–1
    limitations of 76
    neo-physiocracy 61, 80, 81; as defined by the
        political economy of Turgot 61–5, *see also*
        Turgot; on constitutional innovations 68;
        sympathetic to republicanism 61
    on free trade 51, 55, 93
    on republicanism 77
    on sovereignty 52, 55, 61
Picardy, grain trade of 55
Pinel, Philippe, on an educational revolution 139
Pitt, William, prime minister 91, 121
Place, Francis 195, 208
Plato: neo-Platonic philosophy 23
Plutarch 104
Poland 23
    as a physiocratic state 74
    commerce of 176
    economic problems of 55
    mixed monarchy in 20
Polybius 104
Portugal
    collapse of 201
    economy of 175
Prairial, election of 95
Price, Richard 11, 78, 217
    on commerce and labouring class 71
    on American Revolution 80
    *Observations on the Importance of the American
        Revolution* 65
Priestly, Joseph, 217

*Letters to the Philosphers and Politicians of France
    on the Subject of Religion*, on Volney 112
Prinsep, Charles, on English translation of Say's
    Traité 194
Provence, Comte de 189
Prussia 91
Pufendorf 102

Quesnay, François 5, 7, 9, 18, 37, 62, 72
    against French constitutional change 66
    against mixed governments 48–9
    annotations of Mirabeau's *Bref état des moyens*
        47
    first legislative tests of philosophy of 46–7
    his concept of wealth 50–2
    on agriculture 50
    on assemblies 65
    on Britain as a commercial and opulent
        society 47, 48, 50, 66, 162
    on corn trade 50, 54
    on creation of wealth 37
    on decline of France 49–50
    on free trade and public credit 21
    on liberty through 'natural law' 37–8
    on natural law (*or* rationalistic
        providentialism) 49
    political economy of 61
    articles in *Encyclopédie*, esp. *Evidence* and
        Fermiers 46, 48
    Despotisme de la Chine 48
    Essai physique sur l'économie animale 46
    Philosophie rurale 46, 47
    *Physiocratie: Maximes générales du gouvernement
        économique d'un royaume agricole* (collated by
        Dupont) 48
    Tableau économique 46, 48
    Théorie de l'impôt 46

Rameau 104
Ramillies 19
Raynal, abbé 28, 67
    and physiocrats 150
    Histoire philosophique des deux Indes 30, 56
Renaissance 20
Reubell 137
Revolution (1688) 42, 86
Ricardo, David 4, 5, 6, 192, 195, 196, 213
    critical of Say's theory of utility 205–6, 209
    criticisms of Say's third *Traité* 208
    on money 207
    on social usefulness and price of a product
        205
    on value in exchange 205, 211
    Principles of Political Economy, French
        translation of 206

Richelieu, Cardinal 19, 38
Richeraud, Anthelme, *Nouveaux éléments de philosophie* 139
de Rivarol, Antoine, *De la philosophie moderne* 111
  against Condillac 111
  against Revolution 111
  against revolutionary manners 112
  in support of Catholicism 111
Robespierre 93, 98, 112, 116, 118, 119, 193
  his festival of Supreme Being 115
Rœderer, Pierre-Louis, 12, 81, 94, 114, 123, 137, 213, 217, 218
  against Britain 219
  against landed proprietors 74–5
  against nobility 100
  against physiocracy 100
  and Cabanis 113
  and Condorcet 98
  and *Institut national* 112
  and Sieyès 98
  change in political economy of 74
  constitutional reforms of, his 'free constitution' 74, 75, 78
  emphasis on national manners, his science of *mœurs* 95, 98–104
  family history of 74
  importance of national music as 'music for morality' 104
  influences of 74, 75–6, 103, 171
  on 'the principle of conservation' 98
  on an educational revolution 139
  on ancient republicanism 98–9
  on chemical principles behind moral and political science 140
  on communicating feelings of sensibility 103
  on commerce and industry 74, 175
  on Condillac 140
  on control of manners by wise legislators 103
  on debt problem 77
  on failure of republicanism in France 95
  on formation of Estates General 74
  on gender relations and role of women 102–3
  on identifying pain of others 102, 103
  on importance of *philosophes* 116
  on institutions to guide popular behaviour 103
  on large states 75
  on laws to promote virtuous behaviour 103
  on representative government 75, 77, 104
  on securing of safety 102
  on separation of public functions 76
  on setting essay competitions at the *Institut* 125
  on Smith 7, 8, 157
  on social organization 98
  on spirit and temperament 101

  participation of citizens in popular assembly 76
  republican political economy of 76, 80, 100–1, 165, 182
  support for monarchy 189
  Cours 119, 125, 144, 171–2; influence of Smith's *Theory of Moral Sentiments* on 172
  De la Députation 75; and *Second Treatise* and the *Contrat social* 75; influenced by Locke's *First Treatise on Government* 75; links with Sieyès 76–7
  Idées sur un traité de finance 74
  Mémoires sur quelques points d'économie publique 139, 173; constitution necessary for wealth creation 172; interpretation of Smith's *Wealth of Nations* in 172, 174; plutocratic constitutional prescriptions in 172
  Notice sur ma vie, De la députation aux états généraux 74, 75, 76
Rome 99
  empire of 18, 19, 20
  famine of 54
  republican ideas of 22
  supremacy of 45
Roucher 120
Rousseau, J.-J. 28, 29, 37, 58 n. 49, 74, 75, 81, 104, 119, 122, 150
  and Clavière 80
  and Say 212
  as a revolutionary 94
  on commerce 23
  on moral community 167
  on republicanism and commerce 77
  on republicanism in small states 22, 29
  Contrat social 11, 75, 76, 77, 104, 218
  Discours sur l'inégalité 10, 98
  Emile 128
  Gouvernement de Pologne 94; on *mandat impératif* 75
Royalists 95
Royer-Collard 213
Rumford, Benjamin
  and Say 144
  on virtue and self-interest 144
  on workhouses 182
  sources for his ideas 144
  Essays 144
Russia 91, 136

Saint-Cloud 137
St Dominque (West Indies) 89
Sainte-Beuve 76
Saint-Just
  and Clavière 93, 95
  institutions as guarantee of public virtue 94

on liberty of trade with popular manners 93
on popular culture 97
on public virtue as stoicism 94
on reformation of manners 93, 95; in
    economic sphere 93; in politics 94; destruc-
    tion of counter-revolution 94; support of a
    revolutionary government 94
on republican crisis 92
on restoring of republican virtue 93
Saint-Lambert 28
    Principes des mœurs 117
Saint-Lazare, prison 116
Saint-Ouen 189
St Petersburg, Panopticon prison of 208
Saint-Simon, C.-H., de 17, 199, 200, 217
    on creations of laws for new government of
        France 171
    on new religion 191
    on Say's political economy 191
    on supremacy of Britain 190–1
    review of Say's *Traité* (2nd edn) 194
Salaville, J.-B., *De la perfectibilité* 139
Sardinia, trade of 54
Say, Horace, brother of J.-B. Say
    early career of 10
    literary output of 132 n. 19
    against religion 122
    military participation of 125
    on physics and political economy 146
    *Plan d'éducation dans les principes de J.-J.
        Rousseau* 135 n. 91
Say, Horace, son of J.-B. Say 3–6, 217
Say, J.-B.
    Family background and career:
    Calvinist background of 114, 121
    family history and early career of 10–11
    military service of 114
    his stay in Britain 39, 195
    as secretary to Clavière 3, 6, 10
    his *Cours de l'économie politique* 200, 208
    professor of *Économie industrielle* 3, 200, 201
    professor of *Économie politique* 3, 213
    political nomination of to Tribunate of 1799
        136
    ejection from Tribunate 183
    exile of 17
    later career of 183, 200, 213
    possible emigration to America 196
    death of wife of 213
    death of 3
    Ideology:
    against early republicans and *idéologues* 156
    against Jacobins 118
    against luxury 118
    against physiocrats 159, 160

against the Terror 95
and Bentham 132 n. 36, 144; importance of
    manners, republican ideals and against
    social hierarchy 208; influenced by
    Bentham 6, 207–8; influenced by
    Bentham's science of utility 207, 208; meet-
    ing with Bentham 208
and Bourbon monarchy 194, 196–7, 213
and Cabanis 142
and Charles Comte 217
and Clavière 114; as member of Clavière's
    circle at Auteuil salon 12, 137; influenced by
    Clavière 10–12, 31, 118, 199, 217; influenced
    by Clavière (and Brissot) in the promotion
    of manners 82, 85
and Constant 217
and *Courier de Provence* 85
and Diderot 29
and Directory 136, 137
and Dunoyer 217
and Dupont de Nemours 176–7, 217
and French Revolution (1789) 12
and John Stuart Mill 12
and *La Décade philosophique* 85, 117–18
and Malthus 6, 203 n. 56, 217; response to criti-
    cisms of Malthus 206, *and see* Say's *Lettres à
    Malthus*
and Napoleon 17, 125, 136, 170,182–3, 191, 194–5,
    197, 199, 209, 212
and Ricardo 6
and Rœderer 144, 217
and Rousseau on 10
and Rumford, influenced by 144
and Saint-Simon 6, 217
and Sismondi 6, 203 n. 56; response to criti-
    cisms of Sismondi 206–7
and Smith 144–5; criticism of Smith's disor-
    derly ideas 145, 148; criticism of Smith's
    labour theory 145; criticism of Smith's
    theories on wealth 160; interpretation and
    influence of Smith's *Wealth of Nations* on 3,
    4, 5, 6, 7, 9, 12, 17–18, 127; moving away from
    Smith during Restoration 199; on Smith as
    founder of political science 214; republican-
    ism of 145; Say's annotated copy of Smith's
    Wealth of Nations 145
attacks on Staël 210
contributions to *Revue encyclopédique* 206
followers of 193
his 'Boniface Véridick' 128
industriousness *vs.* adminstration 200–1
influences on 73–4
letter to Ternaux 5
liberalism of 4, 5, 6, 7, 9–10, 12; use of the term
    'liberal' 217

Say, J.-B. (*cont.*):
  morality in political economy 12
  on America 127, 217, 219; on America as model
    for France 199, 200, 201, 205; on civil equal-
    ity in 205
  on Britain 17, 127, 136–7, 217, 219; anticipation
    of bankruptcy of 196; as corrupt monarchy
    with overpowerful aristocracy 199; as
    mercantile empire 196; criticisms of British
    economy and corrupt manners 176; in
    favour of Britain's political economy 39;
    investigations concerning Britain 195; jour-
    ney to Britain 195; not a model for France
    123, 196; on Britain's supremacy 181, 195; on
    dangers facing Britain 143; on flaws in
    British economy 195–6; role of Napoleon
    in Britain's supremacy 195, 199; Say's work
    in Britain 39; unemployment in 195
  on Brumaire coup 137
  on Cabanis' *Quelques considérations* 137
  on China as model for France 121, 125, 127, 136,
    143, 181, 199, 219
  on commerce 27, 37, 38
  on constitution of new Consulate 137–8
  on destruction of first estate 26
  on division of constitutional powers 119; influ-
    enced by Duval and Rœderer but not
    Rousseau 119; on Sieyès 'Constitutional
    Jury' 119; on *Conseil des Anciens* 119; on
    Conseil des Cinq-Cents 119; on limited power
    of government to influence public opinion
    120
  on Duval 198
  on education 124–5; his writings as complete
    education for modern citizen 198–9; on
    moral education as responsibility of parents
    181; response to Baron Thénard on educa-
    tion in political economy 200
  on free trade 183
  on Gibbon 121
  on increase of canal system in France 143
  on La Rochefoucauld-Liancourt's prison
    reforms 143
  on legislators 183, 205
  on manners 138, 183; importance of manners
    to constitutional reforms 78; on monarchi-
    cal manners and the Terror 129; on restora-
    tion of manners by political means as his
    most distinctive contribution 199; reforma-
    tion of 144, *see also* Say *on* regeneration of
    French culture
  on Panopticon 208
  on politics in political economy 11–12
  on possible later writings never completed 213
  on reason-of-state philosophy 120, 121
  on regeneration of French culture 120;
    advocating commerce and technology 124;
    against comparing France with ancient
    regimes 123–4, 127; criticism of Gibbon
    122–3; establishing perfect republic in
    France 124; example of Descartes 123;
    example of Diderot 122; influenced by 120;
    on modern republic 124; on dedication to
    patrie 122; on education 124–5; on example
    of Chinese 121, 125, 127, *see also* Say on
    China; on family practice of republican
    duties 124; on importance of virtuous
    manners for republicanism of France
    120–1; on philosophy and republican
    morality 122; on restoration of liberties of
    1789 138; philosophy as more important
    than religion 121–2; religion *vs* virtue 121
  on religion 121–2, 214; against Roman
    Catholicism 10; on political economy and
    religion 214
  on Sieyès 136
  on Switzerland 219
  on Tallyrand 142
  on role of government 200–1
  on self-interest 183
  on theatre 118, 123, 124
  on trade and agriculture 59 n. 55
  on Turgot 7
  on utility: and creation of wealth 205; and
    value of product 205, 218; disputes with
    Ricardo about 205–6; moral perspectives of
    utility 160–1; on defining his political
    economy as 'an extended application of the
    principle of utility' 208–9; *and see* his *Essai
    sur le principe de l'utilité* on the greatest good
    of the greatest number 209, Say's idea of
    utility 160–1
  on violence, justification of 95, 120, 138
  on wealth 183
  political economy: classification 217–18, 219;
    context of political economy of 111, 114;
    contributions of to political science 211;
    controversy over his political economy 3–6,
    esp. 5; distinctiveness of political economy
    of 183; divorced from government 182, 197;
    on violent forms of republican political
    economy 95; popularization of political
    economy 3; *see also* Say *on* utility
  popularity of 218
  republicanism of 12, 17, 18, 27, 31, 118, 194, 218;
    not a liberal 198; on republican morality as
    a restoration of natural liberty in France
    197; on role of republican virtues 183, 206;
    on the republican citizen 104; origins of 62;
    republicanism of his friends 197, 199

Say's 'Law' 218
Works:
edition of Benjamin Franklin's *Poor Richard
  Saunders* as *La Science du bonhomme Richard*
  117
review of Bentham's *Tactique des assemblées
  legislatives* 208
review of Candolle's translation of Rumford's
  Essays 144
review of J.-A. Naigeon's *Œuvres de Diderot* 122
works of edited by Eugène Daire 3
Catéchisme d'économie politique 17, 192
Cours complet d'économie politique pratique 4,
  210, 213; against Britain 212; against empire
  212; against Rousseau 212; based on Traité
  of 1803 211; importance of social structures
  212; influences of Smith on 211; political
  liberty and representative government 211;
  popularity of 219; responses to Ricardo,
  Sismondi and Everett in 211; to popularize
  political science 210
De l'Angleterre et des Anglais 6, 17, 194, 198, 200
De la liberté de la presse 12, 85
Discours d'ouverture 213–14
Essai sur le principe de l'utilité (1829) 209; anticlericalism of 210; debt to Bentham 210; on
  epicureanism 210; on the principle of utility 209–10
*Examen critique du discours de M. MacCulloch sur
  l'économie politique* 206
Lettres à Malthus 206; explanation of poverty
  and unemployment in 206; on social equality and industry 207
Mélanges et correspondance 4
Mémoires 10, 11
*Olbie, ou essai sur les moyens d'améliorer les
  mœurs d'une nation* 86, 126, 136, 143, 144, 156;
  against faith 127–8; against purely commercial nations 126; criticisms of by Guinguené
  130–1, 145; depiction of ideal society in 164;
  distinctiveness of 130; example of Sparta
  128; his republican political economy
  expressed in 129, 167, 171; influenced by
  Rœderer 129; on an analysis of commerce
  127; on Beccaria 128; on combating poverty
  157; on ideal of wealth 128; on political
  economy as essential for education 128–9;
  on principles for legislators to instill
  manners 126; on regeneration of
  Olbie / France 127–9; on Rousseau's *Emile*
  128; on sacrifice of the self for the public
  good 128; origins of as response to essay
  competition set by Rœderer 125–6; republicanism as a reformer of morals 126; two
  editions of 134 n. 83

Petit volume 198, 200; on enlightened
  self-interest 198; on importance of teaching
  of republican morality 198
'Quelques idées sur le projet de constitution
  de la Commission des Onze' 118
Traité d'économie politique (1st edn, 1803) 3, 11,
  17, 131, 136, 146, 198, 207, 210; against division
  of labour, *esp.* in Britain 163–4; against
  inequality of British society 157; against
  mercantile and physiocratic legislator 177,
  180; against mercantile empire 174–5, 176,
  196; against primogeniture 178; against war
  for increase of trade 176; aim of to restore
  French glory 170, 174; analysis of by
  Dupont de Nemours in 37; as response to
  Smith's *Wealth of Nations* 145, 146, 148, 150,
  152, 153, 160, 161, 163, 170, 182, 183; as
  representing intellectual revolution 150;
  audience intended for 153; categories of
  industriousness 158; contents of 146;
  context of 145–6; criticisms of
  Montesquieu, physiocrats (Quesnay and
  Mirabeau), Voltaire and others 149–50; debt
  to French republican political economists
  165, 166; defence of Say's *Olbie* in 131;
  departures from Smith over slavery and the
  grain trade 179; *Discours préliminaire* in 146,
  148, 156–7; distinctiveness of his political
  economy in 151–2, 166; frugality as an
  important virtue 161–2; general fact
  method of 153; importance of defence, esp.
  against threat of Britain 179; influence of
  on his *Cours complet* 211; lack of historical
  analysis in 153; limitations of general rules
  of policy 178–9; on moral community 167;
  on ancient political economy 149; on
  colonial practices 175–6; on combating
  poverty 157; on commerce 37, 38, 175, 176,
  180; on cotton-mill in Aulchy 183; on
  definition of political economy 146–7,
  148–9; on economic mistakes of Sweden
  and Denmark 175; on learning of morals
  through parent and child 156; on legislators
  149, 153, 178, 182, 183, 197; on literary security
  178; on manners 156–7, 164, 165, 170, 171,
  181–2; on natural growth path of ideal
  French state 178–83; on natural liberty
  152–3, 174, 177; on opposing teaching of
  morals 156, 167; on public credit 178; on
  recognition of true happiness and needs to
  create state 165–6; on savings bank and
  productive capital 158, 162; on search for
  general facts 148; on security of property
  177–8; on separating politics from political
  economy 156, 167; on separating wealth

Traité d'économie politique (cont.):
from government 148–9; on Smith and
manners 156–7; on superiority of Britain
162, 168; on taxation policies 177; on the
ideal society 164; on theory of value based
on utility 207; on unemployment 180; on
wealth 157, 167, 170, 174; on well-observed
facts of political economy 146–7; on workhouses and workforce 182; political
economy to be modelled on physics 146;
popularity of 17; 'Say's Law' 159–60; Say's
response to criticisms 162–3; taxation
policies 180
Traité d'économie politique (2nd edn, 1814) 191;
against poverty 192; comparison with first
edition 191–3; criticisms of and borrowings
from Smith 192, 193; criticisms of by
Ricardo 208; dedication of 191; economy
and industry as modern virtues 193;
editions and popularity of 200, 207, 217;
importance of 'general facts' in 192; influenced by Italian political economists 192;
moving away from Smith's influence 191;
on enlightened self-interest 193; on industrious citizens 192; on separating political
economy from government 193; on wealth
192; reception of 193–4
Traité de morale 198
Traité de politique pratique 198, 199, 200
translation of Williams's *Nouveau voyages en
Suisse* 133 n. 63
*Y'a t'il des cas ou il soit permis de violer les
principes?* 120
Say, Jean-Étienne, father of J.-B. Say 10, 15 n. 42
Say, Léon, on his grandfather, J.-B. Say 5
Scotland
commercial relations with France 39
moral philosophy of 141
political economists from 18
political economy of 53
Seneca 30, 122
Seven Years War 19, 46, 168
Sicily, trade of 54
Sidney, Algernon 116
Sieyès, Emmanuel-Joseph 12, 76, 81, 95, 136, 137,
144, 218
and Condorcet 98
and *Institut national* 112
and Rœderer 76–7, 103
assessment of physiocracy 68–9, 70, 73
constitutional reforms of 78
on Britain as physiocratic state 70
on commerce 70
on complex social order of France 69–70
on constitution of 1789 138

on creation of new constitution 137, 138
on cultural regeneration 96–7
on debt problem 77
on primacy of passions 97–8
on public institutions of education 97
on reform of constitution 70–2, 137, 138
on representative government 77
on Smith 8, 9, 157
republican political economy as a 'social art'
68–70, 72–3, 80, 165, 171
Essai sur les privileges 69
*Lettres aux économistes sur leur système de
politique et de morale* 68, 71, 72
Qu'est-ce que le Tiers Etat? 69
Vues sur les moyens d'exécution 69, 73, 74
Sinclair, John 203 n. 37
Sismondi, Simonde de 5, 210, 218
critical of Say's theory of utility 205
dispute with Say on overproduction 206,
211
on commerce 175
on Say 6, 203 n. 56
political economy of 182
use of Smith for new political economy focusing on increase of wealth 171
De la richesse commerciale 173–4, 206
Histoire des républiques d'Italie 210
Smith, Adam 11, 12, 37, 65, 102, 141, 199
and Turgot 6
contributions of to political science 211
influence of on Say 211, 214
interpretation of by later writers 156–7
on liberty of trade 93
on political economy 148
on relationship between political economy,
manners and wealth 144
on social hierarchies 102
Theory of Moral Sentiments 7, 8, 113, 171
Wealth of Nations 71, 86, 87, 88; accessibility of
9; definition of political economy in 18;
different interpretations of 7; French
editions of 8; French translations of 7–8;
importance of in France, 8–9; influence of
on France and England 17; influence of on
Say 3, 127 (*see also* J.-B. Say); interpretations
of concerning the general good 170, 171–4;
on property and citizenship 7, 8; on
sovereignty 7; posthumous disciples of 5;
Say's annotated copy of 145
Société d'encouragement pour l'industrie nationale
203 n. 55
Société des Amis des Noirs 12, 89
Société Gallo-Américain 11, 79
Société libre de commerce et de manufactures 124
Société nationale 96

Société pour l'encouragement de l'industrie nationale 182

Société pour l'instruction elémentaire 203 n. 55

South America 39

Spain 39
  and France 19
  collapse of 201
  economic problems of 55
  political economy of 18
  trade of 54

Sparta 98, 99, 102

Stadholder 20

Staël, Germaine de
  criticisms of Say's theory of utility 210
  on British constitution as model for France 190
  Considérations sur les principaux événemens de la révolution français 190
  Corinne 210
  De l'Allemagne 209, 210
  Du pouvoir exécutif dans les grands états 190

Stanhope, Leicester 215 n. 20

Steuart, James 150

Steven, *Examen du gouvernement d'Angleterre* 67

Stewart, Dugald 31 n. 2, 145, 203 n. 37

stoicism, as advocated by Saint-Just 94

Stradella 104

Stuart, monarchy of 19

Suard 28

Sulla 102

Sully 53, 149

Supreme Being, festival of 115

Sweden
  economy of 175
  mixed monarchy in 20

Switzerland 20, 23, 219
  annexation of by France 173
  economy of 75, 98
  political economy of 74
  wealth of 102

Talleyrand-Périgord 12, 81, 125, 137, 195
  against Clavière's *assignats* 88
  application of 'general fact' to political economy 142
  on commercial independence of America 176
  on development of France as commercial nation 142

Ternaux, letter to from Say 5

Terray, abbé, Controller General 53

Terror, the 95, 96, 98, 104, 111, 112, 115, 119, 122, 129, 139, 219; *and see* Robespierre

Thénard, Baron 200

Theremin, Charles, review of Say's *Olbie* 130

Thermidor coup 111, 115

Thierry, Augustin 190

Timothy of Athens 104

Tocqueville 55, 219

Tooke, Thomas 203 n. 37, 210

Toscan, Georges 115

Tracy, Destutt de 3, 5, 9
  Quels sont les moyens de fonder la morale chez un peuple? 129

Trajan 214

Trégier, Bishop of 68

Tribunate 171, 183

Tucker, Josiah 65

Tully, James 33 n. 29

Turgot, Anne-Robert-Jacques 4, 7, 12, 29, 37, 56, 74, 81, 150
  against popular assembly 76
  and patriotism 79
  as physiocrat 82 n. 2
  as *contrôleur-général* 62
  compared with Smith 6
  disciples of 66; *see also* Dupont, Condorcet
  importance of property 63–4
  liberalism of 9, 10
  on absolute sovereignty 64, 65
  on American Revolution 65
  on Britain's mixed government 65
  on different organization of assemblies 64, 65, 74
  on making of a good citizen 63
  on neo-physiocracy, *e.g.*, combining wealth with agriculture 65, 66
  on public credit 62
  on reforms to political constitution of France 61–5, 66, 68, 71, 72, 75, 77, 78, 79
  on representative government 77
  on republicanism 22
  political economy of 6–7
  resignation of 65
  'six edicts' of 62
  Éloge de Vincent de Gournay 49
  Mémoire au Roi, sur les municipalités 62–4, 65
  Réflexions sur la formation et la distribution des richesses 14 n. 19

Turin 120

Tuscany, famine of 54

United Provinces 20, 23, 24

L'Utilitaire 209

Utrecht, treaties of 19

Vandermonde 95, 107 n. 61, 111

Varennes, Louis XVI's flight to 73, 89, 90, 95

Vendémiaire 120

Venice 20
  commerce of 126

Vergennes 11
Verri, Pietro 192
Vienna 176
Volney 114, 137
　materialism of 112
　morality developed from laws of nature 113
　on education of mind 113
　on reformation of national manners by
　　rational catechism 113
　on separation of religious beliefs and virtuous
　　civil practices 112
　La loi naturelle, ou Catéchisme du citoyen François
　　113
　*Les Ruines, ou méditations sur les révolutions des
　　empires* 112–13
　Voyage en Syrie 112
Voltaire 10, 12, 22, 46, 122, 149
　liberalism of 9

　on need for political change in France 46
　on republics 22
　Dictionnaire philosophique portatif 42
　Letters Concerning the English Nation 41; on
　　Britain's constitutional government 41–2;
　　on evils of social hierarchy 42

War of Austrian Succession 19
War of Spanish Succession 39
Washington, George 209
Waterford (Ireland) 11
West Indies 89
'White Terror' 197
Wilkes 28, 55–6
Williams, David 217
Williams, Helen-Maria 123
　Letters on Switzerland 85
　Nouveau voyages en Suisse 133 n. 63

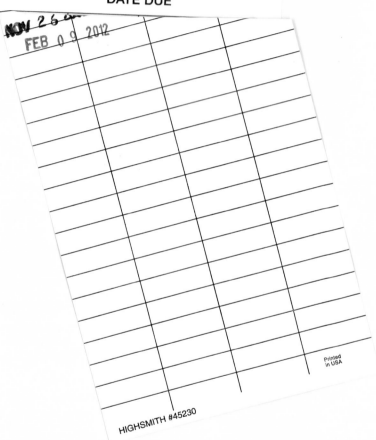

DATE DUE

NOV 2 6

FEB 0 9 2012